TECHNOLOGY O
TEXTILE
PROPERTIES

AN INTRODUCTION

Marjorie A. Taylor

Third edition

fp

First published February, 1972
Reprinted May, 1974
Reprinted January, 1977
Reprinted January, 1978
Reprinted September, 1979
Second edition 1981
Reprinted 1985
Third edition 1990
Reprinted 1993
Reprinted 1994

Forbes Publications Ltd,
2B Drayson Mews,
London W8 4LY

Typeset by Rowland Phototypesetting Ltd,
Bury St Edmunds, Suffolk
Printed and bound in Great Britain
by St Edmundsbury Press Ltd,
Bury St Edmunds, Suffolk

CONTENTS

2 YARN TYPES AND PROPERTIES

3 FABRIC STRUCTURE

Contents

LIST OF ILLUSTRATIONS

LIST OF TABLES

ACKNOWLEDGEMENTS

The author welcomes this opportunity to express her very warm thanks for the active interest and patience shown by many in the textile and apparel industries, associates, and her family, throughout the time devoted to the revision of this book.

The sources of illustrations are gratefully attributed in the text, but it is appropriate to make here a special mention of the following:

- The Textile Institute, for permission to quote some textile definitions and to use certain illustrations from their publications *Textile Terms and Definitions* and *Identification of Textile Materials*.
- The British Textile Technology Group (BTTG), particularly John E. Ford and Maureen Sawbridge.
- The British Standards Institution, particularly David H. Woolliscroft.
- Courtaulds Fibres Limited, particularly Bob W. R. Beath.
- Lewis Miles for his patient and thorough reading of the galleys.
- Joan Forbes, of Forbes Publications Ltd., for her dedicated commitment to the production of this book.

PREFACE

'The manufactory, the laboratory, and the study of the natural philosopher, are in close practical conjunction. Without the aid of science, the arts would be contemptible; without practical application, science would consist only of barren theories, which men would have no motive to pursue.'

Edward Baines, *History of the Cotton Manufacture in Great Britain, 1835*

Since food, clothing and shelter are the most fundamental of our requirements, the textile industry is a subject of very general importance and interest. More particularly, textile fabrics, being the raw material of the clothing industry, are the concern of clothing manufacturers in respect of their aesthetic qualities, their suitability for garment construction, and their behaviour in use. It must be remembered, however, that to consider the textile industry purely in relation to clothing considerably underrates its importance, since clothing takes only about one half of the output of the industry. The other half is divided fairly evenly between household needs and industrial applications.

This newly revised book sets out a technological framework for the understanding of textile materials, their qualities and behaviour in use.

There is an extensive and growing need for users of textiles in the fields of fashion, clothing, furnishings, contract and public authority purchasing, and for retailers, designers and educationists, to grasp the fundamental principles of textile technology. Equally, entrants to the international textile and clothing industries appreciate the value of a broad foundation to the subject.

Many have realised that without a proper understanding their expertise is seriously hampered. Generalised sweeping impressions of the subject of textiles cannot support an efficient and cost-effective performance in any sector of this competitive field.

The development and maintenance of standards is an essential preparation for a 'Single European Market' in 1992 and beyond. The single market of the European Community (EC) will facilitate the free flow of merchandise, personnel and expertise, and this is likely to benefit those who have a command of the subject matter, and an understanding of the requirements of the market. All those with careers involving the use and selection of, or trade in, textiles should now be striving to increase their knowledge and understanding of the properties and limitations of textiles that govern their fitness for particular applications.

While interesting, a study of the details of manufacturing processes is not essential for the intelligent use and appreciation of textiles. It is important, however, to have a knowledge of the properties of fabrics; that is, how they react to the conditions of use, how their characteristics are related to their construction and finish, and why, therefore, fabrics differ in suitability for various purposes. Often, in the study of textiles by those who are not training for positions in the textile industry, these topics are mistakenly subordinated to a study of the manufacturing processes.

It is assumed that the reader has some knowledge of the common methods of producing fibres, yarns and woven fabrics, and of methods of finishing. There is no lack of sources of this information. It has been felt necessary, however, to give information about certain production techniques where this assists in the proper understanding of the product characteristics.

The important changes in this edition consist of the introduction of 'flame retardance', 'colour and colour matching', 'quality assurance' and expansion of 'nonwoven fabrics', and 'coated fabrics and laminates'. A number of other revisions have been necessitated by developments in the textile industry, and the opportunity has been taken to revise the classification of fibres and sewing threads, and to comment on the application of computers in the textile and clothing industries.

'Textile floor coverings' have distinctive properties of sufficient importance to warrant discussion as a separate topic, and this follows the chapter on 'Properties of fabrics'.

Reference is made to the British Standards Institution (BSI), particularly with respect to certain standard test methods, specifications, performance of products, labelling and quality assurance. Each standard and specification is identified by a number followed by the date of publication, such as BS 2543: 1983 'Specification for woven and knitted fabrics for upholstery'. When using a Standard it is important to verify that the current issue or revision is available. Many BSI standards are equivalent to the international ISO standards and this is indicated where applicable. It must now be borne in mind that European Standards are being established for the 'Single European Market' and will come into use increasingly. These will be designated with the prefix CEN (Comité Européen Normalisation) which is equivalent to the BSI at national level. It is expected that many national standards will be in harmony with CEN standards, but it must be understood that once a CEN standard is established by the participating countries, the CEN standard has then to be adopted nationally.

It is hoped this book will provide a basis for satisfaction in the study, use and retailing of textiles, and be a useful introduction to a rewarding career in the textile and clothing industries.

MARJORIE A. TAYLOR MSc CText ATI CGIA
Visiting Fellow, Manchester Polytechnic

INTRODUCTION

The word 'textile' originally meant a fabric produced by weaving, but its application has greatly broadened. Now this term is used for a wide range of products made from fibres or filaments, including not only woven, knitted, and felted fabrics, but also lace, nets, yarn, cord and many other materials. The varieties of these products and their uses are so numerous that textiles have applications in almost all our activities. Clothing fabrics range from gossamer-like silks to the heaviest woollen overcoatings. Textiles used in engineering range from insulating fabric 2·5 hundredths of a millimetre thick to very thick and strong industrial fabrics such as conveyor belting. Household fabrics range from the simplest white cotton cloths used for sheets to the highly decorated materials of complicated construction that may be used in furnishing. Whatever their purpose and method of manufacture, these materials all have one property in common – a certain degree of flexibility which suits them to their various purposes and which arises from the fineness of the ultimate unit of construction – the fibre.

Weaving was one of primitive man's earliest arts, and for many thousands of years the only raw materials were the fibres obtained from nature, that is mainly wool, flax, cotton, and silk. Although man long aspired to produce a silk-like fibre artificially, it was not until about 1900 that the first fabrics made from 'artificial silk', that is viscose rayon, appeared in the shops, and it was not until the '30s that the use of 'rayon' began to expand rapidly. Nylon appeared in 1939 and heralded the polyesters, the acrylics, the polyolefins, the elastane fibres (formerly known as spandex), the new types of viscose and other "man-made" fibres (hence forward referred to as "manufactured fibres"), which have supplanted the natural fibres to such an extent that they now supply over half the textile needs in the United Kingdom.

Research and development

The new fibres are a product of scientific research which has during recent decades brought a revolution to the textile industries of the world comparable with the industrial revolution. The application of research to the textile industry is by no means new, as witnessed by John Mercer's discovery of the effect of cold strong caustic soda solutions on cotton in 1844 and W. H. Perkin's discovery in 1856 of aniline mauve, which initiated the important synthetic dyestuffs industry. However, during the last fifty years all branches of the textile industry have been subjected to scientific investigation on a rapidly increasing scale, and while the production of textiles was until recent times largely in the hands of craftsmen aided by machinery, it is now described as a science-based industry.

The importance of scientific research in the textile field was recognised publicly in the United Kingdom at the end of World War I by the government establishing the Wool Industries Research Association (WIRA), and the British Cotton Industry Research Association, (The Shirley Institute). These, and the younger British Rayon Research Association, were the forerunners, by merging, of the British Textile Technology Group (BTTG). Other research associations working in the interests of the textile industry are the Hosiery and Allied Trades Research Association (HATRA), the Fabric Care Research Association and, in Northern Ireland, the LAMBEG Industrial Research Association. The textile research and technology groups are active in various branches of research development and testing for the clothing industry, and now a Clothing Technology Centre has been formed to coordinate and stimulate research for the clothing industry.

The research associations and technology groups derive their incomes from various sources such as direct subscriptions from member firms, charges which they may make for services of various kinds, and sponsored research.

Research is also an important function of the universities, and the textile and clothing technology departments of the polytechnics and technical colleges, in the important textile areas of the country, as for example the University of Manchester Institute of Science and Technology, the University of Leeds, and a number of polytechnics. Organisations such as these employ scientific workers of international repute.

A third stream of knowledge flows from the laboratories of the large industrial organisations, particularly big fibre producers such as ICI and Courtaulds, who spend large sums on the development of fibres and on research into how they may be used most effectively and economically. Textile research is pursued actively in all other countries that have any pretensions to scientific and technological advancement and has made the production of textiles one of the most rapidly evolving of the international industries.

There is hardly a scientific discipline that does not have its contribution to make to the development of new products and processes, and it would be an impossible task to attempt to summarise in a short space all the fields of scientific activity. It must be sufficient to indicate some of the growing points of the industry, which can be classified as fibres, yarn production, fabric production, and cloth processing.

Fibres

It is considered that the introduction of fundamentally new fibre types has become so expensive that a new fibre can be introduced only if it has considerable advantages in performance or cost. However, this does not exclude the possibility of important developments in the existing fibres. Viscose has already demonstrated its ability to diversify under the pressure of competition from the newer fibres, and now exists in a variety of forms exhibiting a range of properties and uses. A number of different nylons are in use including a variety with a high melting point which is practically non-flammable, and fibres can be modified to give the advantages of a high moisture absorption. Other developments in the fibre field include the production of very fine micro-fibres and bi-component fibres. Bi-components are composed of two different polymers, such as nylon and polyester, extruded together so that the two components fuse to produce a single fibre. Modifications may also be made to the fibre substance by 'grafting on' another polymer under the influence of atomic radiation. Antibacterial and other substances can be introduced into a polymer before it is extruded. Such methods enable the basic properties of the fibre substance to be modified considerably. At the same time there is a constant search for worthwhile modifications that can be made by altering the conditions of fibre production. It must not be imagined that only the manufactured fibres are subject to this constant striving after improvements. For many years the varieties of cotton have been continuously improved by controlled breeding, the aim being to develop new varieties with superior characteristics such as length, fineness, and strength. Qualities which are of economic importance, such as disease resistance and yield, are also sought after. A great effort is also being made to find ways of providing permanent improvements to the cotton fibre, such as providing rot resistance and higher elasticity by chemical treatment of the fibre either in fibre form or at a later stage in manufacture. Similar quests are pursued for breeds of sheep that will provide better wool more economically and for treatments to improve the characteristics of the wool fibre.

Yarn production

In the field of yarn production, important developments have been made, including for example, 'open-end' 'self-twist' and 'jet' spinning. The method of inserting twist used throughout history is to rotate a bobbin (or some other 'package' of yarn) at a high rate in order to twist the yarn and, intermittently, to wind some of the twisted yarn on the bobbin, or alternatively during twisting to feed the yarn at a steady rate to the bobbin as in ring spinning. The disadvantage of these methods is that the size of the bobbin that can be rotated conveniently at high speed is limited. Consequently, the operation must be interrupted at intervals to replace full bobbins with empty ones. A much higher rate of production might be achieved if twist could be inserted by rotating only the yarn. Since yarn is so much lighter than a bobbin, the power requirement would be much less. Methods by which this might conceivably be done have been known for a long time, but until recently little progress towards a practicable solution has been made. Yarn is now being commercially produced by all the above methods and each type has distinctive characteristics and properties.

Fabric production

Cloth production has advanced in various directions. Probably the outstanding change is the replacement of woven cloth, often made from spun yarns, by knitted fabrics, often made of continuous filament textured yarns. This change is largely a result of economic pressure, since knitted fabrics are cheaper to produce than woven ones. It has been made possible by warp knitting machines that work at a much higher rate than was once the case, along with the introduction of knitted structures that have a firm handle and well covered appearance comparable with woven cloths. Many developments have been made in weaving and ancillary processes. Conventional looms insert the weft by hitting a shuttle containing the weft yarn across the warp but, because of the weight and size of the shuttle, there is a limit to the speed and width of fabric that can be produced. Many looms are now designed to dispense with the conventional shuttle so that only the yarn length needed for the weft is inserted singly, and withdrawn from large yarn supply packages stationed at the side of the loom, consequently very high speeds of weaving are possible and exceptionally wide fabrics can be produced for special needs. The main methods of weft-insertion are by using a small metal gripper as a projectile to carry the weft across; "rapiers" which deposit the weft in position; air and water jet looms which project air or water from a jet carrying the weft yarn across the warp. Water jet weaving can only used for continuous filament hydrophobic yarns, usually polyester or nylon. Mention may be made of 'multiphase weaving' which increases the rate of cloth production by the use of a number of shuttles moving simultaneously across the same warp, and this method can be expected to find some applications in the future. Another development, 'triaxial weaving', is a method of producing a new variety of fabrics that contain two sets of warp threads crossing at an angle, both being intersected by the weft yarn. Developments such as these, while improving the competitive position of weaving in relation to knitting, can hardly be expected to regain the ground already lost. Weaving is also subjected to competition from another quarter, namely, 'nonwoven' fabrics. These fabrics are produced by processes other than weaving or knitting and include textiles produced directly from fibres, by fibre bonding techniques, or from yarn and laps of fibre by stitch bonding and other processes (including split film techniques) that are discussed later. These processes produce fabrics more cheaply than weaving, but the fabrics have different characteristics. Developments in the processes and in methods of using the cloths will widen their field of application. One particular use is in inexpensive cloths for disposable or short-life garments and another as durable nonwovens for shoe linings. Current developments are in the production of fabrics for horticulture and agriculture, used in the protection of plants and land, and for increases in crop yields.

Cloth processing

In finishing, there is an important line of progress in 'easy care' fabrics of various kinds. Thus, attention is given to soil release finishes, which improve the ease of cleaning synthetic fibre fabrics, anti-soiling and anti-static finishes, and finishes to promote crease shedding in use and appearance retention after washing. Methods of coating fabrics with, say, polyurethane, have been developed to produce microporous surfaces. There is also scope for the introductions of micron-sized capsules of dye or perfume that is evenly applied to the surface of the fabric so that under certain conditions of use a temporary release of colour occurs as a novelty feature. Besides the quest for better finishes there is a search for improvements in the techniques and control of the finishing process; naturally the consumer benefits from quality improvements and lower finishing costs. Through the use of computers, for instance, it is possible to eliminate very largely the personal skill required to match a given shade, thus enabling the composition of the dye bath to be determined entirely automatically.

Textiles and the consumer

It will be appreciated that the great variety of fabrics now available, differing in respect of fibre, construction, and finish, makes the choice of fabric for a particular purpose much more difficult than it has been in the past and imposes on the garment manufacturer a need, and indeed a duty to his customers, to be much more knowledgeable in textile technology than was once the case. Before the present era of rapid development, say perhaps before 1950, certain types of fabrics had become standardised for certain purposes. So, for any particular end use there would be a commonly known choice of fabrics, suitable for different purses and social classes, which persisted unchanged for many years, or at least only changed slowly. Thus, the classes of society were clearly distinguished by the type of clothes they wore and the fabrics their clothes were made from. The revolution in the textile industry has brought a revolution in this also. The new techniques enable superficially comparable fabrics to be produced in a wide price range and thus allow similar styles to be made for widely different markets. At the same time it must be realised that the mass production of clothing and more efficient methods of retailing have been at least as important in making current fashion widely available.

At one time a garment manufacturer, retailer, or draper was so familiar with the unchanging range of fabrics that he could judge quality by handle and appearance and knew what uses the different fabrics would serve. The situation now is that for any given purpose a wide range of fabrics, differing quite fundamentally, is available. Moreover, the range changes constantly. In order to appraise fabrics nowadays it is essential to have a basic knowledge of the properties of fibres, the effects of finishes, and the types of constructions in use. Even then it may be impossible, in the case of a completely novel fabric, to judge just how satisfactory it will be, and a lengthy laboratory appraisal and carefully conducted service trials may be necessary to establish its acceptability. However, a knowledge of textiles will protect the purchaser to a considerable extent, and will enable him, or her, to judge what credence to give to the shop assistant who is perhaps inclined to confuse viscose and nylon, or to be unduly optimistic about the effects of washing and dry-cleaning.

To the garment manufacturer, a knowledge of the properties and characteristics of textiles is essential if garments are to be provided that are truly suitable for their intended purposes. Too often garments are made from fabrics that are far from ideal for the service they are meant to give. Even if the main fabric is well chosen, the trimmings or lining may be ill-matched, so that perhaps a garment intended to be washed has trimmings that can only be dry-cleaned, or a shrink-resistant outer fabric is made-up with a lining that shrinks.

The retailer has the duty of advising the purchaser on the qualities of the article for sale, and now that it is so difficult to be knowledgeable over the whole field of textiles this function of retailing has become absolutely essential. This is, in effect, recognised by the Merchandise Marks Acts and Trade Descriptions Act, which make it an offence for the retailer to give incorrect information.

Fibre usage

The rapidly evolving techniques of textile production, together with developments in world politics, economics and population, combine to give an overall pattern of world consumption and usage of fibres that has changed considerably since the introduction of manufactured fibres and continues to change. The most important factors are the increase in world population and affluence which are raising both the total of world production of fibres, and also the 'per capita' world consumption. In 1946 world consumption of textile fibres was about 9×10^6 metric tonnes.* It is now about 36×10^6 tonnes. The introduction of manufactured fibres, of which production was negligible before 1930 but accelerated rapidly after 1950, was accompanied by a substantial fall in cotton's share in the world market in textile fibres from 75% in 1946 to 45% in 1981, although the world production of cotton doubled in the same period from 7×10^6 tonnes to

*9×10^6 metric tonnes denotes 9 million metric tonnes.

14×10^6 tonnes. In the last few years cotton has made a recovery to 50% of the world market, and production is now about 18×10^6 tonnes.

The other important clothing fibre, wool, held 14% of the world market in 1946 and this has now fallen to about 5%. Production of flax is only 0.5×10^6 tonnes, and of silk only about a tenth of this. The fibres that are taking an increased share of the world markets are the manufactured fibres, and of these the synthetic fibre group, that is mainly polyamide, polyester and the acrylics, is showing the most rapid expansion. In terms of percentage of world production the breakdown is approximately polyester 18%, polyamide 9%, cellulosic 8%, acrylic 6·5%, polyolefin 5%, glass 2%.

Of course, the pattern of fibre consumption is by no means the same in all countries. In the more affluent countries the important change is the substitution of the more expensive synthetic fibres for the natural fibres, particularly cotton. Since the synthetic fibres are stronger and tend to be made into lighter weights, the weight of cloth needed may be reduced although the yardage may be increased. On the other hand, by far the greater proportion of the world's population live in the under-developed countries where the use of textiles relative to the size of the population has been very low. The standard of living in these countries is now improving, and the population affected is so large relative to that of the affluent countries that the effect on world consumption is very considerable. In these countries, the increase in the use of cotton is very great.

In any particular country the pattern of fibre usage is determined by a large number of factors, such as the standard of living, relative costs of producing the different fibres, the composition of the population in respect of age groups, the effects of government policy in encouraging new industries or protecting established ones, and social habits such as reliance on central heating instead of open fires. It is impossible, therefore, to give figures that could be accepted as representative of the whole, but an indication of the position in the EC will be of interest.

Fibre consumption in the EC

Table 1 shows how the total fibre consumption in 1987 in the EC is used for different purposes. (EC here comprises Benelux, France, German Federal Republic, Republic of Ireland, Italy, Portugal, Spain, UK.) The trend over recent years is for the usage of manufactured fibres to increase, for cotton to remain fairly steady, and for wool to decline slightly.

It is impossible here to give a detailed analysis of the changes that are taking place, but certain factors influencing the changes may be mentioned. An important consideration is the advantages that the manufactured fibres have for the cloth producer. The first of these is a relatively stable price. The annual production of the natural fibres varies, sometimes considerably, largely owing to climatic conditions, and there is a corresponding fluctuation in the price. This is a major factor in the financing of

Table 1   EC TOTAL FIBRE CONSUMPTION FOR MAIN END USES IN 1987 ('000 TONNES)

Use	Manufactured	Cotton	Wool	Total
Clothing	1234·7	802·3	319·6	2356·9
Carpets	475·6	8·6	78·6	562·8
Household other than carpets	512·2	438·0	35·2	985·4
Tyres	85·0	1·0		86·0
Industrial other than tyres	459·7	142·2	9·1	611·0
Total	2767·2	1392·1	442·8	4602·1

(Data derived from CIRFS* 1989)

CIRFS – Comité International de la Rayonne et Fibres Synthetiques

textile production from these fibres, and since the fluctuations are unpredictable, it is a hindrance to the smooth running of a large industry. The prices of the manufactured fibres change relatively slowly and to some extent predictably, which makes planning ahead more accurate. Secondly, the quality of the natural fibres varies from year to year depending on natural causes, that is the weather, pests and disease, whereas the quality of manufactured fibres can be controlled.

Another factor favouring the growth of the manufactured fibres is the development of techniques using continuous filament yarns, particularly for warp knitting. The fibre producers have made great strides in developing continuous filament yarns that give a fabric texture comparable with that produced by staple fibre yarns. And so the development of warp knitting and of textured continuous filament yarns have gone hand in hand. The natural fibres, being all staple fibres (except silk) and less suitable for use in warp knitting, have not shared in this development.

It must also be pointed out that a large part of the increase in manufactured fibre usage arises from the growth in the use of carpets. With the rise in standards of living, there has been an increased demand for home furnishings such as upholstery and carpeting. Traditionally, carpeting has been made from wool, but the properties of certain of the manufactured fibres, particularly nylon and acrylics, make them very suitable for this purpose. Varieties of viscose have also been developed especially for use in carpets. The method of producing carpets by tufting has enabled costs to be kept down and has helped to widen the market. The position now is that viscose has a share of the market comparable with wool, and although synthetics are rather less used, their share is increasing.

The British textile industry

In 1988 the textile and the closely allied clothing industries combined, contributed £5,450 million to the national economy. This is 23% more than the whole of the motor vehicle and engines industry, 58% more than the aerospace industry and more than twice as much as the office machinery and computer industry. Of the above £5,450 million the textile industries' share (including knitting) was £3,500 million and the apparel industries' share was £1,950 millon. Apparel, knitting and the textile industries account for 9% of total manufacturing employment.

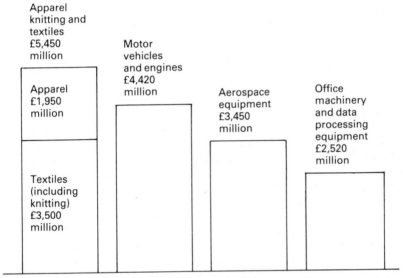

Fig. 1 Comparison of industries in 1987 (estimated value added).
(British Textile Confederation)

Applications of computers in design, manufacture and management

Computers, microprocessors, microchips, electronics, robotics and automation are commonplace tools in this highly innovative and technological industry.

Fashion demands the creation of new products, aesthetically pleasing in design and of suitable and consistent quality, in very short time spans between and within seasons. The delivery of such products is achieved by the use of sophisticated techniques for co-ordinating the wealth of information and expertise in the creative, technological and scientific base. The use of computers widens the range of experimentation, and promotes the rapid generation and testing of ideas prior to manufacture and marketing.

Clearly the use of advanced techniques and equipment demands a reliable and technically sound input by specialised personnel with a well-developed understanding of the subject matter and of the operational structure of the company, the industry and the commercial field.

Computer-aided design (CAD)

The scope of CAD with the usual facilities of keyboard, stylus for drawing and sketching, colour and pattern selection, visual display unit (VDU) with computer graphics, and related software, frees the textile and fashion designers from the many time-consuming activities associated with the traditional 'pencil and paper' approach. It widens the scope for experimentation with shape, dimensions and colour and facilitates rapid three-dimensional visualisation based on the original idea. For this, the computer can provide a library resource of colour, style and fabric.

Though the designing of textiles and clothing is primarily an aesthetic activity, the designer must take into account the feasibility of the design for the range of manufacturing equipment available, the nature and availability of materials and the estimated cost and commercial viability of the product. These activities are the role of the 'Design Manager'.

Constructional design is another important part of textile design. The physical properties of a textile are the product of the inter-relationships of each of its components, and the finishing and chemical treatments which may have been used. It is an impossible task to produce fabrics with all conceivable combinations of structural variations. However, with an understanding of the physical and mechanical properties of textiles, it is possible to process data at speed to investigate the effects of various combinations of the variables of construction and hence to predict fabric properties and performance in use, a process known as 'computer modelling'. It is then possible to select promising fabric constructions for experimental production and testing, probably including service trials, leading eventually to a production specification for a marketable fabric.

Computer modelling is particularly applicable to the design of fabrics for industrial purposes, for which the properties are very carefully chosen, and for functional clothing which usually requires very distinctive properties. As an example, the International Institute for Cotton has established a computer programme for the constructional design and processing of cotton knitted outerwear fabrics to ensure controlled dimensional stability.

The possibilities of 'computer modelling' for the functional design of textiles are at present restricted by the limitations of theoretical understanding and data relevant to the behaviour of textiles in use, a field in which much progress has yet to be made, but which is being intensively explored.

Computer-aided manufacture (CAM)

CAM systems are used throughout industry, from fibre and yarn production, through weaving, knitting and other methods of fabric manufacture, textile coloration and finishing, to the conversion of the textile into clothing, household textiles and industrial items. Continuous on-line

Fig. 2 'Creative Designer' (CAD).
(Gerber Scientific Europe S.A.)

process control, monitoring of production data and product quality are commonplace. For example, computer colour-matching linked with computer recipe specification, is routine. This may be linked with the automatic weighing and dispensing of chemicals and dyestuffs and the control of the dyeing equipment. In carpet 'dye-jet printing' the instant switching over from one design to another during full speed production is activated by computer control.

In clothing manufacture applications of computers are evident in the automatic generation of component pieces, relating to the garment design, and the automatic grading of patterns for size according to the manufacturer's requirements for particular markets.

Maximising the use of the textile material in planning the lay is essential for profitable production, and the computer can manipulate the arrangement of the components of the pattern for the greatest efficiency. Computerised automatic laying-up of the fabric and automatic precision cutting for mass production can be linked to the previously planned lay marker. The computerised cutting table controls the movement of the fabric throughout the cutting process and provision can be made for the automatic marrying of the required parts in striped, checked and printed fabric.

About 80% of the time required for garment assembly is accounted for by handling and positioning of component pieces under the stitching head. To reduce this time it is possible to utilise robotics and mechanisms for the automatic pick-up of components. Programmable sewing and embroidery machines, and garment presses complete the sequences from fibre to fabric and finished garment to customer.

It should finally be observed that the manufacture of a garment can often be achieved by any of a number of options and the choice can be tested by computer modelling of the different strategies. Equally it is possible to investigate the performance of purely theoretical equipment without devoting time and expense to the development of the machine and practical testing.

Computer-integrated manufacturing and management (CIM)

The ultimate presentation of textiles, furnishings, clothing and products for industrial uses is the culmination of a highly diverse range of fascinating steps in design, technology and manufacture. The outlets for these products are through retail, public authority and commercial organisations. Industrial products are destined for use in light and heavy industries world-wide. Textile and clothing manufacture is part of a network of commercial and industrial activities.

Management within an organisation operates most efficiently when in command of all the information relevant to decision making. A factually sound data base is essential for the making of reliable decisions on what to produce, how to produce it, in what varieties and quantities. Such a data base can be held and manipulated best by a suitable computer system, which liberates the flow of information and makes it accessible to all sectors of an enterprise.

The value of CIM becomes clear when one considers how knowledge of fabric, fabric design, availability and price are essential for garment design, simultaneously with information needed about the market and demand, the scope and limitations of equipment, and the administration of the business. Details of costings, processing of orders, stock control, invoicing and credit control can be made readily available besides information about competitive merchandise.

Retailers can now pass information about their requirements by telephone, directly into their supplier's systems, and the computer must be capable of channelling the data through the system to ensure prompt delivery. By such means stock control is made more efficient and capital locked up in unnecessary holdings of stock can be minimised.

Enough has been said to make it clear that the textile industry must not be considered as static. It is changing rapidly in respect of its raw materials, its processes, and its products. Although we have not considered it here, the economic structure of the industry – the size of the commercial and industrial units, the range of their activities, and the nature of their interdependence – is also in a state of rapid evolution. This book aims not only to give an account of the products of the industry as they are at present, but also to provide a basis of knowledge that will enable the reader to keep abreast of developments in the near future.

Chapter 1

FIBRE TYPES AND PROPERTIES

Classification of textile fibres

Confusion sometimes exists as to whether a name associated with a fabric is the fabric name or simply the name of the fibre. 'Cotton/Polyester Denim' refers to the fibre content and the fabric name. So far as natural fibres are concerned the term 'cotton', for example is direct and unambiguous. It is an example of a 'generic name', which for natural fibres refers to the source of the fibre such as 'flax' or 'wool'. The generic name of a manufactured fibre refers to its chemical group, examples being polyester, polyamide. Manufactured fibres would present difficulties in commercial transactions and public use, if the description of the chemical composition were attempted, or if total dependence were placed on the bewildering array of trade-names operated internationally by the fibre producers. Chemical names of fibres are reserved for use within industry and laboratories.

Generic names are used globally and describe unambiguously manufactured fibres of the same chemical group. The use of generic names is a mandatory legal requirement for the labelling of textiles and merchandise, and for Customs and Excise purposes. There is no restriction on the use of trade-names provided it is done in conjunction with the generic name and the prominence and size of the generic name is not diminished in favour of the trade-name.

Polyester, in common with other manufactured fibres, is made throughout the world and each manufacturer gives each distinct product a trade-name. For example, polyester is marketed as 'Terylene' (UK), 'Tergal' (France) and 'Dacron' (USA).

The term 'poly . . .', which is frequently repeated under the heading of Manufactured Fibres in Table 1, simply means 'many', and refers to the many repeating features of the long-chain molecule.

During the manufacture of fibres there is scope for the modification of the fibre by the introduction of additives to the structure. All such variants widen the range of properties on offer. For commercial reasons deviations from the 'regular' fibre can be indicated in the technical literature with the trade-name suffixed by a coded letter or number. Some modified fibres carry distinctive trade-names to highlight the fibre qualities. 'Tactel', for instance, is a very fine nylon fibre, and 'Mitrelle' a very fine polyester fibre.

Where a fibre type is listed as being suitable for apparel, domestic and industrial purposes, it is important to realise that such a range of applications is only possible if chemical and structural variants are introduced to attain the required performance and properties in use.

Table 2   GENERAL CLASSIFICATION OF TEXTILE FIBRES

NATURAL FIBRES	Generic name	Main fibre producers
Cellulose:	cotton	China, USA, USSR, India, Pakistan, Brazil, Turkey, Egypt, Mexico.
	flax	USSR, France, Belgium, Netherlands.
	jute	India, Pakistan.
Protein:	wool	Australia, USSR, China, New Zealand, Argentina, S. Africa, USA, UK.
	hair: alpaca	Peru, Chile.
	camel	China, Mongolia
	cashmere	China, Mongolia, Iran, Afganistan, Russia.
	mohair	USA, Turkey, S. Africa
	rabbit	UK, Belgium, France, Poland
	vicuna	S. America.
	silk: cultivated	Japan
	wild or tussah	China, India
Mineral:	asbestos	Canada, Zimbabwe

MANUFACTURED FIBRES		
Generic names	Some trade-names	Major uses
Natural Polymer Cellulose and variants: viscose		
	'Danufil'[10]*	Apparel
	'Danufil CS'[10]	Fire retardant
	'Danuflor'[10]	Carpets
	'Durafil'[6]	Industrial uses
	'Evlan'[6]	Furnishings

*Superior figures refer to key on page 6.

Generic names	Some trade-names	Major uses
viscose (cont.)	'Fibro'[6]	Staple fibre for apparel and furnishings
	'Lenzing FR'[13]	Apparel, furnishings and industrial uses (flame retardant)
	'Sarille'[6]	Apparel and nonwovens (crimped fibre)
	'SI Fibre'[6]	Hygienic uses. Super absorbent (super inflatable fibre)
	'Tufcel'[22]	Apparel
	'Viloft'[6]	Domestic textiles, apparel including leisure wear and underwear (high bulk fibre)
	'Viscostat'[6]	Anti-static (carbon incorporated)
modal	'Avril'[2] 'Koplon'[18] 'Prima'[12]	Apparel Especially blends with cotton or polyester. (prima-crimped fibre)
Cellulose ester: triacetate	'Lintrelle'[6]	Apparel (made from cotton linters)
	'Tricel'[6]	Linings, blouses, dresses, curtains, cigarette filters, (made from wood pulp)
acetate	'Dicel'[6]	Dresses, linings, knitwear
Lyocell:	'Tencel'[6]	Generic name for a new organic solvent spun cellulose fibre, having 'cotton-like' properties.
Synthetic polymer polyamide (nylon)	'Antron'[8]	Carpets
	'Cambrelle'[11]	Nonwoven fabric (bicomponent fibre)
	'Cantrece'[8]	Hosiery
	'Cordura'[8]	Webbing, luggage
	'Cora'[17]	Apparel
	'ICI polyamide 6.6'[11]	Industrial uses

Table 2 continued

Generic names	Some trade-names	Major uses
polyamide (nylon) (cont.)	'Lilion'[18]	Carpets and apparel
	'Qazul'[11]	Luggage
	'Quintesse'[11]	Upholstery
	'Tactel'[11]	Hosiery, apparel, embroidery thread (textured fine filaments)
	'Tactesse'[11]	Specialised 'wool-like' staple for carpets
	'Timbrelle'[11]	Group of staple and textured continuous filaments of various carpet qualities
polyimide	'Kermel'[17] 'P84'[13]	Industrial high temperature filtration
aramid	'Kevlar'[8] 'Nomex'[8] 'Twaron'[9]	High performance textiles. Heat and flame resistant.
polyester	'Dacron'[8]	Apparel, domestic and industrial
	'Dacron Hollofil'[8]	Filling fibre
	'Diolen'[9]	Apparel, domestic and industrial
	'Fortrel ESP'[10]	Stretch yarn for denim
	'Mitrelle'[11] 'Setila'[18]	Apparel (Very fine fibre)
	'Tendrelle'[11]	Knitting yarn
	'Terinda'[11] 'Terital'[16]	Apparel
	'Terylene'[11]	Curtain nets, industrial uses
	'Tergal'[17] 'Tergal Y'[17]	Domestic and industrial uses Bi-component (PET/PTMT p. 37)
	'Tetoron'[21]	Apparel
	'Trevira'[10]	Apparel, domestic and industrial
	'Trevira CS'[10]	Fire retardant.
polyvinyl derivatives:		
acrylic	'Acrilan'[14]	Carpets
	'Cashmilon'[1]	Apparel, industrial

Generic names	Some trade-names	Major uses
acrylic (cont.)	'Courtek M'[6]	Hygienic uses and barrier clothing. (Bactericidal)
	'Courtek N'[6]	Nonwovens and paper
	'Courtelle'[6]	Knitwear
	'Dolan'[10]	Carpets
	'Dolanit'[10]	Industrial uses
	'Dralon'[3]	Domestic uses
	'Dralon X160'[3]	Knitwear, dresses (fine fibre)
	'Neochrome'[6]	Producer dyed fibres e.g. Courtaulds, Courtelle neochrome
	'Orlon'[8]	Knitwear
	'Sekril'[6]	Cement reinforcement
modacrylic	'Teklan'[6] 'Velicren'[18]	Apparel and toys (fire retardant)
chlorofibre (including PVC and polyvinylidene chloride)	'Clevyl'[17]	Contract furnishing
	'Leavil'[15]	
	'Rhovylon'[17]	Underwear, sportswear
	'Rhovylon FR'[17]	Nightwear and institutional blankets (flame retardant)
	'Thermovyl'[17]	
elastane	'Lycra'[8]	Form fitting textiles
polyolefin polypropylene and polyethylene	'Bluebell'[4] 'Fibrite'[20] 'Leolene'[7]	Industrial uses
	'Gymlene'[7]	Carpets and industrial uses
	'Astra'[7]	Carpets, textured fibre
	'Meraklon'[15]	Carpets, deckchair covers, coverstock for nappies, etc.
PEEK (polyetheretherketone)	'ZYEX'[11]	Tennis racquet strings, sports equipment and industrial uses (high elastic recovery)
Described as polyacrylate (cross-linked)	'Inidex'[6]	Fire blankets, fire blocking layer in upholstery.
fluorofibre (PTFE)	'Teflon'[8]	Industrial uses

Table 2 continued

OTHER MANUFACTURED FIBRES

Generic names	*Some trade-names*	*Major uses*
carbon fibre	'Asgard'[6]	Fire blankets, Fire barrier in upholstery (Partially carbonised and black)
	'Grafil'[6]	Industrial uses.
	'Panox'[5]	Heat and flame resistant.
glass fibre	'Fibreglas'[19]	Industrial uses.

It is inappropriate to provide a comprehensive list of fibre producers but it is useful to note that Japan is a major fibre producer and includes the following manufacturers: Toray Industries, Mitsubishi, Unitika.

Key to fibre manufacturers

1 Asahi Chemical Industry, Japan
2 Avtex Fibers, USA
3 Bayer, Germany
4 Belfast Ropework, UK
5 R K Carbon Fibres, UK
6 Courtaulds Fibres, UK
7 F Drake (Fibres), UK
8 Du Pont, USA
9 Enka, Holland
10 Hoechst-Celanese, Germany
11 ICI, UK
12 Kemira OY Sateri, Finland
13 Lenzing, Austria
14 Monsanto Chemical, USA
15 Montefibre, Italy
16 Rhodia Toce, Italy
17 Rhône-Poulenc, France
18 Snia Fibre, Italy
19 Pilkington, UK
20 Plasticisers, UK
21 Teijin, Japan
22 Toyobo, Japan

What textile fibres are

A large number of fibres twisted together form a yarn. If a thread is untwisted, the fibres can be separated and looked at, and it will be seen that each fibre is long compared with its thickness. In fact, it is said to have 'a high length : diameter ratio'. The length of a cotton fibre, for example, is about 2,000 times greater than its diameter.

Satisfactory yarns can be spun only if the fibres are sufficiently fine and long to grip each other. A large number of long, fine fibres grip each other better when twisted in a thread than a lesser number of coarse fibres. To form a yarn, the fibres are processed by machinery which arranges them parallel and close to each other and twists them together.

The natural fibres, such as cotton, linen, wool and silk, develop naturally in a fibrous form. The manufactured substances used for fibre production may be extruded during manufacture in various forms, such as film or sheet (viscose and acetate are available in this form), or may be moulded into a variety of articles (such as nylon door catches and combs). Before they can be used for the production of textiles, these manufactured substances must be produced in fibrous form, or exceptionally in sheet form.

The fineness and length of some important fibres used for clothing are compared in Figure 3. So far as the natural fibres are concerned, the fibre

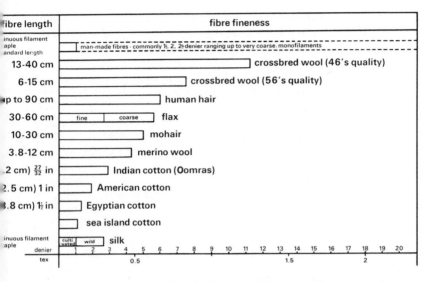

Fig. 3 Length and fineness of natural and manufactured fibres. Fibre fineness is measured by the traditional unit of 'denier' and by the international unit of 'tex'. Denier is the weight in grammes of 9,000 metres of fibre or yarn. Tex is the weight in grammes of 1,000 metres of fibre or yarn. Hence, the denier of a fibre is always equal to nine times its tex. The coarser the fibre, the higher its tex or denier.

characteristics will vary a little according to climatic or other conditions at the time of growth, and also according to the variety of plant or breed of animal. Manufactured fibres, however, have their fibre characteristics determined in the factory. Their diameters can be easily controlled, and they can be made in any length from, say, 1½ in. (3·8 cm) up to continuous filament.

A continuous filament is a fibre of indefinite length, that is, it runs continuously throughout the length of the yarn without a break. Continuous filament yarns are frequently used in such cloths as satin, foulard, and taffeta. If a thread is removed from such a fabric it is possible to verify whether it is made from continuous filament or short fibres (i.e., 'staple fibre') by untwisting it.

Fibre structure

Each fibre, whether it is manufactured or from a natural source, has a characteristic internal structure. Viewing the fibre under the microscope will enable only the surface of the fibre and its cross-section to be examined. This, of course, is a useful aid in fibre identification, but what we are concerned with here is the structure of the interior of the fibre. Scientists may study fibre structure by many techniques, such as X-rays or the electron microscope, and it is necessary for us to have a little understanding of fibre structure, since it has an important bearing on why, for example, some fibres are strong, others weak, or why some absorb water readily and others only a little.

Matter is composed of atoms which join together in groups to form what are referred to as molecules. The shape of the molecule will depend upon how the atoms have joined together. Molecules can link up to form long chains, and it is these 'chain molecules' which are essential to the structure of the long, fine textile fibres. If the molecules do not form long chains they will not be able to form textile fibres. The formation of the long-chain molecular structures from the basic molecules is known as polymerisation.

The term 'polymer' may be used in the context of natural polymer fibres (eg., cotton, viscose, wool) and synthetic polymer fibres (eg., polyamide, polyester).

Whilst all textile fibres are made from long-chain molecules, the substance of which the molecule consists will differ for the various types of fibres. Some synthetic polymer fibres consist of a combination of two or more different chemical units joined together to form a chain; this is known as a co-polymer, and the acrylics are an example of such a fibre construction.

Cellulose in cotton consists of carbon, hydrogen, and oxygen, and the unit or molecule in the cellulose chain is shown in Figure 4. Such units join end to end to form the chain molecule, as shown in Figure 5.

If the molecules inside the fibre lie parallel to each other and to the length of the fibre, they are referred to as being highly oriented. Cotton and flax are both composed of cellulose, and the molecules in flax are highly oriented, whereas in cotton a greater proportion of molecules lie at an angle to the fibre axis. Because of this, all the molecules in flax can share a tension applied to the length of the fibre, whereas in cotton, because some molecules lie across the fibre axis, the load is not equally shared by all. This is one important reason why flax is stronger than cotton.

Since the molecules in cotton are not highly oriented, some of the molecules 'straighten out' in the direction of the axis of the fibre when a

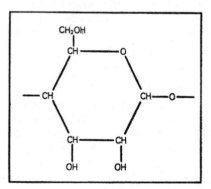

Fig. 4 Each molecule in the cellulose chain consists of carbon, hydrogen, and oxygen.

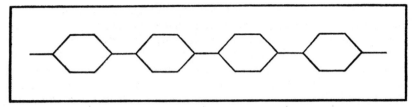

Fig. 5 Molecules as shown in Figure 4 join end to end to form a chain molecule.

tension is applied. Consequently, cotton extends more than flax.

A second feature of internal fibre structure is that the molecules are joined sideways to each other by cross-links which occur at intervals along the molecular length. This cross-linking prevents the molecules sliding past each other and has important effects. For example, the cross-linking of the wool molecules makes the wool fibre springy and gives it good recovery from creasing. The resin treatment of fabrics made from cotton or viscose introduces cross-links between the molecules in the fibre, and so produces a great improvement in crease recovery.

If the molecules are packed together in an orderly fashion the fibre is said to be crystalline. Within all fibres there are both crystalline and non-crystalline regions, and some fibres contain more crystalline regions than others.

Figure 6 shows in a highly diagrammatic fashion a probable arrangement of molecules in a well oriented textile fibre. The regions of orderly crystalline arrangement of the molecules are marked A; B indicates a disordered region. The molecules must be imagined to be joined by cross-links at intervals where they run close together. They are extremely long in relation to their width. Ten million molecules packed side by side would occupy a space of about one millimetre.

It is known that the water molecule is attracted to particular places on the fibre molecule. In the case of the cellulose molecule in cotton there is a fairly large number of such places; triacetate contains

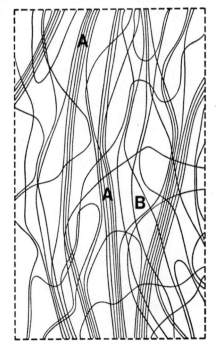

Fig. 6 Arrangement of molecules in a well-oriented textile fibre.

fewer, and polyester fibres very few. In crystalline regions it is difficult for the water to penetrate between the regularly packed molecules and become attached. Non-crystalline regions are more easily penetrated by the water because of the larger spaces between the molecules. Therefore, apart from the known water attraction of a fibre, the extent of crystallinity will have an important effect on the amount of water that can be absorbed. Viscose, which consists essentially of cellulose, absorbs more moisture than cotton. This is largely due to viscose being less crystalline.

Coupled with moisture absorption is, of course, the relative ease or difficulty in dyeing certain fibres, since this is dependent on the ability of water to carry the dye into the fibre. Special methods of dyeing have to be used for such fibres as polyester, which absorbs very little water.

Variations in the manufacturing processes are used to produce several types of viscose having different combinations of properties. For example, high tenacity viscose is stronger and less extensible than regular viscose. Modal and the new solvent-spun lyocell fibre, are more like cotton in character than either of these fibres, particularly in respect of low extensibility.

The aspects of the manufacturing processes that can be varied are the composition of the bath in which coagulation takes place, the degree to which the fibres are stretched during coagulation, and the degree to which they are stretched after coagulation. By varying these details, it is possible to produce fibres having high or low crystallinity, high or low orientations of the molecules, and also fibres with or without a 'skin' in which the molecules are more highly oriented than in the body of the fibre. High orientation confers high strength and low extensibility, and the elimination of the 'skin' improves the strength of the fibre by making it more uniform across its cross-section. Fibres can also be made to have variable thickness of skin, and this causes the fibre to become crimped.

Different varieties of each of the other man-made fibres can be produced by modifying the manufacturing process. In addition, fibre crimping can be achieved in synthetic fibres by extruding two separate polymers, so that the resultant bi-component filament consists of two parts which shrink differently and consequently distort and crimp.

Fibre properties

It must be realised that there is no fibre type that possesses all the properties generally required for most end uses. The properties that are sometimes looked for in clothing are comfort, warmth, easy laundering, and the ability to withstand hard wear, hold pleats, and shed unwanted creases after use. Wool fibres can, for example, provide all these properties except for pleat retention and easy laundering, but these deficiencies can be put right by applying special processes which alter the wool fibre. Many finishing processes are available for modifying particular fibre properties for special purposes.

Another method of obtaining a better combination of desirable properties than is available in one type of fibre is by blending, that is mixing together fibres of different types. What is lacking in one fibre may be supplemented by the others.

Choice of fabric for particular purposes, such as beachwear, evening-wear, rainwear, cool or warm clothing, is consciously or subconsciously influenced by the properties of the fibre. The physical properties of most interest to us are listed and discussed below.

Fineness

The fineness of a fibre is measured by its denier or decitex value. (The decitex of a fibre is equal to ten times its tex; millitex is 1000 times tex.)

Fibre fineness is a fundamental property and governs the use to which the fibre can be put. Thus the coarsest fibres cannot be used in textile applications but may be made into brushes. Horse hair can be made into yarns and woven, but the only clothing use for such fabrics has been stiff interlinings. The fibres used for clothing fabrics rarely exceed 15 decitex and most commonly they are below 5 decitex.

In a yarn of given tex the finer the fibres the greater the number in the yarn cross-section. It is found that a more regular yarn can be spun from a staple fibre if the average number of fibres in the cross-section is high. If the number is too low the yarn is irregular and liable to break at the weakest places. Thus fine staple fibres are needed for the production of fine yarns.

Cloth made from fine fibres or filaments has a softer and smoother 'handle' than an identical cloth made from coarser fibres or filaments, because the finer fibres are much softer than coarser ones. Since the yarns are more regular the cloths are more regular in appearance, and held up to the light are likely to appear better covered. The cloths from the finer fibres are also likely to have a softer and more subtle lustre. Finer fibres are, of course, more easily damaged than coarser ones and for this reason they are associated with a lower resistance to abrasion in the fabric. Being also more flexible they are likewise more liable to become entangled in the little balls of fibre associated with the defect known as 'pilling' (page 181).

Often the choice of tex of manufactured staple depends on the other components of a blend into which it is to be spun, since the various components should not differ widely in this respect. Thus for blending with cotton fibres manufactured staple of 1·7–3·3 decitex may be used, whereas for wool the decitex chosen is more likely to be about 4·5–7. Similarly, manufactured staple fibre will be chosen to match in length the natural fibres in the blend.

Moisture absorption

The amount of moisture which textile fibres are capable of absorbing affects their value in clothing fabrics, since it influences:

a) the comfort of the wearer.
b) the amount of shrinkage that will occur during laundering.
c) the speed with which the textile will dry after laundering.
d) the development of static electricity. (See static electricity, page 14.)

The amount of moisture absorbed by different fibres at a relative humidity of 65% and temperature of 20°C, is indicated in Figure 7.

Definitions

i) *Relative humidity* (r.h.). The ratio of the actual pressure of the water vapour in the atmosphere to the saturation pressure of water vapour at the same temperature.
ii) *Moisture regain* %. The weight of moisture in a material expressed as a percentage of the weight of the completely dry material.

Figure 7 also shows the amount of water vapour absorbed from a moderately humid atmosphere by these textile fibres in normal use. Of course, all the fibres will absorb more moisture when immersed in water.

Comfort

When sitting quietly 'doing nothing', the body transpires through its sweat glands about one pint of water per day. If, on the other hand, there is a rise in environmental temperature and great physical activity, sweat may be secreted at the rate of 1½ pints per hour.

Some of the water evaporates directly from the skin, but some is first absorbed by clothing and then passed on to the air. Whilst the physiology of clothing is discussed on page 212, it must be remembered here that the ability of the textile to absorb water vapour from the skin, and so keep the skin comfortable, is especially important when the wearer is very active.

When fibres absorb either liquid water or water vapour, heat is released, and the claim sometimes made for wool that it feels warm 'even when damp' is to some extent based on this. The fact is that wool is capable of absorbing a large amount of moisture, and therefore provides comfort for quite a time before it becomes obviously wet. But, it is doubtful whether the amount of heat generated on absorption is very noticeable to the wearer and, in any case, once the small amount of heat has been produced it is fairly quickly dispersed.

Shrinkage

A fibre swells when it absorbs water, and the swelling shows as a large increase in diameter and some increase in length. As would be expected, fibres which absorb little water tend to swell less than fibres which are very

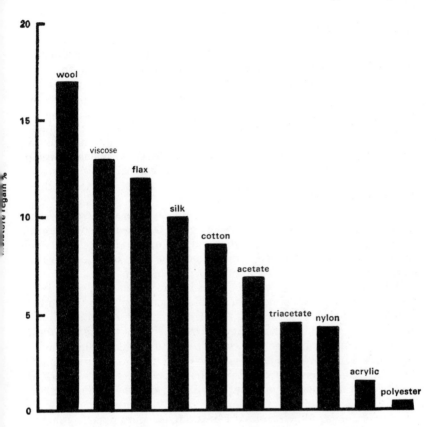

Fig. 7 Moisture regain of fibres.

absorbent, although, surprisingly, wool and silk swell rather less than cotton. Regular viscose shows a very high degree of swelling.

The swelling of fibres is an important cause of fabric shrinkage during laundering, and this is explained under that heading on page 172. However, the ability of fibres to swell in water is used to advantage in the making of crêpe fabrics (see page 84) and is responsible for the closing up or 'sealing up' of the space between threads in 'Ventile' fabrics, which were specially designed for shower-proof garments (page 226).

Rate of drying

Because polyester, polyamide, and polyacrylic fibres absorb only a little water when laundered, they will dry sooner than wool, viscose, and cotton.

Static electricity

The term 'static' means stationary, not flowing. Electricity is known to us usually as a current or flow in a conductor such as a wire or electric lamp. Where static electricity develops there is an accumulation of electricity which does not readily flow away. Static electricity develops when two different substances are rubbed together or even when the surface of two different materials are simply brought together and then separated. If the materials are bad conductors of electricity, the 'static' tends to stay where it is produced. Everyone has experienced at some time the development of 'static' in a comb when it has been used briskly for combing the hair, and then, whilst still charged, it is found to attract small pieces of paper.

The development of 'static' charges results in a negative charge being found on one surface and a positive charge on the other. It is well known that similar charges repel each other and that unlike charges attract one another. Hence, the charged comb attracts the hair, but the individual hairs repel each other and become 'unruly'.

Static electricity in textiles usually leaks away without us ever being aware that it has been generated. It leaks by flowing along those fibres which are good electrical conductors. All fibres are better conductors when damp than when dry; hence, static electricity is more in evidence under dry conditions. Cotton and viscose do not accumulate 'static' unless exceptionally dry: wool, silk, and acetate will show evidence of 'static' only under dry conditions; polyester, polyamide, and the acrylics, which are good electrical insulators with low moisture absorption even under fairly damp conditions, can show evidence of 'static' in the following ways:

Garment clinging. When a top skirt and underskirt are oppositely charged because they have been rubbing together, they stick to one another. In use, one garment will tend to ride up on the other. It is sometimes found effective to rinse the garment in a wetting agent (a number of well-known makes are available) before drying. This agent remains on the surface of the fibre and improves the conduction of electricity, and so helps to increase the flow of static away from the garments.

Fabric soiling. If the dirt and the fibres are oppositely charged, it is found that the fine dirt can become intimately attached to the fibre surface, and afterwards clings so hard that it is difficult to remove by laundering. Underskirts made from certain polyester fibres, for this reason, frequently show soiling or 'greying', especially in the lower part of the skirt where there is a greater amount of movement between the fabric surfaces and consequent development of static electricity.

Sparking and crackling of clothing on removal after being worn. Sometimes, if a shirt or blouse made from one of the fibres which are good electrical insulators is removed fairly vigorously, a spark and crackle may be noticed. Whilst this is of no importance in normal use, it has been found that sparks from clothing can cause an explosion if inflammable vapours are present. This has been of concern in hospital operating theatres, since some anaesthetics are explosive.

In order to overcome these particular defects in fabrics, research continues in the development of durable and inexpensive anti-static finishes which can be satisfactorily applied to fabric.

Tensile strength, extensibility, and elastic recovery

If you take a length of sewing thread, tie one end to a spring balance, and apply a gradually increasing pull to it, a point will be reached when it will break. The load at which it breaks can be read off the scale on the spring balance. In this simple way you can measure roughly the tensile strength of the thread. The amount the thread stretches or extends before it breaks will not be very great. If instead of a sewing thread a similar length of elastic is put in its place, this will stretch a long way before it breaks. So it can be said that elastic has a higher extensibility than sewing thread.

The strengths and extensibilities of the various fibres are known, and some examples appear in Figure 8. Obviously, special apparatus is used in textile laboratories for measuring these accurately. A great deal of importance is attached to knowing the strength and extensibility of a fibre, since the strength of a sewing thread or a yarn in a fabric cannot be greater than the total strength of all the individual fibres which are contained in the yarn, and is usually appreciably less.

As can be seen from Figure 8, there are some differences between the strengths and extensibilities of fibres and, as might be expected from what has been said earlier, these properties are dependent on the chemical

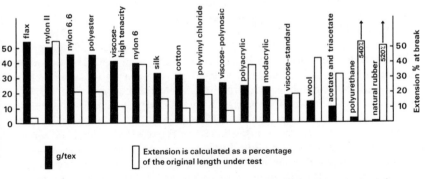

Fig. 8 Tenacity and extensibility of fibres at 65% relative humidity and 20°C.
The strength of a fibre or yarn depends, of course, on its fineness or coarseness. In order to bring all fibres to a common basis, independent of their fineness, it is usual to divide their strengths measured in grammes by the tex of the fibre or by the denier of the fibre. The result is known as 'tenacity' measured in units of g/tex and g/denier. The same units are used for yarn strength.

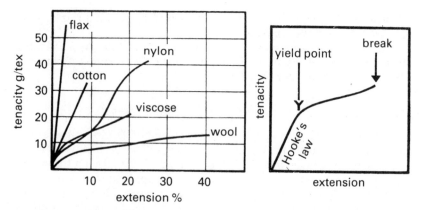

Fig. 9 Load-extension curve

Fig. 10 Diagram of yield point

composition and internal structure of the fibre. For example, viscose used for clothing is not a highly oriented fibre, but if it is stretched during the course of production the molecules turn into the direction of the stretch and the fibre becomes more crystalline, with the result that it is stronger but less extensible.

An easy way of comparing the strengths and extensibility of fibres is to examine Figure 9, which shows how much the fibre extends at certain loads and how much it extends before it breaks.

The graph, or 'load-extension curve', shows that wool is of only moderate strength but is very extensible; nylon is strong and very extensible, and cotton strong but not very extensible. It will be noticed that in most of the curves the first part is almost straight. In this part the extension is proportional to the load applied, and at these low loads the fibre is therefore said to obey Hooke's law.

After the point marked 'Y' (known as the 'yield point') in Figure 10, extension becomes easier with each small increase in load. If the load is removed from the fibre before the yield point is reached it will recover almost to its original length; that is, its elastic recovery is good. If, however, the fibre is loaded progressively beyond its yield point, its ability to recover from being stretched becomes less and less. The reason for this is that in the straight part of the curve as the load is applied the chain molecules are simply stretched, but once the yield point is passed, the cross-links between the molecules, which are under an increasing strain, break progressively and allow extension to occur more easily. Because of this change in the fibre, recovery is not complete.

Recovery from extension is an important property in a fibre for use in clothing. Garments made from fibres having good recovery maintain their shape well and shed creases readily, whereas poor recovery leads to bagginess and unwanted creases.

It will be seen that nylon and wool are good in this respect. This is why nylon is used in tights, since when worn the tights must not look baggy about the knee.

It must be appreciated that Figure 11 compares the recoveries of fibres after they have all been stretched to the same small extension, *not* when they are all loaded equally. If a comparison of recoveries is made after the fibres have all been subjected to the same *stress*, the results would be different. This is important when the recoveries are applied to particular conditions of use.

The effects of moisture, temperature, and light on the strengths and extensibilities of fibre will now be briefly discussed.

Effect of water

Cotton and linen become stronger when wet and all other fibres become weaker, although to different extents, as shown in Figure 12. Nearly all fibres are more extensible when wet.

Obviously, those fibres which show a large drop in strength when wet require more careful laundering.

Effect of temperature

Whilst most of us will be spared the rigours of an Arctic expedition or high altitude or outer space exploration, it is of interest to note that the behaviour of textiles under these conditions has been investigated. At temperatures ranging from 57°C to 177°C, fibres are always found to be

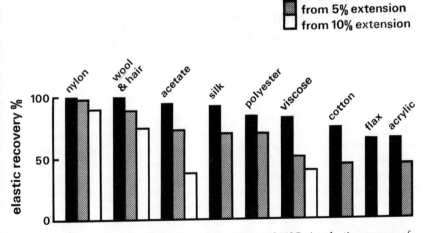

Fig. 11 **Elastic recovery at 65% relative humidity and 20°C.** An elastic recovery of 100% indicates complete recovery from the imposed extension. Recovery of 50% indicates that half the imposed extension is recovered, and so on.

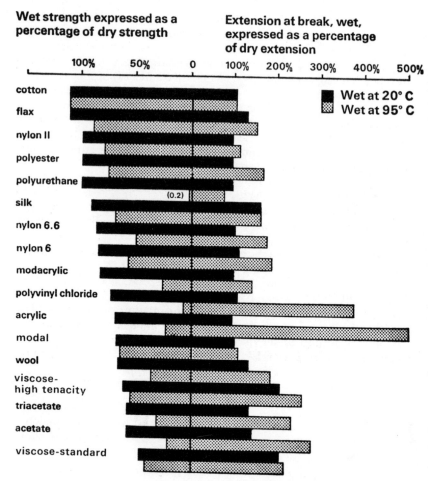

Fig. 12 Strengths and breaking extensions of some fibres when wet.

strongest at the lowest temperature, with a progressive drop in strength as the temperature increases. The effect is particularly marked in acrylics, which show a very large drop in tensile strength and a large increase in extensibility, especially in the presence of moisture.

Because of these changes special care is required in dyeing, which is nearly always conducted in hot water. It is essential that garments should be pressed in the dry state and at as low a temperature as convenient.

Effect of light

Light produces very complicated changes in widely different substances, such as green chlorophyl in leaves and silver compounds in photographic emulsion. When textiles are exposed to light, changes are liable to occur.

Oxidation by atmospheric oxygen can be activated by ultraviolet (UV) light and this is sometimes referred to as photochemical degradation. Heat has a similar activating effect. The degradation of textiles arises from the breakdown of chemical bonding within the fibre. A decrease in wavelength of light below 380 namometre (nm) accelerates the rate and extent of fibre damage by reducing the molecular length. This can be further accelerated by an accompanying rise in temperature and humidity.

The eventual drop in strength and extensibility due to 'light' tendering is important for such items as curtains, and for textiles used outdoors such as tents and awnings, but less so for clothing in temperate climates.

Delustred or dull manufactured fibres show a bigger drop in strength upon exposure than bright fibres and some dyes increase the sensitivity of the fibres to light. An example of light tendering is the loss in strength that occurs in curtains at a sunny window, although the presence of glass tends to filter out some of the very short wavelengths to advantage. Polyester shows a high resistance to light tendering under these conditions and is therefore a good choice for window curtains.

Polypropylene is particularly sensitive, cellulosic and protein fibres, nylon and polyester, are all affected to some degree. Acrylic fibres show particularly high resistance to UV. Coated fabrics, depending on the composition of the coating, can be liable to such chemical tendering.

Textile finishes and chemical modifications during the production of manufactured fibres have been devised to prevent the oxidation processes.

Tests are available to determine the degree of chemical damage due to a reduction in molecular length. The principle of the method is to measure the 'fluidity' of a solution of the fibre in a suitable solvent. The more fluid the solution, the greater is the reduction in molecular length associated with chemical damage; the more viscous the solution the less chemical damage. BS2610 'Methods of test for the determination of the cuprammonium fluidity of cotton and certain cellulose man-made fibres' is an example of such a test.

Resistance to abrasion

Fabrics are abraded in use against various materials (elbows on tables, fabric against fabric under the arm); under various pressures (the seat of a pair of slacks); under dry and wet conditions (a wet gabardine raincoat or fabric in the washing machine). The life of a fabric is very dependent on its resistance to abrasion. Apart from abrasive actions, there are other causes of breakdown such as continual flexing at the elbow of a sleeve. There are many different types of wear, and for this reason it has been difficult for textile laboratories to imitate them satisfactorily. One way of finding out how textiles will wear is to put them into service, but such a consumer trial is a slow and expensive way of comparing fibres.

However, it may safely be stated that nylon has an outstanding resistance to abrasion compared with all other fibres, and this property is of great value, especially when nylon is blended with other fibres. Polyester fibre is excellent also in this respect. Cotton and wool have good resistance to abrasion, and the other fibres show adequate durability in the types of end uses for which they are intended.

The abrasion resistance of a fabric is very much influenced not only by the choice of fibre but also the construction of the yarn and fabric.

Crease recovery

All textiles to be used in clothing must be flexible and capable of being creased and folded to conform to the figure and be comfortable to wear. If they are to retain a good appearance, however, they must have good crease-shedding properties; that is, recovery from unwanted creases that occur in a fabric in use and during laundering.

When a fibre is bent, two things can happen:

1) The cross-links may break and join in new positions. When the load is removed, recovery from the crease is restricted by the new positioning of the cross-links, and the textile will show poor crease recovery.

2) The cross-links may be stretched without actually breaking, so that when the load is removed they will tend to return the fibre to its original shape.

Figures 13 and 14 show in schematic form the behaviour of the cross-links during creasing.

The recovery of textiles from creasing will be influenced by whether the fabric is in the dry or the wet state, or at an elevated temperature. The presence of water weakens the cross-links, and this is why creasing is

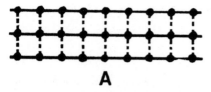

A

B   **C**

Fig. 13 Creasing and crease-recovery.
A – Schematic representation of fibre structure with cross-links.

Fig. 14 Creasing and crease-recovery.
B – Formation of new cross-links, giving a crease.
C – Straining of cross-links, leading to crease-recovery.

Figs 13–14 from *Physical Properties of Textile Fibres*, by Morton and Hearle.)

usually more evident in fabrics which are made from fibres with high moisture absorption* and which have been creased whilst wet.

Certain fibres are softened by heat, and unwanted creases formed in these fibres at elevated temperatures may become set in the fabric on cooling. (The explanation of this is given on page 22.)

A comparison of the crease recoveries of various fibres is given below, but it must be realised that the crease recovery of a fabric is dependent on the details of its construction as well as on its fibre composition.

Table 3 RATING OF FIBRES IN RESPECT OF RECOVERY FROM DRY CREASING

Poor	*Fair*	*Good*	*Very good*
acetate	silk (Tussah)	acrylic	polyester
cotton	triacetate	modacrylic	wool
viscose	polyvinyl chloride	nylon	
		polypropylene	
		silk (Bombyx)	

Stiffness

When fabrics are handled, one often comments on their stiffness, draping quality, softness, firmness, and similar properties. These characteristics of a fabric help to determine what style of garment can most suitably be made from it. They depend on the construction of the yarn and cloth and the way in which it is finished, but also on the fibre from which it is made. The most important fibre property in this connection is the fibre *stiffness*.

By the stiffness of a fibre is meant its resistance to bending. This is governed mainly by two features, the fibre fineness and the resistance of the fibre to stretching.

Fibre fineness

Fine fibres in a given material are less stiff than coarse fibres. Compare, for example, the stiffness of the coarse nylon filament in a toothbrush with fine fibres used in a nylon fabric. One reason why fibres are made available in a range of fineness is to give scope for variations in the 'handle' of fabrics.

However, it must be added that the stiffness of a filament depends not only on its fineness but on the shape of the cross-section.

Resistance to stretching

It will be appreciated that when a fibre is bent, the outside of the curve must be longer than the inside of the curve. One side of the fibre must therefore be stretched relative to the other side. It is only because part of the fibre has to be stretched when it is bent that it has stiffness; that is, a

---

* This statement is not applicable to some fabrics with special finishes. (See page 9.)

resistance to being bent. Fibres which are the easiest to stretch are also those which are easiest to bend. Looking back to the load-extension curves for wool and flax, it will be seen that wool extends more easily than flax at low loads and, in fact, measurements show that wool is less stiff than flax when fibres of the same fineness are tested.

Thermal conductivity

The warmth or coolness of clothing is sometimes ascribed to the fact that the wool fibre is a poor conductor of heat and so feels warm, and that linen is a good conductor of heat and therefore feels cool to the touch. This is only a small part of the truth. The insulating effect of clothing is greatly influenced by the structure of the yarn and fabric. (This is discussed on page 214.)

Heat setting

Certain fibres, such as polyester, polyamide, and triacetate, are known as thermoplastic fibres because they become soft and plastic at elevated temperatures, returning to their normal state on cooling. When a fabric made from such a fibre is taken to a high temperature and then cooled, it becomes 'heat-set'. The cross-links between the molecules are broken by the heat, and new cross-links occur whilst the fabric is in its new shape. When the fabric is cooled it is difficult to disturb the new cross-links, and the fabric will retain its new shape in spite of the conditions of use. Because moisture-absorbent fibres such as cotton and viscose have their cross-links broken by the entry of water into the fibre, it is impossible to heat-set these fibres without the application of special finishes.

If a fabric made from thermoplastic fibres is given a flat, smooth surface free from creases and is then heat-set, it will retain its good appearance provided that the temperature at which it was set is not exceeded again, as in laundering, for example. Seam-free nylon stockings are knitted without any shaping of the leg. In this form each stocking is placed on a 'leg shape' which is then heated and cooled, thus setting the standard leg shape which is available in seam-free and other stockings.

Heat-setting of thermoplastic fibres is a very important property which is used for forming permanent pleats in garments, embossing effects in fabrics, and in the production of textured yarns (see page 67). The pleats, size, and shape of garments made from textiles which have been heat-set will be retained provided that, as mentioned before, high temperatures are not applied in use.

Flame retardance

Attention has been focused on the flame retardance of textiles because of the deaths and injuries caused by inflammable garments. The problem of providing safe clothing, especially for children and the elderly, resulted in the Home Secretary issuing the Nightwear Safety Regulations 1985, under the Consumer Protection Act 1987.

The flame retardance of a fabric depends to a large extent on the fibre or blend of fibres from which it is constructed. The relative flame retardance of fibres is considered on page 233.

Heat sensitivity

Heat sensitivity of fibres during laundering and ironing is indicated on pages 266 and 267.

Friction

The interest in friction extends here particularly to its connections with:

a) the ease with which a thread passes through the sewing machine;
b) the fraying of fabrics;
c) the laddering of tights;
d) the felting of wool.

When two threads, or for that matter any two materials, are made to slide past each other, they tend to stick, and force is required to keep them moving. The magnitude of this force indicates the level of friction between the two surfaces. For instance, sliding on an icy road surface is easier than on the road itself because the friction between the shoe and the surface has been greatly reduced by the presence of the ice.

A thread made from short fibres twisted together depends upon the friction between the fibres to prevent them slipping past each other when a load is applied. This should remind us of the almost parallel need of the long-chain molecules to have cross-links which prevent them slipping past each other and so help to maintain the fibre structure. A thread of a given thickness will be stronger if it is composed of a greater number of long, fine fibres than a similar thread containing fewer coarser fibres, because it has a greater area of fibre surface over which friction can act.

Too high a fibre friction, however, can be troublesome in sewing threads. The thread is required to pass with ease over various metal parts and through the eye of the needle, since if the friction is high the thread may break. Lockstitch sewing machines used in the clothing industry may operate at up to 5,000 stitches per minute, whilst machines used in the home run at a maximum speed of 1,000 stitches per minute. At high sewing speeds it is even more important to have a very low friction thread, because there is a rise in the temperature of the needle in the vicinity of the eye due to the friction of the thread and, in the case of threads made from thermoplastic fibres, this may cause melting or fusing of the fibres. In order to reduce the thread friction, sewing thread manufacturers always apply a lubricant.

The ease with which threads fray out of a piece of fabric when cut and the tendency for some fabrics to fray at seams is largely due to low friction between the threads which allows the threads to slip past one another. Smooth, continuous filament yarns are liable to do this. Fraying can be greatly reduced if the cloth is closely woven, but this closer structure would, of course, affect the character of the fabric. Special finishes can be used on the fabric to increase the inter-fibre and inter-yarn friction. Resin finishes are often used for this purpose, and are frequently used on tights made from nylon.

The felting of wool depends on the friction of its surface scales being greater when a fibre is pulled against the scales than when it is pulled in the opposite direction. This effect is utilised in wool fabric finishing and in the production of woollen felts. As discussed on page 173, it is the cause of unwanted shrinkage in fabrics made from wool. The frictional effect can be reduced by modifying the scales in finishing.

Density

The density of a substance is its weight in grams per cubic centimetre. Alternatively, the reciprocal of density, 'specific volume', tells us how many cubic centimetres of the material weigh one gram. (Obviously, a gram of cork occupies a greater volume than a gram of lead.)

The density of a fibre depends upon the weight of the molecules of which it is made and how closely they are packed together. Glass has a high density because of the fairly heavy atoms that are present, whereas the bulky shape of the molecules in wool and nylon prevent them packing closely, and result in fibres of low density. In highly crystalline fibres, the molecules are densely packed, and the fibres have high densities.

The fibres having the lowest densities are polyethylene and kapok. The former is made into ropes which will float in water (whereas hemp and cotton ropes sink), and the latter is used for filling life-jackets.

Yarns made from low density fibres are more bulky than yarns of the same count (or tex) made from fibres of higher density. Hence a knowledge of fibre densities is necessary in the development of cloth constructions.

Since the densities of fibres are known, it is possible to identify fibres by observing whether they sink or float in liquids of known density.

Lustre

The term 'lustre' refers to the manner in which light is reflected from a surface. If the surface is very smooth the light is reflected as from a mirror, and this is referred to as specular reflection. No cloth reflects light as perfectly as this, but ciré fabrics have a hard, shiny lustre of this kind. On the other hand, a surface which reflects light equally in all directions is said to be 'matt', and is practically without lustre, such as winceyette. The most interesting surfaces tend to reflect light strongly in particular directions, with a background of scattered light. The attractive lustre of fabrics such as satins and taffetas is produced in this way.

Whilst lustre can be changed or improved by fabric finishing, according to the requirements of fashion, the fibre itself makes an important contribution to the nature of the lustre, and in this connection the following points are of importance:

1) Fine fibres provide a greater number of reflecting surfaces than fewer coarse fibres in a similar thickness of yarn. Hence, fine fibres produce a softer sheen than coarse fibres.

2) Fibres that are uniform in diameter along their length have a greater lustre than fibres that are not regular. For example, silk and manufactured fibres have a greater lustre than fibres which are not so regular, such as cotton and wool.

3) The shape of the fibre cross-section affects the degree of lustre. Circular fibres are very lustrous. Triangular fibres such as silk have a soft lustre. Tri-lobal nylon shows a sparkling type of lustre. Cotton, after mercerisation, has a more circular cross-section, and this improves the lustre of the fibre.

4) Manufactured fibres can have their lustre subdued by introducing fine particles of, say, titanium dioxide into the fibre during production. Since the fibres are translucent, that is, they allow the passage of light, the presence of the delustring particles within causes the light to be scattered and so makes the fibre appear to be dull.

5) Yarns made from continuous filaments are more lustrous than those made from short fibres, that is, staple fibre.

Microbiological attack

Micro-organisms such as fungi and bacteria abound in the air, water and soil, and in warm humid conditions they proliferate on substances such as textiles and on adhesives, starch, plastics, finishes and coatings that are applied to textiles and that provide the nutrients needed.

Such microbiological activity is described as an attack since the basic textile is liable to be damaged chemically, and weakened by substances produced by the micro-organisms. Visible evidence of this type of activity may often show as the development of dark or coloured spots or stains ('mildew') that may be difficult to remove. In a severe attack the textile may disintegrate completely, that is become 'rotten'.

Natural cellulosic fibres, jute in particular, are susceptible to such attack, the non-cellulosic constituents of the fibres providing the nutrients. Protein fibres and the acetates are more resistant, and the synthetic fibres are the most resistant. However, the activity of micro-organisms living on plasticisers and other additives may damage even synthetic fibres by the substances this activity produces.

Biocides, which prevent the development of micro-organisms, are included in a variety of fabric finishing treatments that confer water repellancy and fire retardance, and for products such as shoe linings, garden umbrellas, sails, boat covers and uniforms.

The risks of biological degradation of textiles is particularly high in the tropics, where there is a combination of high humidity and high temperature.

Weathering

Microbiological attack is one of a number of causes of weathering, a term applied to the deterioration of textiles, used or exposed out-of-doors. Deterioration may become apparent by fading, or yellowing, or loss of strength, and is attributable to any of a range of climatic conditions including sunlight and the presence of ozone.

The various fibre types react differently to the range and combinations of weather conditions, and it is necessary, therefore, when assessing the probable behaviour of a product in out-of-doors use, to consider its reaction to all the variables of exposure, including ultraviolet (UV) radiation and micro-organisms.

Insect attack

Moths are responsible for a great deal of damage to wool. About 50 eggs are laid by each female clothes moth on fabric in dark, usually unventilated, places. When the ravenous grub emerges from the egg it needs large quantities of protein, which is provided by wool. The protein in silk is somewhat different from that in wool and is less acceptable to the grub. If the grub has to contend with a blend, wool and acetate for instance, this will not deter it, since the unwanted fibre will simply pass unchanged through the digestive tract. The grub has a preference for greasy wool and, therefore, used garments are less liable to attack if they are cleaned before they are put away. Fresh air and sunlight discourage the insects. It is possible to dislodge the eggs by shaking the fabric, but it is obviously advisable to apply a mothproof finish to wool fabrics. Dry-cleaners can do this if required.

Tests to assess the effectiveness of mothproofing are frequently carried out, and this is done by putting the larvae with the fabrics under test in dark, temperature-controlled conditions and then weighing the cloth to assess the loss in weight. If the wool is well proofed, the grub is unable to digest the treated protein and dies.

Chemical properties

The behaviour of fibres towards chemicals is of particular importance in:

Textile processing where the scouring, bleaching, dyeing, printing, and finishing have to be carefully controlled, and the chemicals at various concentrations have to be carefully selected in order to avoid damage to the fibre. This aspect of the behaviour of textiles towards chemicals is not of special importance to most users of textiles, provided the final quality of the textile is up to standard.

Fibre identification. The known sensitivity of different fibres to various concentrations of chemicals is a useful means of fibre identification, and some indication of this is given on page 53. In the quantitative analysis of fibres in a fabric, appropriate solvents are used.

Laundering and dry-cleaning. Generally speaking, cellulosic materials are less sensitive to alkaline than to acid treatment, and the reverse is true of protein fibres. Manufactured fibres are usually stable to dilute concentrations of acids and alkalis, except for cellulose acetate, which is rather sensitive to alkalis.

Acid treatment of textiles in domestic use is usually restricted to the removal of stains. If a spot-removal procedure is being followed, it is important to ensure that the area of fabric is either neutralised or washed after the treatment. Otherwise, a low residual concentration over a lapse of time may damage the fibres.

Alkalis are much used in laundering, and are of value in assisting the emulsification of grease by soap. However, no textile material should be subjected to strong alkali.

The importance of dissolving detergents in the washing liquor prior to the immersion of the fabric cannot be over-stressed, because sprinkling the detergent on the fabric in the water may result in heavy concentrations of powder and severe localised chemical damage.

Dry-cleaning of clothing makes use of organic solvents such as perchloroethylene and trichloroethylene, which remove oil-borne soil and stains. Perchloroethylene is more commonly used than trichloroethylene, which has the disadvantage that triacetate is damaged by it. Since these organic solvents do not cause fibre swelling, no shrinkage occurs on this account, although inherent relaxation shrinkage in the fabric may occur.

Water-borne soil and stains can only be effectively removed by the use of water, and for this purpose a controlled amount of water and detergent is introduced into the solvent during some dry-cleaning processes, and this is known as the 'charged system'.

Bleaching is the process of removing or destroying discolouring matter. This may be done by what is known as a reducing process which is not permanent, since the treated fabric, upon exposure to air, is liable to show a reversal to its original colour. Far more important are the oxidising bleaching agents such as chlorine, hypochlorous acid, perborates, per-

27

manganates, and peroxides, which are effective because they cause the colouring matter to decompose and to be washed away. Hydrogen peroxide is being used increasingly in the textile industry on cellulosic fibre, and is particularly suitable for protein fibres, which are readily dissolved by hypochlorite. At one time some resin finishes used on fabrics absorbed and retained the chlorine liberated by the hypochlorite, and there followed a drop in strength and yellowing of the fabric. If bleaching is carried out for too long or at too high a temperature, the textile is liable to be chemically damaged and to suffer a serious drop in strength. In addition, if the fabric has been dyed with dyes sensitive to bleach, the colour may be destroyed or may bleed.

Synthetic detergents, which are generally innocuous to most fibres, often contain fluorescent brightening agents, generally referred to as 'optical bleach'. Fluorescence describes the ability to absorb invisible ultra-violet 'light' and re-emit the energy as visible light. Whilst fluorescent brighteners do not bleach and cannot be regarded as a substitute for bleaching, they do improve the white sufficiently to permit a reduction in the amount of bleaching required and the risk of damage to the fibres.

SUMMARY OF THE PROPERTIES OF INDIVIDUAL FIBRES

The following section contains information about the sources and properties of the more important fibres.

In dealing with the sources of the synthetic fibres it has been necessary often to refer to chemical compounds by names which may be quite unfamiliar to the reader. These names have a clear significance to a chemist, but it is realised that they will mean little to most of the readers for whom this book is intended. It has, however, been thought advisable to use these names, primarily because the reader will find these substances referred to elsewhere in the literature of textiles.

No information is given on the chemical process involved in the manufacture of the manufactured fibres, but the raw materials which the processes use are stated. If these are stated to be, for example, coal, lime, and salt, it must not be imagined that the fibre is made directly from these. The raw materials are the starting point of a complicated chain of processes in chemical engineering. If the source of a fibre is stated to be 'coal industry' or 'oil industry', it will be understood that these industries provide the raw materials.

The properties are discussed in general terms. It is hoped that the reader will consider the remarks made about the properties of the individual fibres in the light of the information given in the section entitled 'Fibre Properties'.

Natural fibres

Cotton

Source of fibre. Cotton grows from the surface of seed in pods on the Gossypium plant which belongs to the Mallow family. Geneticists continually create complex hybrids to provide good crop growth and fibre quality.

General properties. The principal growers of cotton are listed in the table on page 2, according to the quantity of cotton grown, with Japan as the major importer of raw cotton. Imports of cotton to this country come mainly from the USA, Turkey, Sudan, and West Africa. In common with other natural fibres, cotton is available in a great variety of fibre qualities, which are determined particularly according to fibre length and fibre fineness. The West Indies produces a small quantity of cotton compared with world production, but its supreme excellence is well known and it is commonly known as 'Sea Island'. Its length of about 6 cm (which is extra long for cotton), lustre, fineness, and accompanying softness make it suitable for fine, best quality yarns and fabrics. 'Egyptian type' cotton is classed as a long fibre whereas 'Asiatic' cottons are coarse and have a short staple length, making them suitable only for coarse yarns and fabrics. The official categories of staple length are: short <26 mm, medium 26–29 mm, long 30–38 mm, and extra long 39 mm and over.

Generally speaking, it can be said that all cotton fibres exhibit good moisture absorption, good wet and dry tensile strength and resistance to abrasion, and that they withstand frequent laundering at a high temperature. Fabric finishing is necessary to achieve minimum-care properties, pleat-retention, and minimum shrinkage. Some finishes may restrict the permissible laundering procedures.

Cotton is put to a wide range of uses, such as underwear, blouses, T-shirts, dresses, suits, pocketings, overalls, rainwear, sewing threads. Fabrics which may be made from cotton are voile, poplin, denim, satin, winceyette, corduroy, velveteen, single jersey, terry towelling, lace, and a host of others. Fortunately, cotton is an inexpensive fibre.

Flax

Source of fibre. The fibres are extracted from the stem of the annual plant *Linum Usitatissimum*.

General properties. In common with fibres such as jute and hemp, flax is classed as a bast fibre because it is obtained from the stem of a plant. When flax is converted into yarn and fabric it is known as linen.

The fibre, when first removed from the stem, is about 1 metre long, but during processing some reduction in fibre length occurs. By the time it is ready for spinning, the best quality flax will be about 40 cm long. The length of the fibres contributes to the lack of hairiness and to the lustre of the fabric.

Flax is stronger but less extensible than cotton and has a lower resistance to abrasion. It is more moisture-absorbent and can be laundered similarly to cotton. High fabric shrinkage and creasability of linen is overcome by finishing processes.

Flax forms only a small part of the world's textile fibre production, but its interesting slub texture and thready 'linen-look' have prompted users of manufactured fibres to develop the effect in other fabrics. Up to now it has been easier to bleach the linen fabric after it has been woven rather than bleach the fibres alone, and this has made fibre blending a little difficult. A development in processing enables the flax fibre to be bleached and blended with a wide variety of fibres.

Examples of fine linen fabric are batiste, lawn and handkerchief cambric. Heavier weights of fabrics are used for dresses, suits, and furnishings. Linen sewing thread is used for heavy-duty anchoring of some buttons and the stitching of some footwear.

Wool

Source of fibre. Wool is obtained from the fleece of sheep which comprise many breeds, differing significantly in the characteristics of the fleece.

General properties. The characteristics mainly associated with wool are its warm, soft, full handle, arising largely from the natural fibre crimp and resilience. The handle and other properties, however, are influenced by the type of wool fibre used; e.g., merino being the finest fibre, through crossbred wools, to the coarse wool from mountain sheep.

The fine fibres are up to 12 cm long, the medium wools between 6 and 15 cm, and the long coarser wools up to 40 cm in length. The characteristics of these groups of fibres are reflected by the fabrics into which they are made.

Wool sheds unwanted creases in use, and the fabric can be shaped in the presence of steam to hold a crease and other desired shapes. Special finishes are available to give durable creases. Untreated wool shrinks when washed and is attacked by moths, unless special fabric finishes are applied.

Overcoats, suits, dresses, and carpets are commonly made from wool. Apart from being suitable for knitted fabrics and sweaters, the two big distinctive woven fabric groups are woollen and worsted. Examples of woollen fabrics are afgalaine, flannel, blazer cloth, melton, and tweed. Worsted fabrics include georgette, gabardine, whipcord, and barathea.

Hair

The description 'hair' fibres includes animal fibres other than sheep's wool or silk. The coats of many animals consist of identifiable layers, namely the long coarse outer coat made up of the guard-hairs, and the softer, downy, shorter undercoat.

Hair fibres are generally regarded as rare and expensive, except that obtained from the wild rabbit. Consequently, hair fibres are used as effect fibres in a blend, to modify the handle or appearance of the fabric. Worsted mohair fabrics for suits are expensive, and vicuna overcoating is a rare luxury.

However there is growing interest in developing the use of rare fibres in distinctive fabrics for high value clothing. Fibre price is about £150 per kilogram to £6 per kilogram. This price level raises the possibility of unfair dilution of the fibre by blending with a less expensive hair, and the need to establish a precise method to differentiate between closely related hairs (page 57). Research into the acclimatisation and breeding of selected hair producing animals is occurring in New Zealand, Australia and in Britain, the result so far being 'Cashgora'.

Alpaca

The alpaca, an animal related to the llama, has a fairly fine soft fibre, which can be up to 60 cm long if not sheared. The lustrous black, brown, fawn, or white fibres can be used for tropical suitings, dress fabrics, and pile fabrics. Owing to difficulty experienced in bleaching the fibre, the colour range of resulting fabrics is rather restricted.

Camel hair

The bactrian camel produces an undercoat of strong, soft fibre up to 16 cm long, which has been used for overcoats and dressing gowns. The surface scales enable felted fabrics to be produced. Because of difficulty in bleaching the fibre, it is used undyed, in its natural colour.

Cashgora

This new fibre has the characteristics of cashmere from China but is reared in the climates of New Zealand and Australia. It is a recent breed of animal, the result of a cross between the Angora goat and the wild goat. The white fibre and the quantity of soft down produced per animal are good.

Cashmere

The Tibetan goat's downy undercoat is very fine and about 9 cm long. It has a warm, soft handle and is considered to have attractive properties for clothing. It may be used for knitwear, and at one time was associated with the cashmere shawls.

Mohair

The lustrous, springy, hard-wearing fibre of the angora goat has relatively few surface scales and is therefore mainly used in worsted fabrics. Mohair can be up to 30 cm long and may be used for long pile fabrics.

Rabbit

The common wild rabbit and the angora rabbit have both guard-hairs (about 7·5 cm long) and the undercoat (about 2 cm long). They are used separately for textiles. These very soft fibres often appear in knitted goods as effect fibres in blends. In the manufacture of felts and felt hats, these fibres are felted together to form the fabric. Pure white fibre is associated with the angora rabbit.

Vicuna

The fibre obtained from the vicuna, a type of small llama, is very expensive, fine, and soft and is about 5 cm long. Generally, the natural colour of brown, fawn, or white is utilised in the garment.

Silk

Silk, because of its price, is regarded as a luxury fibre of the *haute couture* class. It accounts for a very small share of the world fibre production.

Cultivated silk

Cultivated silk is produced by the caterpillar of the *Bombyx Mori* moth in continuous filament form. Silk yarn produced by combining several cocoon threads is known as nett silk. It is also available as staple fibre.

Its smooth appearance, soft lustre, fairly good crease-shedding properties, and warm handle are its most valued characteristics. Its draping qualities are excellent, especially when used in lightweight fabrics. Because of the fibre's high tensile strength, sheer fabrics of adequate strength may be produced. Care in washing is necessary owing to the reduction in strength when wet.

Chiffon, jappe, surah, brocade, and velvet are a few fabrics in which silk may be used.

Wild silk

The Tussah variety of wild silk is produced by the caterpillar of the Antheraea type moth. The cross-section of the filament is very irregular throughout its length and this causes the resultant fabric to have a characteristic irregular appearance. Otherwise, wild silk has somewhat similar properties to cultivated silk.

Shantung and tussore are examples of fabrics made from wild silk. However, a wide range of satin back and plain woven wild silk fabrics are used for more expensive formal dress.

Asbestos

Source of fibre. There are many types of asbestos, all of which are mined, the most important being chrysotile.

General properties. This fibre is not used in conventional clothing but since it is quite non-flammable has been used in some protective garments where non-flammability and thermal insulation are required. It is resistant to most common chemicals and to insects and micro-organisms, but its use is restricted because it is a health hazard.

Manufactured fibres

Natural polymer:
Cellulose and variants

Viscose
Special characteristics of fibre production. Cellulose obtained from wood pulp is made into a solution and then extruded through holes in a spinneret, followed immediately by the coagulation of the cellulose in filament form in an acid bath. In this process the fibre is said to be wet spun. Various modifications to the process may be introduced to control the fibre properties, some of which are mentioned below.

Regular viscose
The filaments are stretched sufficiently after extrusion to orient the molecules to the axis of the fibre, thereby developing adequate fibre strength.

This type of viscose has dry strength adequate for many clothing purposes but is weak and extensible when wet. Appropriate finishing reduces fabric shrinkage and produces good crease recovery, but resistance to abrasion is not very good.

The scope of fabric designing is greatly widened by the availability of fibres (as with most manufactured fibres) in both filament and staple forms. Filament viscose, both bright and delustred, is used, for instance, in satin, foulard, and brocade fabrics. Staple fibre is used alone or in blends with other fibres in standard fabrics traditionally made from cotton. Viscose, in common with many other manufactured fibres, may have colour incorporated in the solution before extrusion.

High-tenacity viscose
If a high degree of stretch is applied to the filaments after extrusion, the molecules are better oriented to the fibre axis and the fibre is more crystalline. Consequently, the fibre is stronger and has a lower extension than regular viscose. Although there is a drop in strength when wet, there is an improvement compared with the regular fibre.

Continuous filament of the high-tenacity type finds many applications in industry. High-tenacity staple fibre with an enhanced resistance to abrasion is also available and is utilised in clothing for purposes such as pocketings and in blends with wool for blazer cloths.

Crimped viscose
During fibre production a thicker skin is formed down one side of the filament. This swells differently from the core and so crimps the fibre. On drying, the crimp develops and is permanent. Crimped fibres are valuable where increased resiliency and bulk is required. Fabrics made from crimped fibres have a warm, soft, and full handle.

Deep dyeing viscose

This type of viscose dyes to a deeper shade in the dye bath than standard viscose. Thus by the use of the two kinds together in a fabric, cross-dyed effects can be obtained and a variety of shade combinations can be economically obtained from the same stock or undyed fabric.

Modal

In the production of modal fibre the coagulation and stretching stages of production are modified to obtain a fibre of reduced extensibility when wet, and of good dry and wet strengths. Its water absorption is less than that of regular viscose, and it has, therefore, better dimensional stability. Modal fibres are widely used, often blended with polyester or cotton, in knitted fabrics for undergarments and apparel.

Ribbon-like viscose

The former hollow fibre produced by Courtaulds known as 'Viloft' has been replaced by a solid cross-section, ribbon-like fibre also bearing the 'Viloft' brand name. This fibre is now being used in 50/50 blends with polyester or polypropylene and its prime claims are of increased level of moisture absorption and an improved capacity to transmit moisture from the skin by wicking. Such properties are an advantage in leisure and sportswear and for undergarments.

The dry and wet fibre tenacities are about 21 and 10 cN/tex, with dry and wet extensions at break of about 20% and 27% respectively (cN = centi Newton).

Lyocell

This is a new generic name for a solvent spun cellulose fibre with 'cotton-like' properties, bearing the Courtaulds brand name 'Tencel'. An important advantage of the process environmentally is that the solvent can be reprocessed with practically no effluent problems.

The molecular structure is very different from that of regular viscose, and the fibre has a circular cross-section and smooth surface (Figure 33). The fibre profile is similar to that of a melt-spun synthetic fibre. Currently the fibres are either of bright lustre or matt in staple form. The fibre is receptive to reactive, direct and vat dyes.

The dry and wet fibre tenacities are about 40 and 36 cN/tex, with dry and wet extension at break at about 15% and 17% respectively. Compared with regular viscose, 'Tencel' offers higher tenacities with a lower extension and is very suitable for fibre blending with cotton and polyester. Its moisture regain is 11.5%. Comparison of the stress-strain characteristics in relation to cellulosic fibres and polyester is given in Figure 15. At present the fibre is being used in woven fabrics and it is expected that knitted and nonwoven fabrics will benefit from the inclusion of the new fibre. It is expected that fabrics of appropriate weights and structures will be used for blouses,

ad (cN/tex)

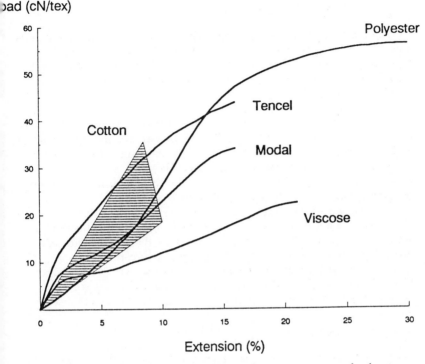

Fig. 15 Stress-strain properties of 'Tencel', modal, viscose, cotton and polyester fibres. *(Courtaulds Fibres Ltd.)*

dresswear, and high-performance home furnishings, and in technical fabrics such as coating substrates and abrasive belts.

Cellulose ester

Whereas viscose manufacture involves the conversion of natural cellulose into cellulose in fibrous or filament form, the production of acetate and triacetate begins with pure cellulose but the final filament is a chemical derivative of cellulose known as an ester. As a result of this chemical modification, the properties of these fibres are different from those of cellulosic fibres.

Triacetate

Special characteristics of fibre production. The filaments are precipitated by evaporation of a solvent. In this process the fibre is said to be 'dry spun'. Each of the three OH groups in the cellulose molecule is replaced by an acetate group, hence the name triacetate.

Acetate

Special characteristics of fibre production. The manufacture of triacetate in its liquid state is a primary step in the production of secondary acetate. Secondary acetate, known as 'diacetate' or simply 'acetate', is produced by putting back one OH group for about every six that were replaced in the previous stage.

General properties of cellulose acetate and triacetate. Acetate is known for its excellent draping qualities and attractive soft handle, and is used for lingerie, dress fabrics, and linings despite its low wet and dry strengths and poor resistance to abrasion. Its moisture absorption is fairly low, and consequently the material dries quickly. The fibre is softened at low temperature and, therefore, care must be taken in laundering. If washed in hot alkaline liquors, the fibre becomes delustred.

Triacetate possesses all the properties mentioned in connection with acetate, but in addition absorbs less water, is more crease-shedding, and softens at a much higher temperature. This thermoplasticity enables durable pleating and heat-setting of the fabric to be carried out.

In dry-cleaning, trichloroethylene is liable to cause shrinkage and colour bleeding, but perchloroethylene is satisfactory as a cleaning solvent.

Triacetate is more expensive than acetate and has similar end uses.

Synthetic polymer fibres

Synthetic polymer fibres are formed entirely by chemical synthesis.

Nylon (polyamide)

Special characteristics of fibre production. The generic group of polyamide fibres is classified according to the number of carbon atoms in the repeating amide group, and three important members are nylon 6·6, nylon 6, and nylon 11. Nylon is melt spun. Hexamethylene adipamide, derived from coke and tar, both based on the coal industry, is the constituent of nylon 6·6 which forms the bulk of nylon in use.

General properties. The nylon fibres are known for their high tensile strength, excellent resistance to abrasion, good elastic recovery from extension, and low moisture absorption. Crease shedding properties are good and are greatly improved by the use of BCF yarns, that is 'bulked continuous filament' produced by heat treatment. BCF and air-jet textured yarns (page 69) are used in socks, upholstery, warp knit decorative furnishings, leisure and lightweight sportswear, and carpets. About 2,690 million tons of the fibre is continuous filament whereas 675 million tons of staple fibre is available worldwide.

Since the fibre is thermoplastic, nylon fibres are heat-set to ensure dimensional stability and relatively durable characteristics such as embossed surfaces, pleating, and shaping of stockings and tights.

The melting points of nylon 6·6, 6, and 11 are 250°C, 210°C and 185°C respectively. Very little nylon 11 is produced. The thermal difference between nylon 6·6 and 6 is utilised in the production of nylon bicomponent fibres in which the nylon 6 outer sheath of the filament melts during heat treatment thereby bonding a web of filaments to form a nonwoven. If overalls were to be seam welded, instead of conventionally stitched, the lower fusing temperature of nylon 6 would be an advantage, apart from the benefit of its soft pleasant handle.

It is estimated that of the total world production of nylon, 27% is currently used in carpets, 31% in the home and clothing, and 35% in specialised uses in industry and in resins. Versatility in fibre manufacture provides fibre variants which contribute to the technical design of carpets. For instance, a four-hole hollow filament nylon increases fibre bulk in the pile and improves stain resistance and control of static.

Aramid

Characteristics of fibre production. This is a generic term of a group of fibres, (for example Nomex, Kevlar and Twaron), which was at one time included in the nylon category. The aramid fibres are composed of aromatic groups joined together by amide or sometimes imide linkages. The filaments are produced by extrusion from solutions in powerful solvents or strong acids.

General properties and uses. Aramids are highly flame retardant and able to withstand high temperatures. They ignite with difficulty at 538°C. These expensive fibres may be put to use in firemen's clothing, racing car drivers' suits and laundry presses. These uses highlight their important role in resisting burning. 'Nomex' at 317°C begins to degrade but does not melt, whereas 'Kevlar' fails at 425°C. However, 'Nomex' can be chemically treated to increase its thermal stability and neither produce dangerous fumes. Apart from these uses 'Nomex' is of special value in aircraft furnishings where the elimination of flammable material is essential.

'Kevlar' has the distinction of having a high strength/weight ratio, four times that of steel wire, which is particularly valuable in industrial, and other special applications, where an overall reduction in the weight of the product together with resistance to chemicals is needed, for instance in cables for oil-rigs, boat rigging, conveyor belts, and high-performance tyres. Bulletproof vests are made from 'Kevlar'.

An extension of the use of aramid fibres is in composite structures in which the fibres are embedded in synthetic resins to form rigid light-weight material for use in the bodies of racing cars, in yachts, and in aerospace.

Polyester

Characteristics of fibre production. Polyethylene terephthalate polymer (PET), and polytetramethylene terephthalate (PTMT), with limited production for specialised uses, derived from the petroleum industry, are melt spun to form the filaments.

PET yarn may be continuous filament or produced as staple fibre in a range of fibre lengths and fineness according to whether it is to be processed with cotton or wool, or is required to possess silk-like, cotton-like or other distinctive handle. The filament yarn or staple tow is stretched to orientate the molecules and increase fibre strength. Staple fibres are crimped. Extruded hollow filaments are used as filling fibres for duvets, sleeping bags and anoraks.

General properties and uses. PTMT has a lower melting point and is more readily dyeable than PET. It may be used for textured yarn in 'stretch' denim, and as PET/PTMT bicomponent yarn for panty hose and other apparel where the differential shrinkage develops bulk and stretch.

Standard polyester (PET) provides good resistance to extension and this gives a crisp handle, crease recovery, and good dimensional stability in use. Polyester is not used for tights because it does not extend easily at low loads although PTMT performs better in this respect.

Polyester has good resistance to abrasion but, when used in blends, fibre pilling is likely to occur unless special 'low pill' fibres or special finishes have been used. A build-up of static charges is associated with low moisture absorption unless an appropriate anti-static finish has been applied. Polyester is used in spun and continuous filament sewing thread. The fibre is resistant to degradation by ultraviolet light and for this reason, among others, is used for curtains.

The thermoplastic properties contribute to the durability of pleating and the thermal stability of fabrics resulting from heat-setting.

Air-jet and false twist methods of texturing (page 70) are applied to continuous filament yarns, giving a 'crimp' which modifies handle, bulk and elastic recovery. Depending on the level of extensibility introduced, textured polyester is used effectively in sportswear. The use of micro-filaments in conjunction with air-jet texturing provides a range of fabrics with modified fabric handle. Suitably chosen polyester fibres are used for protective clothing, sails, filter fabrics, and other industrial and functional uses including soft composites (page 154) which are used for car rooffliners and interior panels, and hard composites for the moulding of car exteriors.

Polyvinyl derivatives

These are co-polymers of vinyl with some other chemical unit.

Acrylic

Characteristics of fibre production. The polymer is a product of the petroleum industry and is defined as having at least 85% by weight of acrylonitrile units. The filaments are usually wet spun, but for end uses requiring a higher resistance to abrasion dry-spun acrylics are used. About 2,400 millions tons of staple fibre as against 3 million tons of continuous filaments are used globally.

The yarn is mostly produced by stretching tows or 'ropes' of filaments to the point where the filaments break at random into short lengths, and its main use is for knitted apparel, the typical characteristics of knitwear being enhanced because the fibre is in staple form. Producer-dyed fibre is fibre that has been dyed immediately after the wet-extrusion of the fibre. By this means more interesting colour effects can be developed than in garment dyeing which is almost limited to socks.

General properties and uses. The general characteristics of the fibres in this group are a full, warm soft handle, similar to that of wool, and good dry crease-shedding properties, particularly in knitted structures. Extra high-bulk is introduced by side-by-side bicomponent fibres which crimp when relaxed, and by high-bulk yarns created by stretching the tow, steaming and relaxing with consequent high shrinkage.

When used for hand-knitting yarns, coarser staple fibres tend to be used to increase bulk and, combined with continuous filament viscose, or acetate, to influence lustre. Finer spun yarns in weft-knit jersey fabrics covering the range of Single Jersey, Interlock and Pont Roma are used for dresswear. The level of resistance to abrasion of 100% acrylic is adequate for most apparel.

The acrylic fibre's soft lustrous properties are utilised to advantage in the pile of simulated fur fabrics; by introducing a range of fibre fineness and length, the simulation to natural fur is enhanced.

The appearance, handle and aesthetic properties of acrylic products can be varied by the choice of fibre fineness, cross-sectional shape, high-bulk yarns, blends with natural fibres such as wool, mohair and cotton, and the use of plasticisers and finishes.

Extensive application is made of acrylic woven and knitted velvets for furnishings and seat covers, but account needs to be taken of its high level of flammability. The use of acrylics in nonwoven blankets and in carpets has declined for commercial reasons.

Modacrylic

Special characteristics of fibre production. The fibre forming polymer consists of 35 to 85% by weight of acrylonitrile units, and is known as a modified acrylic.

General properties. These fibres also have some of the wool-like properties of the acrylics, but they are even more heat-sensitive. The heat-sensitivity of the fibre is valuable when it is combined with a less sensitive fibre in a pile fabric, since suitable heat treatment during finishing will cause the modacrylic to retract to form an undercoat. Some of the fibres in the group, for example Teklan, have medium flame retardance.

Chlorofibre

Special characteristics of fibre production. Polyvinyl chloride is the main polymer forming substance. It is extruded in a molten state and solidified by cold air, in other words, 'melt spun'.

General properties. At present this fibre is not widely used, primarily because it softens and shrinks at low temperature; consequently, care has to be taken in laundering. It must not be dry-cleaned in trichloroethylene

39

solvent. PVC shrinkage in boiling water (it does not absorb water) can be used to produce novelty, cloqué-type effects in fabrics.

Its chief merit is that it has a warm handle, is non-flammable, and is resistant to chemical damage, and for these reasons it finds use in protective clothing.

Polyvinyl chloride is occasionally blended with other fibres such as wool.

PVC in the form of semi-transparent sheeting is used for rainwear and is also applied as a coating on fabrics for the same purpose.

Polyvinylidene chloride

Special characteristics of fibre production. Vinylidene chloride is used either by itself or co-polymerised with other substances.

General properties. The amount of this fibre used in clothing is negligible, but it may be of interest to know that it is used for manufactured eyelashes and wigs. The more important outlets for polyvinylidene chloride are furnishings, car upholstery, and deck-chair covers.

It is easy to keep clean because of its very smooth surface. It does not absorb water and therefore does not stain easily. Like PVC, it is non-flammable and has a high resistance to chemical attack.

A film or transparent sheet of this substance shrinks when warmed and is suitable for making skin-tight packages which can be heat-sealed.

Polyolefin

Both types of polyolefins are based on the petroleum industry and are melt spun. Polyethylene and polypropylene have very limited outlets in clothing.

Polyethylene

Polyethylene, because of its low melting point, has been used in fusible interlinings to produce stiff collars. On account of its high resistance to acids and alkalis it is suitable for protective overalls. Some of the uses of the fibre, in monofilament form, are for car upholstery, awnings, and fishing nets. Polyethylene is also known as 'Alkathene' and 'Polythene'.

Polypropylene

Characteristics of fibre production. Polypropylene, a low priced fibre, is produced by the polymerisation of polypropylene, a gas liberated in the refining of crude oil, and also a component of natural gas. The molecular chains are packed very closely and regularly in the polymer, and as a consequence polypropylene is completely lacking in water absorbency and therefore cannot be dyed by conventional methods. Coloured fibres are produced by incorporating pigments in the molten polymer before extrusion.

Fibres can be produced by extrusion, but a greater quantity is extruded as tape, or film that can be slit into tape. Tapes are twisted to form string, cords or rope, and are used directly for weaving. Tow is produced for cutting into staple fibre. Twisting tape under tension causes fibrillation and hence yields a fibrous twine.

Properties and uses. Polypropylene has a low melting point (165°C). Although the fibre is strong (70–80 cN/tex) and retains its strength when wet, its tensile modulus (resistance to extension) is on the low side, similar to regular polyamide, and it has low elastic recovery and poor creep behaviour (continuous stretch under load).

It has the lowest density of textile fibres (0·9 g/cu ml) and therefore provides good cover relative to its weight. It has good crease shedding properties, and in the form of fine fibres a soft handle. Water moves freely between the fibres which therefore show good wicking. It is flammable but in 100% polypropylene constructions is self-extinguishing. On the other hand its flammability is very pronounced if it is in a supporting structure of other flammable fibres. It has good chemical resistance but is unsuitable for dry-cleaning. Polypropylene has satisfactory stain and soil release, but tends to retain oil and grease.

Polypropylene may be used in the form of tapes or fibre. Tapes of 2–3 mm wide may be woven directly in shuttless looms that lay the tape flat without twisting. The main purposes of such fabric are those once served by jute fabric; that is backing for tufted carpets, sacks, webbing and bale wrappings. Tapes 10 mm or more wide are twisted to make twine which has largely displaced sisal agricultural twine. Polypropylene twines and cordage are made into nets for fishing, for industry and other purposes. Heavier products such as ropes find many applications in industry, agriculture, shipping and fishing.

An important use of polypropylene fibre is for the pile of carpets, for which purpose it has been found to be very durable, with a soft feel, and satisfactory crush recovery.

Mostly the yarns used are spun, sometimes in blends with nylon or wool, in both tufted and needle punched constructions. Textured continuous filament yarns are also used in carpets but in lesser quantities. Upholstery fabrics are another outlet for the fibre, providing the advantages of durability and easy removal of soil and stains.

Polypropylene fibres are made into nonwoven fabrics used for carpet underlays and hygiene textiles, the latter making use of the good wicking characteristics of polypropylene.

The only clothing outlets at present are knitted items that are unlikely to be dry-cleaned such as 'thermal' underwear and footwear. Coarser varieties of polypropylene fibre are used in building, civil engineering and a range of other purposes.

Elastane

This fibre consists of a complex co-polymer, of which the polyurethane elastomer comprises not less than 85%. The molecules are in the form of spring-like coils.

41

The elastane filaments may be considered in conjunction with natural rubber, since both are elastomeric fibres and are used for similar purposes. Elastane is considerably stronger than natural rubber, has a very high (300–700%) capacity for extension, and offers excellent recovery to its original length after extension. Consequently it provides support to different degrees in foundation garments and support hose, good fit of figure contours in swimwear, and comfort in clothing such as bra straps and knitwear which require ease of movement in use.

Elastomeric fibres may be used bare, within a woven fabric structure, but for knitted structures are commonly covered whilst stretched, with an inelastic yarn which spirals round. 'Core-spun' yarns are produced similarly but with a covering of staple fibre instead of yarn. The yarn may be warp- or weft-knitted and used in narrow fabrics.

Unlike rubber, synthetic elastomers are white and are particularly resistant to repeated laundering at low temperatures, and the effects of sun-tan oils and perspiration.

FIBRE IDENTIFICATION

The number of fibres and combinations of fibres used in textiles make their identification sometimes difficult but always interesting. The approach to fibre identification depends on whether the sample consists entirely of one kind of fibre or a blend of fibres. In the case of blends the quantitative analysis of the fibres may also be necessary.

Fibre identification may be carried out by:

a) Microscopical examination of the longitudinal and cross-sectional views of the fibre.
b) Burning test.
c) The use of solvents.
d) Other chemical tests.
e) Staining.
f) Melting point determination. } Methods *f* and *g* are not included in
g) Fibre density. } the text.

It should be remembered that sometimes no single method gives a completely reliable indication of the identity of the fibre and that confirmatory tests are often advisable.

In order to determine whether more than one type of fibre is present, microscopical examination of the fibres is convenient.

Microscopical examination

Examination of distinctive sets of yarns must be made separately e.g., warp and weft.

Longitudinal view

Procedure. A thread is removed from the fabric and a length of a few millimetres is cut off. The fibres are spread out to lie parallel without overlapping in a drop of liquid mountant. This is then covered with a clean cover slip and air bubbles are excluded. If too much liquid has been applied the cover slip will float and this must be remedied. Magnifications between 100 and 500 are needed.

The most generally useful mountant is liquid paraffin, in which all fibres except acetate and triacetate may be examined. For the acetate and triacetate fibres n-decane is suitable.

Cross-sectional view

Plate method. A metal plate is required, 0·5 mm (0·020 in.) thick, of the size of a microscope slide, containing one or two holes 0·75 mm ($\frac{1}{32}$ in.) in diameter. The plate is preferably made from stainless steel, and it is important for it to be flat, smooth, and free from ridges round the holes; the edges of the holes should be rounded.

Procedure. A tuft of delustred cellulose acetate fibres is pulled through the hole by means of a loop of strong fine thread, such as nylon. The protruding tuft is opened out as in Figure 16 so that the specimen may be inserted vertically. It is necessary for the fibres in the specimen to be reasonably parallel, and for this reason yarn must be untwisted before being examined. The tuft containing the specimen is pulled a little further through the hole until it seems to be just firmly held. Undue compression of the fibres may deform the cross-section.

Figure 17 shows a new degreased safety razor blade being used to cut the tuft flush with the surface of the plate (Figure 18). The plate is now supported on a thin microscope slide and the second surface is cut. The side cut last is kept uppermost and is the one to be viewed. A drop of n-decane and a cover slip are applied. When viewed under the microscope, the fibres appear light against a dark ground. After the cutting of cotton, flax, or delustred viscose, black oil colour is rubbed into the section with a piece of cotton fabric over the finger. The excess colour is then removed with a clean part of the cloth moistened with n-decane. A drop of n-decane and a cover slip are then applied.

Heavily dyed and pigmented fibres require modifications to the technique to produce good cross-sections. Full details of the methods are obtainable.*

Appearance of fibres

Photomicrographs of the longitudinal and cross-sectional appearance of a selection of fibres are shown on pages 45–48, 50–51. They provide a basis for the comparison of observations made during practical work. Even

---

* *Obtainable from Shirley Developments Ltd., Stockport.*

Fig. 16 To obtain a cross-sectional view of fibres by the plate method, a tuft of fibres is first inserted into a hole in a metal plate and the protruding tuft is opened out.

Fig. 17 After the specimen is inserted vertically into the tuft, the tuft is cut flush with the surface of the plate with a safety razor blade.

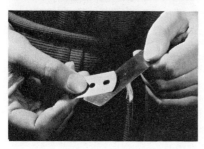

Fig. 18 Then the plate is ready to be examined.
(Shirley Developments Ltd.)

more satisfactory is to examine authentic specimens by the techniques outlined, in order to acquire familiarity with the microscopical appearance of fibres and fibre sections. It is often found that within one class of fibre some variation in appearance occurs.

A few comments on the visual characteristics of some fibres are given below. It would be useful to link this with an examination of the photo-micrographs which illustrate most of the fibres mentioned.

Natural Fibres

Wool. The surface of wool is characterised by overlapping scales. The prominence of these depends on whether the wool has had an anti-shrink finish, or has been damaged in use as in the case of remanufactured wools. The scale pattern depends on the variety and fineness of wool. The cross-sections are of various diameters and tend to be oval or circular. (Figures 19 and 20). *Cont. on p. 49*

Longitudinal   *Cross-section*

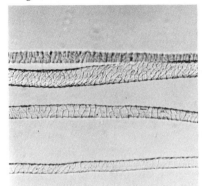

Fig. 19 Wool fibres from 64s top ×180.

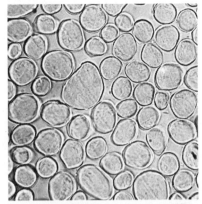

Fig. 20 Wool fibres from 64s top ×500.

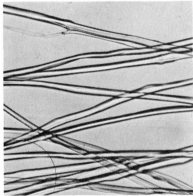

Fig. 21 Silk, *Bombyx mori*, degummed ×180.

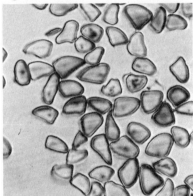

Fig. 22 Silk, *Bombyx mori*, degummed ×500.

Fig. 23 Wild silk, Tussah ×180.

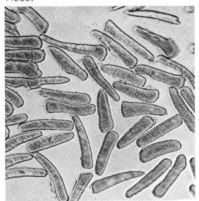

Fig. 24 Wild silk, Tussah ×500.

45

Longitudinal

Cross-section

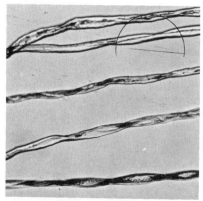

Fig. 25 Cotton, raw ×180.

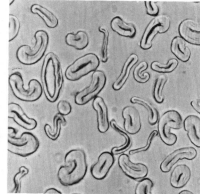

Fig. 26 Cotton, raw ×500.

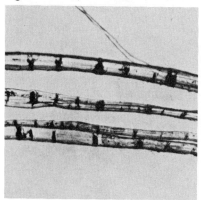

Fig. 27 Flax (ultimates) ×180.

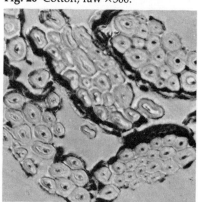

Fig. 28 Flax (bundles) ×340.

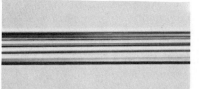

Fig. 29 Viscose, standard tenacity ×750.

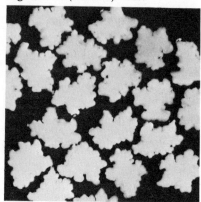

Fig. 30 Viscose, standard tenacity ×750.

Longitudinal

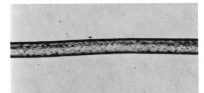

Fig. 31 Modal fibre ×750.

Cross-section

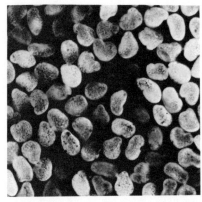

Fig. 32 Modal fibre ×750.

Longitudinal

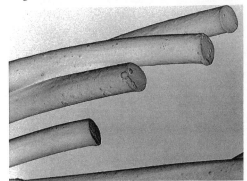

Fig. 33 Lyocell 'Tencel'.

Fig. 34 Secondary cellulose acetate ×750.

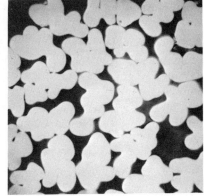

Fig. 35 Secondary cellulose acetate ×750.

47

Longitudinal

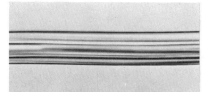

Fig. 36 Cellulose triacetate (Tricel) ×750.

Cross-section

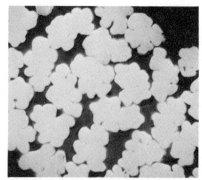

Fig. 37 Cellulose triacetate (Tricel) ×750.

Longitudinal

Fig. 38 Polyamide (nylon 6.6). This photograph shows the appearance of fibres with three levels of content of titanium dioxide delustrant. Left, dull fibre; centre, semi-dull fibre; right, bright fibre ×180.

Cross-section

Fig. 39 Polyamide (nylon 6.6) ×750.

Cross-section

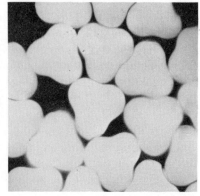

Fig. 40 Polyamide (nylon 6.6), tri-lobal ×500.

Hairs. No attempt is made in this book to distinguish between the hairs. They differ mostly in fibre fineness and the patterns of the scales.

Silk. Degummed *Bombyx Mori* or cultivated silk has fine, smooth feature-less filaments, but the cross-section is distinguished by its triangular shape with rounded corners. (Figures 21 and 22).

Tussah silk, on the other hand, has a flat, irregular, twisted appearance with fine longitudinal ridges or striations. The triangular cross-sections are rather elongated. (Figures 23 and 24).

Cotton. The flattened ribbon-like appearance, with frequent convolutions that reverse direction, is typical of cotton. (Figure 25). In cross-section it looks like a collapsed tube. (Figure 26). Mercerised cotton, however, shows a large proportion of round, smooth fibres with few convolutions.

Flax. Cross-markings and nodes occur frequently along each fibre and the cross-section shows the outline of fibre ultimates to be rather angular and to have several sides. The ultimates lie in bundles or groups. (Figures 27 and 28).

Manufactured fibres

Regular viscose. The fibre has many striations throughout its length and these correspond to the indentations which are a feature of the cross-section. (Figures 29 and 30).

Modal fibre is free from striations but has a rather granular appearance. In cross-section it is off-round or bean-shaped. (Figures 31 and 32).

Lyocell. The characteristics of 'Tencel' are discussed on page 34. The circular cross-section and smooth appearances are shown in Figure 33.

Secondary cellulose acetate and triacetate. It is difficult to distinguish between these two fibres by their appearance. Compared with viscose, each has fewer indentations and the fibres are lobed. Corresponding with the lobes there are only a few striations along the fibre length. (Figures 34, 35, 36 and 37).

Polyamide (nylon). A circular cross-section and a smooth surface are generally typical of the appearance of nylon 6, 6·6 and 11. As with most manufactured fibres, it is possible to incorporate delustrants in the fibre and they show as dark speckled marks. Tri-lobal nylon is not uncommon. (Figures 38, 39 and 40).

Polyester. Under the microscope nylon and polyester fibres are not easily distinguished by their shapes. (Figures 41 and 42).

Acrylics. There is a large variety of acrylic fibres. The longitudinal appear-ance of these fibres is usually smooth and regular with only a few striations, but the cross-sections of some provide distinctive shapes.

Long

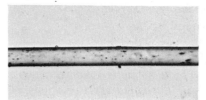

Fig. 41 Polyester (Terylene), bright ×750.

Cross-section

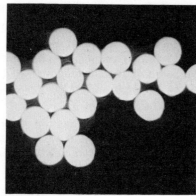

Fig. 42 Polyester (Terylene), bright ×750.

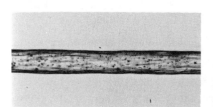

Fig. 43 Acrylic fibre (Courtelle) ×750.

Fig. 44 Acrylic fibre (Courtelle) ×750.

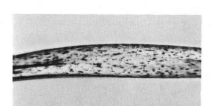

Fig. 45 Acrylic fibre (Orlon) ×750.

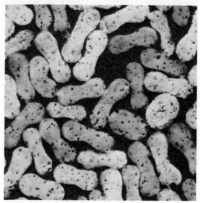

Fig. 46 Acrylic fibre (Orlon) ×750.

Cross-section

Cross-section

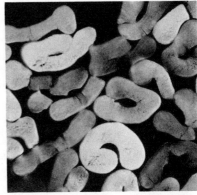

Fig. 47 Acrylic fibre (Acrilan) ×750.　　**Fig. 48** Modacrylic fibre (Dynel) ×750.

(Photomicrographs by courtesy of The Textile Institute)

'Acrilan' has a roughly circular outline slightly flattened in places. (Figure 47).

'Courtelle' is almost circular, but with very fine indentations round the edge, visible only at a magnification of about ×750. Fine streaks are apparent on the fibre surface. (Figures 43 and 44).

'Orlon' has the shape of a peanut shell for its cross-section and this gives the longitudinal appearance of the fibre a ribbon-like twist. (Figures 45 and 46). Another type of 'Orlon' has a bi-component structure and this produces a lobed shape.

Modacrylics. 'Dynel' has a folded peanut cross-section, and 'Teklan' is square or trapezoidal in shape with indentations. See Figure 48.

Natural fibres are easily distinguished under the microscope, whereas manufactured fibres may be more easily confused. For this reason additional tests to provide the necessary confirmation are more important for manufactured fibres.

Burning test

Observations on the manner in which textiles burn can be misleading, since this is influenced by the finish applied and whether the sample being burnt is a blend of fibres. However, for samples consisting of only one kind of fibre, which may be checked by viewing under the microscope, burning can serve as a preliminary sorting test, as shown in Table 4. One or two of the threads to be examined are held in forceps and advanced slowly up to the flame, observing their behaviour closely.

Table 4   BEHAVIOUR OF FIBRES IN BURNING TEST

Before touching flame	In flame and after leaving flame	Classification of fibre
Does not melt or shrink from the flame.	Burns with some spluttering. Leaves an inflated black ash, which is easily crushable. Smells like burning hair.	Protein
	Leaves a white ash skeleton, which becomes incandescent in the flame.	Tin-weighted Silk
	Burns rapidly, leaves a small soft grey ash, and smells of burnt paper.	Cellulose
	Burns rapidly, leaves a black skeleton of the original yarn or fabric. Emits a smell of bad fish.	Resin finished Cellulose
Shrinks and melts from flame. Forms a bead.	Burns and melts from the flame.	Thermoplastic Fibres
	Additional observations:	
	Burns readily with luminous flame. Leaves hard, brittle, black, irregular bead.	Secondary Cellulose Acetate, Triacetate
	Burns with difficulty. Melts and drips. Leaves a hard, round, fawn bead.	Nylon
	Burns with luminous sooty flame. Hard, round, black bead.	Polyester
	Hard, irregular, black bead.	Acrylic
	Rubbery, black, irregular bead. Self extinguishing.	Modacrylic

Use of solvents

This method of identification is particularly useful in distinguishing between fibres that have no morphological peculiarities. Assuming that the burning and microscopical examinations have been carried out and the possibilities as to the identity of the fibre have been narrowed down, it may be necessary to distinguish between or apply confirmatory tests to fibres within small groups.

A mere introduction to the subject is outlined here and, as with all aspects of fibre identification, more comprehensive information is available in the publications listed in the bibliography.

If it is known that the sample is composed of one type of fibre only,

Table 5   FIBRE IDENTIFICATION BY THE USE OF SOLVENTS

A fibre is considered to be *insoluble* in the tests listed in this table if it does not dissolve within thirty minutes. Solvents are used at room temperature unless otherwise stated.

Yes = Soluble   No = Insoluble

CELLULOSE AND PROTEIN FIBRES

		Solubility	*Reagent*
Wool		Yes 18 min.	1% Sodium Hydroxide
Regenerated protein		No	at the boil
Silk	Bombyx	Yes	Cold conc.
	Tussah	No (swells)	hydrochloric acid
Cotton	Scoured	Yes	Cuprammonium Hydroxide
	Resin treated	No (may swell)	for 15 minutes
Viscose	Untreated	Yes	
	Resin treated	No	
Cotton	Scoured	No	60% w/w
			sulphuric acid
Viscose	Untreated	Yes (7 min.)	at 60°C

THERMOPLASTIC FIBRES

	70% v/v Acetone	Glacial Acetic Acid	4·4 N Hydrochloric Acid	5 N Hydrochloric Acid at 65°C	Conc. Nitric Acid	Meta-cresol	Tetra-hydro-furan
Secondary cellulose acetate	yes	yes	no	no	yes	yes	yes
Triacetate	no	yes	no	no	yes	yes	no
Polyamide							
nylon 6	no	no	yes	yes	yes	yes	no
nylon 6.6	no	no	no	yes	yes	yes	no
nylon 11	no	no	no	no	yes	yes	no
Polyester	no	no	no	no	no	no	no
Acrylics	no	no	no	no	yes	no	no
Polyvinyl chloride	no	no	no	no	no	no	yes

solubility tests may be carried out in a test tube or on a watch glass. However, the behaviour of blends of fibres can be examined only under the microscope. The procedure is to disperse the fibre on a dry slide and to cover it with a clean cover-slip. The solvent is carefully applied to the side of the cover-slip and the liquid flows underneath. It is important that the reaction of the fibres to the reagent should be observed immediately.

Reagents which are heated will have to be used in a test tube. It will be noted that some of the reagents are strongly corrosive, and especial care must be observed in their use. For example, the use of concentrated nitric acid under the microscope should be avoided by inexperienced workers.

Staining tests

The identification of fibres by the use of stains depends on the fact that particular fibres absorb only certain dyes from the mixture of dyes contained in the stain and the resultant colour identifies the fibre. This test is suitable only for textiles which are free of dye and finishes.

A set of stains, under the trade-name of 'Shirlastain' are available.* These enable the range of fibres in common use to be identified by simply immersing the fibres in the appropriate stain. After rinsing the fibres in water the colours are compared with a stained standard fabric woven with stripes of yarns containing different fibres.

General observations which may aid identification

Often the identification of fibres in a fabric will be assisted by general considerations before the tests are applied. A knowledge of the fabrics currently in use is particularly helpful; for example, shower-resistant raincoats are commonly made from cotton, a cotton and polyester blend, or wool. Linings are often made from nylon, acetate or viscose. False twist stretch fabrics are nearly always polyester. If the length of staple fibres is very uniform, the fibres have been manufactured; if variable, the fibres are natural. If a fibre removed from a durably pleated fabric appears under the microscope to be either acetate or triacetate, the latter is the more likely – and so on. Thus the labour of fibre identification may often be much reduced by making tests on the most likely fibres first.

Other tests that assist identification

Certain fibres may be distinguished by the elements they contain. Table 6 is a classification of fibres according to whether they contain sulphur, chlorine, or nitrogen.

---

* *Obtainable from Shirley Developments Ltd.*

Table 6   TESTS FOR THE PRESENCE OF ELEMENTS IN FIBRES

Sulphur	wool
Chlorine	polyvinyl chloride
Nitrogen	nylon, acrylic, elastane, rubber
Chlorine and nitrogen	modacrylics
Chlorine and nitrogen absent	secondary cellulose acetate, triacetate, polyester

Test for the presence of sulphur with alkaline lead acetate

A strong caustic solution is added to a saturated solution of lead acetate until the precipitate that is formed begins to dissolve. When the precipitate that remains has settled, pour off the clear liquid. After immersing wool in this solution at room temperature, it will be found to be stained dark brown. Thoroughly wash the sample in cold water and neutralize it in dilute hydrochloric acid. Rinse and dry the sample. Wool is the only fibre that stains dark brown.

Test for the presence of chlorine: Beilstein test

Heat a copper wire in a bunsen flame until the flame is no longer green coloured. Then take the wire from the flame and, while still hot, touch the fibres. Thermoplastic fibres will adhere. When the wire with the fibres attached is placed in the flame, a green colour will indicate the presence of chlorine.

Test for the presence of nitrogen: Soda-Lime test

Cover a few fibres in a small ignition-tube with soda-lime, plugging the mouth of the tube with glass-wool to prevent spluttering. When the tube is heated strongly, ammonia will be found in the vapour if the fibre contains nitrogen. In this case, the vapour will be strongly alkaline and will turn litmus paper blue.

Test for mercerised cotton

Mercerised cotton is stained dark blue, but bleached and unbleached cotton remain unstained when a tuft of fibres is immersed for about two minutes in a few ml of Hubner's reagent and then washed.

The reagent is prepared by dissolving 10g of iodine in 50ml of a saturated solution of potassium iodide in distilled water.

Test for formaldehyde in resin-treated fabric

If one boils a piece of fabric about 2·5 cm square in a test-tube with about 10 ml of 10% hydrochloric acid and a smell of formaldehyde is released, formaldehyde is present.

Another method of identification is to boil a tuft of fibres for 5 minutes in 10 ml of 0·5% hydrochloric acid. Add a few crystals of phloroglucinol and neutralise the solution with 5% caustic soda. If formaldehyde is present, a deep red colour develops.

Quantitative chemical analysis of fibre blends

The measurement of percentage of fibre content in a blend cannot be carried out until the fibre composition of the blend is known.

It is possible under some circumstances to obtain an approximate idea of the percentage by counting the different kinds of fibres in the field of view under the microscope. Several samples of fibre from the blends have to be examined in this way before an estimate is made. If the different kinds of fibres differ in denier, it will be necessary to multiply the proportion of each fibre by its denier to obtain the relative weights of the kinds of fibres present.

Having determined the nature of the fibres present, it is possible to select a reagent that will dissolve one of the components, and by means of accurate weighing and control of other conditions, the percentage by weight of each fibre in the blend is calculated. To help the fibres to be more readily dissolved, the threads are removed from the fabric and untwisted. If any substance such as oil, size, or resin is present, this must be removed according to established methods. Special methods exist for the analysis of triple blends.

The equipment required for the quantitative analysis of fibres consists of a weighing bottle; sintered-glass filter crucible (porosity 1 or 2) with ground-in stopper; suction flask with adaptor for filter crucible; a desiccator containing anhydrous calcium chloride; a chemical balance capable of weighing to 0·5 mg.

Analysis of mixture of protein and non-protein fibres

The method is based on the dissolution of protein and is only suitable for a binary blend; that is, a mixture of only two types of fibre. The method is unsuitable if the non-protein fibre is acetate or a bast fibre and if added matter has not been removed.

Take about 0·5g of the textile, cut into convenient-sized pieces, and dry it at 110°C for 3 hours in a weighing bottle with its stopper removed. Replace the stopper on the bottle, the weight of which is already known, and allow to cool. Weigh the bottle and its contents accurately. From this the dry-weight of the specimen is known.

Place the specimen in a 100 ml-beaker and add about 50 ml of alkaline sodium hypochlorite (5 g/litre of sodium hydroxide is added to normal sodium hypochlorite). Stir vigorously at intervals for 30 minutes. Now filter this through a weighed sintered-glass crucible. Wash the beaker with a little hypochlorite solution and pour this into the crucible. After the crucible has drained, wash the residue with cold water, 0·1 normal acetic acid solution, and then water again, draining the crucible thoroughly after each rinse.

Dry the residue in the crucible for at least 3 hours at 110°C. Cool in a desiccator with the lid of crucible on before weighing. Express the dry-weight of the residue as a percentage of the original dry-weight of the blend of fibres.

Analysis of mixture of secondary cellulose acetate with cotton, nylon, polyester, viscose or wool

The determination involves dissolving the secondary cellulose acetate and weighing the residue. The moisture content of the mixture is determined on a separate sample weighed at the same time.

Weigh about 0·5 g of the blend accurately in a stoppered conical flask. Add 20 ml of acetone, shake, and leave for half an hour at room temperature. Pour off the liquid through the tared sintered-glass crucible. Repeat this twice more at quarter-hour intervals. With more acetone pour the residue into the crucible. Rinse with water and press the residue against the filter with the suction on in order to remove excess liquid. Dry the crucible for 3 hours at 110°C and cool in a desiccator, as described above, before weighing. Express the dry-weight of the residue as a percentage of the original weight corrected for moisture content.

Bio-chemical method

Normal methods of fibre identification cannot be applied with accuracy to distinguish between certain hair fibres. Since hairs such as Vicuna and Cashmere are expensive it is necessary to guard against unlawful blending of such fibres with less expensive types. The presence of such adulterants would contravene the 'Brand Name' and the 'Labelling Acts'.

Research into the examination of the DNA chain in a fibre 'finger printing' technique to distinguish between the various hair fibres is being pursued, with the intention of learning how to authenticate the fibre content of the product.

Fibre content labelling

Fibre content labelling is compulsory under the 'Textile Products (Indications of Fibre Content) Regulations 1986'. It initially came into effect in 1976, in accordance with a Directive of the EC which required member states to introduce compulsory labelling of textile products. The purpose of this labelling scheme is not merely to provide information to the purchaser but to facilitate trade in textile products inside the EC, by harmonising the names of fibres and the method of labelling throughout the Community.

The scheme applies, generally speaking, to all new (unused) textiles sold to the public, containing more than 80% of textile fibres, or in which the properties of the textile component are very important. Among the articles excluded are felts, various technical items such as conveyor belts, and trivial items such as pin cushions. More important to the clothing industry is the exclusion of fabric used for interlinings, stiffening, and backing. The main lining of outerwear is not exempt.

Fibre content may be shown on a permanent label, or a gummed label attached to the packaging. For cloth sold by the metre a ticket may be attached to the roll. The retailer has the ultimate responsibility for ensuring that goods offered to the public are labelled, but manufacturers and distributors are also obliged to indicate the fibre content of goods passing through their hands. This information may be supplied on commercial documents.

If a textile product is made from a single unblended fibre type, it may be described by the use of the fibre name, by the fibre name prefaced by '100 per cent', by 'pure' or by 'all'. A tolerance of 2% or 5% of other fibres, according to the method of manufacture, is allowed and it is not necessary to take into account sewings, fastenings, trimmings, stiffening fabrics, etc., nor a variety of finishing additives used to improve handle or facilitate dyeing and printing.

For other products composed of more than one fibre, none of which accounts for 85% or more of the product, the two most important fibres must be named with the percentage by weight of the product which each represents, followed by the names of the other fibres in order of proportion by weight. The declaration of the percentages of these fibres is optional. Fibres which separately represent less than 10% of the product weight may be classed together as 'other fibres' followed by their total percentage weight. If, however, the name of the fibre that accounts for less than 10% of the weight of a product is given, then the name and percentage weight of every fibre in the product must be given.

For other products composed of more than one fibre the percentage of the most important fibre must be stated, followed by the names of the other fibres in order of proportion by weight. The declaration of the percentages of these fibres is optional. Fibres which separately represent less than 10% of the product weight may be classed together as 'other fibres' followed by their total percentage weight. When the percentages of the fibres are given they must be accurate to within 3% of the total.

Certain textile products may be made from more than one fabric with different fibre content: for example, jerkins where the sleeve may be different from the body. In such a case, where any component accounts for

30% or more of the weight of the product it is necessary to provide an indication of its fibre content. It is permissible to label a component separately, even when it does not account for 30% of the weight of the product.

In determining the fibre content of a product, or a component, as pointed out above, many small items are to be left out of account. These include sewn-on frills, decorations, ribbons and elastic. Thus in an article such as a brassiere consisting of many diverse components it will probably be found necessary for the label to refer only to the face fabric and the wings.

The regulations require that any advertisement intended for retail customers, which enables the product to be ordered by reference only to the description in the advertisement, shall carry an indication of the fibre content of the product.

The regulations provide a list of 39 names which are to be used. Of these, 22 are generic names for manufactured fibres, the others being the well known names of natural fibres, such as wool, cotton and silk. An expression such as 'metallised yarn' or 'paper yarn' may also be used.

The terms 'fleece wool' and 'virgin wool' may be used only if the wool has not previously been incorporated in a finished product, and with certain other restrictions. In the UK the term 'pure new wool' may still be used as previously and other terms such as Shetland wool, botany wool and lambswool may also be used.

It will also be permissible to continue to use terms such as Sea Island Cotton, Irish Linen, mercerised cotton, when such descriptions are consistent with fair trade practices.

Although it is obligatory to use the names listed in the Regulations to describe the fibre content, a trade mark may be used in conjunction with this name, as for example, 'Brand X' polyester, or may be placed anywhere else in the article.

Chapter 2

YARN TYPES AND PROPERTIES

All yarns, however they are made, are long continuous strands, and this is the form into which the fibres must first be put for processes such as weaving, knitting, and lacemaking. When a yarn is woven into a fabric it is often referred to as a 'thread'. There is a very wide range of yarns having different characteristics for different purposes.

Yarn strength depends on spinning method, eg ring, open-end or self-twist, which also affects extensibility, bulk and handle. Longer and finer versions of a fibre produce stronger yarns and there is an optimum value for twist.

Spun versus continuous filament

Spun yarns are those which are made from 'short' fibre; that is, fibres with lengths ranging from about 2 cm to say 26 cm (page 6) twisted together. All the natural fibres, except silk, are short or 'staple' fibres. Continuous filament yarns are composed of filaments that run continuously the full length of the yarn. Silk and manufactured fibres may be either continuous filament or spun yarns.

Smoothness

If the two types of yarn are examined closely it will be noticed that the spun yarn is hairy and the continuous filament yarn smooth (Figures 49 and 50). The hairiness of staple fibre yarns is influenced by the length of the fibre; for instance, smoother yarn is produced from flax than from cotton.

Handle

A smooth yarn helps to make a fabric feel compact, whilst a hairy yarn gives a fuller handle.

Lustre

Because long staple yarns are less hairy than short staple yarns, they are often more lustrous. Yarns made from continuous filaments are likely to have a high degree of lustre.

Regularity

When spinning a yarn from staple manufactured fibre it is impossible to achieve the regularity in thickness of the yarn that would be obtained with

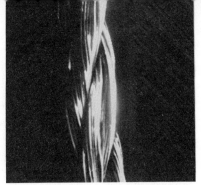

Fig. 49 Single spun yarn

Fig. 50 Two-fold continuous filament yarn. *(UMIST)*

continuous filament yarn of the same fibre. Irregular yarn tends to be weaker.

Combed versus carded

If a yarn is produced simply by drawing out and twisting fibres from a handful of fibres it will be noticed that the fibres are tangled and lying in all directions, and for this reason the yarn is irregular.

Before a thread can be spun, it is necessary for the fibres to be prepared. The two ways in which this is done are known as 'carding' and 'combing'. All staple fibres go through a machine which 'cards' them so as to disentangle and make them lie fairly straight. If a better quality thread is needed, the fibres, after carding, pass through a machine where combing takes place. Here the fibres are made to lie very straight and parallel to each other, and all very short fibres are removed. 'Combing' adds to the cost of the yarn and is only done when better quality yarns are required, or when a smooth, compact characteristic is needed, as in worsted yarns. Woollen yarns, which have a full hairy handle, are not combed.

The advantages of combed yarn over yarn that has only been carded are: improved yarn strength, regularity of thickness, and increased lustre. Combed yarns are used in worsted suiting, cotton sewing thread, the better qualities of cotton poplin and cotton knitwear.

Single, folded and cabled yarns, and direction of twist

The description 'single yarn' (Figure 49) refers to a yarn composed of either: (a) fibres of regular or irregular length twisted together, or (b) continuous filaments with a very slight amount of 'producer twist', or firmly twisted together.

Filaments issuing from one spinneret are brought together to form a single yarn, as are the filaments from a number of silk cocoons.

A folded yarn (Figure 50) is one in which two or more single yarns are twisted together, making 'two-fold' or 'three-fold' yarns, for example.

A cabled yarn (Figure 51) consists of two or more folded yarns twisted together.

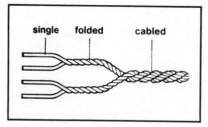

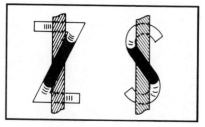

Fig. 51 Single, folded and cabled yarns

Fig. 52 Direction of twist
(The Textile Institute)

Direction of twist

Twist can be inserted in either of two directions, and is described as 'S' or 'Z' twist (Figure 52). It will be seen that the centre stroke of the letter S or Z coincides with the direction in which the fibres lie in the yarn.

If a sewing thread or knitting yarn is untwisted, the twist in the folded yarn will be found to be in the opposite direction to that in the singles. This combination of twist direction helps to make the thread 'balanced' that is, less liable to 'snarl' or to untwist.

Fabrics made from spun yarn usually have 'Z twist' in the warp and may have 'S twist' in the weft. Light is reflected in opposite directions from the two types of yarn, and so lustrous stripes can be introduced in fabrics by having alternate groups of 'Z' and 'S twist' yarns in the warp.

Why folded yarns?

The question now arises, why are these different types of yarn used? Obviously single yarns, either from staple fibre or continuous filament, are fairly easily made and less expensive to produce. However, when two single yarns are twisted together, the thick and thin places tend to average out and consequently give a folded yarn that is more regular in thickness than either of the single components. Since the strength of a yarn is that of its weakest places, the folded yarn is relatively strong. Also, the folded yarn, if twisted in the 'S' direction on 'Z' single yarns, or 'Z' on 'S', is more lustrous, because the fibres on the surface lie nearly parallel to the yarn axis. Generally, therefore, better quality fabrics are made from folded yarns which, in a woven cloth, may be found sometimes only in the warp direction. Two-fold yarns have been used in velvets and velour carpets to achieve the spreading out and development of the 'bloom' in the cut pile during the brushing process. Sewing threads are required to have a uniform diameter and no very weak places. Consequently, they are folded or cabled for this purpose. Cabled yarns are not much used for clothing but may be found in industrial fabrics such as conveyor belting.

Systems for the designation of yarn and thread 'size'

Yarns, filaments and fibres are produced in a very wide range of 'sizes' (diameters) and the natural fibres also show considerable variations in diameter. In choosing a fibre, filament or yarn for a particular purpose, it is necessary to consider what size is suitable and to have a means of specifying this size. Diameter is an unsuitable dimension to use since, particularly for spun yarns and the natural fibres, it varies considerably from point to point along their length, and it cannot be measured easily with simple apparatus. Traditional methods that have been in use for a long time, and newer methods appropriate to modern industry, both express the size of a yarn by the relationship between length and weight. They are of two kinds: *'Direct' or Linear density systems* are based on the expression of mass per unit of length. In the 'Universal' system for designating linear density of textiles, **Tex system** BS 947 (1981), the size for yarns and filaments and fibres is expressed in units of tex given in grams per kilometre. For filaments and fibres, linear densities are expressed in decitex (dtex) to avoid fractional values: for cotton hairs the unit is millitex (mtex). (A value of 1 tex is equivalent to 10 decitex or 1,000 millitex.) Thus the structure of a textured yarn could be given as 60 dtex/80, indicating that the yarn is composed of 80 filaments each of 0·75 dtex or 75 mtex.

Denier is the name of the unit used in a traditional direct system, originally used for silk. It is being superseded, slowly, by the tex system. The denier of a yarn or filament is given as its mass in grams per length of 9 kilometres.

Both tex and denier are determined by weighing a measured length of the filament or yarn. The coarser the filament or yarn the greater is its tex or denier.

Length per unit mass: 'count' or 'numbering' systems

Historically there have been quite a variety of methods for designating the 'count' of woollen, worsted, linen, cotton and jute yarns and these have almost been phased out. Each is based on the number of specific lengths of yarns for a fixed weight. There are two methods of continuing interest, Metric count (Nm) which is in use in continental Europe, and the English Cotton Count (Ne) which is in use in the USA and the Far East, but has largely been replaced by tex in the UK.

Metric count (Nm) is the number of kilometre lengths of the yarn per kilogramme, and *cotton count* (Ne) is the number of 840 yard hanks per pound weight. Both these systems are described as 'indirect' because the coarser the yarn the lower is its count or number.

Conversion formulae	Cotton count (Ne)	=	591 ÷ tex
	Metric count (Nm)	=	1000 ÷ tex
	Denier	=	9 × tex

Designation of the size of folded yarns

When two or more yarns are twisted together the resultant yarn is known as 'two-fold', 'three-fold' and so on. During folding a slight contraction in length usually occurs so that linear density of a two-fold yarn is slightly greater than double that of the singles. Thus a yarn described as R48 tex/2 is a yarn of 48 tex made by twisting together two singles yarns slightly finer than 24 tex, the R standing for 'resultant tex'. The description 24 tex × 2 would signify two 24 tex yarns twisted together, making a yarn slightly coarser than 48 tex.

Note that R40 Ne/2 implies that 2 singles of approximately 80 Ne have been twisted together, and R20 Nm/3 that three singles of approximately 60 Nm have been twisted together.

Twist level and twist factor

The purpose of twist in a spun yarn is to bind the fibres together and so give the yarn strength. If the level of twist is low, the yarn may break under tension by the fibres slipping apart without any fibre breakage. An increase in twist will increase fibre binding, and the yarn will be stronger and more compact. A very high level of twist increases the liveliness of the yarn which will have a tendency to untwist and 'snarl', that is twist upon itself.

Twist level is defined as the amount of twist per unit length of yarn, that is turns/m or turns/cm. Whilst the level of twist is of interest for a particular yarn, it is the angle at which the fibres (or other yarn components) lie to the axis of the yarn which is fundamental in influencing the yarn tensile strength and the other properties mentioned above.

A convenient way of quantifying the angle is by calculating the 'twist factor' from the twist level and tex value of the yarn.

$$\text{Twist factor} = \frac{(\text{turns/m}) \sqrt{\text{tex}}}{100}$$

Yarns with the same twist angle have the same twist factor (TF).

A coarse yarn with fewer turns/cm may have the same twist factor as a finer yarn with more turns/cm, as shown in Figure 53.

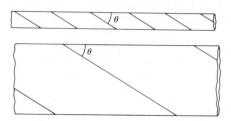

Fig. 53 Two yarns with the same twist factor but differing in turns/cm.

The type of fabric in which the yarn is to be used influences the choice of tex and twist factor. Cotton has a TF about 40 for warps and 32 for knitting. Crêpe yarns have the highest twist factor at about 70. Cotton yarn for knitted outerwear will have different requirements compared with a worsted yarn from the point of view of its behaviour in knitting and formation of the loop. Equally, yarns for the weft of fabrics, which are to be raised or 'brushed' during finishing need to have a low twist factor so that the fibres can be easily teased apart to form the nap without breaking in the process. Such yarns will be less strong than yarns of a somewhat higher TF. However, a round compact thread for use in voile fabrics will require a much higher TF.

If the twist factor is increased still further a crinkly crêpe yarn will be produced suitable for crêpe dresswear and for crêpe bandages, according to fibre content and fabric construction. Such a yarn is very extensible and has good elastic recovery. Because of its tendency to snarl the fabric develops its characteristic crêpe effect in various suitable constructions.

For the maximum tensile strength of a particular yarn there is an optimum TF which is dependent on fibre content and staple length.

In a woven fabric it is necessary to have the stronger and more compact threads in the warp (parallel to the selvedge) because it is the warp which is liable to break down under the severe load it has to bear during weaving. Weft yarn generally has a lower TF.

During the production of continuous filament yarns a small amount of twist, known as 'producer twist' is inserted and there is no need for additional twist to bind the filaments together. Highly lustrous filaments may have the lustre subdued by an increase in twist, but generally the modification of the yarn properties is achieved by texturing (page 70).

Corespun yarns

Corespun yarns are produced by twisting a fibrous sheath round a continuous filament or a spun thread.

The uses of yarns having this type construction are:

- In the production of sewing threads (page 295) where continuous filament polyester is surrounded either by cotton or polyester fibre.
- To combine the strength and elasticity of a continuous filament yarn with the handle, cover, and surface interest of a staple fibre such as wool.
- In support garments, to combine the elastomeric component with a fibrous cover, so disguising its presence.
- Rubber thread is often covered by a close wrapping of one or two textile yarns, but this type of product is not described as a 'corespun yarn' but as a 'wrapped yarn'.

A variation on the above constructions is one in which a continuous filament polyester core is covered by air-jet intermingled (or air-entangled, page 70) polyester multi-filaments, which modifies the handle and surface characteristics. This is, of course, produced by a different method from that for core-spun.

Wrap-yarn

This consists of an untwisted strand of fibres, fibre wrapped spirally with, usually, a fine continuous filament yarn. This is less expensive to produce than a two-fold yarn and is more bulky. It is sometimes used in interlinings.

Fancy yarns

When fashion fabrics require interesting visual effects and texture, fancy yarns are often incorporated in the construction. Sometimes the fabric bears the name of the fancy yarn it contains, such as 'bouclé' or 'ratiné'. Examples of fancy yarns are given in Figures 54, 55 and 56.

Fancy yarns are made by manufacturers who specialise in their production. They differ from the simple construction of single, folded, and cabled yarns by having deliberately introduced irregularities or intermittent effects along their length. When incorporated in a fabric, these yarns may alter not only its appearance but also its handle. It is quite interesting to remove such yarns from fabrics and examine them to see how they are constructed.

Fancy yarns can be made from any fibre in continuous filament or staple fibre form. Usually the yarn consists of three components. A ground thread is the base, round which is twisted the effect thread. In order to stabilise the structure, a 'tie' thread is used to bind the two together. Often the components of the fancy yarn are of unequal thickness, and this can be an important feature of the yarn.

It is possible to obtain considerable variety in fabric appearance by making two-fold yarns with single yarns of different colours; these are known as 'grandrelle yarns', and in worsted construction as 'twist yarns'. By varying the combination of colours and the amount of folding twist, subtle modifications to the hue of the fabric can be achieved. These yarns are commonly used in gabardines and worsted suitings.

Chenille yarn is characterised by fibres projecting more or less all round a central core of threads. It is unusual in that the yarn is produced by first weaving a leno fabric (page 87). The groups of warp threads are arranged at a suitable distance apart so that when the weft threads, which span between them, are cut after the fabric has been woven, long lengths of chenille yarn are produced. The chenille yarn is then woven into a fabric which bears the name of the yarn.

Metallized yarns are not generally classified as fancy yarns, although they have similar uses. Generally, sheets of aluminium foil are sandwiched between clear plastic film, and the laminate is then cut into strips to

Fig. 54 Slub yarn *(UMIST)*

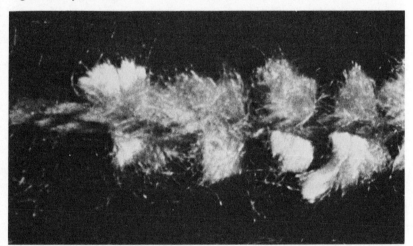

Fig. 55 Chenille yarn *(UMIST)*

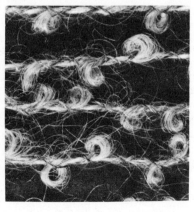

Fig. 56 Loop yarn. *(UMIST)*

Table 7 METHODS OF PRODUCING TEXTURED CONTINUOUS FILAMENT THERMOPLASTIC YARN

	World Production (198 Tonnes $\times 10^3$
False-twist The yarn is highly twisted, heat-set, and untwisted.	675
Modified false-twist (polyester) Stretch-textured modified by further heat treatment to reduce stretch, but retaining a suitable level of bulk	1540
Bulked-continuous-filament (BCF Yarn) Yarn is propelled forward by a jet of hot fluid against a porous cooling surface. Filaments develop a saw-tooth edge slope. Nylon and polypropylene filaments are used.	540
Knit-deknit The yarn is knitted, heat-set, and then unravelled from the knitting. Polyester and nylon used. **Gear-crimping** Crimp is heat-set by running yarn between intermeshing cog wheels. Method little used. **Edge-crimping** The yarn is heated and drawn over a knife-edge and this causes it to curl. Method little used	143
Air-jet texturing A jet of compressed air is directed at the continuous filament yarn which causes the individual filaments to form tiny loops along their length. Mainly polyester and nylon filaments are used, but this method is applicable to any continuous filament since it does not depend on the filaments' thermal properties. The prospects for future development and use are high.	110

ical yarn appearance	Yarn characteristics	End uses

57a False-twist yarn
ley Institute)
	Bulk
	Stretch
		Hosiery
		Knitted
		    outerwear
		Swimwear
		Skiwear
		Gloves
		Surgical
		    stockings

	Bulk Reduced stretch	Knitted outerwear
 57b BCF yarn *(Shirley Institute)*	Bulk Little stretch Resilient	Carpets
 57c Knit-deknit yarn *ile News Services)*	Lustrous, crêpe, crinkle or bouclé appearance with little stretch.	Knitted outerwear

57d Air-jet textured yarn
N Components, Darwen)
	Textured without
	creating high
	extensibility. Increased
	fabric cover and
	regularity, and slightly
	fuller handle. High
	strength. Use of very
	fine filaments creates
	fabric handle similar to
	staple fibre-yarn.
		Woven
		    lightweight
		    fabrics
		Menswear
		Skiwear
		Car interiors
		Suitcases
		Sewing threads.

form a flat ribbon-like yarn. In order to produce special visual effects and to provide additional strength, the metallized yarn may be combined with another yarn, round which the metallized yarn is made to spiral.

Textured yarns

Yarns made from continuous filaments are usually smooth and compact because the filaments from which they are made are very straight and uniform in diameter throughout their length. This smoothness affects the feel and appearance of the cloth and distinguishes it from fabrics made from staple fibre yarns. Continuous filaments can have their characteristics modified by passing the yarn through processes which introduce crimps, coils, snarls, or crinkles into the filaments. With one exception, these modifications are introduced in thermoplastic filament yarns whilst the yarn is heated, and become permanently set as the yarn cools. According to the configuration introduced and the heat treatment applied, yarns can be produced with various levels of increased bulk and accompanying opacity and warmth of handle, and may in addition have high extensibility and good recovery from stretch. A range of textured yarns is available, and from these fabric producers can select those suitable for any particular purpose; for example, knitted outerwear, which requires increased bulk but minimum stretch, ski- and swimwear, which require a good level of stretch and elastic recovery, and resilient carpet pile.

One process which does not use heat is known as *'air-jet texturing'*, and this may be applied to any continuous filament yarn. Because of the low extensibility of this type of yarn, it is very suitable for woven fabrics where improved texture and reduced transparency are required, compared with regular continuous filament yarns.

Table 7 summarises the properties and applications of textured yarns, and indicates world production figures. Other methods of producing stretch are given on pages 42 and 100.

BCF yarns (Fig. 57b) are also referred to as having been produced by 'hot-fluid texturing' where a jet of hot fluid (air or steam) projects the yarn into confined space to develop the texture. 'Cold-fluid texturing' covers air-jet texturing methods described in 'Textile Progress' Vol. 16, No. 3. Comparison of the properties of textured yarns have been made with standard closely packed continuous filaments (CF), but great interest has centred on developing and modifying CF yarns to have the tactile and comfort properties of natural fibres, such as silk, cotton and wool, when the yarns are incorporated in woven fabric. This has resulted in polyester, with its high strength and regularity, giving a 'silk-like' handle (for instance) to the fabric.

It has been possible to develop such fabric characteristics because of the availability of fine and microfine polyester and nylon fibres ranging down to 0·1 dtex, and the development in techniques of air-jet texturing. The surface characteristics of the fibres themselves can also be suitably modified, for instance, with micro-'pits' which, together with the air-texturing process, imparts to the fabric a natural or 'spun' sensation when handled. The main outlets for all these air-textured yarn types is in woven and knitted apparel where there has been substantial stimulation of interest in marketing and retailing.

Air-jets are also used for 'Intermingling' or 'Comingling' filaments. This process simply entangles the filaments, without the formation of loops, thus reducing the need for twisting the yarn to increase cohesion. It is also used for filament blending.

The purpose of these developments is not only to control and improve aesthetic and performance characteristics but to give added commercial value to the product. In relation to this it is essential to consider costs of production and the marketability of the product.

'High-bulk yarns'

Yarns described as 'high-bulk' differ from texturised continuous filament yarns in that they are spun from staple fibre. The yarn consists of a blend of fibres, usually acrylic, of low and high shrinkage potential. When the yarn in the knitted or woven fabric is subjected to high temperature and/or wet treatment during finishing, a proportion of the fibres contained in the yarn shrink and the remainder, because of their excess length, become highly crimped and so give the yarn and the fabric increased bulk and warmth of handle.

'Bicomponent fibre yarns'

Bicomponent fibres are mentioned on page 10. Yarns made from these filaments have an inherent tendency to develop bulk, due to the crimping of the filaments on relaxation. Bulked yarns can therefore be made from bicomponent filaments without special processing. 'Cantrece' is a trade-name given to one such continuous filament nylon yarn. Staple fibre yarns having the same characteristics are made from the acrylic fibres, e.g., 'Latent-crimp Courtelle'.

Blended yarns

Evidence in historical writings and in the remains of textiles shows that fabrics made from two different fibres were quite common even in ancient times. The combination of fibres was, and still is, achieved by using one type of fibre in the warp and another fibre in the weft direction. Such fabrics are known as 'union fabrics' and are different from fabrics made from a blend of fibres. The combination of different fibres in 'union fabrics' gives the textile designer opportunity to produce striking effects. Many museums have examples of wool/linen, linen/silk, and wool/silk 'union fabrics' of Egyptian and other sources about 2,000 years old. An example of a 'union' which has been used for school uniforms consisted of a cotton warp and a wool weft; such a fibre combination is less expensive than an all-wool fabric, which it closely resembles.

True blending is achieved by spinning yarns from a blend or mixture of two or more types of fibre. Blending has been extended to the mingling of two types of continuous filaments to produce a 'hetero' or 'multi-filament' yarn. The possibilities of blending can be summarised as follows:

1) To achieve a particular end use, some fabric properties may have to be gained by blending, even at the expense of some other property. On the whole, good blending aims at combining the most desirable properties of different fibres in one fabric.

2) Effects of texture and handle may be secured by blending suitable fibres. For instance, triacetate tends to give a soft handle. The addition of wool increases the fullness and warmth. Mohair can improve the fabric lustre and softness.

3) Novelty effects may be achieved by dyeing fabrics made from blended yarns. The different dyeing affinities of the fibres may result in one fibre component remaining undyed or the fibres being dyed different colours. This is known as cross-dyeing.

   The sensitivity of one fibre to acid has been used in fabrics made from polyester/cotton yarns, by printing a paste containing an acid which attacks the cotton and leaves the polyester fibre intact. The result is that the printed design appears more transparent since the cotton component has been removed.

4) The cost of producing a fabric is nearly always important, and blending is often used to control the price.

A few comments on the principles involved in blending to modify important physical properties will help in understanding the available range of blends.

Resistance to abrasion

As has already been mentioned, nylon has a very high resistance to abrasion. The inclusion of 20% nylon in a cotton yarn will approximately double the resistance to abrasion of the yarn and the fabric made from it. Nylon is frequently blended with wool solely to improve resistance to abrasion. The above blend of nylon and cotton will probably be no stronger than the all-cotton yarn, whereas the blend of nylon with wool will show some improvement over the all-wool yarn. The explanation for this is given below.

Tensile strength

If you take a strip of paper and an elastic thread which have been twisted together and then pull on the two-fold structure, it will be found that the strip of paper, which is very inextensible, supports the load, while the elastic will make little contribution to the strength of the combination. In the same way, if a rather extensible fibre, such as nylon, is combined with a comparatively inextensible fibre, such as cotton, the cotton fibre will bear most of the load. For this reason there may be a drop in tensile strength when a small percentage of nylon is added to cotton yarn, even though the nylon is stronger than the cotton. With the addition of more than 50% nylon, the strength of the yarn begins to increase. The effect of combining fibres of similar extensibilities is that the load is more uniformly shared, and in the example of the wool and nylon blend the strength of the small percentage of nylon present is added to that of the wool since these two fibres are rather similar in extensibility. Thus, when a strong fibre is blended with a weaker fibre to improve abrasion resistance, it cannot be assumed that tensile and tearing strengths will also necessarily be improved. Whether this is or is not the case depends on how well matched the two fibres are in respect of extensibility.

Crease recovery

The addition of a fibre with known good crease recovery to a yarn containing fibre of inferior crease recovery will improve this property according to the amount of fibre added. The percentage of fibre added will depend on how far the other properties, such as strength and handle, and cost can be allowed to change.

Pleat retention

Thermoplastic fibres can be used to confer pleat retention, and the degree of pleat retention attained depends on the proportion of thermoplastic fibre present. The amount of assistance needed to give good pleat retention depends upon the components of the blend. For example, the percentage of polyester fibre needed in a polyester/wool blend is less than that needed in a polyester/cotton blend because wool has a better capacity for pleat retention than cotton.

Drying properties

Fibres of low moisture absorption produce fabrics which dry quickly. The speed with which a fabric dries after laundering increases with the proportion of hydrophobic fibre included.

Dimensional stability

The causes of shrinkage, that is relaxation, fibre swelling, and felting are discussed on page 170, and it is pointed out that fabrics made from synthetic fibres are immune to shrinkage arising from swelling and felting. Thus, fabrics made from a blend of the synthetic fibres with such fibres as viscose or wool will be more stable than fabrics composed entirely of the non-synthetic fibres. Most of the common non-felting fibres may be added to wool to reduce felting. The acrylic fibres are particularly suitable for blending with wool because of a similarity in handle. Polyester fibres are also very suitable because of the improved durability they provide.

Pilling tendency

This is a defect which is especially troublesome in certain blends. It is discussed on page 181.

Blends in common use

It is useful to examine garment labels which indicate percentage fibre content and to consider, in the light of the above information, why particular fibre combinations are used and how the percentage composition is chosen. Blends commonly encountered are 55% polyester/45% wool, 67% polyester/33% cotton or viscose, 85% viscose/15% polyamide. Other combinations are wool/acetate, wool/acrylic, wool/viscose, triacetate/viscose, polyester/modal, and polyester/flax.

In order to further the sale of their fibres and to maintain satisfactory standards, producers of manufactured fibres sometimes stipulate the minimum percentage of their fibre which must be included to permit the use of their fibre trade-name on the garment. Many fabric and garment manufacturers are pleased to exhibit such trade-marks, since they can benefit from the advertising of the trade-marks by the fibre producers. A commercial reason for blending has been the attractiveness, from a sales point of view, of the claim that the fabric contains a 'quality fibre' such as mohair.

Yarns from split film

There is great interest in a development that enables fibres, yarns, or fabric to be produced directly from films. The polymer used is usually polyethylene or polypropylene, both classed as 'polyolefins'. These films have the property that under suitable conditions, even simple lengthwise tension, they can be induced to fibrillate (that is, to break up into a network of fibres). It is possible to separate the fibres, which vary in length and diameter, to obtain staple fibre that can be spun conventionally. Or, a tape of film may be fibrillated and converted directly into yarn by twisting. A fibrillated tape may be spread out sideways to yield a textile web that may have various uses. By first embossing a plastic sheet with a suitable pattern and then stretching it, a regularly formed network is produced. These products already have industrial uses (e.g., as twine), but clothing applications are under consideration.

Chapter 3

FABRIC STRUCTURE

Cloths produced by weaving have been in existence since the earliest times when only the natural fibres were available. From these fibres a wide variety of cloths have been made, each easily recognisable by such characteristics as weave, appearance, weight, and drape. In order to facilitate buying and selling, names became associated with the different types of cloth, and now we have a large choice of standard woven fabrics such as denim, poplin, gaberdine, serge, crêpe, and grosgrain.

Many fabric names have long histories and, from time-to-time, the fabrics are discontinued and then reintroduced according to current fashion trends. Definitions and constructional details of such fabrics are therefore of interest. Those whose responsibility it is to collect for textile archives will, of course, also need to define and classify fabrics in their care. The 'Glossary of Fabrics' – page 313 contains fabrics of both current and historical interest.

Many cloths originally made from silk bear French names. This may be largely due to the development of sericulture in France when silk first found its way to Europe, and later to the development by a Frenchman, M. Joseph Marie Jacquard, of the sophisticated method of producing pattern in weaving, known as Jacquard weaving, which at the time utilised silk to the full in complicated woven designs such as brocades.

However, with the introduction of manufactured fibres it is now common for standard cloth constructions to be made not only from the natural fibres originally associated with them but also from appropriate selections and blends of manufactured fibres.

Weaving is, of course, not the only method of producing textiles. The techniques of knitting, lacemaking, braiding, and felting have been known for a long time. Newer methods of producing fabrics cheaply include fibre bonding and various methods of stitch bonding. Laminating and foam backing are methods for extending the use of fabrics produced by the traditional methods. These techniques will be discussed in turn.

WOVEN FABRICS

Woven fabrics are produced by interlacing two sets of threads, known as warp and weft, at right angles to each other. Darning by hand produces a somewhat similar effect to that obtained by weaving cloth on a loom, in which the warp threads are lifted automatically so that the weft can be inserted. The warp threads run parallel to the selvedge down the length of the cloth, and each warp thread is known as an 'end'. The weft threads, which are referred to as 'picks', run across the cloth from selvedge to selvedge.

Classification of weaves

The interlacing pattern of the warp and weft is known as the weave. There are a number of important weaves which are worth knowing because they are so often used in making useful fabrics such as foulard, gabardine, poplin, satin, and taffeta. The weave influences not only the appearance of the cloth but also its handle and behaviour in use.

In order to identify the weave of a fabric it will be necessary to view the cloth on the right side with a magnifying glass. Since the weave is sometimes difficult to describe, it is useful to illustrate what you see on squared paper. Let us suppose the spaces between the vertical parallel lines in Figure 58 correspond to the warp threads, and the spaces between the horizontal parallel lines represent the weft threads. Then each square in the diagram (obtained by combining the vertical and horizontal lines) can be considered to indicate the intersection of an end and a pick. To show that an end is on the surface of the fabric a square is filled in. When the pick is visible the square is left white. Now compare the weave diagram with the adjacent fabric in Figure 59. It will be seen that the first end passes over one, under one, over one, and under one pick; and the next end under one,

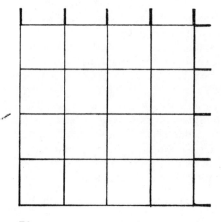

Fig. 58 Squared or point paper. The spaces between the vertical lines correspond to warp threads and the spaces between the horizontal lines correspond to weft threads.

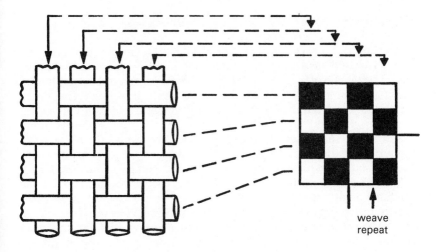

Fig. 59 Plain weave fabric.

over one, and under one pick. The third end repeats the pattern of interlacing of the first end and so on. This is PLAIN weave and the pattern repeats on two threads; the weave repeat is outlined in the diagram.

Plain weave

The plain weave is the simplest and most frequently used weave of all. Because it has the maximum number of interlacing or binding points possible, the fabric will be firmer and stronger than a fabric otherwise identical but made in a twill weave. Lightweight, sheer fabrics, such as chiffon, voile, and georgette, have to be made in a plain weave. Otherwise, the ends and picks, which are few in number, would slip over each other very easily and the fabric would distort.

Fabrics with ribs running in the weft direction, such as poplin, taffeta, poult, and grosgrain, are made in a plain weave. The ribs are caused usually by having many more ends than picks per centimetre, the ends bending round the rather straight picks which lie across the cloth. Since it is the warp that is visible, such a cloth can be described as warp-faced with a weft-way rib. This can easily be checked by comparing threads taken from both directions, from say a grosgrain or poplin, when it will be found that the ends will be more heavily crimped than the picks.

A variety of decorative effects can be produced in a plain-weave cloth. For instance, stripes, or checks as in a gingham, are often made by including dyed yarns. Coarse yarns, fancy yarns, and variations in the amount or direction of twist provide some interest to what may be an otherwise featureless weave. Cramming the ends close together in groups can introduce an interesting stripe effect.

The various characteristics shown by fabrics are governed not only by the weave used but also by the weight of the cloth, how close or open the fabric is, the ratio of the number of ends to picks per centimetre, the type of yarn used, the fibre content, and also the finish. If a cloth has approximately the same number of threads per centimetre and count of yarn in both the warp and the weft, it is said to have a 'square construction'. Examples of such a cloth would be voile and jappe. If only a small proportion of the area of a fabric is covered by, say, the warp yarns, the warp is said to have a 'low cover', whereas the weft may provide a higher degree of cover, perhaps by virtue of its coarser yarns. In fact, the combination of the amount of cover provided by the warp and weft yarns determines the openness or closeness of the cloth. A voile will have a much lower cover than a cambric, and a dress poult will have a greater cover than either.

Some fabrics made from the plain weave are listed below and are defined on pages 313–342.

Table 8   FABRICS MADE FROM PLAIN WEAVE

Group 1	Group 2	Group 3
batiste	afgalaine	chiffon
buckram	crêpe	crêpe-de-chine
cambric	delaine	grosgrain
lawn	domet	jappe
organdie	flannel	organza
poplin	panama	poult
voile	thornproof tweed	shantung
	tropical suiting	taffeta

The fabrics in Group 1 were commonly produced from cotton or linen, those in Group 2 from wool, and those in Group 3 from silk. Nowadays some of these fabrics may also be made from manufactured fibres.

Weaves derived from the plain weave

Warp rib weaves

Warp rib weaves are made by running two or more picks together, as shown in Figures 60 and 61. This produces pronounced weft-way ribs, the surface of which consists of warp threads. The rib effect is emphasised by the use of a greater number of ends than picks and the insertion of coarser weft yarns. Consequently, the picks tend to lie rather straight with the ends bending round them, thus producing a warp rib structure in which the warp is mainly visible. The advantage of introducing two fine weft yarns instead of one coarse yarn is that a broad rib is achieved without greatly increasing the thickness or weight of the cloth.

Since some confusion can arise in the terminology used, it is worthwhile drawing attention particularly to the fact that 'warp rib' weaves produce ribs running weft-way. Cloths known as repp utilise this weave.

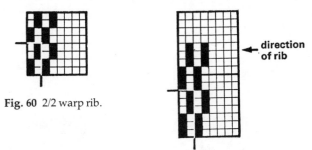

Fig. 60 2/2 warp rib.

Fig. 61 3/3 warp rib.

Weft rib weaves

Weft rib weaves are the opposite to warp rib weaves, as shown in Figure 62. The weft is prominent on both sides of the cloth, which has warp-way ribs or cords running lengthwise. Such weaves are not commonly used in fabrics for clothing because it is uneconomic in weaving to insert the large number of picks which are required.

It may be noted that in Oxford shirting the two ends weave as one (and help to increase the tearing strength of the fabric), but the other details of fabric construction, such as threads per centimetre and yarn count, are not designed to produce or emphasise a rib effect. This type of fabric is sometimes referred to as a double-end plain.

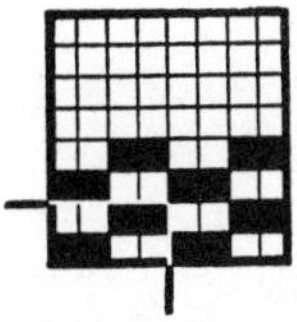

Fig. 62 2/2 weft rib (two ends weaving as one.)

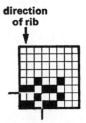

Fig. 63 Haircord.

Haircord

Haircord was used for cotton dress fabric, especially in children's wear. The weave is characterised by the use of a plain weave in which pairs of ends weave as one and alternate with single ends, as shown in Figure 63. The cloth has a fine warp-way rib caused by the pairs of ends.

Hopsack weaves

Hopsack weaves (synonym 'matt') are produced as 2/2 or 3/3 hopsack, for example. See Figures 64 and 65. It will be seen that two or more ends and two or more picks weave as one, giving a fabric with a smooth surface but with a greatly enlarged coarse plain-weave structure. Fabrics bearing the name of this weave are commonly made from worsted yarns. If two fabrics of otherwise similar construction are woven as a plain and a 2/2 hopsack, it will be found that because of its fewer intersections the hopsack weave will tend to be less stiff. In addition, when a 2/2 hopsack fabric is torn, the threads will break in pairs and the cloth will, therefore, have a greater resistance to tearing than a comparable plain cloth, in which the threads break one at a time.

Fig. 64 2/2 Hopsack.   **Fig. 65** Twilled hopsack.

Twill weaves

These weaves are characterised by continuous diagonal lines; they cannot be produced on less than a three thread repeat. See Figures 66, 67 and 68. It will be noticed that some of the twill lines run up to the right and are known as right-hand twills or 'Z twills'. Twills with their diagonal lines running in the opposite direction are known as left-hand twills or 'S twills' (the centre stroke of the letters Z and S denote the direction of twill).

Taking a '2/2' as an example, the term 2/2, which may also be written $\frac{2}{2}$ signifies that each end floats over two successive picks and under two successive picks, with each adjacent end to the right stepping up one pick, resulting in a 'Z twill'. It is possible to have a 2/2 twill stepping down one, which of course, would produce an 'S twill'. Twill weaves with a 2/2, 3/3, or 4/4 repeat are regarded as balanced twills. If they are used in a fabric of square construction, the warp and weft will be equally prominent on both faces of the fabric. Such a fabric is a serge, which is made in a 2/2 twill.

On the other hand, weaves such as 1/2 and 3/1 twill are regarded as 'unbalanced' twills, since in the first example the right side of the fabric will be composed mainly of weft threads. The cloth is, therefore, referred to as 'weft-faced', and the 3/1 twill produces a 'warp-faced' fabric such as a denim. See figures 67 and 68.

The prominence of the twill lines in a simple twill weave depends to some extent on the length over which the threads 'float' across each other: a 2/1 twill has a shorter float than a 4/1 twill. There is, of course, a limit to the length of float that can be used, since fabrics with very long floats may

Fig. 66 2/2 Twill
(Z direction).

Fig. 67 1/2 Twill
(S direction).

Fig. 68 3/1 Twill
(S direction).

be unstable and liable to snag. The use of warp and weft yarns differing in colour, diameter, or twist may also enhance the twill effect.

The angle at which the twill line runs is influenced by the ratio of ends to picks and the stepping number used in the weave. A stepping number of one in a fabric of square construction will produce a twill line at an angle of 45°. (The angle of twill is taken as that formed by the twill line and the weft.) If the ends per centimetre are greater than the picks per centimetre, the twill line will be steeper and will run more closely to the warp direction. Comparing a serge and gaberdine, both of 2/2 twill construction, it will be found that the serge with its square construction has its twill line running at a lower angle than in the gaberdine, which has about twice as many ends as picks. If an even steeper twill line is required, a stepping number of more than two will achieve this. Some whipcords which have bold, steep upright twills utilise twill weaves with fairly long floats and big stepping numbers. See Figure 69.

Fig. 69
Whipcord

It is possible in a twill weave to accommodate more ends and picks in the fabric than the maximum that can be accommodated in a plain weave using the same count of yarn. Consequently, similar yarns can be made into heavier fabrics by using twill rather than plain weave. Twill weaves are always less stiff than plain weaves made from the same yarns and with the same ends and picks per centimetre.

Twill weaves are often used simply to create surface interest. It is possible for the fabric designer to use attractive or expensive yarns in the warp, which will show, and incorporate the less attractive or inexpensive yarns in the weft, which may be scarcely visible on the face of the cloth.

Some fabrics made from twill weaves are listed below and are defined on pages 313–342.

Table 9 FABRICS MADE FROM TWILL WEAVE

Group 1	Group 2	Group 3
denim	dog's-tooth check	foulard
jean	flannel	surah
regatta	gabardine	
regina	Glen check	
silesia	whipcord	

Weaves derived from twill weaves

Fancy diagonals

Numerous twill weave variations are possible, some of which are used in worsted fabrics known as fancy diagonals. Here, two or more weaves are combined together as, for example, 3/1 and 1/3 twills. See Figure 70.

Cavalry twill

The cavalry twill, with its characteristic double twill line, commonly uses a weave of the type shown in Figure 71.

Pointed and herringbone twills

Pointed and herringbone twills are produced by the combination of 'Z' and 'S' direction twill weaves, and are illustrated in Figures 72 and 73. Both examples are based in this instance on the 2/2 twill. Generally in a fabric of a given construction the herringbone would provide a firmer cloth than the pointed twill.

Diamond designs

Diamond designs can be obtained by the arrangement of pointed and herringbone twills, as shown in Figure 74.

Fig. 72 Pointed twill (based on 2/2 twill).

Fig. 70 Fancy diagonal.   **Fig. 71** Cavalry twill.

Fig. 73 Herringbone (based on 2/2 twill).

Fig. 74 Diamond weave (based on pointed twill).

Satin and sateen weaves

Fabrics made from these weaves have a typically smooth and generally lustrous appearance without strong diagonal lines of the type associated with twill weaves. The satin weave is used in fabrics made from a wide range of fibres. Flat continuous fllament yarns are very commonly used, since their bright lustrous surface enhances the smooth appearance of the fabric. However, cotton yarn, mercerised or unmercerised, and worsted yarn are both put into these weaves, and it follows that whilst a satin has a smooth surface it may not necessarily have the lustre which is sometimes erroneously considered to be an essential requirement of the fabric.

A satin is warp-faced, whereas a sateen is a weft-face fabric. An examination of the weaves illustrated in Figures 75, 76 and 77 shows the intersections between the warp and weft to be distributed so that they can be somewhat concealed on the face of the fabric. In fact, in a closely woven cloth the floats tend to overlap the binding points and consequently make them less conspicuous. Satin and sateen weaves commonly repeat on 5 or 8 threads and are generally called a 5-end or 8-end satin or sateen.

Fig. 75 5-end satin.   **Fig. 76** 8-end satin.   **Fig. 77** 5-end sateen.

Satin fabrics are available in a range of weights suitable for lightweight linings, lingerie, slippers, foundation garments, heavy dress fabrics suitable for evening wear, and bridal gowns. Generally, the heavier satins are made with an 8-end repeat, and the threads per centimetre and cloth 'cover' are greatly increased.

The smooth surface of a satin lends itself to printing, machine embroidery, and embossing to produce lustrous patterned effects. Sateens are frequently made from cotton, and apart from being printed and being suitable for dress fabrics, the weave is used in such fabrics as Italian for lining and closely woven downproof sateens for eiderdowns.

Some fabrics made from satin and sateen weaves are listed below and defined on pages 313–342.

Table 10 FABRICS MADE FROM SATIN AND SATEEN WEAVES

Group 1	Group 2	Group 3
Italian	doeskin cloth	duchesse satin
satin drill	satin-back gabardine	satin-back crêpe
Venetian		satin marocain

Construction of other important groups of fabric

Fabrics with a crinkled or puckered surface

This appearance is typified by fabrics such as georgette, moss crêpe, and seersucker.

Georgette, crêpe-de-chine, marocain, crepon

In this group the effect is achieved by the use of crêpe twist yarns in plain-weave fabrics with various fibre contents and degrees of cover. It will be remembered that crêpe twist yarns, when woven into a fabric, snarl and shrink during the wet finishing treatment applied to the fabric (see page 64). The size of the 'pebble' or 'figure' on the surface of the fabric is governed by:

1) The amount the fibres swell when immersed in water or other swelling agent. Viscose, cotton, wool, and silk fibres are all suitable in this respect for producing crêpe fabrics.

2) The amount of twist in the yarn. A high twist is required, and the higher the twist the greater the shrinkage.

3) The combination of 'S' and 'Z' twist yarns in the weft direction. Crêpes are usually woven with a pair of 'S' and a pair of 'Z' twist yarns alternating in the weft. If only one direction of twist is used, the fabric will develop a fluted appearance like a crepon.

4) The closeness of the threads in the cloth. The more widely spaced the threads, the greater will be the freedom with which the yarns can snarl, and consequently the figure will be coarse. Closely woven cloths, on the other hand, provide greater control on the distribution of the crinkles in the yarn, and a finer figure is produced.

5) The rate with which the fabric is allowed to shrink during finishing. Before a crêpe fabric is woven, the crêpe yarns in both warp and weft are stabilised by sizing to enable the fabric to be woven easily and to help the crêpe yarns to lie straight in the loomstate cloth without distortion. After the cloth has been woven, it is often embossed by a heated metal roller engraved with the fine pattern associated with a good quality crêpe. For the embossing to be effective, acetate yarns are commonly used in the warp because of their thermoplasticity. Embossing is followed by allowing the fabric to develop the crêpe in hot, soapy water. The temperature and crêpeing conditions influence the character of the pebble; in any event the crêpe is contained within the embossed pattern. If the fabric is allowed to shrink to its fullest extent, it may develop a coarse rough appearance. Consequently, it is usually stretched a little and dried in that state on the stenter to improve its appearance and handle.

Fabrics made with continuous filament yarns without crêpe twist are embossed after weaving, as described above to simulate a crêpe surface.

This is obviously a less expensive way of producing a 'crêpe' fabric but it lacks the full character and draping qualities that are expected from true crêpes.

Another method of producing a crêpe effect without the use of crêpe yarns is to weave a fabric with a crêpe weave (Figure 78), the simplest of which is shown repeating on eight threads. This gives the cloth an irregular surface, and to quote *Textile Terms and Definitions*, 'Having a random distribution of floats so as to produce an "all-over" effect in the fabric to disguise the repeat.'

Fig. 78
Crêpe weave.

Moss crêpe

Moss crêpe fabrics not only require the special moss crêpe yarn construction but also a moss crêpe weave. It is usual for such a weave to repeat on 66 ends and 40 picks. The intention is effectively to obtain a random distribution of floats without any patterning or weave repeat being evident. It is possible, however, to use a moss crêpe weave with standard continuous filament yarns instead of the usual moss crêpe yarn, which is a two-fold yarn consisting of a viscose crêpe twisted with a flat acetate yarn. This results in a more stable fabric, less liable to shrink (because of the absence of the crêpe component). It is lighter in weight than the true moss crêpe.

Seersucker, Plissé

The cockled effect associated with these fabrics is produced by causing small areas of fabric to shrink, with the result that the excess length of yarn in the intervening fabric cockles. There are three important ways of producing this type of cockling:

Choice of yarn or fibre

Nylon plissé is frequently made by using heat-set and unset yarns either in the warp or weft or in both directions. The unset yarns can shrink as much as 10% when the fabric is passed through hot water during finishing or dyeing. Consequently, the heat-set yarns will now have an excess length over the unset yarns and will cockle.

Apart from utilising the differential shrinkage of heat-set and unset thermoplastic yarns, it is possible to introduce a yarn of different fibre content which has a higher shrinkage potential than the yarn used in the basic fabric. A good example of this would be a fabric made from nylon, in which polyvinylchloride yarn is woven at suitable intervals. The shrinkage of a PVC yarn in hot water could be as high as 35%, and this would cause a pronounced blister effect in the fabric.

Conditions of weaving

Instead of using one weaver's beam at the back of the loom, as is usual, two weaver's beams are used, enabling alternate groups of ends to be delivered to the loom at different tensions. In finishing, the groups of ends woven at a high tension will contract, and the slacker ends will cockle. This method of manufacture has often been used for cotton seersucker, in which case the cockled stripes follow the same ends exactly throughout a piece of cloth.

Finishing

Seersucker effects can also be obtained in cotton cloths by printing small designs on the surface with paste containing caustic soda. Where the caustic soda is absorbed, the fibres swell and consequently the yarns shrink. As a means of identifying the method used in producing the cockles, it is worth noting that the cockled stripes produced by this method do not follow the same ends exactly.

Special finishing treatments may be applied to fabrics made from nylon to develop cockling. One method is to calender unset fabric between a pair of metal rollers, one of which is engraved with a pattern. Where the fabric comes in contact with the prominent parts of the engraving it shrinks, and consequently the intervening areas of fabric cockle. Another method which has been used is printing nylon fabric with phenol, and in these areas the fabric shrinks.

Cellular fabrics

'Cellular' is defined as: 'A term describing a fabric having a close and orderly distribution of hollows or holes. In woven fabric, this can be achieved by honeycomb, leno or mock leno weaves.' (*Textile Terms and Definitions*).

Honeycomb

Ridges and hollows produced by any one of three standard honeycomb weaves gives a cellular effect which may be evident on one or other, or both faces of the cloth. The weave diagram of the ordinary honeycomb can be seen in Figure 79. The vertical ridge of the fabric is composed of warp floats, and the horizontal ridge of weft floats, while the hollow is formed where the two opposite twill lines cross.

Leno

In a leno weave some of the ends are made to weave first to one side and then to the other of adjacent ends. Sometimes the leno weave is used to produce decorative stripes, as in voile fabrics. If the whole of the fabric is made from the leno weave, it is possible to produce a very open structure which is reasonably stable and not easily distorted because the crossing ends tend to lock the weft threads in position. Quite a number of cellular blankets utilise the leno weave. (Figure 80).

Mock leno

In this weave it will be seen that the ends are not made to cross each other,

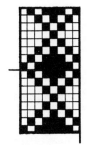

Fig. 79
Honeycomb.

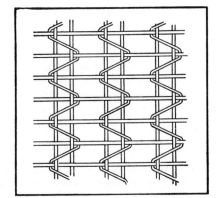

Fig. 80 Leno. *(The Textile Institute)*

Fig. 81
Mock leno.

and it is less expensive to produce than the true leno. The cellular or open-mesh effect is achieved by the spaces which develop in the directions indicated on the weave diagram. The effect produced by this weave, which is shown in Figure 81, may be used in a plain-weave fabric, for instance, to produce a decorative 'open-work' feature for dresses, blouses and table-cloths. In addition, it is commonly used for hand embroidery 'canvas'.

Double cloths

A double cloth consists of two separate fabrics, woven at the same time on one loom, and held together by the ends of one fabric sometimes weaving with the picks of the other fabric. Examples of this type of structure are cloqué, matelassé, double plain, and reversible cloths.

Cloqué

This type of cloth is characterised by a figured blister effect, produced by the use of two warps and two wefts. One set of warp threads and one set of weft threads weave together and consist of yarns which shrink only a little. The other warp and weft consist of yarns capable of high shrinkage, either because they are highly twisted crêpe yarns or because they are made from fibres or filaments which will shrink considerably when the cloth is finished. The figure or design is produced by uniting the two sets of yarns to form one layer on the perimeter of the design, and by the underlayer of cloth shrinking and the top layer cockling to accommodate the excess cloth length within the perimeter of the design.

Matelassé

Matelassé has a quilted appearance. Whilst this cloth is made from two warps and two wefts, unlike cloqué a differential shrinkage between the two sets of yarns is not required. In order to emphasise the quilted effect extra warp threads, known as wadding ends, are introduced between the two layers of cloth during weaving.

Double plain

Here two plain-weave cloths of different colours are woven, one above the other, and, according to the design required, such as a check, stripe, or figure, the different coloured threads interchange with each other and so produce a compound fabric. This principle of cloth construction can be developed to produce a wide variety of reversible cloths.

Bedford cord and piqué

Both of these weaves are characterised by rounded cords with fine sunken lines between. The distinction between a Bedford cord and a piqué is that in the former the cord runs along the length of the cloth, whereas in a piqué the cord runs across the cloth. However, very few true piqués or 'welts' are made now. Instead, lightweight Bedford cord structures made from spun cotton or modal fibre, or flat continuous filament yarns, are sold commercially as piqué.

The weave used is quite distinctive. See Figure 82. The face of the cord is generally a plain weave. A twill is sometimes used instead, in which case the cloth was known at one time as 'London cord'. The rounded cord effect is achieved by pairs of weft yarns floating across the back of the cord and being woven in to form the sunken lines. Bedford cord can have the cord emphasised further by the introduction of wadding ends.

Definitions of fabrics which take their names from the Bedford cord and piqué weaves are given in the Glossary of Fabrics.

Pile fabrics

A definition of the term 'pile' is: 'A surface effect on a fabric formed by tufts or loops of yarn, introduced into the fabric for the purpose, which stand up

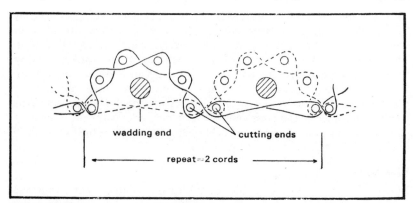

Fig. 82 Bedford cord: section through warp.
(The Textile Institute)

from the body of the cloth.' Attention must be drawn to the distinction between the terms 'pile' and 'nap'. Whereas a 'pile' is produced by weaving, a 'nap' is developed on the fabric surface during cloth finishing processes such as brushing and raising. Usually the fibres are teazed out of the fabric by the action of fine wire teeth, by teazles, or by carborundum as in sueding. A nap or suede effect can also be produced by flock printing.

Pile fabrics can be produced by weaving, knitting, or tufting. Here we are concerned with woven pile fabric, which may be classified in the following way:

> Warp pile: cut loops; (velvet)
> > uncut or loop pile; (terry towelling)
> Weft pile: cut; (velveteen and corduroy)

Velvet

The uniform dense pile is produced by cutting warp yarns which have been specially woven in to form the pile. There are three principal methods of weaving velvet, two of which involve lifting the pile warp over wires or metal strips, which determine the height of the pile. The pile is cut at the loom by different techniques. The third method is to weave two cloths face to face, as shown in Figure 83, with the pile warp alternating between the upper and lower fabrics. At the front of the loom a knife moves back and forth across the width of the cloth and cuts the pile warp as the cloth moves forward during weaving. In this way two separate pieces of velvet are produced simultaneously.

The bloom and attractive appearance of velvet is developed after dyeing during fabric finishing when the pile is cut level by cropping or shearing. Then, by brushing and the use of steam, the fibres in the cut yarns are

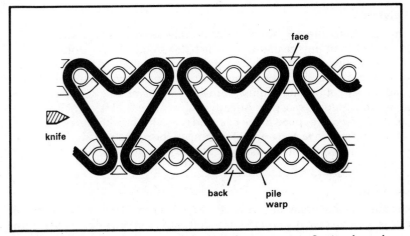

Fig. 83 Velvet: two fabrics woven face-to-face prior to cutting. Section through weft. *(The Textile Institute)*

splayed out and are made either to stand erect or are laid at an angle. A variety of velvets made from various fibres are in styles such as Brocaded, Genoa, and Nacré.

Terry

This cloth consists of a loop-pile and is sometimes known as 'Turkish towelling'. The method of manufacture differs from that for velvet because here no wires are used. During weaving the reed beats forward completely only on every third pick and, consequently, three picks are carried forward at the same time, thus causing the pile-warp, which is slack, to loop above and below the fabric to form the pile. The loops are anchored in position by the interlacing of the weft yarn and the firmly woven ground-warp. (Figure 84).

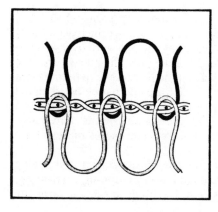

Fig. 84 3-Pick terry: pile on both sides.
(The Textile Institute)

Velveteen

The pile in velveteen is short and uniformly dense and is produced after weaving by cutting the pile-weft, which floats on the surface of the cloth. The weft pile is of very high density and this is attained by using fewer warp yarns than would be required for a velvet. Velveteen is commonly made from cotton and requires brushing and cropping to develop the lustre and uniformity of pile. After dyeing, in order to obtain a rich bloom a solution of dye is applied to the pile, and revolving brushes spread the dye on the surface. In fact, frequent brushing of the pile is an essential feature of the finishing of such cloths. Figure 85 shows a cross-section of a velveteen.

Corduroy

Corduroy is sometimes known as corded velveteen. The distribution of the pile is such that the floats of the pile-weft yarn lie in rows down the length of the cloth, as shown in Figure 86. When the weft is cut the pile forms lines or cords, which run in the warp direction.

For satisfactory wear it is important for the pile to be firmly anchored in the ground structure. It is possible to have the tufts held in place by only one warp thread, as illustrated, with the result that the tuft forming the pile is V-shaped. A much firmer structure is achieved by having W-shaped tufts. The back of pile fabrics is sometimes lightly raised or sized to improve the fastness of the pile.

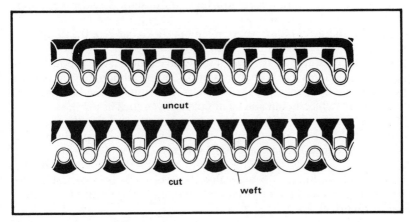

Fig. 85 Velveteen: section through warp. *(The Textile Institute)*

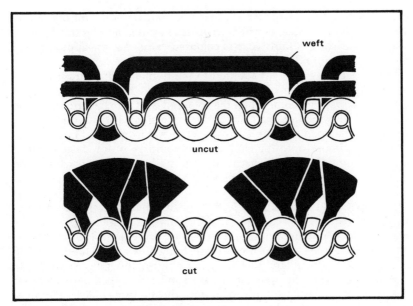

Fig. 86 Corduroy: section through warp. *(The Textile Institute)*

Special visual effects produced by weaving

Tappet, dobby, and Jacquard shedding mechanisms

In addition to the basic weaves and the special cloth constructions outlined above, interesting modifications in fabric appearance can be obtained by designing a pattern on paper which is translated into a fabric by the skilful combination of different weaves to achieve the design. An example of such a fabric is brocade. Depending on whether the warp or weft is prominent, and on the character of the weave in any particular area of the design, so the light, shade, and texture of the design is developed.

Any loom is limited by the size of the weave repeat it can produce, and this is governed by what is known as the shedding motion, which controls the lifting and lowering of the heald shafts. The simplest shedding motion is the tappet, which is suitable for simple weaves such as plain, twill, and satin, and weaves derived from these. The next most versatile shedding mechanism attached to the loom is the dobby, which can produce more complicated effects. The term 'dobby' is freely used to indicate the size of the woven design. For instance, a cloth may be described as a dobby striped poplin. The most complicated designs, such as large-scale floral effects, are produced on the Jacquard loom. These fabrics may be referred to as Jacquard fabrics.

Swivel, lappet, and clip-spot effects

Cloths of simple construction can have decorative motifs introduced by swivel or lappet weaving or by the clip-spot technique. The small figure, usually consisting of fairly coarse, coloured yarns, has the appearance at first sight of embroidery.

Swivel weaving uses, in addition to the normal weft, extra yarn contained in a number of small spools which are located just above the warp at intervals across the loom. When the coloured weft is to be introduced the spools are lowered into the warp and move a short distance through the section of the opened warp. Each swivel thread is traversed from side to side and is bound into the cloth at the boundary of the design and at intermediate points by the yarns used in the basic fabric structure. The distance between adjacent figures is governed mainly by the size of the mechanism used.

In lappet weaving, which is less expensive than swivel weaving, the variously coloured special warp threads are traversed horizontally in front of the reed and produce a figure on the surface of the cloth. They are bound in by the weft at the limits of the traverse. Long unwanted floats extending between one motif and the next down the length of the cloth are cut away.

Warp and weft clip-spot effects are similar in appearance to those described above. The weft method of introducing spots utilises a normal-type shuttle to contain the novelty yarn, in addition to a shuttle for the weaving of the ground fabric, and this crosses the full width of the cloth. Where the effect yarn is not woven-in but merely floats on the surface, it is cut off. Weft clip-spot is limited to the introduction of one colour across the cloth.

Warp clip-spots require an extra weaver's beam at the back of the loom to contain the novelty yarn. The effect is very similar to the weft clip-spot and, similarly, the long floats between each repeat of pattern in the warp direction are sheared during fabric finishing.

Colour woven fabrics

Colours may be introduced in cloths by dyeing the cloth, the yarn, or the fibre before it is spun, or by printing. Colour weaving is a method of introducing colour and pattern into a cloth that utilises coloured yarns which have been either yarn-dyed or fibre-dyed before spinning. However, identical effects are produced by weaving undyed yarn of different fibres followed by cross-dyeing. In this way it is possible for an undyed cloth to be held in stock ready for dyeing to meet the customer's demand for any colour range.

Patterns produced during weaving fall into two categories:

a) Those which depend largely on the character of the weave for their ornamentation, such as brocade and cavalry twill. These cloths may be either self-coloured or have a contrasting warp and weft.

b) Those which depend solely on colour as the predominant decorative feature.

The use of dyed yarns in weaving provides considerable patterning scope for the cloth designer, who must take into account the effect of factors such as the presence of neighbouring colours; the ratio of areas of the colours used; and the influence of fibre, yarn, cloth construction, and cloth finish on the prominence of the colours. It is obvious that if a coloured stripe is woven in plain and twill weaves, the plain weave provides a more subdued effect than is achieved by the twill weave with its long floats, which enable greater clarity of colour to be attained. Cloth finishing techniques can emphasise the brightness of the colour by clear finishing, which removes projecting surface hairs, or can subdue the colours by raising the fibres to form a nap.

Colour woven cloths fall into the following categories according to the way the coloured threads are combined:

Shot effects – the warp is one colour and the weft a different colour.

Stripes – different coloured yarns in the warp and only one colour in the weft direction. There is a variety of style of stripes according to the colour arrangement in the warp; some of the more common ones are known as chalk stripe, pin stripe, and pyjama stripe. Coloured weft-way stripes may similarly be introduced.

Checks – simple checks are produced by different coloured yarns arranged in both warp and weft. An example of such a cloth is a gingham made in a plain weave.

Colour and weave effects

By combining two or more colours in the warp and weft with plain, hopsack, or twill weaves a great variety of small patterns are produced, such as hairline, step effect, dog's tooth check, shepherd's check, and also more elaborate designs in which small patterns are integrated to produce a Glen Urquhart check or basket designs. Colour and weave effects are extensively used in woollen and worsted cloth for men's and ladies' wear.

At first sight some patterns give an impression of dobby and Jacquard designs, but in fact they simply depend upon the weave and the arrangements of the colours, the weave being responsible for the breaking up of the colour, as can be seen in the examples given below. In each illustration the diagram gives an impression of the appearance of the fabric. The weave is indicated by placing a dot wherever the warp is on the face of the fabric, and the arrangement of the coloured warp and weft threads in the cloth is shown in the margin round the diagram. These designs are not restricted only to the weave and order of colouring given for each example, since selected colour and weave combinations may produce similar effects.

Hairline – Plain weave with a 1:1 order of colouring, that is, with one thread of each colour alternating both in the warp and in the weft directions. This effect is one of solid coloured vertical lines on the face of the fabric, the reverse side of the fabric showing horizontal coloured lines. (Figure 87).

Step effect – 2/2 twill weave with a 1:1 order of colouring. It will be noticed that whilst the twill weave has the twill line running to the right, the coloured effect runs to the left. (Figure 88).

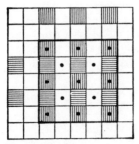

Fig. 87 Hairline.

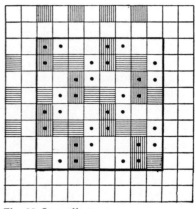

Fig. 88 Step effect.

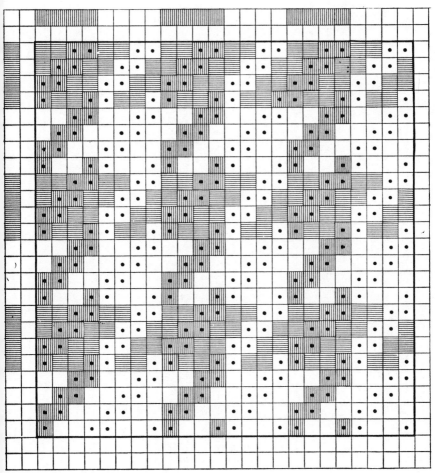

Fig. 89 Dog's tooth check.

Dog's tooth check – 2/2 twill weave with a 4:4 order of colouring. This distinctive design when produced to give a large pattern is known as hound's tooth. (Figure 89).

Shepherd's check – 2/2 twill weave with a 6:6 order of colouring. Here a bolder effect is achieved than in a dog's tooth by having pronounced coloured squares. (Figure 90).

Glen check – 2/2 twill weave with a 4:4 and 2:2 order of colouring in both warp and weft.

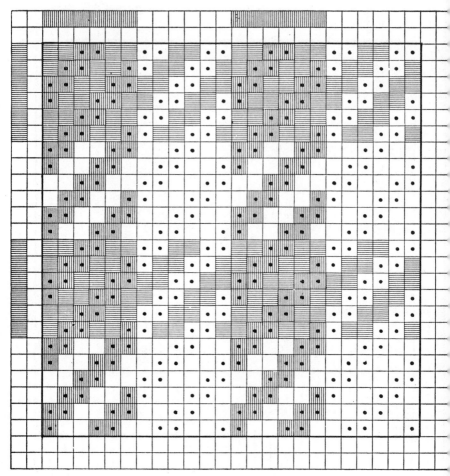

Fig. 90 Shepherd's check.

KNITTED FABRICS

Machine knitting is an important method of fabric manufacture now that, in addition to its rapid rate of production, the limited range of fabrics and end uses with which it was at one time associated has been widened to such an extent that knitted fabrics compete with fabrics traditionally made by weaving.

There are two main industrial categories of machine knitting: weft knitting and warp knitting. Fabrics in both these categories consist essentially of a series of interlinked loops of yarn.

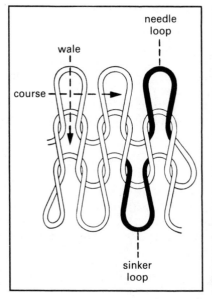

Fig. 91 Plain weft knitting – face side.

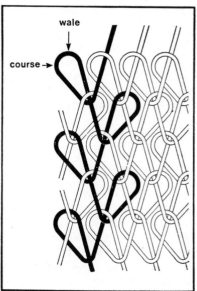

Fig. 92 Back of warp-knitted half-tricot.

In *weft knitting*, these loops are formed in succession one loop at a time when the yarn travels across the fabric as it is being formed. Each new row of loops is drawn through the previous row of loops in the fabric. All the loops in one row are produced from one yarn, unless special colour effects are required. It is evident that weft knitting is liable to ladder if a loop is broken, and may be unravelled course by course. (Figure 91).

Each horizontal row of loops is known as a 'course', and each vertical line of loops is known as a 'wale'. This description applies to both weft and warp knitting.

Warp knitting is produced from a set of warp yarns, normally using at least one yarn per wale, knitted parallel to each other down the length of the fabric, Figure 92. These yarns are fed downwards to the knitting zone and all the loops in one course are knitted simultaneously. If each yarn were continuously knitted in the same wale, a series of unconnected chains of loops would be produced. To make a fabric it is, therefore, necessary for the chains of loops in the wale direction to be inter-connected. This is done by moving the threads sideways at intervals to be knitted on adjacent wales. Warp knitted fabrics do not ladder and cannot be unravelled course by course.

Formation of the stitch in the knitting process

Needles as shown in Figure 93 are used in machine knitting. In weft knitting, latch and bearded needles are used, whereas in warp knitting, 'compound needles' are also used. One needle is required for each loop or wale. The term 'gauge' is used to indicate the closeness of spacing of the needles. An explanation will now be given of the formation of a stitch by both latch and bearded needles. The series of diagrams shows the action of one needle, stage by stage, and the photograph compares the appearance of the two needles.

Action of bearded needle

The yarn is laid across the needle when it is in the position shown in the first diagram in Figure 94, and slides under the beard. The presser bar now moves forward to close the beard. The needle travels down until the tip of the beard, pressed into the eye of the needle, is below the level of the old loop. After the old loop has landed on the beard, the presser bar moves away and releases the beard. The needle continues its downward movement and pulls the new loop through the old one. The needle then returns to its original position, ready to knit the next course.

Action of latch needle

The action of the needle is the same in both warp and weft knitting, the distinction between the two methods being in the way the yarn is pre-

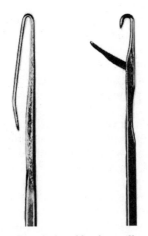

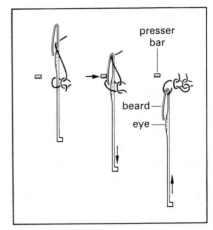

Fig. 93 Bearded and latch needles.
(Hollings Faculty, Manchester Polytechnic)

Fig. 94 Action of bearded needle.

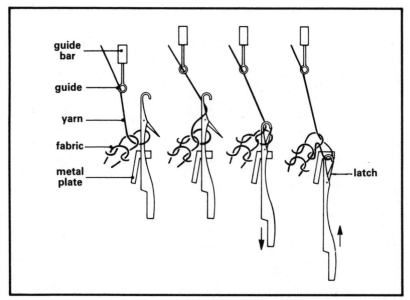

Fig. 95 Action of latch needle.

sented to the needle. Figure 95 shows the situation in warp knitting, where an individual yarn guide for each needle swings round the needle and laps the yarn round the needle above the latch, laying it in the hook. As the needle descends, the old loop closes the needle latch, and when the needle arrives below the metal plate the old loop is knocked over. The knitting cycle is completed by the needle rising, and in so doing the newly formed loop opens the latch. The guide is moved sideways to lay the same thread in the next or some other needle in readiness for knitting the subsequent course.

Compound needle

The compound needle consists of a grooved stem with a hook at the top. A slider can move up and down in the groove to close and open the hook. As the needle moves down, the stitches are displaced over the closed needle heads and are cast off. The method of formation of the loop is very similar to that already described above. This type of compound needle is particularly suited to the knitting of staple fibre and textured yarns.

End uses of knitted fabrics

The scope of knitted fabrics is extensive, permitting the use of the natural fibres, textured or untextured nylon and polyester yarns, as well as yarns made from acetate, triacetate and acrylic fibres. The use of stretch and elastane yarns provides additional stretch and recovery to the fabric.

Although knitted fabrics, and most particularly warp-knitted fabrics, have replaced a substantial part of the market for woven fabrics in recent years, the two classes of textile differ essentially in certain basic characteristics and each has an area of use for which the other is unsuitable.

Knitting consists of interlinked loops of yarn, and since these are very easily distorted the fabric is also easily distorted and is very extensible. It conforms easily to the shape of the figure and drapes very softly. Woven fabrics are naturally much less extensible, particularly in the direction of the yarns. They can be distorted by pulling in the bias direction, but if the cloth is closely woven even this distortion is fairly limited. The properties of both types of fabric are highly dependent on the choice of fibres, yarn type and constructional details, but it is possible to generalise and state that knitted fabrics excel in softness of handle, and drape. Because of the mobility of the loop knitted fabrics do not crease readily and are quick to shed creases. The loops of yarn immobilise air and this promotes a good relationship of warmth to weight. On the other hand, woven fabrics are firm, stable and strong and can be woven to have a resistance to air penetration far in excess of what is possible in knitting.

It is possible to attain a much greater degree of firmness and stability by warp knitting than by weft knitting, and it is partly for this reason that in certain fields warp-knitted fabrics have been able to compete successfully with woven fabrics, but the dominant reason for this success is the high rate of production of the knitting processes. In addition, because of their inherent crease shedding characteristic they make up into highly successful 'wash and wear' garments.

In weft-knitted fabric the problem of dimensional stability is more marked, and it should be noted that the dimensions of the fabric are sensitive not only to mechanical stresses but also to the effects of washing. It is one of the aims of the finisher to ensure that on washing the fabric will change its dimensions as little as possible. Excessive tension in finishing will stretch the fabric in length and cause a contraction in width and these changes will be reversed when a garment made from the fabric is washed. Care in finishing and the choice of suitable finishing processes will minimise this behaviour, but it is necessary for the garment manufacturer to learn from the fabric supplier and from his own tests what standard of stability he can expect in a particular fabric. It is also essential that the fabric should be handled carefully throughout garment manufacturing processes to ensure that it is not stretched or distorted since this would render a garment liable to shrinkage and loss of shape in use and in cleaning.

In contrast to weft knitting, which requires various sizes of machines in order to produce a range of fabric widths, warp knitting permits the production of various widths of fabric within the working width of the one machine. This flexibility of choice is useful in meeting customer needs, both in clothing manufacture and household textiles. Sheets and net curtains are examples of products requiring a range of fabric widths.

Weft-knit

Of the two methods of knitting, weft knitting is the older. The fabrics produced by this technique are characterised by a flexible structure accompanied by a soft handle which is often enhanced by the inclusion of staple fibre yarns. It is the shape and mobility of the loops of yarn within the fabric structure that influence the extent to which the fabric conforms to the figure and drapes easily. Such a flexible structure also permits crease shedding, easier laundering and soil removal. Weft-knitted fabrics lend themselves to the comfort of informal casual wear, underwear and hosiery. The range also extends from light weight sheer fabrics to thick pile fabrics.

The knitting pattern, the closeness of the structure measured by the number of wales and courses per centimetre, the length of yarn per stitch (which determines the size of the loop), the linear density of the yarns used in the construction, and the fibre content all influence the appearance and physical properties of the material.

Apart from the usual facility for using a yarn composed of a blend of fibres there is opportunity in weft-knitting to feed in separate yarns of different fibre content during the knitting process. Consequently individual courses may consist of a yarn of a different fibre content from that in adjacent courses. This is known as 'feeder blending' and enables the appearance, texture and properties of the fabric to be modified.

Weft-knitting machines are either *flat* or *circular*. The flat machines have all the needles arranged in straight rows. Usually there are two beds in an 'inverted V' position to hold the needles. The yarn is fed back and forth across the width of the fabric, and flat lengths of fabric or garment parts are produced. Circular machines feed the yarn continuously in one direction to the needles, which are arranged in circular formation, and consequently the fabrics or garment blanks produced are usually tubular. Instead of feeding only one yarn to the circular machine, and having most of the needles idle whilst the yarn is being knitted on its circuit, a succession of yarns are fed to the needles with the result that there are a number of knitting zones around the periphery. In a multi-feed system, if 24 yarns are supplied there will be 24 points at which knitting occurs and 24 courses knitted simultaneously. The rate of production in this multi-feed knitting will be 24 times that of single-end knitting and the tube of fabric will be composed of spirals of yarns as illustrated in Figure 96.

Dependent on the choice of flat machine and the way it is operated garments, as opposed to fabric lengths, may be formed during the knitting process. Knitwear, such as sweaters and cardigans, may have parts of the garment made on the machine. This consists of either producing body lengths with ribbing attached for the waist and cuffs, or introducing shaping in flat pieces of fabric by 'fashioning', which widens and narrows the fabric automatically as required. The panels are seamed together in a separate operation. Knitwear is also made by simply cutting lengths of

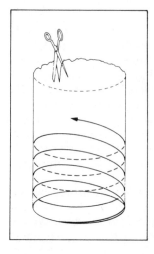

Fig. 96 Tubular weft-knit fabric slit open to full width.

knitted fabric to shape and sewing, this being known as the 'cut-and-sew' method.

Tubular fabric of the appropriate body size, produced on circular machines, eliminates the need for side seams in T-shirts and underwear, for example. Such garments are completed by cutting out and seaming the neckline and armholes. Socks are made on small diameter machines. Larger diameter machines may be used to make garment blanks which are slit in such a way to reveal the sleeve material as an integral part of the garment. The process used for the manufacturing of tights and one-piece seamless pantihose are highly automated.

The seaming and other operations required to finish the knitwear garments referred to above are normally carried out by the knitwear manufacturers themselves, but the weft-knit sector of the textile industry is primarily involved in the high speed manufacture of single and double-jersey fabrics for supply to the clothing industry. For this purpose the fabric may be slit and opened to full width during finishing (Figure 96) so that garments may be cut from flat single layers. A study of the basic fabric structures (Table 11) would lead to an appreciation of the wide choice of fabrics available.

It is on circular weft-knitting machines that simulated fur fabrics are made. These high-pile fabrics are known as 'sliver-knit' since ropes of fibre, known as slivers, are fed into the knitting zones and cut tufts of fibres are trapped securely in the structure. The pile is commonly made from acrylic fibres since these provide the desired handle.

Warp-knit

Warp-knitted fabrics are used extensively in clothing and household textiles, and it is the outerwear section of the clothing trade that uses the bulk of the fabric. The range of fabrics and uses to which warp knitting may be put is still being increased by developments in the technical design of the machines, fabric structures and choice of yarns.

The two main categories of warp-knitting machines are tricot and raschel. Machine widths of up to 180 inches are common, operating up to 2,000 courses per minute: in other words, 50 metres of fabric 4 metres wide can be produced per hour. The greater part of tricot production consists of a range of much used standard constructions, typically in weights suitable for dresses, blouses, lingerie and sheetings, made from continuous filament yarns such as polyester and nylon. This type of fabric is often printed by transfer or screen printing techniques. Cotton yarns can be knitted to produce sheets and duvet covers.

Raschel knitting provides greater scope for the production of a more extensive variety of constructions and weights, giving, for example, relief or three-dimensional effects in which coarser and novelty yarns may be used (Figure 97). However, there are some warp-knitted constructions that can be produced on either machine, and therefore the demarcation between the two is not always clear. These include fabrics as diverse as curtain nets and power nets for foundation wear using continuous filament yarns; men's underwear, string vests, swimwear, crochet-type dress fabrics, cellular blankets and fringed scarves made from spun yarns. Pile fabrics of the plush type or of the terry type, with loops on either one or both faces, are also in production. Special raschel machines can produce patterned tights.

In addition to what has been mentioned above, the range of end uses for warp-knit fabrics includes suits, slacks, raincoats, overcoats, linings and pocketings, and these supplement the existing woven and weft-knitted fabrics.

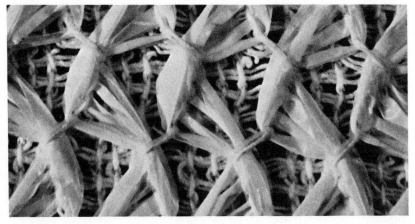

Fig. 97 Raschel fabric. *(Hollings Faculty, Manchester Polytechnic)*

Lingerie and nightwear are commonly made from tricot-knitted polyester or nylon fabric. Until 1968 there was a dramatic rise in the use of warp-knitted nylon for shirts, but since then there has been a decline in its use for this purpose because customers preferred the comfort and visual effects provided by polyester/cotton woven fabrics. Interlinings are being made by the 'weft-insertion' technique, in which a weft is introduced in front of the needles and is trapped in position during the tricot knitting operation. This structure has better stability, which is important in interlinings. For other applications the texture of weft-insertion yarn, and its fibre content, influence the warmth and handle of the material. If the 'weft' yarns are coloured, interesting effects can be achieved.

In the warp-knitting sector of the textile industry, interest centres on developing the capacity to shape garments in the knitting operation in order to minimise, or even eliminate, subsequent making-up operations. Ladies' panties have been produced that are ready to wear, without any making-up operation. The idea of reducing the need for seams, and thereby the cost of sewing operations, has led to the production of one-piece seamless and moulded brassieres, and body-stockings and swimwear that only need edge finishing. Further developments have been the production of carpets by raschel knitting. This method, however, is expensive since the pile yarn is incorporated in the whole fabric structure, whereas carpets made by tufting, for example, have the pile built on to a less expensive base fabric.

Nets were traditionally made by knotting yarns together to form a mesh and the finer meshes were made by twisting yarns together as in lace making. Now warp-knitted nets are used, for example, for fishing, produce-bags, meat wrapping and shoelaces. In this field circular fabric, produced on flat warp knitting machines with two sets of needles, is the means by which seamless tubes for container bags are manufactured, and these meet high performance standards and specific properties. Truly circular warp-knitting machines are also now available, but very rare.

Car upholstery made from corded or ribbed warp-knit fabric is now often preferred to PVC coated fabric, because the superior moisture and air permeability ensures greater comfort.

Basic fabric structures

Weft-knit

Single jersey and double jersey are the two main categories of fabric structures. Single jersey requires only one set of needles; double jersey can only be made on flat or circular machines with two sets of needles positioned at right angles to each other. Purl structures, however, are distinctive from single and double jersey fabrics in that they are made on double headed latch needles (Figure 98), which are made to slide in either direction to knit yarn that is delivered to either hook.

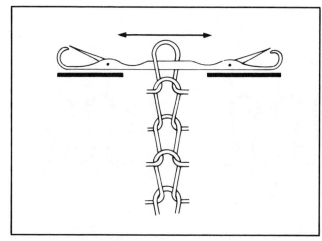

Fig. 98 Double headed latch needle.

Both single and double jersey fabrics are available self-coloured, or patterned by the introduction of dyed yarns. Such patterning may consist of horizontal or vertical stripes, or of designs made by coloured yarns incorporated by 'Jacquard knitting'.

In addition, fabric texture and surface appearance can be modified by the introduction of special stitches in the basic structure. For instance, in single jersey, relief or knop patterns (page 109) develop from the introduction of a 'Miss Stitch', and the 'Tuck Stitch' is similarly useful. 'Cellular' or 'Eyelet' fabrics, which depend on the introduction of a 'hole' in the fabric, utilise the 'Pelerine' stitch (page 110). 'Laid-in' fabrics and 'Plated' fabrics, based on the single jersey structure, provide scope for production of fleecy and pile fabrics, and the high-pile fleece fabric known as 'sliver knit' also utilises the single jersey structure.

The basic stitches used in weft-knitting, and the modifications that are commonly introduced, are summarised in Table 11 (pages 106–113). It will be appreciated that some stitches, such as the 'Tuck Stitch', can be used only as a feature, whereas the plain knit and rib structures are commonly used alone. But note that the introduction of tuck stitches can modify fabric dimensions and hence fabric properties.

Knitting patterns for double jersey structures

The two most important groups of double jersey fabrics are based on structures produced by 'Interlock gating' and 'Rib gating'. To explain these double jersey fabrics, it is necessary to consider the significance of knitting patterns.

As in hand-knitting, interesting fabric structures can be achieved by selecting simple stitches and building up the pattern course by course. Double jersey knitting requires the two sets of needles to be specially

Table 11   WEFT KNITTING

Basic structures	*Characteristics of stitch*

Plain

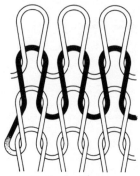 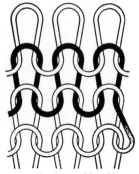

Technical face	Technical back

Rib
  1 × 1 rib

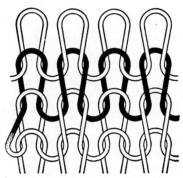

(Fabric extended widthways)

Rib
  'Double' 1 × 1 rib

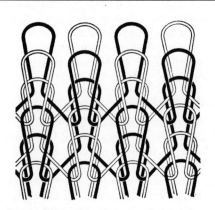

ame of fabrics or effects	Characteristics of fabrics produced from these structures
ngle jersey Stockinette	This is a fairly elastic fabric in which face and reverse side are different in appearance and which tends to curl. Pattern may be obtained by the introduction of float or tuck stitches, for example. The fabric is produced at a high rate on only one set of needles on either circular or flat-bed-machines. It is used for sweaters, T-shirts, underwear, and piece goods. Fully fashioned garments are commonly made in this structure.
b	The 1×1 (English rib) is the simplest rib fabric, and alternate wales are intermeshed in opposite directions. The fabric has a similar appearance on each side and, like most ribs, does not curl. In the relaxed state it is about half the width of a similar plain knit fabric produced on the same machine. Examples of other typical constructions of ribs of different widths are 2×2 (Swiss rib), 2×1 (Richelieu rib), and large ribbing such as 6×3 (Derby rib). Rib fabrics are characterised by being bulky and very elastic widthwise, but a reduction in elasticity occurs with an increase in width of rib. A greater quantity of yarn is required in a rib fabric than in a plain fabric of similar general construction and width. Thus, rib fabrics are heavier and slightly more expensive. Rib fabrics may be produced on either circular or flat machines having two sets of needles working at right angles to each other. They are used for cuffs, collars, and trimmings, as well as piece goods and garments.
)uble jersey Interlock	This structure consists of two 1×1 rib fabrics knitted together by means of two yarns which knit alternately on the face and back of the fabric. Consequently, it is reversible and has a similar smooth appearance on each side. It does not curl, is firmer and less extensible than most weft knitting. For the same stitch spacing Interlock is heavier and thicker than rib knitting, but in order to reduce the weight fine yarns are used. The rate of production is slower than for rib knitting and stitch patterning is more restricted, although coloured patterning with two or more colours is common. Special machines with two sets of needles are required, of two lengths in each set. Double jersey is used for outerwear and is often made from wool or acrylic fibres, whereas cotton interlock is also used for underwear. A 'double' 2×2 rib is called an Eightlock.

Table 11 (cont'd)

Basic Structures	*Characteristics of stitch*
Purl 1 × 1 purl (Links-Links Knitting)	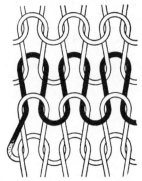

(Fabric extended lengthways)

STITCH MODIFICATIONS THAT MAY BE INTRODUCED IN THE BASIC FABRIC STRUCTURES

Miss stitch

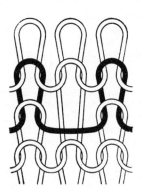 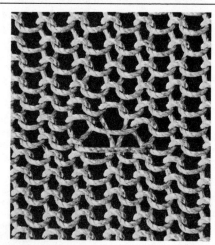

Float stitch

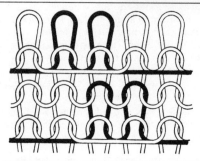

ame of fabrics or effects	Characteristics of fabrics produced from these structures
ırl	Both sides of the fabric are rather similar in appearance to the reverse side of plain knitting, and the fabric does not curl. 1×1 purl is produced by knitting alternate courses in opposite directions, but a number of courses can be drawn in either direction to produce variations in the design; e.g. 3×1 purl. The fabric extends easily lengthwise and for this reason is commonly used for children's wear. The rate of production is relatively slow on the double-ended latch needles that are used in flat or circular machines. There is good scope for patterning, and sometimes the purl structure is used as a means of introducing pattern into plain knitting.
elief or Knop patterns ords pples ıce effects	This consists of a loop that is 'held' by the needle and not knitted for one or more courses, whilst the threads fed to these courses float across the back. Compare with float stitch.
ock intarsia	This stitch is introduced into plain knitting to produce patterning in which colour appears intermittently on the face of the fabric. Two or more colours are used and the yarns float on the back of the fabric when not required as part of the design. The yarn that floats connects two loops of the same course and colour that are not in adjacent wales. Frequent floating of threads reduces the fabric extensibility widthwise. For the definition of true Intarsia see note 1 on page 112.

Table 11 (cont'd)

Stitch modifications	*Characteristics of stitch*

Tuck stitch

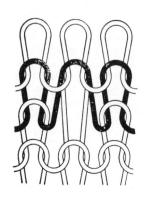
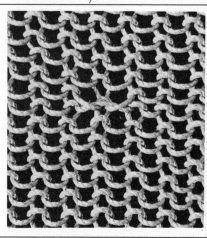

Pelerine

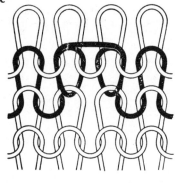

Stitch transfer

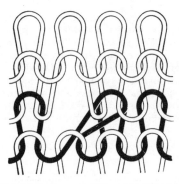
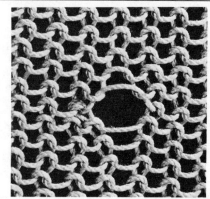

Name of fabrics or effects	*Characteristics of fabrics produced from these structures*
plain knitting: Hopsack	This stitch is produced by accumulating two or more loops on a needle and casting them off together. If in plain fabric the tuck stitch extends over more than one course, pronounced raised designs develop in the structure and these can be used in such a way as to produce figured shapes.
rib knitting: Half-cardigan or Royal Rib Full-cardigan or Polka rib interlock: Single piqué Texipiqué	The tuck stitch is more generally used in rib knitting and produces greater fabric width than ordinary rib from the same number of needles. If tucking is introduced in the rib only, a 'Half-cardigan' stitch is produced. However, a 'Full-cardigan' stitch is made by tucking a 1×1 rib on face and back stitches on alternate courses. These stitches are used for garment lengths and sometimes for piece goods. The presence of a tuck stitch in a fabric gives it a ladder resistant property which when introduced in tights is known as 'micromesh'.
Eyelet Cellular effects	Here the Sinker-loop (page 97) is transferred from its normal position and knitted in with the needle loops. This produces a hole in the fabric. It is mainly used for underwear and to a limited extent for sports shirts. Special circular knitting machines are needed to expand the loop for it to be knitted on two needles.
plain knitting: Lace effect rib knitting: Relief patterning e.g. cable stitch	The simplest example of stitch transfer is when a single loop is transferred to the next wale. The stitch is also used in the narrowing of fully fashioned garments.

Table 11 (cont'd)

Stitch modifications	*Characteristics of stitch*
Roll welt	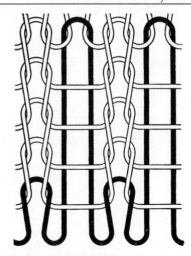
Laid-in yarn	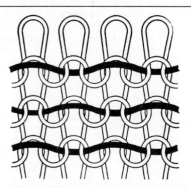
Plated loops	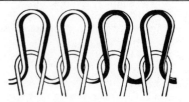

Note 1 Intarsia

This term refers to knitted fabric in which coloured designs are solid from the face to the back, and the fabric is reversible from the coloured design point of view. Each coloured yarn knits only in its specific area of the design, and where the coloured parts of the design abut they have to be joined together in a special way on a hand-operated flat knitting machine.

me of fabrics or effects	Characteristics of fabrics produced from these structures
1 × 1 rib fabrics: Roll welt Bourrelet Cloqué Honeycomb Piqué Ripple	The basis of this stitch is to knit a 1 × 1 rib followed by a few courses in which knitting occurs only on alternate stitches or needles. If this stitch is used at the start of a fabric a slight roll is produced at the edge. This gives a neat and firm structure. In addition to being used as a welt, this stitch sequence may be introduced in a 1 × 1 rib fabric generally by continuously knitting on one set of needles to form the face and occasionally knitting as required on the other set of stitches at the back of the cloth. This will cause ripples or ribs to develop across the face of the fabric. This type of fabric is widely used in piece goods for dresswear and swimwear in which ripples run horizontally or diagonally across the fabric.
ecy fabric	Coarse yarn, often acrylic, is laid-in at the back of a plain-knitted fabric and the fabric is raised during finishing to produce a fleecy appearance. Its presence tends to reduce the elasticity of the fabric. Such fabric is suitable for sweaters, tracksuits, dressing gowns, underwear, and children's wear.
f supporting garments or parts of garments	Wrapped rubber or elastane yarns may be laid-in in various ways in plain or rib knitting. This is made in tubular form so as to avoid cutting the fabric during making-up. It is used for foundation garments, tops of self-supporting socks, and surgical stockings.
corative effects	If interesting yarn is laid-in in rib fabrics so that it is visible between selected ribs, decorative effects are produced. This is mainly used for outerwear.
fferent characteristics face and back	Two yarns are knitted together as one so that the loops lie back to back; one yarn is visible on the face of the fabric and the other on the back. This provides the possibility of having a soft yarn with a pleasant handle inside the garment and a yarn made from hard-wearing fibre outside.
loured designs	If two different coloured yarns are used, it is possible to interchange their positions as required to produce a coloured design. (Note 1)
ish fabric rry' fabric lour	By arranging for one of the plated yarns to have long loops during knitting a loop-pile fabric is made suitable for leisure and sportswear fabric and socks, giving good fit and elasticity. Velour is developed by cropping or shearing the loops to produce a velvety surface. (Note 2)
te 2 Two-way stretch	Plush is knitted in a variety of ways, one of which produces a two-way stretch structure known as 'Babygro' for baby wear.

positioned relative to each other and capable of being selected to knit according to the requirements of the knitting patterns. The range of possible combinations produces a variety of double jersey fabrics going by such names as Punto-di-Roma, Piquette, Ever-Monte, Texipiqué, Pin Tuck, Single-Piqué, Swiss Double Piqué, French Double Piqué, Milano Rib, for example. Bourrelet in particular produces a surface relief effect.

To appreciate these fabrics consider and visualise the disposition of the needles in a circular knitting machine where two sets of needles, located in slots, are arranged at right angles to each other. The two sets of needles may be staggered as in Rib gating (Figure 99A), or opposite to each other as in Interlock gating (Figure 99B). The needles that lie radially are known as Dial needles and those arranged vertically round the circle are referred to as Cylinder needles. All the mechanisms that control the selection and movement of the needles have been excluded from the illustration, but suffice it to say that each needle rises as required to knit the yarn delivered or fed to it.

Rib gating

By looking at the fabric structure illustrated in the diagram showing rib gating (Figure 99A) it will be seen that the knitted fabric produced is a 1×1 rib, and, because the needles are staggered, all the needles can be brought into action to knit the same thread successively without the danger of the two sets of needles colliding.

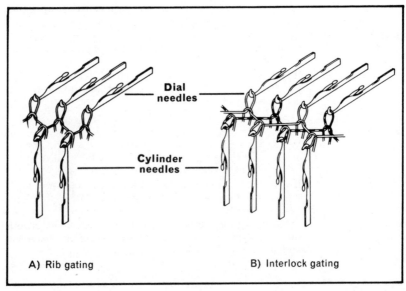

Fig. 99A and B Rib and Interlock gatings.

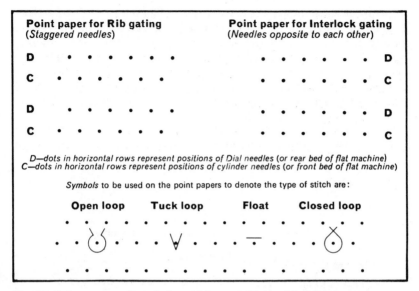

Fig. 100 Point paper and symbols used for recording weft-knit fabric structure.

Interlock gating

Since the dial and cylinder needles are aligned opposite to each other, alternate needles in the dial and cylinder are operated at any one time, and the opposing needles never rise simultaneously.

This arrangement of needles (Figure 99B) and their operation enables two 1 × 1 rib structures to be knitted in combination, with the result that the face and the back of the fabric have a similar smooth appearance. *Interlock* is the name given to the fabric made in this structure.

Weft-knit: thread path diagrams

Having established the principles of Rib and Interlock gatings, and appreciated the knitted loop formations obtained by these methods, it is now useful to know how to record the knitted structures on point paper. Agreed procedures for this and for warp-knitted fabrics are laid down in BS 5441: 1982 'Methods of test for knitted fabrics'.

Two styles of point paper are available for this purpose. Figure 100 shows the distribution of the dots, which correspond with the relative positions of the dial and cylinder needles in the Rib and Interlock gatings. It will be seen that two rows of dots represent one course of knitting; therefore, there is provision in the illustration for two courses to be recorded, or it may be preferred to think of it as two separate deliveries or feeds of yarn which produce the two courses. (For plain knitting, which utilises one set of needles, only one row of dots would be needed).

The use of the point papers is illustrated in Figures 101 and 102 and the thread path diagrams shown should be compared with the successive courses in both the 1 × 1 Rib and Interlock fabric structures shown in Figure 99 and also illustrated by the stitch diagrams on page 106. The continuous line round the points on the point paper indicates the path of the thread from needle point to needle point during knitting. Examples of thread path diagrams are also given for 2 × 2 Rib produced on Rib and Interlock gatings in Figure 102.

As mentioned earlier fabric structures are developed by building up a pattern course by course. To determine their constructions, weft-knitted

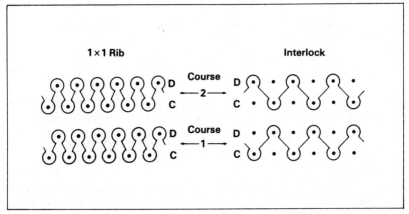

Fig. 101 Thread path diagrams for 1 × 1 Rib and Interlock fabric structures.

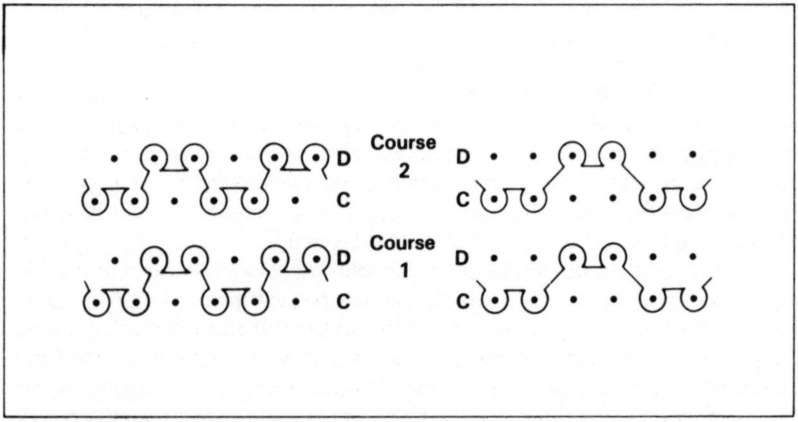

Fig. 102 Thread path diagrams for 2 × 2 Rib structures produced on Rib and Interlock gatings.

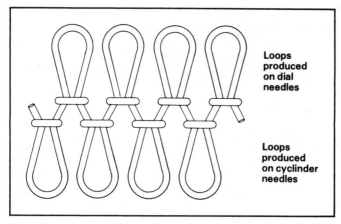

Loops
produced
on dial
needles

Loops
produced
on cyclinder
needles

Fig. 103 1 × 1 rib – end view of structure.

fabrics are best examined by viewing the fabric 'end on' at the edge which unravels and was knitted last. (Figure 103).

Keeping the edge of the fabric under tension over a short length in one hand, in order to splay out the loops, it is possible to trace the path of the yarn. Sometimes it helps to withdraw one thread at a time with the other hand. In so doing the path of the yarn may be observed and recorded on the point paper, noting whether the unravelled looped thread had been knitted on all needles or alternate needles, and whether it was knitted only on dial or cylinder needles, for example. To determine the knitting pattern successive courses must be examined in this way. Usually the pattern repeats on four courses and occasionally up to eight courses.

Summary of plain double jersey fabrics

Whilst there is a choice of commercially produced fabric structures, two well-tried fabrics are to the fore – Swiss Double Piqué and Punto-di-Roma. These have been popular because they are relatively easy to knit free from faults and are more predictable than other structures in meeting pre-determined fabric weight, width and length standards. An unwanted increase in fabric weight is the consequence of some structures using more yarn and this inevitably increases the cost of the fabric. Deviations in fabric width beset the garment manufacturer with difficulties in planning efficient cutting of the material to best advantage and economy.

In the following fabric structures it will be observed that where Tuck stitches are included, for example, the fabric width is liable to be increased and so is the mass per unit area. The extent to which such characteristics are modified for a particular structure is probably influenced by the choice of fibre and yarn apart from the structural details.

Swiss double piqué (4 course repeat) (Figure 104)

This is a very popular firm and stable fabric based on the rib gated structure. Its success is also due to an attractive diagonal effect produced by the cylinder needles, moderate fabric weight and suitable fabric width as it comes off the machine. Floats occur on what in effect is single jersey or plain knitting on courses 2 and 4. It is used for women's dresses and suitings.

French double piqué (4 course repeat) (Figure 105)

The minor difference between the Swiss and French Double Piqué structures is apparent if courses 1 and 2 are compared in each example and similarly courses 3 and 4. Even such a deviation alters the properties of the fabric, giving an increase in fabric width and more pronounced visual effect.

Milano rib (3 course repeat) (Figure 106)

This is simply a 1 × 1 rib, with single jersey or plain knitting on the cylinder dial needles of course 2, and the needles of course 3. The fabric is reversible and has a slightly horizontal effect. It is not a stable structure and therefore has limited use.

Interlock (2 course repeat) (Figure 107)

The plain appearance of this structure is not considered to be specially attractive as a fashion fabric but generally it has been made from cotton for underwear and some outerwear.

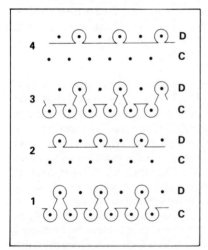

Fig. 104 Swiss double piqué (Rib gating).

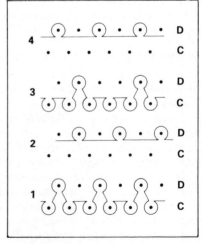

Fig. 105 French double piqué (Rib gating).

Eightlock (Figure 108)

This is a similar fabric to the Interlock except that it is based on the 2 × 2 Rib. It provides greater widthwise extensibility and a softer handle.

Punto-di-Roma (Ponte-Roma) (4 course repeat) (Figure 109)

This is a very successful and popular fabric based on the Interlock structure with the plain knit (or single jersey) structure introduced on courses 3 and 4. It is reversible, provides good width stability and is not too heavy a fabric.

Piquette (6 course repeat) (Figure 110)

This is characterised by float stitches occurring on the course 2, 3, 5 and 6. The interlock structure can be seen on courses 1 and 4. The float stitches account for the narrower fabric width compared with the width usually attained with the Punto-di-Roma structure

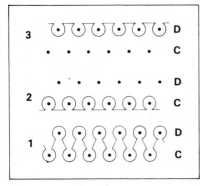

Fig. 106 Milano rib (Rib gating).

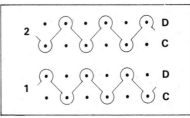

Fig. 107 Interlock (Interlock gating).

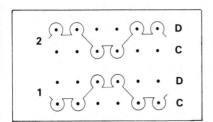

Fig. 108 Eightlock (Interlock gating).

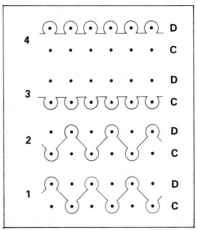

Fig. 109 Punto-di-Roma (Interlock gating).

Single piqué (6 course repeat) (Figure 111)

This structure is characterised by the introduction of tuck stitches on the dial needles of courses 3 and 6. Tucking tends to reduce the fabric length and increase the fabric width compared with the Interlock. A 'piqué' surface effect is produced which provides a certain appeal.

Pin-tuck (6 course repeat) (Figure 112)

Compared with the Single Piqué there are a greater number of 'tucking' courses, all of which are on the dial needles. This, therefore, creates an imbalance between the two faces of the fabric. The appearance of the fabric is considered to be less attractive than the single piqué. In addition, the fabric is heavier and wider.

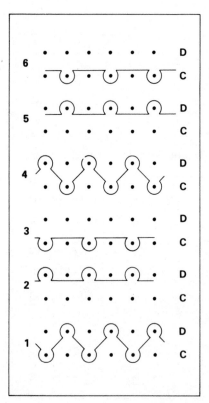

Fig. 110 Piquette. (Interlock gating).

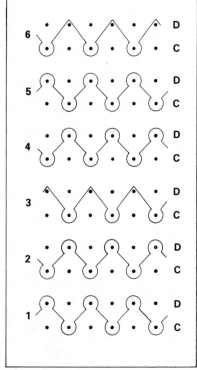

Fig. 111 Single piqué. (Interlock gating).

Texipiqué (6 course repeat) (Figure 113)

Tuck stitches occur on both dial and cylinder needles on courses 3 and 6. This tends to reduce the widthwise extensibility of the fabric and results in a somewhat heavier fabric. The fabric appearance is rather featureless and is somewhat like Interlock.

Ever-Monte (8 course repeat) (Figure 114)

This fabric is composed of Tuck stitches introduced into the Interlock structure, and plain knitting produced on the dial needles of courses 3 and 8 and the cylinder needles of courses 4 and 7. Compared with the previous structures manufactured under the same conditions the Ever-Monte fabric tends to come off the machine wider and shorter.

Other double jersey fabrics

Apart from plain double jersey structures, relief features may be developed on the fabric surface in the form of blisters and cloqué effects. These may be self-coloured or enhanced by the introduction of a selection of colours in Jacquard patterning.

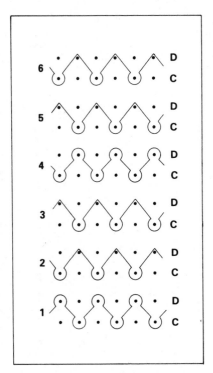

Fig. 112 Pin-tuck (Interlock gating).

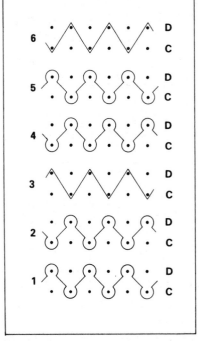

Fig. 113 Texipiqué (Interlock gating).

Fabric Structure

Bourrelet (Figure 115)

This fabric provides an example of a relief effect. On one face there is a horizontal roll or ripple and this is produced by the rib needles holding loops for a number of courses (roll welt) whilst the other needles knit continuously. It is on this principle that blisters and cloqués are produced.

Jacquard

These fabrics may be divided into two groups, blister fabrics and flat fabrics. Colour effects in flat Jacquard fabrics may be achieved by feeding

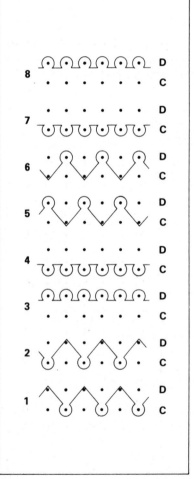

Fig. 114 Ever-Monte (Interlock gating).

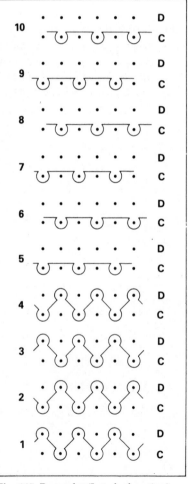

Fig. 115 Bourrelet (Interlock gating).

122

in different coloured yarns during knitting so that colour-patterns extend over several hundred stitches. Colour and structural Jacquard effects may be combined.

The Jacquard mechanisms select the yarns, the needles and regulate the stitch patterning which is produced only on the cylinder needles. These mechanisms may be used for Intarsia effects.

Sliver knit or high-pile fabric

Sliver knit fabric is weft-knitted on circular single jersey knitting machines and is used for a wide range of popular simulated furs, warm linings, gloves, cushions and paint rollers.

The pile is produced by feeding tufts of staple fibres from untwisted dyed slivers (made on mini-carding machines) directly into the knitting zone. The tufts of fibres are held in the latch needle hooks together with the ground yarn which knits the ground structure and traps the pile in the process (Figure 116). The pile is commonly modacrylic or acrylic fibre with a polypropylene ground, but polyester sliver knits are also available.

Subsequent finishing treatments of the pile surface after knitting are essential for the creation of a uniform effect in the direction and levels of

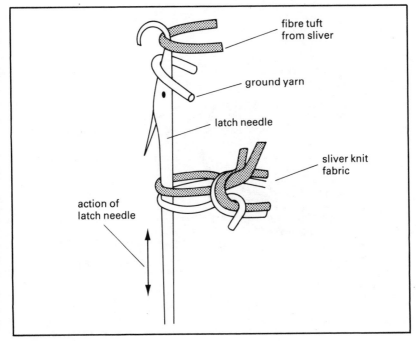

Fig. 116 Sliver knitting.

pile, apart from the need to develop the character of simulated fur. The security of the pile is ensured by backcoating the fabric with resin or latex, and fabric stability in garment manufacture and in use may be attained by bonding it to a lightweight fabric.

Warp-knit

The distinction between tricot and raschel knitting may be traced to the characteristics of the two types of warp-knitting machines.

Tricot machines use needles of either the bearded or compound type and are generally capable of a higher rate of production than the raschel machines. A particular feature of this machine is that the fabric is withdrawn at right angles to the vertically mounted needles.

Raschel machines, which use the latch needle, are designed for the production of a greater variety of fabrics. This is achieved by the use of one or two banks of needles and special devices which, for example, make it easy to use coarse or novelty yarns. From this machine the fabric is drawn downwards, at an angle of about 20° to the vertical needles.

Despite the difference between tricot and raschel machines they both employ the same basic knitting principles, tricot producing fine gauge fabric and raschel in coarse gauge structures.

The diagram of a warp-knit structure, Figure 92 on page 97, is a

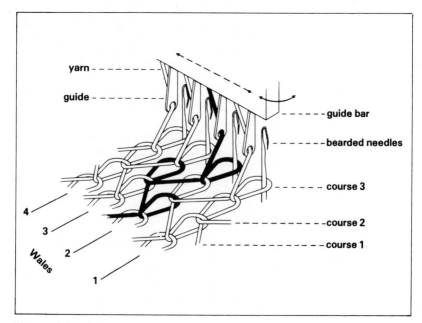

Fig. 117 Warp knitting with one guide bar producing a half-tricot.

half-tricot and illustrates the fundamental structure of warp-knitting. (It is an unsuitable fabric for clothing, since it is not stable.) Only one warp thread is available for each needle in this structure. Each thread travels through the eye of a thin metal guide, which is attached to a guide bar, as shown in Figure 117.

The guide bar moves sideways and, when in position, swings the guides and yarns between the needles. In this way each guide laps a yarn round each needle and places it over the beard. The needle then rises to allow the loop to slip onto the stem (see Figure 94). The stitches are formed by the collective downward movement of the needles when the new loops are drawn through the old loops on the previous course. Consequently, only one bar carrying the guides is necessary for a half-tricot, since all the threads which pass through the guides are required to traverse and knit identically on each course. While the needles are down the guide bar is traversed to its next required position. The yarn is knitted first on one needle and then on the adjacent needle on the next course. Development of this simple and fundamental warp-knit, half-tricot fabric structure results in such well known fabrics as Locknit, Reverse Locknit, Satin, Sharkskin and Queenscord.

In order to recognise and appreciate these standard warp-knit fabrics more easily, attention must first be given to the method by which the pattern of a warp-knit structure is recorded on point paper.

Pattern notation

The point paper in Figure 118 consists of dots which represent the needles in the warp knitting process. On this the traverse of the thread in the knitted structure caused by the movement of the guide bar is recorded, together with an indication as to whether the loops formed are *closed* or *open*. This is illustrated in Figure 120.

The dots inserted in the fabric structure diagrams in Figure 120 represent the needle positions and the broken line, superimposed on the diagram for

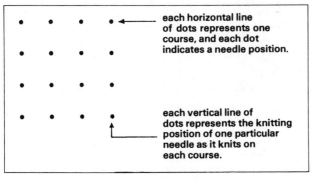

Fig. 118 Point paper for warp knit structures.

the sake of explanation, traces the path of the yarn. It is this yarn path that is used in the lapping diagrams on the point paper. In this example of open and closed loop structures, there is only one set of threads, with all the threads moving together across the structure at any one time.

The pictorial representation of lapping movement of the yarn is com-

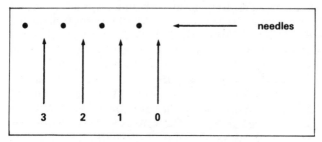

Fig. 119 Numbering of spaces between needles.

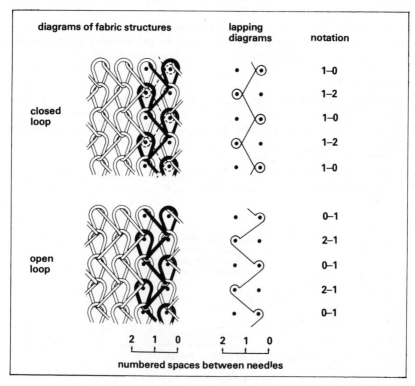

Fig. 120 Lapping diagrams and notations of half-tricot fabric structures with open and closed loops.

monly described more concisely in numerical form. This is done by first attributing numbers to the spaces between the needles or dots. If one considers a line of four needles then the spaces between the needles are numbered as shown from right to left in Figure 119.

This may be compared with the space numbering given to the fabric structures in Figure 120. Now the lapping diagrams may be interpreted numerically by reading upwards on the diagrams.

Closed Loop   1–0/1–2
Open Loop   0–1/2–1

This means that in the closed loop yarn has been guided through space 1 passing between two needles to space 0, having *overlapped* the needle in between (1–0) to be knitted by this needle. Similarly on the second course the yarn has been passed through space 1 to space 2 and *overlapped* the intervening needle (1–2). The traverse of the yarn across the 'technical' back of the fabric from the knitting position on the first course to that on the next course is referred to as an *underlap*.

From this the significance of the symbols used may now be understood.

Hyphen '–' shows that the thread has been guided from a space between the two needles and has *overlapped* a needle, for the purpose of knitting, en route to its next location.

Oblique Stroke '/' indicates that the thread has been traversed to another position ready for knitting the next course without having laid the thread in a needle en route. This movement is known as *underlapping*.

When more complicated warp-knit structures are produced, two or more sets of warp threads are used, and therefore an appropriate number of guide bars are required. The relative positions of the two guide bars to the needles at a particular stage in the knitting process are shown in Figure 121 (overleaf).

Here two yarns are lapped round the needle in the same or opposite directions. The guide bar at the front of the machine delivers one set of threads to the needles in one direction and the back guide bar takes care of the delivery of the second set of warp threads to the needles in the opposite direction. Tricot, Locknit, Reverse Locknit, Satin, Sharkskin and Queenscord, are all examples of fabrics made from two sets of warp threads with the guide bars laying the yarns in opposite directions.

The pattern notation of the fabric structures made with two or more guide bars requires a record to be made of the movement of each guide bar separately, even though their traverses are superimposed on each other within the structure. The definitions of the standard warp-knit fabrics which follow give the notations for the front and back guide bars against the letters F and B respectively.

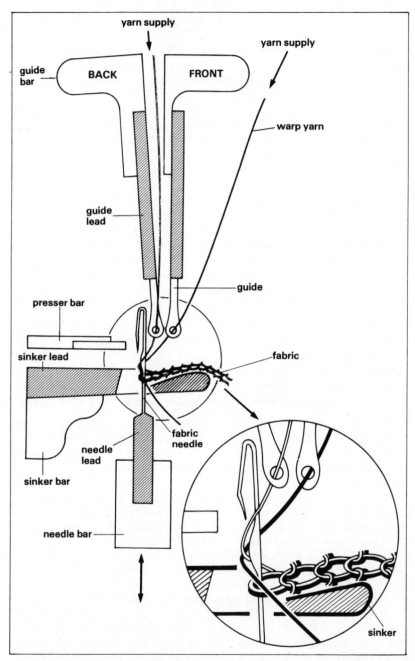

Fig. 121 Warp knitting with two guide bars – diagrammatic representation of knitting elements in tricot machine. The guide bars, presser bar, sinker bar and needle bar are fixtures on the machine to which are fastened, as required, the appropriate guides, presser and needles which are embedded in lead.

128

Summary of standard warp-knit fabrics made with two guide bars

Warp-knit Tricot fabrics can be considered in terms of range of fabric effects and choice of properties, such as handle and fabric extensibility.

The scope of visual effects is widened by an increase in the number of guide bars used. It is possible to thread each guide bar with different coloured or types of yarn and this, together with the relative traverses of the guide bars, governs the pattern or effect produced. Another design possibility is to thread some guides and leave others unthreaded within a particular guide bar. This introduces more open or less pronounced effects along the fabric length.

Fabric handle and extensibility is influenced by the traverse or length of underlaps of each guide bar, apart from the choice of fibre and yarn. Fabrics made from two guide bars generally have the yarn laid in opposing directions. The yarns delivered by the guide bars tend to be located within the fabric thickness according to the position of the guide bars in the machine. This can be understood if it is realised that the yarn delivered from the front guide bar in Tricot knitting appears on both faces of the fabric, whereas yarn from the second guide bar is sandwiched next in position inside the structure, with the result that if three guide bars are used it is the yarn from the third (i.e. back) guide bar which is knitted and trapped within the middle of the structure. This being so, if the front guide bar provides a relatively short underlap compared with the others the yarns within the fabric structure will be firmly clamped. Conversely, if the traverse of the front guide bar is greater than the others greater mobility of all the yarns will be possible. Consequently, the handle of the fabric will be less firm and the draping quality will be improved.

The two faces of warp-knit fabrics are referred to as the 'technical face', which is composed of rounded tops of the loops in the wale direction, and the 'technical back', on which the underlap or horizontal traverse of the yarn is the main feature. In practice the technical back may provide the design feature or special textural characteristics enabling it to be used as the 'right' side of the fabric.

Tricot

Tricot is the simplest fabric made from two sets of warp threads. The two threads to each needle make similar 1×1 lapping movements as in the half-tricot but in opposite directions, knitting on adjacent needles alternately in each consecutive course. Close examination of the fabric shows fine vertical wales on the face and crosswise ribs on the back. If different coloured yarns are used in the warp, vertical stripes are produced, and because of the symmetry of the overlaps the definition of the edges of the stripes is sharp. Tricot is frequently used for lingerie, blouses, dresses, and linings laminated to other fabrics. Its chief characteristics are softness of handle, good drape and elasticity.

Different qualities will be found to vary in respect of courses per cm. For

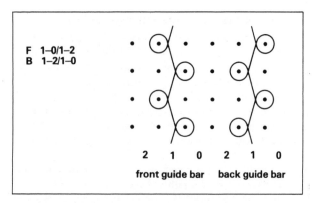

Fig. 122 Tricot.

example, linings may have only 7 courses per cm compared with 18 per cm in dresswear.

Fabrics knitted from staple fibre yarn and from continuous filament yarn have very different characteristics. It should be noted that Tricot is a term commonly applied to the group of warp-knitted fabrics produced on Tricot machines.

Locknit

This important two-bar fabric, Figure 124, differs from Tricot in that the front guide bar has a longer underlap between courses. The fabric has a softer and more elastic handle than Tricot because there is greater freedom for the yarns to move within the structure and it is heavier and has better cover. Locknit fabric, Figure 124, has a smooth face and a comparatively coarse appearance on the back. Patterning, such as stripes and other

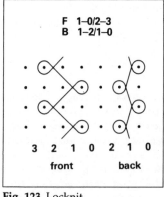

Fig. 123 Locknit.

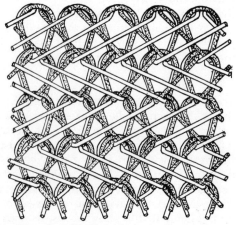

Fig. 124 Locknit fabric – reverse side. Here the white threads on the face of the fabric are made to traverse across the back to their new knitting positions by the front guide bar. *(The Textile Institute)*

designs, is easily introduced by the use of coloured yarn. The definition of colour at the edge of the stripe is somewhat diffuse because of the wider traverse of the front guide bar. The fabric is extensively used for lingerie, blouses, shirts and dresses. It is interesting to note that the technical back of the locknit fabric is often made up as the face side.

Vertical cords (sometimes known as 'piqués') can be introduced into a locknit structure by the partial threading (or part setting) of the back guide bar, and the width of the cord is controlled by the interval at which yarns are absent in the threading of the bar.

Reverse Locknit

The reverse locknit is widely used for dresses, shirts and sheets and has been found to be easier to print than locknit. It is lighter in weight and more extensible than sharkskin, given the same yarn construction, and is less extensible than locknit.

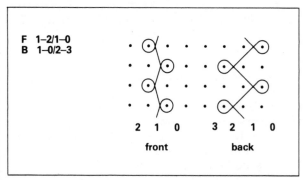

Fig. 125
Reverse Locknit

Satin

The smooth features of the satin and the soft handle are due to the greater length of yarn used in the underlaps of the front guide bar on the technical back. A satin structure intermediate between this and the Locknit is given with F 1–0/3–4   B 1–2/1–0. A problem associated with satin structures is their liability to be snagged.

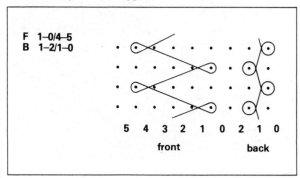

Fig. 126 Satin.

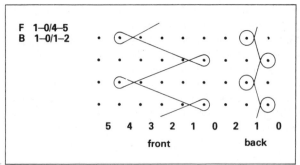

Fig. 127 Raised loop.

The back of these fabrics is used as the effect side because of the smooth lustrous appearance; a brushed effect may be produced by subjecting the technical back to mechanical finishing.

All satin structures may be 'loop-raised' as discussed immediately below. The greater the height of the pile produced the less stable is the fabric.

Raised Loop

To facilitate the extraction of filaments from the technical back to form loops over the surface, the front and back guide bars work in unison. This, together with the freedom of movement allowed by the length of underlap on the front guide bar, enables the loops of yarn to be withdrawn during fabric finishing, as shown in Figure 128. The above diagram represents only one example of the structures that are used for this purpose.

A distinction must be made here between loop-raised and brushed

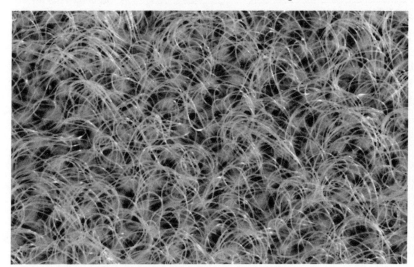

Fig. 128 Loop-raised nylon. *(Shirley Institute)*

fabrics. Where the filaments have been withdrawn from the structure without breaking them, the fabric is known as 'loop-raised'. 'Brushed' fabrics are those where most of the filaments have been broken. Raised-loop fabrics are used for nightwear and sheets.

Sharkskin

The traverse of the front guide bar is very much shorter than that of the back guide bar, with the result that the fabric is rather inelastic and has a firm handle. This was very popular at one time for shirting (comparison with the satin structure shows that the distinction lies in the interchange of the role of patterning between the two guide bars.)

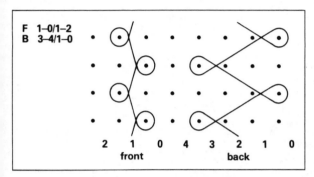

Fig. 129 Sharkskin.

Just as the 'raised loop' is a method of modifying the fabric surface, so can the sharkskin be given a less slippery handle by overfeeding the yarn delivered by the back guide bar. The excess yarn appears discreetly over the surface and this effect is known as 'airloop'. This type of fabric has been used for bed sheets. If the method is developed further, a terry-type effect is obtained.

Queenscord

Another method of increasing the firmness of the fabric and its dimensional stability is for the front guide bar to knit continuously on the same

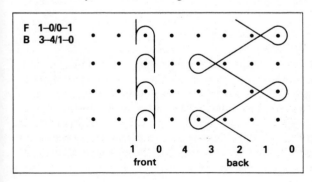

Fig. 130 Queenscord.

needles. This provides a clamping effect on the yarns supplied by the back guide bar.

Queenscord has been popular for shirting and, like Sharkskin, has provided a good basis for roller printing because of its stability and resistance to distortion whilst printing. Coloured stripes with good definition at the boundaries can be obtained by the introduction of coloured yarns in the front guide bar.

Laid-in fabrics are made with special warp threads which are trapped between the face loops and the underlaps of the warp-knit structure. Novelty yarns can be incorporated into the fabric since they are not knitted by the needles to form loops.

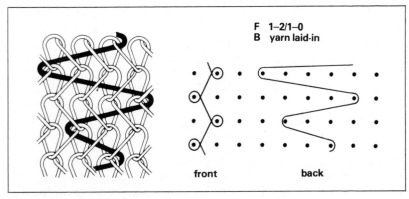

Fig. 131 Warp-knitted laid-in fabric.

Weft insertion is characterised by weft threads being introduced across the full width of the warp-knit structure. This increases the stability of the fabric and may give the impression of a woven structure. Now being used for interlinings.

Pile fabrics

Velour and velvet – Tricot structures

These fabrics, made from continuous filament yarns, are similar in construction to satin and raised loop fabric (page 131). The long underlaps on the technical back are brushed and broken during finishing, and this is followed by cropping to produce tufts of filaments, which stand erect from the surface. Velour has a shorter, denser pile than velvet and, according to its density, is used for furnishing or apparel. The pile may be viscose or, for softness of handle, acetate, whilst the strength of the ground is attained by the use of polyester or nylon filament yarn.

Other warp-knit structures

Check designs

Checks are commonly used in warp-knit overalls and shirtings. Three methods are available for introducing such effects.

Gingham patterns are produced by threading each of the two guide bars with colours arranged in groups of, say, six. The guide bars are given appropriate movements to distribute the colour repeat over a few courses to produce the pattern.

Fine checks in shirting depend on the 'inlaying' of coloured yarn in the course direction to match the chains of coloured yarns introduced in the wale direction by the front guide bar. The back guide bar is fully threaded to produce the ground fabric.

Plated checks depend on the back guide bar being threaded one colour with the front guide bar a different colour but with, say, every 14th guide carrying the colour of the back guide bar. When normal knitting proceeds narrow stripes will appear on the face of the fabric at an interval of 14 wales. To produce the check effect the front guide, at intervals, does not knit for two courses – consequently it is the coloured yarn from the back guide bar that is revealed and appears as a horizontal line across the fabric to form the check.

Atlas

'Atlas' describes the lapping movement in a one- or two-guide bar warp-knitted fabric. If two guide bars are used each set of yarns is moved in opposite directions, so that each thread is knitted on successive needles on successive courses. After knitting a number of courses, the traverse of the yarn is reversed and knitting continues course by course until the yarn returns to its original needle. The traverse of the warp can extend over as many as 48 courses before the direction of movement of the guide bar is reversed.

If only one set of yarns is used, the fabric is known as 'Single Atlas'. If two sets of threads are used, it is known as a 'Double Atlas'.

If different coloured warp threads are arranged in a single guide bar, zig-zag effects can be produced, sometimes known as Vandyke. Such fabric, depending on its weight and design, may be used for lingerie and cut-and-sewn gloves.

Milanese fabric

Atlas lapping is the basis of Milanese fabrics which are produced on special machines in which two sets of yarn traverse diagonally across the full width of the fabric. Milanese fabrics drape well and have an attractive handle and appearance. However, the rate of production is low and because it is uncompetitive little of the fabric is made.

Simplex fabric

Simplex is generally a high quality double-face reversible fabric suitable for cotton glove fabric which is often finished by gently sueding the surface with emery-covered rollers.

Bearded needles are used in this process and are arranged in two needle beds, similar to that shown in Figure 132, with the fabric travelling downwards through the gap between them. Atlas lapping is used to contribute to the widthway stretch necessary for gloves. The rate of production is low.

Raschel warp knitting

Raschel fabrics are produced at a profitable rate on either single-needle-bar machines or double-needle-bar machines which have two sets of needles positioned back to back as in Figure 132.

In fine gauge Tricot knitting (Figure 121) the fabric comes off at right angles to the machine, whereas, in the coarser gauge Raschel, it is drawn off downwards almost parallel to the needles.

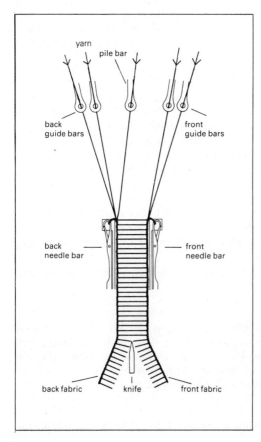

Fig. 132 Raschel knitting on double-needle-bar machine producing two pile fabrics simultaneously. *(Shirley Institute)*

Fig. 133 Warp-knit cut pile fabric. *(Shirley Institute)*

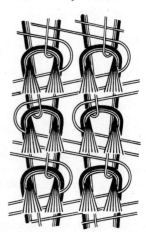

Dependent on details of machine design, fibre and yarn type, such products as tubular sacks for vegetables, briefs, string vests, elasticated fabrics for foundation wear, curtain net, lace-like fabrics and trimmings, and fashion fabrics are made. Raschel knitting provides the facility for incorporating very coarse and unconventional (e.g. ribbon-like) material into the knitted structure by in-laying.

Pile fabric is produced on the double-needle-bar machine, its main outlet being for apparel. Attempts to produce carpeting in this way have not been commercially viable. Separate ground fabrics are produced by the back and front needle bars, which are joined by the lapping movement of the pile yarn. The knife slits the pile to produce two cut pile fabrics suitable for simulated fur and upholstery, for example.

Point or *loop pile* fabric is produced by substituting a point or peg for the front needle bar. Chains of loops form the foundation of the fabric on the back needle bar whilst the pile yarn is first passed round the point to form the loop and is subsequently knitted into the ground structure. The distance between the latch needle and the point determines the pile height.

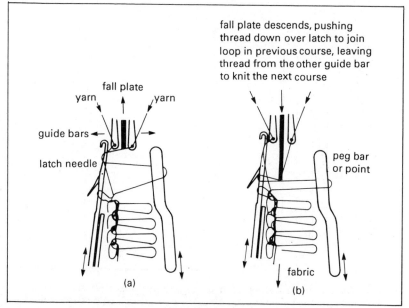

Fig. 134 Raschel, point or loop-pile, knitting. The latch needle, two guide bars, fall plate, the peg bar round which the loop pile is formed, and the paths of the yarn are shown, together with part of the action of loop formation.
(a) Fall plate in operative position is ready for the knitting cycle.
(b) The fall plate now descends, pushing the thread delivered by the front guide bar down over the latch to join the loop from the previous course, leaving the thread from the back guide bar in the latch needle ready to knit these two loops.

The pile may be retained as loops or cut on the machine by means of rotating blades or the substitution of sharpened points instead of rounded pegs. Loop pile is sometimes known as Bouclé and cut pile as Velour.

LACE

Hand-made laces are of two important types. One is made on a pillow with bobbins and pins and known as 'pillow' or 'bobbin lace'. The other is made by using needle and thread to produce 'point lace', which is based on loops of thread and buttonhole stitches.

The structure of machine-made lace is based on the hand-made bobbin lace, in which the threads are twisted about each other to form a mesh of holes. The essential action of twisting threads by machine is shown in Figure 135.

The bobbin, known as a 'brass bobbin', consists of two thin brass discs held together near the centre by rivets. The space between the discs, which

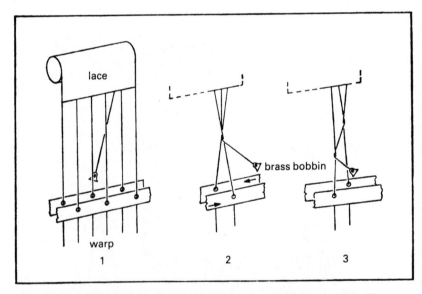

Fig. 135 Illustration of twisting action during lace-making. Diagram 1 – The bobbin containing the bobbin thread is held in a carriage a little distance behind the warp threads. Diagram 2 – Pairs of warp threads are crossed and the bobbin is swung between them and is caught by a catch bar on the near side of the warp. From each bobbin thread is simultaneously run off as required. Diagram 3 – The warp threads are now uncrossed to their normal position, and this reveals the twisting that has taken place. The bobbin is now swung back between the warps to its original position behind warp threads. After each twisting, the warp is moved to the next position to the right or left.

is only about 1mm wide, contains up to 100 metres of thread. The thread in the brass bobbin tends to cause it to bulge, and the bobbins are therefore compressed before use, so that they will pass easily between the closely spaced warp threads.

There are two distinct groups of machine-made dress nets and laces known as 'Bobbinet' and 'Leavers lace'.

Bobbinet

The bobbinet machine, based on John Heathcoat's invention, produces a net consisting of a mesh of small holes. Bobbins and warp threads are used in equal numbers in such a way as to produce diagonal lines of twists to the front and the back of the warp threads as shown in Figure 136. The warp threads run lengthwise in the fabric, and half the number of bobbin threads traverse in opposite directions. This type of net is also known as 'plain net' or 'traverse net'. 'Tulle' is the name given to pure silk bobbinet. It is interesting to compare this with a net structure produced by knitting. See Figure 137.

Bobbinet may be decorated by flock or metallic particles applied with an adhesive by printing, by machine embroidery, and by the introduction of a tiny spot effect made by filling in a single mesh with thread during manufacture. This spot effect is known as 'Point d'Esprit'. There is a wide choice of nets made from nylon, cotton, silk, or elastic, and the uses vary accordingly from bridal veils to dresses and foundation wear.

Leavers lace

Historically, John Leavers' lace machine was a development on Heathcoat's net machine. In addition to having warp threads and bobbin threads which form the background net, a separate supply of threads known as beam threads is introduced to outline and produce the figuring. The sideways movement of the warp and beam is actuated by a Jacquard to

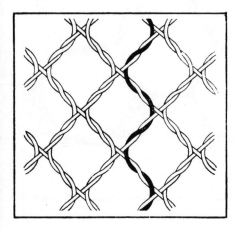

Fig. 136 Leavers lace net – twist structure.

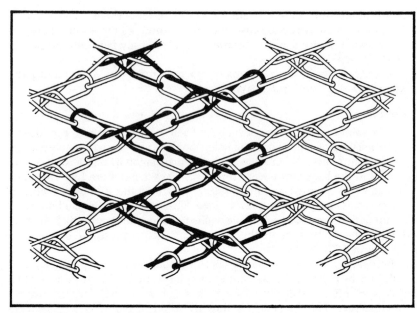

Fig. 137 Warp-knitted net – loop structure.
(*After the diagram in* Warp Knitting Technology, Columbine Press)

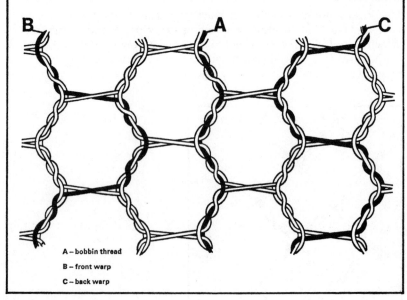

A – bobbin thread
B – front warp
C – back warp

Fig. 138 Ensor net.

produce the pattern. The beam threads are usually coarser than, or of a different character from, those used for the net, and a greater length of beam thread is required because the pattern utilises more thread than the ground net.

A variety of net structures, from the simple to the most complicated, can be produced on the Leavers machine. They vary in density and sheerness, shape and size of mesh, and firmness and stability of structure. Each design and shape of mesh bears a name such as Ensor (hexagonal mesh – see Figure 138), Filet (square mesh), or Valenciennes (round or diamond holes). Generally, when one buys lace one does not consider the detail or the name of the basic structure, but rather the width and general style of the lace.

The product of the Leavers machine is available in narrow widths or as wide dress laces. Fibres such as cotton, nylon, bulked nylon, viscose, or acetate may be used. A cross-dyed effect may be obtained by a combination of two suitable fibres. Leavers lace may be classified as follows:

Narrow laces

This style of lace is available in widths from ⅜ in. to 10 ins. During manufacture, these narrow laces are part of a full working-width of lace, joined together sideways and running together the full length of the piece. After manufacture, the narrow widths are separated either by the removal of draw threads or by dissolving away special threads which have been twisted-in at the junction of each width.

Edgings

These have one straight edge strengthened with several threads running parallel along the edge to facilitate sewing to fabric. The other edge may have scallops or picot edging.

Galloons

A fancy or scalloped effect occurs on both edges of the trimming.

Insertions

These narrow laces have two straight edges, both reinforced by having threads running parallel to the edge. They are suitable for stitching between the edges of two pieces of cloth. Insertions are also available with slots through which ribbon may be threaded.

Motifs

The decorative figure of a lace pattern may be cut out and used separately.

Wide dress lace styles

Allovers

This refers to lace in which the closely-spaced pattern repeats regularly over the full width and length of the piece. No scallops are present. The maximum width of the piece may be as great as 5 metres. However, if narrower widths are required, these may be obtained by splitting the full width fabric lengthwise, after finishing, by removing the draw threads which were inserted at appropriate intervals to give the required selling width.

Flouncing

This lace may be from 30 to 180 cm wide and has one scalloped edge and one straight edge. It may be made with the scallops horizontally or vertically arranged in the machine. Flouncings are more expensive to produce than allover laces and, consequently, the more complicated and costly designs of lace are used in this style. An example of such a design is Chantilly.

Lace designs and re-embroidery

Different designs of lace may be produced in allover or in flouncing styles. Alençon, Chantilly, and Cluny are examples, and their names indicate the origin of the design. 'Bobbin Finings' refers to a Leavers lace in which the brass bobbin thread is used to fill in the design. Since the brass bobbin yarn is fine, it produces a design with a light or delicate effect.

In addition, the designs may be outlined by 're-embroidering' the lace after manufacture with a heavy cord, ribbon, or other suitable textile. The term 'rebrodes' is sometimes used to describe these laces, which, because of their cost, are somewhat restricted to use in *haute couture*. A re-embroidered effect is, however, successfully obtained by using rather heavy cord (Cordonnet) to outline the design during lace manufacture. This, of course, may be identified by the fact that the cord is twisted-in and not stitched on.

Embroidery

Embroidery is commonly used on nets and woven fabrics. Machine-embroidery on nets is somewhat similar in its effect to hand-made 'point lace' mentioned earlier.

Single-needle sewing machines, such as chain stitch or Cornelly lock-stitch, are used for embroidering veils to form a border round the edge. However, where the embroidered design is required to spread over the whole surface of the net, a multi-needle Schiffli machine is used, operating on the lockstitch principle. The net or fabric is moved according to the design in the required direction relative to the needles, which operate in unison.

Multihead machines are in use, which operate at a higher rate than the Schiffli machines, and which can embroider directly on garment panels or on individual articles.

The development of the fusible motif offers interesting possibilities. To produce this type of decoration a fusible nylon thread is used in the shuttle, and this lies on the back of the carrier fabric, just as the shuttle thread does in lock stitch sewing. This thread can be fused to a garment by placing the embroidery in position and applying heat by means of an iron. The carrier fabric has been chemically treated so that it is broken down by the heat and can be brushed away, leaving a design apparently embroidered on the garment.

Guipure lace embroidery is made using a Schiffli machine to embroider a heavy textured, bold pattern of thread on a woven ground, which is dissolved away with a suitable solvent, leaving the embroidered design. Acetone is commonly used to dissolve woven acetate base fabric. An important characteristic of Guipure is that there is no background mesh.

Broderie Anglaise is another example of a Schiffli embroidered fabric. The woven textile base is not dissolved away but is an essential part of the final fabric, which has regularly-spaced holes in the design. Batiste and cambric are often used as base fabrics, and boring needles make the eyelets, the edges of which are embroidered as the work proceeds.

'Braid' lace

This type of lace is produced by a plaiting technique on a Barmen machine. The machine utilises large bobbins of yarn travelling in interlacing tracks so that the yarns are plaited with each other, and the newly formed lace can be drawn upwards. The path of the bobbins is controlled by a Jacquard to produce the required design. Only one breadth of lace is produced at a time.

Barmen or 'braid' lace is always of narrow width. It is used for trimming lingerie, for example, and for some purposes contains elastic. Coarser textures are suitable for glove-backs.

NONWOVEN FABRICS

The conventional methods of fabric formation have in the past required the use of yarns, except for true felt, which consists of those animal fibres that can be made to matt together, because of their scaly surface, to form a fabric.

Generally nonwoven fabric is made from 'webs' or 'batts' of fibre held together and strengthened by bonding.

Such fabrics lower the cost of textiles by increasing the rate of cloth production, reducing the amount of labour and the number of operations needed in manufacture.

The properties of nonwovens are determined by the way the batt of fibres is prepared, the type and fineness of the fibres used, the thickness of the batt, and the method(s) used in bonding the structure.

The early nonwovens were unattractive in appearance, in handle and drape. The characteristics of these fabrics can now be more readily engineered, but it is still difficult to achieve the desired level of handle and drape associated with woven and knitted structures. The bonding of the fibres in a nonwoven prevents them from skewing and shearing sufficiently to develop the required double curvature of the fabric when the material is intended to drape.

In addition to the properties mentioned the following requirements may have to be met according to end use: good conformability, adequate strength in wet and dry states and in dry-cleaning solvents, high absorbency, non-toxic and non-allergenic, non-linting surface, absence of fraying, dimensional stability, shape retention, defined levels of stiffness and crease recovery.

Of particular interest are interlinings and insulation waddings used in the clothing industry, but it is necessary to be aware of the importance of nonwovens in other spheres. Nonwovens are used as disposables, as semi-durable and as durable products. Hygienic and absorbent products account for the greatest use and there is an increasing use in civil engineering. In the list below, 'other uses' includes non-fibering nonwovens for clean room use, resin-free liners for floppy disks, and artificial leather.

Data* on nonwoven consumption in the USA reflect the situation also in Western Europe.

Table 12   NONWOVEN CONSUMPTION IN THE USA (1985)

End Use	Value ($millions)
Diaper cover stock	330
Surgical packs and gowns	230
Wipes and roll towels	210
Filtration media	175
Interlinings	145
Bedding and home furnishings	140
Coated and laminated fabrics	140
Carpet components	135
Civil-engineering applications	100
Other	450

The two important stages in the manufacture of nonwovens are the formation of the batt or web and its consolidation. The choice of fibre can influence the method of manufacture.

Manufactured fibres account for most of the fibres used in nonwovens. Of these micro-fibres provide a softer handle and modify other physical properties. Cotton is used to a limited extent for industrial applications, and for cleaning/wiping cloths. Wool has its main but limited use in nonwoven carpets. The following summary ranks the use of manufactured fibres in decreasing order of consumption.

Thermoplastic synthetic fibres account for more than 60% of the fibres used in nonwovens, about 30% is manufactured cellulosic fibre, the balance comprising natural and other fibres.

*J. R. Starr in 'INDEX' 81 Conference Papers Vol. 1, 'The European Disposables and Nonwovens Association', EDANA, Brussels.

Web formation

The formation of the web is important because it affects the character of the cloth. The method will differ according to whether the fibres are in staple or continuous filament form.

Dry-laid

Manufactured and natural staple fibres are passed through a carding process which separates the fibres and forms a gossamer web which is built up in sufficient layers to form a batt of the required mass/unit area. Special attention is given to the uniform distribution of the fibre to avoid thick and thin places in the fabric. The batts may be formed by one of the following methods:

Parallel-laid

By superimposing an appropriate number of layers of web as they come off the carding machine, according to the thickness and mass required.

This is the least expensive method, but it has serious disadvantages. Most of the fibres lie in the lengthwise direction, with the result that the final structure is extensible and weaker across its width. This type is only suitable for a few types of interlinings, and cleaning cloths.

Cross-laid

By laying the web in a criss-cross overlapping fashion so that the batt finally consists of fibres which lie at an angle to its lengthwise direction. This method of 'cross-laying' tends to equalise the properties of the cloth in the two directions. Stretching of the web during production improves its regularity. The nonwoven is stable diagonally but has some stretch width and lengthwise. Heavier fabrics can be produced by this method than by parallel-laying. This method is suitable for the production of interlinings.

Air-laid

Fibres, emerging from a carding process, are carried by an air stream and sucked on to a perforated drum. The mass of the batt can be controlled between 10 and 200 g/m^2.

Because the fibres in the batt are randomly oriented the stiffness, drape, and strength of the fabric is uniform in all directions. This method is particularly suitable for interlinings, and for the manufacture of very lightweight batts from fine fibres.

Wet-laid

The wet-laid process is similar to that used in paper-making. The dispersion of fibre in water, is followed by the formation of a web by the settling of the fibres on a moving perforated screen through which the water

Table 13   MANUFACTURED FIBRE CONSUMPTION IN EC
for dry-laid and wet-laid nonwoven fabrics
(Indication of use derived from data published by EDANA*)

Application	Manufactured fibres ranked in order of consumption
Garments	Mainly cellulosic, and polyester, polyamide
Furnishing and household fabrics	Cellulosic, polyester, polyamide, polypropylene
Cleaning and wiping cloths	Mainly cellulosic; and polyester, polyamide, polypropylene
Medical and sanitary uses	Primarily cellulosic; and polyester, polyamide, polypropylene
Industrial applications	Polyester, cellulosic, polyamide, polypropylene
Floor coverings	Polypropylene, polyamide, polyester.

*J R Starr in 'INDEX' 81 Conference Papers Vol 1. 'The European Disposables and Nonwovens Association', EDANA, Brussels.

drains. The web is now treated with a binding agent and then dried. Its great advantage is the very high speed of production, but the product does not have a textile application because of the 'paperiness' of the product.

Web consolidation

Various methods are available for the consolidation of the dry-laid web of fibres and the choice depends on the ultimate properties required and the target price. The nature of the adhesive chosen and the frequency of bonding between fibres in the batt influences the flexibility of the material and other aspects of performance.

Interlinings, for instance, may be paste-dot coated or powder-dot coated. The dot distribution of the adhesives leaves the intervening areas unbonded, thus contributing to the flexibility of the material. Scatter coating is also used for flexibles and here the distribution of the adhesive does not form a prescribed pattern.

Synthetic rubber latices based on butadiene and acrylic derivatives are common adhesives, the former giving a fairly soft, extensible structure, the latter being less extensible.

All such variables in bonding, considered in conjunction with the fibre content, widen the range of qualities available for a variety of end uses. The following summarises methods of bonding and their implications.

Impregnation

This is an old and simple technique in which the bonding agent is applied to the batt from a bath, followed by drying and polymerisation. It is necessary to take steps to minimise the fabric stiffness. Current developments centre on the uniform application of the adhesive from a foam carrier.

Spray-bonding

Adhesive applied as a spray is used for abrasive pads. It is also used for the consolidation of insulating wadding, as for anoraks, by spraying on both faces to ensure penetration.

Thermo-bonding

Thermo-bonding is being used increasingly because of its lower energy costs, variety of techniques of manufacture, and the possibility of producing a resin-free product. Binder thermoplastic fibres, or polyester powders ('Powder bonding') contained in the batt, function as adhesives when the batt is hot calendered, and a dense compact material results. Alternatively the application of a stream of hot air passing through a perforated conveyor facilitates localised bonding of the batt and produces an open, lightly compacted and more drapable structure. A variety of other methods of thermobonding are used.

Typical thermal bonding fibres are polypropylene and low softening point polyester. Bicomponent fibres may function as a bonding agent if they comprise of two types of polymer lying side by side, or a core and a low melting point sheath. Where the filaments are in contact in the batt the sheath softens on heating and, upon cooling, creates a bond between the filaments.

'Melded' fabrics are made from heterofilaments, but modifications to the fabric properties can be achieved by the introduction of non-thermoplastic fibres e.g. viscose, the presence of which reduces the strength of the bond locally.

Applications of thermobonded fabrics include interlinings, upholstery, filtration fabrics and other industrial uses.

Spunlacing

This method relies on the mechanised entanglement of staple fibres in a batt by means of high velocity jets of water. By modifying the base structure against which the fibres are entangled, attractive 'lace-like' designs or simple patterns can be produced. Spunlaced fabrics have a soft handle and good drape, but the material lacks recovery from distortion. Polyester fibre has been used in this way for home furnishings, bedding and garments.

Spunlaid fabrics

These nonwovens are produced in a continuous process starting with the extrusion of the continuous filaments, through the stage of filament drawing on emergence from the spinneret, to the random deposition of the filaments on to a moving belt. By this method fabric weights of less than 10 g/m^2 may be produced. Apart from thermal bonding of the batt, chemical and physical means can be employed. The spunlaid fabric also known as spun-bonded, may be dyed, printed or receive a finishing treatment as required. Polyester, polyethyene and polypropylene are used in this sytem of manufacture which produces fabrics having particular applications in civil engineering. Spunlaid SI fibres are used for fabrics requiring low linting tendency, high absorbency, suitable capacity and texture intended for, say, wall coverings, disposable clothing, medical and domestic uses.

Melt-blown fabrics

These fabrics are produced from extruded filaments of molten polymer which are attenuated into very fine filaments by jets of hot air. On cooling, the filaments break into fibres of variable length. The fibres are air-laid on to a moving belt to form a batt, which can range in mass from 5–1,000 g/m^2, followed by thermal bonding. Polypropylene is commonly used in this process, although most fibre forming polymers can be used, save for acrylics. Because the filaments are very fine the fabrics feel soft and drape well. Possible uses include insulation waddings and fabrics for clothing, tentage, filters and battery separators.

Needle-punched fabrics

The principle involved here is the penetration of a large number of barbed needles, with the barbs pointing downwards, through a supported batt of fibre (Figure 139). As the needle travels down it carries with it fibres which

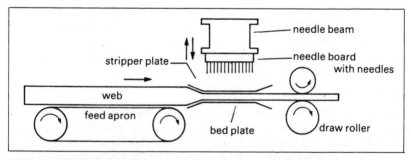

Fig. 139 Needleloom machine. A machine for producing *needlefelt* or *needle-punched* nonwoven fabric. A needle beam reciprocates vertically at rates up to 33 cycles per second. Barbed felting needles are mounted in a board at a density of 300–5,000 per metre width and pass through a web or batt of fibres which is supported between bed and stripper plates. In some machines the needles work from both the top and under-sides of the batt giving increased strength.
(Illustration – The Textile Institute)

are caught by the barb. The needle then withdraws, leaving the fibres entangled in the batt. It is, therefore, the fibres from the web itself which hold the batt together. The batt is passed through the machine several times. Sometimes scrim is sandwiched between layers of web to increase stability, and the needle punching binds the layers together. Fabric produced by this method is usually fairly thick. Its most important outlets are for carpets and for use as blankets, in which acrylic fibres are used. It is interesting to note that the blankets (which are napped after manufacture) are produced at about thirty times the speed of conventional methods.

Pile fabrics with corduroy effects can be created. Needle-punched material has been used for shoe-liners. An industrial use is filtration.

Stitch-bonded with thread

This method uses yarn to consolidate the batt of fibres and therefore does not conform to the definition of nonwoven, although, for convenience, it is included here in this section. Stitch-bonding originated in East Germany and Czechoslovakia.

The web of fibre is passed through a warp knitting machine, and the web is penetrated by specially designed needles, each of which hooks on to a nylon or high-tenacity sewing thread (presented to it by a guide on the

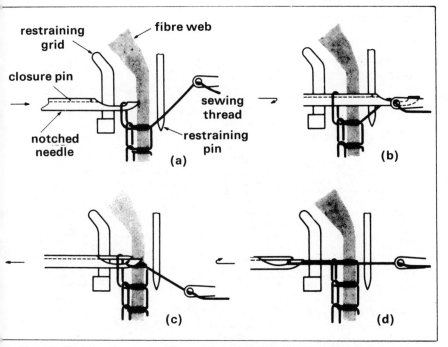

Fig. 140 Stitch bonding web of fibre with thread to form fabric. *(Shirley Institute)*

Fabric Structure

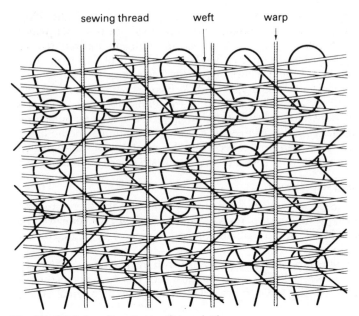

Fig. 141 Stitch bonding sheets of cross-laid yarn.
(Shirley Institute)

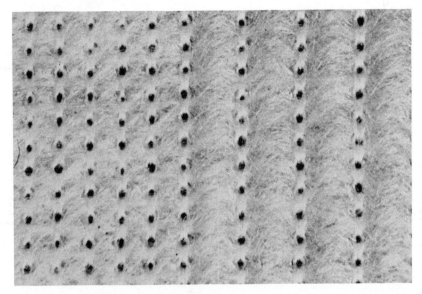

Fig. 142 Stitch bonding without thread.
(Hollings Faculty, Manchester Polytechnic)

150

underside) which it withdraws through the batt to form a simple chain of tricot stitches. The stitch-bonding or sew-knitting continues along the full length of the cloth, the separation between the chains of loops being equal to the spacing between the needles. The rate of production may be up to 350 metres per hour. (See Figure 140.) This method of manufacture can be applied to sheets of yarn instead of a batt of fibres (Figure 141).

Stitch bonding without thread

Here the needles are designed to pull small loops of fibre out of the web, and these are then used as the means of chain-stitching in lines along the fabric length.

Stitch-bonded fabrics have considerably greater strength in the length-wise direction of stitching than across the width. Depending on the fibre content and mass of the fabric they have a wide range of uses such as: self-coloured and printed curtains and soft furnishings mostly made from viscose, with the substitution of a chloro fibre providing flame retardance. Other applications are vertical blinds from polyester fibre, polyester and viscose footwear linings, polyester roofing felt substrate, carpet backing, vehicle upholstery, medical products and industrial wipes.

COATED FABRICS AND LAMINATES

Coating is the process of applying a layer or layers of a polymer film to the surface of a woven, warp- or weft-knitted, or nonwoven base fabric. Lamination is the process of combining two or (more rarely) more layers of fabric by an intermediate layer of a polymer adhering to both. This layer may be sufficiently thick and substantial to form a significant part of the sandwich, or it may merely act as an adhesive to join the two fabrics together.

Coated and laminated fabrics are made in a very wide and diverse range of weights and constructions to meet a very extensive range of applications. These include clothing for which a coated fabric may be chosen mainly for aesthetic appeal, as for example simulated leather, or clothing in which a coated fabric is chosen for its ability to keep the wearer dry in a storm, while still permitting water vapour released from the body as perspiration to escape. Such garments are used by many kinds of outdoor workers, and for leisure pursuits such as mountaineering and golfing. Simulated leather fabrics can be made to imitate real skins very closely, while having the aesthetic and physical properties required for footwear, hand-bags, luggage and fashion wear. Heavy duty uses of coated fabrics include tarpaulins and wagon covers.

The lightest laminated fabrics, which are essentially merely two conventional fabrics held face-to-face by an adhesive, may be used for various conventional purposes, such as clothing, but can provide a convenient way, for example, of combining the attractive appearance of an unstable knitted or lace fabric with the stability of a woven fabric. Such a combination may also have a firm handle in place of the limpness of the 'top' fabric.

Laminated fabrics for demanding engineering uses may be made in a considerable range of weights, and find many applications.

Methods of coating

Direct coating

In this method the cloth passes over a supporting roller or plate, and a 'doctor blade' held very close to its surface spreads a layer of the polymer in a uniform thickness before curing at a suitable temperature. More than one layer of polymer may be applied. Such a process permits the addition of fabric before curing to provide a laminated structure, the polymer holding together the two layers of fabric.

Transfer coating

In this method the layer of polymer is formed on a 'release paper' before being applied to the fabric to which it adheres. The polymer may be built up in layers on the paper, with what will be the top coat applied and cured first. A final coat to serve as an adhesive follows, and the polymer is then transferred to the fabric. Finally, the release paper is removed. This method is particularly suitable for fabrics that are easily stretched or distorted such as knitted, loosely woven or nonwoven structures. By using embossed release paper, leather grain effects may be produced.

In coating by either the direct or the transfer method, the intermediate polymer layer may be of the 'expanded' or 'foam' type, which is described as 'microporous'. This produces a softer more flexible product.

Clothing fabrics

The earliest clothing fabrics were the 'oil skins' used by outdoor workers. These were made by applying a linseed oil to a cotton base fabric. This oil oxidises to form tough water impermeable skin. Waterproof coats, ground sheets and other articles were made by applying rubber coatings, also to a cotton base. 'Double texture' fabrics were made by laminating two cotton fabrics with rubber and these were used for heavy duty articles such as riding coats, fishermen's waders, and superior raincoats. Rubber has now been superseded by synthetic polymers of which polyurethane (PU) is quite the most important except for special protective clothing.

One of the important disadvantages of rubber was that the coated fabrics did not 'breathe', that is, they did not permit the transmission of water vapour (perspiration), and they were, therefore, uncomfortable to wear. Ordinary PU is not permeable to water vapour but two varieties that have this property are in common use. The 'poromeric' coatings contain numerous very fine pores that permit the passage of water vapour, but are too fine to allow liquid water to penetrate. Examples of these are 'Entrant' and 'Cyclone'. Hydrophilic PU coatings transmit water because a chemical modification to the PU renders them capable of allowing water vapour to diffuse through as fast as the best poromeric PU. Such a fabric is marketed as 'Witcoflex'.

Both these varieties of PU coated fabrics are used for rainwear and can be worn with comfort because, unlike the earlier 'rubberised' fabrics, perspiration can escape and does not condense on the inner surface of the clothing. There are numerous other applications of these fabrics such as in tentages and surgeons' gowns.

Protective garments are required in agriculture and industry and in specialised occupations where operatives may be exposed to various hazards such as splashes from dangerous liquids, high voltages, and flying sparks. These garments are usually heavy and durable and must be capable of being laundered frequently. PVC coatings on cotton or viscose fabric give protection against acid and alkali splashes but 'Neoprene', 'Hypalon' and PU or Nitrile rubber are required where organic liquids are the hazard. Fire retardant grades of these coatings are available for application to fire retardant fabrics where there is a fire risk.

PVC coatings are less suitable for ordinary clothing use than PU; since they have a tendency to become brittle, stiffness varies with temperature and they are not suitable for dry cleaning. They are much used in accessories, however, handbags for example.

Upholstery and soft furnishings

The appearance, durability and feel of the leathers used in upholstery can be very successfully simulated by PVC and PU coatings, but the former probably have the larger share of the market. The base fabric is commonly knitted or open weave on which a soft microporous coating is applied, followed by a top coating for scuff and soil resistance. The coating is embossed with a leather grain effect. In cheaper grades the microporous layer may be omitted.

Plastic coatings find a variety of uses in the house as for example a foam polymer layer (natural rubber, PVC, PU or acrylic) backing for tufted or needle punched carpets, improving tread and durability. Vinyl wallpapers are an important example of domestic application, to which may be added luggage.

Industrial uses of coated and laminated fabrics

The most striking example of the industrial use of these products is in the construction of buildings. So-called 'air-houses' are built entirely of impermeable plastic-coated fabric supported by a slight internal pressure

(Workfoto OC TIEF, Essen)

Fig. 143 Haj air terminal in Saudi Arabia covering 370 acres and topped by the world's largest translucent fabric roof; 510,000 sq. metres of glass fibre material coated with Teflon.

(Owens-Corning Fiberglas Corporation, Toledo, Ohio)

maintained by an air pump. These buildings are ideal for temporary purposes such as exhibition halls. Much larger buildings such as sports stadia may have a steel framework or be supported by external wire ropes attached to tall posts. PVC coated or laminated nylon or polyester are often used for these purposes but polymer coated glass fabrics are more durable and translucent.

154

In some buildings only the roof is made from textile (Figure 143) which is usually translucent to provide excellent illumination, and may be supported either by an internal framework, or external guy ropes.

Other industrial uses are almost too numerous to mention, but reference must be made to balloons, covers of various kinds including wagon covers, storage vessels, hoses ranging from very small to very large, capable of transporting liquid in large volumes at high pressure, and conveyor belting, often for the movement of coal, rock, or similar loads. Inflatables include lifejackets, rafts and dinghies.

Leather substitutes

Reference has been made above to simulated leather for use in clothing and upholstery. We are now concerned with simulated leather for use in shoe uppers. Such a material must simulate the desirable properties associated with leather, that is, it must be capable of moulding to the foot in use, be vapour permeable, resistant to scuffing and cracking, abrasion resistant and fast to dyes. It must also be capable of being bonded to the sole.

Natural leather is composed of a fibrous network of thick fibre bundles which are themselves composed of smaller and smaller bundles coming down to the collagen protein molecule itself. It is this structure that

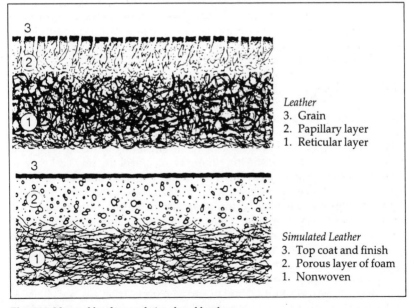

Leather
3. Grain
2. Papillary layer
1. Reticular layer

Simulated Leather
3. Top coat and finish
2. Porous layer of foam
1. Nonwoven

Fig. 144 Natural leather and simulated leather.
(SATRA Footwear Technology Centre).

accounts for the distinctive properties of leather. Near the grain side of the skin the fibres are finest and form a web-like structure interrupted by hair cavities which can be seen on the surface and characterise the grain of the leather.

For footwear the base fabric is commonly a specially soft nonwoven made from synthetic fibre or a cotton-blend fabric, capable of absorbing moisture. On this is coated a flexible PU foam inner layer, and finally a scuff resistant flexible top coat. Poromeric PU is used to permit the passage of water vapour from the foot, and the top layer is embossed to imitate the required visual characteristics of leather.

The above is a description of the structure of a typical simulated shoe upper leather but, of course, variations are possible to produce cheaper or more expensive versions. For example, a less expensive product is made by omitting the foam layer and putting the top coat directly on the raised surface of a woven or knitted fabric. A superior product is formed on a base of a nonwoven made from very fine polyester or polyamide fibres arranged in very small bundles, imitating the structure of leather.

Seams for waterproof coated fabrics

Special attention must be given to the way seams are made in waterproof fabrics (page 309). Conventional stitching will let water through. The seam may be made watertight by applying a tape with an adhesive or using a heat sealing tape. Treated sewing thread that will not encourage the wicking of water is available and special seam constructions are used to ensure waterproofness. The performance of the final product depends not only on the quality of the fabric and other components, but on the design and method of, and care in, assembly.

INTERLINING

The interlining of garments is an essential feature, both in tailoring and dress manufacture. An interlining is a suitably chosen fabric interposed between the outer cloth of the garment and the lining or under collar, for example. The function of the interlining is to control the physical characteristics of the garment assembly and to meet specific aesthetic requirements. For instance, in localised areas of shirt collars and cuffs, dresses, suits and top coats it may be important to increase as appropriate the stiffness, resiliency, stability, bulk and warmth, and to improve the retention of a smooth surface or a curved shape in use. Interlinings are of value in controlling the extensibility of curved seams and improving the appearance and strength of buttonhole stands.

To meet the wide range of demands made on interlinings in clothing manufacture, woven, knitted and nonwoven fibre structures are all used. This choice of structure, combined with the range of fabric weights, fibre contents, and fabric finishes, enables a careful selection to be made for a particular style and end use. The needs of the home dressmaker are met by a smaller range of interlinings.

Interlinings are either of the 'sew-in' variety or are capable of being fused to the garment part. Wherever practicable, fusible interlinings have by now almost superseded 'sew-in' interlinings. Unstructured garments that are unlined provide a casual silhouette which makes little use of interlinings. Such a trend is often also based on economy in manufacturing costs.

Sew-in interlining

Woven non-fusible interlinings include stiff organza and soft mull, both of which are light weight and are suitable for light-weight dress and blouse wear. Plain weave fabrics in various medium weights, say 100 g/m², made from resin-treated cotton or viscose, or blends with nylon, are used for shirts. The interlining must have easy care properties and shrink resistance equal to that of the fabric used in the garment and, if the garment is to have durable press treatment, the interlining must be fully shrunk and satisfactorily meet the conditions of curing.

Canvas used in tailoring is a heavier fabric than those mentioned so far. Even here, a wide range is available of weights and qualities made from cotton, linen, wool, or horse hair (which is now little used). Some canvasses incorporate manufactured fibres or mono-filament to obtain the requisite stiffness, but these may be inferior in handle. The yarns used at one time in the weft of some good quality canvasses consisted of horse hair wrapped with cotton yarn and this contributed to the stiffness of the structure. Cotton warp and resinated viscose weft has now substantially replaced the wrapped hair interlinings.

An interlining to be used as the chest piece in a tailored jacket is required to be stiffer and more resilient across the jacket to give full support and resistance to deformation in the chest area, whilst the warp direction running the length of the chest piece should have a softer handle and be more pliable in use. The interlinings are constructed with differing numbers and types of yarns in the two directions to produce the desired effect. Woven interlinings for chest pieces have been produced with graduated stiffness, being firm at the top in the shoulder area, where extra firmness is needed, and diminishing in firmness towards the lower part of the chest.

Nonwoven fabrics are discussed on page 143. The properties of bonded-fibre interlinings depend on the orientation of the fibres within the batt, the type of fibre used and the choice of agent used to bond the fibres together. Thick bonded-fibres are used for padding in tailoring, whilst lighter weight varieties are used for blouses, dresses, suits and rainwear.

Despite the availability of various techniques for the preparation of the nonwoven interlinings, they lack the combined handle and resiliency associated with woven structures, but their chief merit is reduced cost of the interlining itself and economy in the utilisation of the material because the general non-directional characteristics allow components for the garment to be cut at random.

Knitted interlinings may be either weft or warp-knitted, but the structure showing the greatest potential is the warp-knit with weft-insertion. Traditional yarns may be used in the weft-insertion, and commonly viscose or polyester is inserted across the nylon structure. This enables an interlining to be designed which is lighter in weight than the conventional canvas, while providing the handle and stability to complement the characteristics of the top fabric and meeting the requirements of styling most outerwear.

Fusible interlinings

Interlinings which are fused to parts of garments during the garment manufacturing process reduce the production time and operator training costs normally associated with the sewing in of non-fusible interlinings. The fusing or sticking of interlinings to the outer fabric requires the use of a hot press to cause the coating of synthetic resin (which has already been applied to the surface of the base fabric by the interlining manufacturer) to soften and stick to the top fabric.

The characteristics of the 'sew-in' interlining have to be built into the interlining fabric structure, whereas for the fusible interlining, it is the role played by the adhesive and the production of the laminated structure itself which primarily governs the resultant physical characteristics of the composite structure in the garment. However, woven, knitted and nonwoven structures are available with a range of fibre contents for use as a base fabric in fusible interlinings. To further modify the structure, deviations have been introduced such as inserting fine slits in bonded fibre fabrics to improve flexibility.

The combination of upper fabric and interlining is likely to be much stiffer than would be expected from the stiffness of the two fabrics judged individually. To bend the fused combination, the fabric on the outside of the bend must be stretched, and the fabric on the inside must be compressed in its own plane, and the bending forces must be sufficient to produce this stretching and compression additional to bending the individual fabrics. Thus the stiffness of the combined fabrics is always greater than the sum of the stiffness of the individual fabrics, and is often considerably greater. The ability of a fusible interlining to increase the stiffness of a fabric is therefore out of proportion to its own stiffness and is very dependent on its resistance to stretching and compression in its own plane.

The drape of a fabric is governed partly by its stiffness but also by its resistance to being deformed by stretching, compression in its plane, and skewing. Thus if an interlining is particularly resistant to such deformation it may produce an important modification in the drape of the top fabric. A light-weight but inextensible and rigid interlining may therefore help to control a much heavier but soft and loosely constructed top fabric.

The choice of synthetic resin used to coat the base fabric, and the form in which the resin is distributed over the fabric surface, influences the effectiveness of the bond between the fusible and the top fabric, the handle and drape of the fused material, and the performance of the composite structure in use, in laundering and dry cleaning.

Conditions of fusing

To function as an adhesive, the resin coating must soften and become tacky in the temperature range of 110–175°C and harden again on cooling. The hot press of the steam or electric type used for fusing the garment parts must be controllable within narrow tolerances with respect to temperature, the pressure applied to the fabric, and the duration of fusing in the press. The temperature and pressure within the press must be uniform over the area of fabric to be fused, otherwise uneven bonding can result. The specified operational temperature associated with a particular resin must be attained at the 'glue-line', that is the point of contact of the resin with the fabric.

Uncontrolled deviations from fusing conditions needed to effect a bond may result in faults such as 'strike-back', which is the penetration of the adhesive to the outer surface of the interlining, or 'strike-through', which is the penetration of the adhesive from the interlining to the surface of the outer fabric. In addition, the handle of the laminate can be substantially modified by the conditions of fusing and the bond may be weak or not resistant to washing and dry cleaning.

There are two main categories of electric or steam presses, those in which the components to be fused are placed between two flat surfaces brought together under controlled pressure, and presses that have a conveyor which carries the prepared components to a fusing zone. Top fabrics which are liable to shrink when heated or are susceptible to a change in colour when exposed to high temperatures, may be particularly liable to develop these defects when being fused on continuous fusing presses in which the components are not clamped firmly through the operation.

The resin

The types of resin used for fusible interlinings* are summarised on page 160 together with their associated properties. The resin used governs the conditions of fusing to obtain satisfactory results, and the permissible method of cleaning. From this it will be seen that certain interlinings are destined for particular end uses.

To appreciate further the importance of the resin, it is necessary to be aware of the influence that the distribution pattern of the resin over the base cloth can have on the ultimate handle. For instance, a continuous film of resin will result in a stiff laminate, but the application of dots of resin of various sizes and spacing introduces greater scope in specifying the

* *British Interlining Manufacturers' Association, London.*

Table 14 SUMMARY OF THE PROPERTIES OF RESINS USED IN THE PRODUCTION OF INTERLININGS

Resin Type	General observations and recommendations for use
Polyethylene	
High density FE * * * FC * * CL * * * CP * * * Dry cleaning in Trichlorethylene is fair to good	The viscosity of the molten resin during fusing is higher than that of the low density type, and therefore, to effect a bond of adequate strength with the top fabric, greater pressure is required during the fusing operation. This makes it particularly suitable for use in collars and cuffs of shirts which benefit from a stiffened flat effect. These garments are also subject to frequent washing.
Low density FS * FE * * * FC * * CL * * CP * Trichlorethylene must not be used	This resin costs less than the high density type. Because of its greater fluidity when molten the penetration into the structure of the fabric is easier, and there is not the same need to apply high pressure during fusing. Low density polyethylene powder is often blended with resins that have a high performance in dry-cleaning in order to reduce costs. The polyethylene provides a good initial bond when fusing, accompanied by durability in washing and improved dry-cleaning performance.
Polyamide FS * * FE * * * FC * * * CL * CP * * * Satisfactorily dry-cleaned in Trichlorethylene	The polyamides used generally are Terpolymers (i.e. consist of three different polymers), and by varying the proportions of each and the addition of plasticisers a range of polyamide resins are produced to provide a choice of characteristics. These may be grouped as having a 'higher melting' and 'lower-melting' characteristic. The cost of such resins is high and their possible application wide, excluding shirts.
Polyvinyl acetate FS * * FE * * * FC * * * CL *	The plasticised resin is applied as a continuous coating to the base fabric, and this is used with leather, in millinery, for furs, and the backing of belts. Some of these compounds harden after fusing. It is not dry-cleanable.

Table 14 cont.

Resin type	General observations and recommendations for use
Polyvinyl chloride FE * * * FC * * * CL * * CP * * * Trichlorethylene must not be used on some types of PVC	The properties of PVC depend on the amount of plasticiser included in the mix, and it is this that determines the temperature range permissible in fusing. According to type it has a wide range of applications from shirt collars to men's and women's outerwear. Whilst the resin may be distributed in granular form over the surface of the interlining it is more commonly printed on as dots. Sometimes on dry cleaning the plasticiser is partially removed. This results in a stiffer handle accompanied by an improved bond strength in the laminate.
Cellulose acetate FS * FE * * * FC * * * CL * * CP * * Trichlorethylene may be used in dry cleaning	Plasticisers are used in conjunction with the resin to provide a range of interlinings, responsive to fusing temperatures of 120°–165°C, suitable for inclusion in the body of the garment in addition to small areas.
Phenolic resins FS * FE * * * FC * * * CL * CP * * Trichlorethylene must not be used	Other resins and plasticisers are generally blended with the phenolic resins in order to extend the range of uses, excluding shirts and blouses. A disadvantage is the discoloration which occurs during fusing operations and on exposure to light. After fusing some tend to harden and affect the handle of the composite.

Key to performance of resins

Type of fusing press
FS Steam
FE Electric flat bed
FC Continuous fusing

Method of cleaning
CL Laundering
CP Dry cleaning (perchlorethylene)

Level of performance after cleaning
* * * Very good
* *   Good
*   Use this method with caution

ultimate handle of the laminate. The distribution of the dots results in discontinuous bonding, which allows greater flexibility within the laminated structure. On the other hand, the less expensive method of scattering powdered resin over the base cloth, which is subsequently heated to make the resin adhere to it, produces a fusible interlining which does not attain the same level of uniformity and flexibility as that provided by printed coatings when fused to the top cloth. Double sided fusibles consist entirely of an adhesive in the form of a web or net. This is available with or without a carrier paper for temporary support. Unsupported webs of adhesive may be sewn into a garment and fused later.

The design of clothing requires the choice of components on technical grounds and taking full account of the compatability of the materials. Unstructured loose-fitting lightweight jackets, such as safari jackets and casual wear, only require sufficient interlining to stabilise the front edge to support the buttons and buttonholes. Formal type coats may require a combination of various interlinings to build up the shape. Rainwear often incorporates fusible interlining in the pocket trim, cuff tab and collar, but with a sewn-in interlining along the front edges.

An example of incompatability of materials is particularly evident in rainwear when the presence of an absorbent interlining accelerates the passage of water through an otherwise satisfactory shower-resistant top fabric.

Pocketing

Not all pockets in garments are subject to the wear and tear of the trouser pocket in men's suits. Trouser pockets are made from cotton fabric or 'cotton pocketing', as it is referred to in the trade. These generally give good service if they are made in closely-woven constructions, in twill or plain weaves, preferably from two-fold yarns. However, good durability cannot be attained with a more open construction which has been calendered or finished to flatten the threads, producing the appearance of cloth with a good cover. Rubbing is the chief cause of wear and, whilst cotton fabric of reasonable construction has a good resistance to abrasion, the inclusion of nylon greatly improves it in this respect. Since nylon is more expensive than cotton, some pocketing is manufactured so that only a broad band of the fabric contains nylon. The nylon section falls only at the portion of the pocket where all the abrasion occurs.

Warp-knitted nylon fabric is also used for trouser pockets, especially in washable garments. Such warp-knitted structures are very stable, are not bulky, and have the advantages associated with nylon.

Jacket pockets receive less severe treatment than trouser pockets, and are generally of light construction such as silesia. These are often dyed a dark colour, whereas trouser pockets are cream or dove grey.

Overcoat pockets generally have a soft warm feel so raised cotton fabrics are used. For expensive garments, a short pile velvet may be chosen.

Chapter 4

PROPERTIES OF FABRICS

The demands made on a fabric, and hence the properties and characteristics it must have, are determined by the use to which it is put and also the requirements of satisfactory behaviour in making-up. Certain requirements are common to most fabrics, adequate strength and durability for example, whilst other properties such as waterproofness or resistance to agencies such as acids or alkalis are demanded for fabrics to be used for special purposes. The uses to which fabrics are put are extremely wide and diverse and the properties and characteristics which are of importance are correspondingly diverse, as are the corresponding methods of examining and testing fabrics.

The performance characteristics of fabrics can be grouped in a number of broad categories as follows. The entries in each category are illustrative only, since they cannot be exhaustive.

Mechanical properties important in use:
Tensile, tearing and bursting strengths, resistance to abrasion, dimensional stability, stretch and recovery.

Properties relating to aesthetic acceptability:
Handle and drape, crease recovery, easy care properties, lustre, appearance retention including colour fastness, and colour matching.

Physical requirements relating to comfort:
Permeability to air and moisture vapour, thermal insulation, stiffness, and smoothness.

Properties important in garment manufacture:
Sewability, dimensional stability, tailorability, and freedom from static.

Requirements for special applications:
Flame retardance, waterproofness, wind resistance, resistance to acid, alkalis and industrial solvents.

The above classification is mainly applicable to clothing fabrics but it should be remembered that the textile industry produces a vast range of industrial fabrics from the extremely lightweight to very heavy fabrics, for uses such as conveyor belts and other engineering purposes.

MECHANICAL PROPERTIES

Strength

Tensile strength

A textile may have all the qualities and properties needed to fit it for some particular purpose, but unless it is strong enough to resist the forces it will encounter in use it is of no value. In use cloth may be liable to fail by breaking when a straight pull is applied, by ripping and tearing, and by bursting when a force is applied normal to its surface. Laboratory test methods are used to measure the resistance of cloth to each of these forces and generally tests are made on the fabric in the unused state, which may be referred to 'as received'.

When fabric has been in use under a variety of conditions, including possibly cleaning processes, exposure to light and other agencies, the performance of the fabric will gradually diminish. It is therefore important for an appropriate level of strength to be set and attained so that, despite a subsequent drop in performance, the material will still give reasonable satisfaction throughout the 'life' of the garment or other textile product.

The tensile strength of a fabric, that is its strength when a load is applied in either the warp or weft direction of the fabric, is affected in some degree by almost every feature of construction or finish. It is for this reason that the minimum tensile strength is commonly laid down in fabric performance specifications drawn up by large organisations or government departments. A minimum level of performance is set for each product and the testing and monitoring of the newly manufactured material is judged against the specified values. Any drop in strength signals a possible change in fabric structure, fibre content or finish.

The warp direction of woven fabrics is often stronger than the weft simply because there may be more threads in that direction. Also, the warp yarns probably have more twist than the weft to give them the greater strength they need during weaving.

Normally and preferably the tensile strength is set for each direction of a woven fabric but, for the sake of expediency, some organisations simply monitor the least strong direction and on that basis accept or reject the fabric.

The tensile strength of a fabric is measured by taking a strip, generally 5 centimetres wide, cut parallel to the threads, and finding the force necessary to break it. Clearly, the strength of the strip is mainly determined by the strength of the individual threads and the number of threads per centimetre. However, a simple calculation based on these quantities might be in error by as much as 20%, for it is found that the pressure of the warp and weft yarns on each other may increase the fibre binding and hence the strength of the yarns. Other effects also are important, such as the support of weak places in yarns by the neighbouring threads. The result is that generally fabrics made from spun yarns are stronger than might be expected from a consideration of the yarn strength.

Besides the factors that contribute to yarn strength (page 60), cloth strength is influenced by weave. The firm, closely bound weaves such as plain and simple twill and matts are stronger than the looser weaves such as the satin.

Values for minimum tensile strength for clothing can range, for example, from about 12 kg for blouse fabric to about 30 kg for active sportswear. Test conditions and specimen size are of course standardised to ensure reliable comparative assessment. The fabric strip method for determining the breaking strength and elongation of woven fabric is given in BS 2576.

Tearing strength

It will be seen in Figure 145 that during tearing the load acts upon each weft thread in turn and consequently, tearing strength is much less than tensile strength, when a large number of threads must be broken together. If in tearing the threads slip, they will bunch together to some extent and support each other. Hence, the more easily the yarns slip the greater the tearing strength.

It will be realised that in a plain weave, which has the maximum number of thread intersections possible, yarn slippage will be restricted, and that in twill weaves, satins, and sateens, in which the long floats are a characteristic of the fabrics, the floats will permit easy slippage of the threads. A very closely woven fabric may restrict such movement. It is for this reason that closely woven fabrics in plain weave can have low tearing strengths, whereas twills and loosely constructed cloths, particularly those in weaves with long floats, often have high tearing strengths.

If a finish, such as a synthetic resin or starch, is applied to the fabric, this often increases the friction between the threads and reduces their freedom of movement and so causes a fall in tearing strength. Obviously, finishes which incorporate lubricants will improve matters.

Yarns made from fibres which are easily extended, such as wool and nylon, will also yield and bend under the load applied, thereby sharing the load with the adjacent yarns.

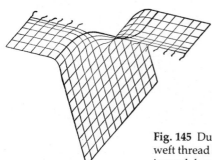

Fig. 145 During tearing, the load acts upon each weft thread in turn. Consequently, tearing strength is much less than tensile strength. *(Shirley Institute)*

If a very high tearing strength is required, in excess of what is normally needed for clothing, it is necessary to include fibres in the fabric which are inherently very strong, since the tearing strength of a fabric depends upon a combination of all the points that have been made.

Garment construction, such as correct placing of pockets and adequate seams, can help to prevent tears starting, but once it has started in a fabric of low tearing strength, a tear will easily continue.

Various methods are used to measure the resistance to tearing of woven fabrics and these are given in BS 4253 and BS 4303.

Knitted fabrics are usually very difficult to tear and are therefore not commonly subjected to tear tests.

Bursting strength

The tensile strength of knitted fabrics cannot be accurately measured by taking a strip and pulling on it because the fabric distorts considerably, as can be easily verified. These fabrics are therefore subjected to a 'bursting test' which avoids this effect. In the test for bursting pressure, a specimen of the fabric to be tested is clamped by a circular clamp against a rubber diaphragm resting on a flat plate. A liquid or gas under pressure distends the diaphragm and specimen until the latter bursts, and the corresponding pressure is registered on the pressure gauge. (The pressure required to distend the diaphragm is usually negligible). Figure 146. The pressure required to burst the fabric is noted and termed the 'bursting strength' of the cloth. This depends not only on the strength of the yarns but also, in a complicated way, on the extensibilities of the yarns and the cloth construction.

A method for determining the bursting strength and bursting distension of fabric is given in BS 4768.

Brushed knitted fabrics and resinated fabrics tend to have lower bursting strengths than the original fabric. For such fabrics it is necessary to

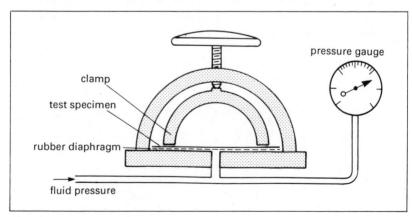

Fig. 146 Bursting strength tester.

indicate the minimum permissible level of bursting strength. When fabrics are to be screened say for anoraks, or close fitting skirts and trousers, minimum values of the order of 430 kPa may be recommended whereas knitted fabric for blouses, shirts, nightwear and body lining could be of the order of 250–300 kPa. Knitted pocket linings are subject to much stress in use and provision is made for this by ensuring the fabric quality is about 400 kPa (kPa is the abbreviation for kilo Pascals).

Shear strength and peel strength

These two aspects of strength are used in the performance assessment of multi-layers of material which are required to adhere to each other either permanently or temporarily in use.

Shear strength (g/cm^2) is defined as the resistance of layers of fabric to sliding laterally over each other (Figure 147), whereas *peel strength* (Kg/cm width) refers to the force necessary to separate the layers by peeling apart (Figure 147).

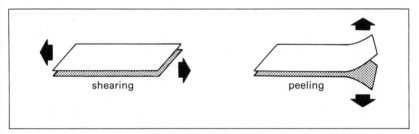

Fig. 147 Illustration of direction of fabric movement (shear strength; peel strength).

When an interlining is fused to a fabric the peel bond strength must be sufficient for the laminate to remain intact throughout the life of the product. In contrast 'touch and close' fasteners, such as 'Velcro', are required to maintain adequate strength after several thousand repeated separation and closure cycles of the layers in use, and after exposure for instance to, cleaning, heat and sterilisation treatments.

These fasteners in certain locations are subject to shear stresses in use, and for these shear strength is important in addition to peel strength.

'Velcro' fasteners consist of a pair of narrow fabrics, the inside surface of each being of distinctly different structures, that is, a monofilament hook structure on one face which engages under pressure with multifilament loops protruding from the other (Figure 148a), usually made from nylon 6.6.

Another 'Velcro' structure is composed of mushroom shaped elements (Figure 148b), usually of polypropylene, which engage the loops when pressure is applied. However, this is intended for applications where repeated opening and closing is infrequent as for furnishings, upholstery,

 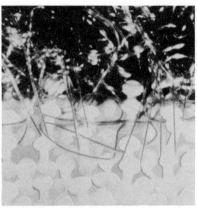

Fig. 148a Standard 'Velcro' with monofilament hooks and multifilament loops. *(Selectus Ltd.)*

Fig. 148b Mushroom shaped elements engaging the loops. *(Selectus Ltd.)*

carpets, medical disposable garments and bandages. Mushroom fasteners are less expensive to manufacture than the nylon hook type which provides the necessary functional life-span for clothing.

Stretch and recovery

The comfort of a garment, its closeness of fit, and appearance in use, are influenced by the extent to which the component fabrics will stretch and recover from extension. The stretch and recovery of common woven and knitted fabrics made from conventional yarns is limited, but by the inclusion or substitution of textured yarns, elastane fibres, or the application of special fabric manufacturing and finishing procedures, a range of fabrics offering different degrees of stretch and recovery is possible.

The range includes such categories as 'comfort stretch' in which the garment conforms to the body contours without providing extra support, e.g. leotards, swimwear, skiwear and other sportswear. 'Power stretch' fabrics are used for garments required to compress and control the shape of the body, e.g. foundation wear and bras. To provide localised support garments need to extend sufficiently to enable them to be drawn over the larger parts of the body and yet, in use, to give the required figure control. Narrow elastic fabric can be woven, knitted or braided for use as straps to provide support and ease of movement, the elastic threads running along the length of the fabric.

For the comfortable use of relatively loosely fitting garments it may be advantageous to make provision for the stretch that occurs over curved areas in such locations as across the back, around the seat, knees and elbows during natural movement or in more active use. This may be done by garment design and choice of fabric. Weft-knitted fabric in particular responds well to movement in such locations, and may also be improved by fibre choice. However, another factor to be considered is the facility with which the underside of the fabric slides over the knee in slacks, for example, or over an undergarment, since drag in these areas could be discomforting. The introduction of a lining with suitable physical properties will reduce the intersurface friction.

Stretch fabrics produce garments with good shape-retention and freedom from puckering and fabric buckling in use.

'Comfort stretch' fabrics stretch and recover from about 25% extension but fabrics classed as 'power stretch' have high extension up to 200% with snap recovery. Good examples of 'stretch' yarns are those used in knitted socks and tights, which stretch to accommodate a large range of foot sizes.

It is useful to know how much 'body' stretch occurs at various parts of the anatomy in sitting, bending, and flexing knees and elbows. The illustration in Figure 149 indicates possible levels of 'body' stretch compared with measurements taken on the figure standing at the rest position. Differences will be found between such measurements made on women and men.

An important non-clothing use for stretch fabrics is as 'stretch covers' for chairs and settees. These knitted covers do not require careful 'tailoring' and make it possible to provide a mass produced range of covers which are much cheaper than the custom-made article.

Assessment of fabric stretch

The choices of test and conditions of testing are governed by what force is required to stretch the material and to what percentage of its original length it can be extended, and for what purpose the material is intended.

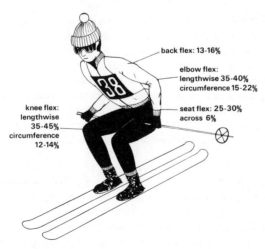

Fig. 149 Stretch requirements.

Two BS tests are available, namely:

BS 4294: Methods of test for stretch and recovery properties of fabric.
BS 4952: Methods of test for elastic fabrics

A relatively simple test known as the 'Fryma Extensiometer' requires a measured strip of fabric to be mounted horizontally in the apparatus under an applied load of 1·4 kg; its extension under this load, and its residual extension following the removal of the load, being measured and expressed as a percentage of the original length. However, it will be appreciated that it is usually of greater interest to determine residual extension after the sample has been held for a specified time at a fixed elongation rather than at a fixed load. For example, it may be specified that a fabric would be acceptable for a particular purpose provided its residual extension is not greater than 3% after a 30% elongation held for a specified time. Requirements for the two directions are likely to be different.

Garments, of course, are likely to make some recovery from residual extension while out of use overnight or for longer periods, and also during washing.

Dimensional stability

When a fabric is stated to lack dimensional stability this usually refers to either shrinkage or extension in one or both directions of the fabric.

Fabric shrinkage is a great inconvenience since it may result in a garment becoming too small or too mis-shapen to wear. There is a slightly greater tolerance of shrinkage in curtain materials since the question of 'fit' is not so critical. Carpets, and carpet tiles in particular, need to be very stable dimensionally once laid to cover the floor area.

The user of the product requires dimensional stability particularly in washing and drycleaning, but it must also be borne in mind that fabric stability during garment manufacture is a pre-requisite for quality merchandise and efficient production management.

If fabric changes dimensions on the cutting table it will result in the garment parts not being of the correct shapes with consequent mismatching of parts in garment assembly. Check patterns, for instance, may become distorted sufficiently to create problems when matching up the patterns during seaming. Serious dimensional change will affect garment sizing and quality.

Heat is applied when fusing interlining to garment parts, when transfer printing, and during the application of fusible embroideries. Such processes utilising heat require the fabric to which these applications are made to be thermally stable.

Steam pressing is another process used in garment manufacture, particularly for outerwear. Here interest centres on ensuring the stability of the fabric in the presence of free steam.

Attention will now be directed to an understanding of the causes of fabric shrinkage, since this may provide a better appreciation of the function of finishes applied to control shrinkage.

Relaxation shrinkage

It is difficult to avoid stretching the fabric during manufacture and finishing. This stretch becomes set in the fabric when it is finally dried after finishing, but at the first opportunity the fabric will relax and return to its most stable, that is, most natural state. This change will occur completely only if the cloth is washed several times with agitation in hot water. But merely damping the fabric will cause some shrinkage, as for example during pressing in making-up. Dry cleaning solvents themselves do not cause this relaxation to occur, but some shrinkage may occur in dry cleaning, partly because of the agitation and partly because a small amount of water may be present.

It has been explained that relaxation shrinkage is a result of the stretching that occurs in manufacture. The threads of a woven fabric must bend up and down to pass over and under each other. When the cloth is stretched lengthwise, the warp threads are made straighter with the result that the weft must bend more. Hence, when the cloth is stretched it also becomes narrower, and sometimes a fabric that shrinks in the length direction when washed may extend a little in the weft direction.

A very old method of reducing relaxation shrinkage in worsted fabric was known as 'London Shrunk'. This consisted of interleaving the fabric with wet pieces of blanket – a process which produces some relaxation. The fabric was then allowed to dry in a current of warm air, and finally was subjected to a special pressing process to improve its appearance. Prior to such a process the worsted fabric passed through a number of finishing processes including heat-setting by 'crabbing' and 'blowing', which are more important than the 'London Shrunk' process itself in producing fabric stability and are still in use.

Fabrics made from cotton, especially overalls and shirtings, are frequently pre-shrunk by the Sanforized or Rigmel processes, both of which apply 'compressive shrinkage'.

In these processes the cloth is passed through a machine which compresses the cloth lengthwise by an amount sufficient to ensure that it will not shrink by more than 1% when washed. Before compressive shrinkage, the cloth is adjusted to the width it would settle to if washed.

Fabric is usually delivered to garment manufacturers wound onto a roll or sometimes in plaited form. The method and care with which the fabric is wound, and subsequently unwound as the fabric is laid-up on the cutting table influences the extent to which the fabric is stretched and is subsequently liable to relax to reduced dimensions. Ideally all fabrics to be cut are already in a relaxed state and, if not, sufficient time must be allowed for fabric relaxation prior to cutting. Knitted fabric in particular needs to be handled in such a way as to be tension-free.

Shrinkage due to fibre swelling

The swelling of fibres was discussed on page 12 and it was seen that some fibres swell more than others when they absorb water. This causes the fabric to shrink, and the more the fibre swells the greater the fabric shrinkage. This can be illustrated first by considering what happens to a thread when the fibres in it swell, and then what changes take place in the woven fabric itself.

Let us imagine that we are examining under a magnifier a dry thread which is held so that it will not untwist. If we now submerge this cotton or viscose thread in water the fibres and hence the yarn will swell in diameter, but there will be no big change in the lengths of each fibre. Since the yarn circumference is increased, the yarn must shrink in length to accommodate the unchanged fibre length (Figure 150).

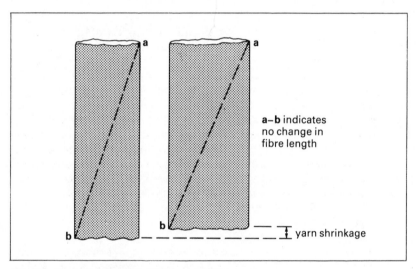

a–b indicates
no change in
fibre length

yarn shrinkage

Fig. 150 Yarn shrinkage due to fibre swelling.

In comparing the shrinkage of a softly twisted yarn and a crêpe twist yarn, the crêpe yarn would be expected to swell and shrink more because there would not be as much 'free space' between the fibres within the yarn into which the fibres could swell. In a softly twisted yarn, the fibre swelling is first accommodated by the existing 'free space' before the yarn will begin to swell and shrink.

Now consider a piece of woven fabric in both dry and wet states (Figure 151). We know that the yarn will swell according to the fibre used and the amount of twist. This yarn swelling forces the threads to bend more as they interlace, and this is described as an increase in yarn crimp. Since the yarn does not get any longer the cloth must shrink and the fabric becomes

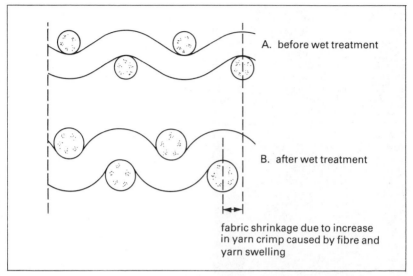

Fig. 151 Section through fabric before and after wet treatment, showing swelling of intersecting yarns.

thicker. In viscose fabrics, shrinkage due to swelling may be large, and compressive shrinkage is unsuccessful. In order to reduce cloth shrinkage due to fibre swelling, a finish may be applied which will reduce the absorption of water. For this purpose synthetic resins are frequently applied to viscose and cotton fabrics. The presence of the resin reduces fibre swelling and yarn and fabric shrinkage.

Shrinkage due to felting

Fabrics made from wool show shrinkage due to the causes discussed above, but also they may shrink by felting. Felting is the entanglement of wool fibres caused by the differential frictional properties of the wool fibre (page 24). The felting which occurs is accompanied by the fabric shrinking and becoming thicker, and the detail of the fabric structure becomes less visible because of the development of surface hairiness. When a wool fabric is rubbed in hot soapy water each squeeze and pressure applied causes the elastic wool fibres to move in direction A (Figure 152), which is easiest for it to do, but it is not possible for the fibres to return to their original positions in the yarn because the fibres are unable to travel easily in direction B. In other words, the entanglement of the fibres and the felting of the fabric are not recoverable. Generally speaking, the lighter and more open the construction, whether woven or knitted, and the more loosely twisted the yarns, the greater is the liability of the fabric to felt. Felting can also occur under the arm of a garment where there is constant rubbing, moisture in the form of perspiration, and warmth.

↑
B

↓
A

Fig. 152 Wool fibre as seen by the
scanning electron microscope.
(Dr J. Sikorski)

Shrinkage due to felting can be reduced to such a level that knitting wool, wool fabric, and wool garments, are labelled 'Machine Washable'. This may be achieved by masking the scales to some extent with a synthetic polymer which eliminates fibre migration and hence felting. A light application of polymer may also be used to produce some fibre to fibre bonding, so that there is no movement of the fibres relative to each other during the washing process. (IWS Superwash).

Wool yarn for hand or machine knitting is first treated lightly and uniformly with chlorine whilst the wool is in the form of a 'top' before spinning. This renders the surface more receptive to the polymer which is required to form a smooth even film on the individual fibres. The amount of polymer is quite small (1–3%) and the effect on handle, strength, and resistance to abrasion, for example, is only slight.

Some knitted garments such as lambswool sweaters, require a soft, slightly hairy surface, and this is produced by lightly felting or 'milling' the garments prior to their shrink-resist treatment. This treatment depends on first processing the garments in a bath containing the polymer, followed by chemically curing the polymer to provide a durable flexible bridge between the fibres which prevents them being displaced when the garment is washed. A batch of about 500 garments may be processed at a time. Polymer fibre bonding is used to ensure the dimensional stability of woven and knitted piece goods when subsequently made into garments. The solution of polymer in water is applied to the fabric in open width, then dried and heated to convert the polymer into its insoluble form in the fabric without affecting adversely the aesthetic properties associated with wool fabrics.

Easy washability of wool is very important if wool dress fabrics and knitwear are to take their place among the great variety of easy care fabrics. Worsted fabrics such as gabardine, serge, barathea, and calvalry twill are generally only dry cleaned, and consequently they are not finished to make them washable. Felting may be reduced by blending in a suitable non-felting fibre such as polyester.

The felting properties of wool are applied deliberately in the manufacture of woollen fabrics such as flannel, melton and duffel since these woollen fabrics are required to be thick and hairy, with a soft full handle. 'Milling' or 'fulling' are the names given to the felting process which is applied to the fabric after it has been woven.

Real felt is neither woven nor knitted but made by causing a mass of wool fibres to felt together to form a uniform matted layer of fabric. Felts for hats, for instance, are produced by this method.

Fabrics made from synthetic fibres

From what has been said so far it is obvious that fabrics made from synthetic fibres do not have the properties to cause felting. They are, however, heat-sensitive and can be deformed above certain temperatures unless they have been heat-set. Heat-setting of fabrics made from thermoplastic fibres is a very important process, and it is usually carried out before the woven or knitted fabric is dyed and finished. The essentials of the process are that the fabric is held flat, with the two directions of the fabric at right angles, and subjected to an appropriately high temperature for a sufficient time. Provided this temperature is not exceeded in the dyeing and other finishing processes in garment manufacture or in use, the fabric will retain the dimension to which it was set.

Dimensional stability of knitted fabrics

So far consideration has been given to ways in which fibres affect fabric shrinkage, and to the behaviour of woven fabric. Knitted garments have the additional possibility of stretching and 'going out of shape' because the loops can be made to slip and alter shape. In use knitted fabrics are liable to deform under the weight of the garment when it is hung vertically to dry, hence the need to 'dry flat'.

Generally, knitting composed wholly or mainly of thermoplastic fibres can be stabilised by heat-setting, but knitted cotton fabrics require special consideration to meet the high standards for outerwear.

The behaviour of weft-knit cotton fabric arises from the construction details, the manufacturing history during the knitting process, and particularly by fabric finishing. Cotton fabrics for underwear can be compressively shrunk mechanically, somewhat similarly to the Sanforizing process. However, the resultant fabric appearance is not of sufficient uniformity and quality to be acceptable for outwear. For outerwear, therefore, greater consideration is given to the specification and control of the knitted structure, particularly in conjunction with subsequent finishing processes. 'Starfish' (International Institute for Cotton page xxviii) is a computer-aided system for the prediction of the stability of certain knitted cotton fabrics.

Assessment of dimensional change

There is no one single method of testing the dimensional change of fabrics. The reasons being that fabrics are composed of different fibre types, and require different washing or dry cleaning conditions. Tests are required also for fabrics that may be exposed to steam during garment manufacture, or may be subject to effects of immersion in cold water.

Consequently, a choice of test methods is available, some of which are scheduled as BS or ISO methods. The following test method titles indicate the range of possibilities.

Determination of dimensional change of textiles in domestic washing and drying.	BS 5807
Dimensional stability of textiles to dry cleaning in tetrachloroethylene.	BS 4931
Procedure for the preparation, marking and measuring of fabric specimens and garments in tests for assessing dimensional change.	BS 4961
Dimensional changes of fabrics induced by cold-water immersion.	BS 4736
Dimensional stability of textile floor coverings.	BS 4682
Dimensional change of elastic fabrics during washing and drying.	BS 4600
Dimensional change of fabrics induced by free steam.	BS 4323
Dimensional changes of wool-containing fabrics during washing.	BS 1955

The common procedure for most tests is to cut out flat specimens of a given size from the material and to mark out permanent reference lines as shown in Figure 153.

The distances between pairs of marks are recorded for each direction of the specimen, all the specimens are then washed, immersed in water, or dry cleaned as specified, and then allowed to dry and condition horizontally in a tensionless state. Other drying conditions may be specified, such as line, drip, flat dry, flat-bed press and tumble dry. Calculation of the dimensional change for each fabric direction is derived from the measured

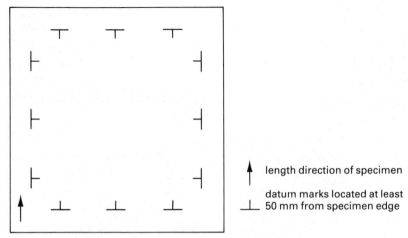

Fig. 153 Measurement of dimensional change of fabric.

length differences, before and after the test, as a percentage of the original length. Shrinkage is indicated by a minus sign and fabric extension by a plus sign. The mean dimensional changes are given separately for each direction. Knitted fabrics may be tested with specimens of double thickness stitched together.

Washing stability

Cloth specifications include the maximum permitted level of shrinkage according to what is attainable for the particular fabric or what is required for the intended garment fit. Fabric for most garments is acceptable if it is within the limit of ± 2·5%. Shirts and shirt collars have more stringent requirements and these are set at less than ± 1·5%.

Weft-knitted fabrics, as already discussed, provide great mobility of fabric structure, hence a maximum shrinkage of 6% or a maximum elongation of 2% may be acceptable. It is, however, not uncommon to consider the area rather than the linear change when judging the suitability of a knitted fabric.

Certain fabrics such as cotton terry towelling may have an 8% limit set for a 60°C wash.

Reference has been made earlier (p. 171) to the fact that the whole relaxation shrinkage potential of a fabric may not be realised in a single wash. In subsequent washes further shrinkage may occur in decreasing amounts. For this reason alone it is desirable that screening tests for shrinkage, based on a single wash, should be severe, if they are to ensure satisfactory fabric and garment performance in normal use. A further point to be brought into consideration is that garments often are assembled from several different fabrics and it is very necessary, if garment distortion is to be avoided, that their different components should be of similar stability.

Fig. 154 WIRA steaming cylinder for the prediction of cloth shrinkage – BS4323. *(Shirley Developments Ltd.)*

Thermal stability

Woven fabrics containing thermoplastic and wool fibres need to be within the limit of 2% shrinkage when tested at say 175°C. This test is carried out by placing the measured specimen between two temperature controlled plates for a given time.

Steam stability

This test is used to predict fabric relaxation shrinkage when steam pressed in garment manufacture. The WIRA steaming cylinder shown in Figure 154 is used for this purpose.

Measured fabric specimens are supported on a metal frame placed inside a chamber and steamed for a total of 90 seconds, following which the specimens are allowed to condition and are re-measured. Normally shrinkage values of up to 2% and 3% can be considered for woven and knitted fabrics respectively.

Whole garment testing

This method of fabric and garment assessment, in which the garment is washed under controlled conditions in a washing machine, or drycleaned in a commercial drycleaning unit, has much to commend it. Any abnormal dimensional change within and between components, and along seams and within collars can be judged subjectively in addition to the assessment of the dimensions of the re-measured garment.

178

DURABILITY OF FABRICS

Causes of failure:

- flat abrasion
- edge abrasion
- flexing and cracking
- loss of pile
- pilling
- snagging

The degree to which a fabric withstands mechanical action in use may be regarded as one aspect of durability.

Resistance to abrasion

Abrasion may occur on localised areas of a flat surface of the fabric or an edge (e.g. a cuff edge) or fold of a fabric. Coated fabrics are liable to crack if they are flexed repeatedly along the same line, and this may be worse at low temperatures.

Pile fabrics such as corduroys and velvets may show loss of pile if they are abraded on the back since this can drag the pile out if the pile is not bound in very well. Abrasion on the pile surface can also drag out pile or may wear it down. The wear of the pile on carpets is discussed elsewhere.

Abrasion may cause a loss of appearance by disturbing the surface of a fabric, and particularly by causing pilling, as discussed below.

In clothing the durability of a fabric depends to some extent on the use to which the garment is put. Evening wear is normally not required to be in use over very long periods. Children's clothes should last at least as long as they fit the child. Protective clothing such as overalls and men's working clothes, which are subjected to severe use, must be hard-wearing. The way a garment wears out is affected not only by the choice of fibres and fabric, but by the wearer's size and shape, suitability of garment size and style (which affects the tensions and pressures on the fabric), occupation (which governs the preferential wearing out of a garment; for example, a heavily worn right-hand cuff of a desk worker). Examples of specialised wear are: a man's chin rubbing on the knot of his tie; the points of a collar rubbing on particular spots at the front of the shirt; dresses wearing under the arms of an active person.

The factors of concern here are the choice of fibre and fabric. The relative resistance to abrasion of fibres is given on page 19, but obviously the selection of the fibres must be balanced against the other properties required of the fabric. It cannot be emphasised sufficiently that the causes of poor wear are varied and very complicated. For fabrics made from fibres that show a big drop in resistance to abrasion when wet (e.g., triacetate, acetate, and viscose), a certain amount of wear takes place during the rubbing action in laundering. If a fabric becomes damaged and tender in use by the effects of, for example, bleaches in laundering or by excessive exposure to a hot iron or light, this will be reflected in a reduction in abrasion resistance. Mention has already been made of the drop in abrasion resistance of resinated fabrics. Whilst it is very difficult to predict with accuracy the expected life of fabrics in particular applications, it may be useful to make the following observations.

Protective clothing, such as overalls, are often offered with a choice of cotton, nylon, or polyester fibres, or blends of cotton with polyester or nylon. Whilst there is the advantage of easy washability and lightness in weight of overalls made from synthetic fibres, cotton overalls will absorb splashes of liquid and so prevent them from penetrating through to the clothes beneath, whereas lighter fabrics will allow the liquid to pass right through and possibly do some damage.

For outerwear such as coats, overcoats, and rainwear, if warmth is not the criterion, hardwearing fabrics, as for rainwear, are chosen from cotton or cotton polyester blends. Alternatively, if warmth is required, wool is frequently used, sometimes with the addition of polyester fibres. The acrylics, whilst they have a warm handle, are not so hard wearing.

Dresses and blouses made from cotton, polyamide, and polyester fibres are harder-wearing than those made from viscose or triacetate, but these last-named can have great aesthetic appeal and may be appreciably cheaper.

Having become generally aware of the importance of the type of fibre, other features must be considered.

Fibre fineness

If two identical cloths are compared, both of which contain fibres of the same type, but one being made from coarse fibres and the other from fine fibres, it will be found that the fabric from the coarse fibres will have the greater resistance to abrasion. For example, carpets which have to be very hard wearing are made from coarse wool. It must be remembered that fibre fineness influences other fabric properties also, and these must be brought into account when deciding what denier of fibre is to be used in a particular fabric.

Folded yarns

If two apparently identical cloths are offered but one is made from folded yarn instead of single yarn of equivalent size, the fabric made from the folded yarn will be found to withstand rubbing a little longer.

Closeness of threads in the cloth

A cloth that is firmly woven wears longer, since the tighter construction helps to hold the yarns in position and also prevents the fibres from being pulled out by rubbing.

Weave

Twill, satin, and sateen weaves have a preponderance of either warp or weft threads on the face of the cloth; in fact, they may be said to be either warp-faced or weft-faced. If such fabrics are rubbed, it is obvious that the rubbing action is concentrated on one set of threads, whereas in a plain weave of square construction the effects of abrasion are equally shared by both warp and weft threads. Such a fabric will show a more rapid fall in strength in use in one direction than in the other.

Fabric thickness

As might be expected, the thicker the fabric the longer it takes to 'wear'. Thick fabrics, however, are not always convenient because of their bulk and probably their stiffness, but they are frequently used as coatings for reasons of insulation. Generally, such a garment is discarded because it looks shabby rather than because it has worn through.

Pilling

Why do we discard clothing? Generally, a garment is not discarded because a hole has developed or because it is torn, but more often because of loss of appearance. Consequently, in assessing a fabric's durability one has to judge how soon it becomes 'shabby' and unacceptable. Causes of shabbiness are, for example, loss of shape or fit, fading, loss of nap, and pilling. 'Pilling' is the rubbing up of the fibres on the fabric surface into small balls, an unsightly defect that only occurs in fabrics made from spun yarns. See Figure 155.

Fig. 155 Pilled fabric. *(ICI Fibres Ltd.)*

Fabric-to-fabric contact can account for much wear in clothing as inside trouser legs, at the knee, and the inside of sleeves against the body in knitwear. Such abrasion may result in the fabric becoming theadbare, but in fabrics made from spun yarns pilling may develop. The rubbing action eases the fibres to the surface where, instead of being shed or worn-off, the tangled mass is held by a few strong fibres (Figure 155). Wool fabrics sometimes 'pill' but the defect is more pronounced in fabrics containing synthetic fibres. The reason for this is that wool fibres are weaker than the synthetics and consequently such 'pills' as form are readily shed, whereas if some synthetic fibres are present, they serve to anchor the pills to the fabric surface where they become soiled and conspicuous. Blends of strong fibres with weak fibres are, therefore, very prone to pilling. For this reason synthetic fibres are available as special 'low pill' types, which are of lower strength than regular type.

'Pilling' in both woven and knitted fabrics is more severe in open constructions with loosely twisted yarns, since the more firmly twisted the yarn, the less is the chance of the fibres being pulled out. Because the projecting surface hairs facilitate the development of pills it is necessary that they should be removed in finishing. This can be done by cropping the cloth or singeing it, which burns the fibres off or melts the synthetic fibres back. It is possible to reduce the pilling tendency by special finishing techniques.

Assessment of resistance to abrasion and pilling

From the foregoing it is apparent that fabrics are subject to a wide range and combination of types of mechanical action and therefore no one single laboratory test method will forecast precisely resistance to abrasion or 'wear'.

Laboratory tests accelerate the screening of fabrics but the results must be interpreted by experts with caution. Wearer trials, if they are well planned and monitored, provide useful data but are time consuming. A selection of tests will now be outlined to indicate some aspects of testing for durability.

The '*Martindale Abrasion Tester*' conforms to BS 5690. Four specimens are mounted in holders which, facing downwards, rest at an agreed pressure on a fabric abradant. The specimens are abraded as the holders move in a prescribed pattern in all directions. After a certain number of rubs the condition of the specimens is judged from the points of view of loss in weight and change in appearance.

Using the above abrasion tester under agreed conditions and procedure it may be found that a knitted fabric for ladies' and children's outerwear would be acceptable if no breakdown occurs after 20,000 rubs whereas a woven fabric for trousers should show no failure up to say 30,000 rubs. These figures are given for illustration and are not intended to be universally applicable.

The *ICI Pilling Tester* conforms with BS 5811. Woven or knitted specimens are fitted over polyurethane tubes and these tumble about inside rotating cork lined boxes for an agreed number of revolutions according to the nature of the fibre and fabric (Figure 157). The severity of pilling and hairiness is judged and rated against five standard photographs of acrylic

Fig. 156 Martindale abrasion tester. Specimens mounted in downward facing holders which are abraded against standard material. *(James H. Heal)*

Fig. 157 ICI pilling tester. *(Shirley Developments Ltd.)*

Fig. 158 Pilliscope. Tested specimen mounted and viewed under incident light and compared with five standard photographs of either pilled, knitted or pilled woven fabrics. *(Shirley Developments Ltd.)*

double jersey, or woven fabric, under standard viewing conditions, as in the Pilliscope, Figure 158. Most fabrics may be rated at least to the 3–4 level whereas acrylics will be expected to be not less than 2–3 against the photographic rating. (Number 5 rating is the best). The pilled specimens may be rated, however, against standard descriptions of different degrees of pilling.

Snagging

Assessment of fabric snagging

Knitted fabrics composed of textured continuous filament yarn are particularly liable to snag in use. By snagging is meant the catching of a thread on a point or rough surface, so that a short length is pulled out, forming an unsightly loop on the surface, while the adjacent part of the thread is pulled tight and shows as a shiny line in the fabric. Fabric snagging is a serious problem for outerwear.

The susceptibility of the fabric to snagging depends on the yarn type, knitted fabric structure and fabric finish. The ICI 'Mace Snag Tester' provides an accelerated means of predicting fabric snagging. Tubes of fabric mounted over cylinders are exposed to the action of a spiked ball, the 'mace', bouncing on it as it rotates for 600 revs in 10 minutes. The tested samples are compared in a viewing cabinet with photographs covering five standards. Ratings greater than grade three are normally required unless a higher minimum grade of four is required to meet special needs as for some trouser fabrics.

AESTHETIC PROPERTIES

Easy care properties

This expression signifies that the garment or other article does not develop creases easily in use and that the few creases that remain after washing and drying can be easily removed by gentle ironing or pressing.

Previously terms such as 'non-iron', 'drip-dry', 'crease resist' and 'wash and wear' were intended to advertise the easy care characteristics of the garment but these are no longer in use. It is useful, however, to be aware of how current performance standards for cellulosic fibres have arisen.

Resin finishes on cotton and viscose

In 1930, before any of the modern synthetic fibres had been developed, the cellulosic fibres – cotton, viscose, and linen – had the disadvantage of creasing very readily compared with the other natural fibres, wool and silk. It was to remove this deficiency that Tootal Broadhurst Lee Co. Ltd., of Manchester sought, and eventually found, a finish that would give good crease-recovery to the cellulosic fibres. The finish consisted of the application of synthetic resin (urea-formaldehyde) to the fabric.

There have been great developments since then and a wider variety of such finishes are now available. Some of these are particularly suitable for dresses because they do not affect the fastness of the colour to light, or for sheets which are to be subjected to chlorine bleach.

Essentially the process involves the penetration into the fibre of a liquid carrying constituents which combine to form the resin, which makes chemical cross-links between the long-chain molecules. The cross-linking only becomes permanent after the fabric has been baked or, as it is commonly termed, 'cured'. This is often referred to as resin finishing. It is essential for the fabric to be perfectly smooth and flat during curing because the purpose of the cross-linking is to provide the fabric with a 'memory' so that it will return to the smooth flat state that we require. Fabrics so finished show reduced shrinkage in laundering and quicker drying because of reduced moisture absorption.

Unfortunately such finishes sometimes result in undesirable changes in the fabric such as reduced tearing-strength, tensile-strength, and resistance to abrasion. Because of this, finishes are a compromise giving a satisfactory level of crease-recovery while avoiding an excessive deterioration of mechanical properties. The finished fabric may also be more prone to stitching damage (page 302).

In its original form the reduction of abrasion resistance was such that the finish was not applied to many cotton fabrics. Although they also had reduced abrasion resistance, viscose fabrics were improved by the finish in two respects. The fibres of the treated fabrics absorbed less water and, therefore, swelled less. As a result, viscose fabrics, when resinated, show a much reduced shrinkage in laundering. Also, the fall in strength on wetting is much reduced. These benefits made the finish very useful for viscose fabrics which, untreated, show a high shrinkage and a serious fall in strength on wetting. Modern resin finishes have been improved by various additives that reduce sewing damage and a loss of abrasion resistance, tearing-strength, and 'handle', but some loss in abrasion resistance and tearing-strength is still inevitable.

The easy care fabrics, often of cotton or cotton blended with synthetic fibre, are resistant to creasing during laundering with the result that when they are dried they may be smooth enough to be worn, or at most, may require only a touch of the iron. These fabrics have a lower absorption of water than the untreated cloth and, therefore, dry more rapidly. The easy care effect has been achieved by applying the finish under conditions that improve crease-recovery not only when the fabric is dry but also when it is wet.

Some fabric finishes, if inadequately cured and rinsed after processing, may release a 'fishy' smell when the fabric is pressed with an iron, and the cloth may have a harsh handle. This is not now a very common occurrence. Whilst traces of unfixed chemicals are normally removed when the garment is washed for the first time, certain individuals have an allergic response when the new material comes in contact with the skin. An obvious precaution is to wash the new garment first before wearing it.

Soiling during laundering (page 209) may be due to the presence of certain additives which may have been used to improve the fabric handle, but it can be greatly reduced by the use of fluorocarbons. It is worthwhile knowing that some finishes are affected by the presence of bleach in laundering, and others have their effectiveness gradually reduced by constant laundering in the presence of alkali. However, those finishes sensitive to bleach are usually indicated by the instructions on the garment label. A number of new finishes combine effectively with the fibre so that the finish becomes very durable.

Wool and silk

Fabrics made from wool or silk have naturally good recovery from creasing. Their good crease-recovery is illustrated by their use in men's ties, which need to be made from cloth having excellent crease-recovery. This property also makes wool suitable for dress fabrics and suitings which are not to become creased in use; silk similarly provides good recovery from creasing and for this reason was at one time much used for velvets.

Wool fabrics may show creases after wet treatment, but these are generally easily removed by the use of steam and a hot iron.

Synthetic fibres

Many of the manufactured fibres show very good crease-recovery, the best being polyester, acrylic and nylon. These fibres, therefore, can be used for crease-shedding fabrics, either as 100% in fabrics or in blends. Polyester in particular is often blended with cotton to provide good crease-recovery.

The thermoplastic fibres show good easy care characteristics. That is, they will dry without creases or at least require only slight ironing, if washed correctly. 'Correctly' in this case means that they must not be washed at an excessive temperature, put in the spinner after a hot rinse, or left too long spinning. Creases inadvertently introduced into fabrics made from these fibres, while hot, may be set in and become impossible to remove.

Pleats and pressed-in creases

The retention of sharp pleats and intentional pressed-in creases in use and after repeated laundering is also regarded as a major attribute of an easy care garment, and this will now be discussed. Other properties that might be included such as seam pucker, pilling, retention of colour, ease of cleaning and soil release are omitted here since they are dealt with elsewhere in the book.

The capacity for fabric to retain pleats depends primarily on the fibre used, and the choice of method by which pleats and creases are made durable also depends on the fibre type.

Cotton and viscose

Cotton and viscose, as already discussed for easy care fabric, need suitable synthetic resin to be fixed within the fibre, and this is done whilst the smooth fabric is held flat and is passed through a heated zone in the fabric finishing process. The desirable 'springiness' of the resinated fabric does not make it easy to produce garment styles with pleats and flat seams. Garment manufacturers have overcome this by using special high temperature presses which temporarily break the cross-links and then re-form them whilst the fabric is creased or, in the case of seams, held in a flat position.

Alternatively it is possible for the process begun by the cloth finisher to be completed by the garment manufacturer. This may be done in one of two ways. The cross-linking agent applied may be partially fixed by the finisher and finally 'cured' by the garment manufacturer by applying heat for a short time after the garment has been pressed flat and the pleats or creases located. Some clothiers undertaking this process have special ovens installed into which garments are put or through which they pass, hanging on a conveyer. Figure 159 shows trousers passing through such an oven.

Since such a garment will have durable pleats and shaping as required, together with good wet and dry crease-recovery for the fabric as a whole, and good dimensional stability, it is essential for all other components of the garment to have similar performance characteristics. For instance, the interlinings, linings, pocketings, and zip fastener tapes, must be specified. Equally the choice of sewing thread, since the possibility of shrinkage is important at high temperatures, or in washing, when seam puckering will

Fig. 159 Garment curing oven. *(The Spooner Dryer and Engineering Co Ltd.)*

develop. The dyes used, including those for sewing threads, must be fast at temperatures up to 170°C.

Thermoplastic fibres

Thermoplastic synthetic fibres are very suitable for producing durable pleats, which may be introduced:

- by the fabric finisher, who pleats the full fabric length by machine producing, for example, pin pleats;
- by a pleater, who pleats skirt panels before the garment is assembled;
- by the clothing manufacturer when the garment is pressed.

The conditions of temperature and time under which the pleats are introduced, which are adjusted according to the fibre, are very important, since if the process is incorrectly carried out the durability of the pleats in use and in laundering may be unsatisfactory. Here again care is taken to ensure that the dyes used are not sensitive to high temperatures.

Blends

Blending different fibres is used extensively to obtain durable pleating. Well-known combinations are 55% polyester/45% wool, 67% polyester/ 33% cotton, 67% polyester/33% viscose. It will be noticed that a greater percentage of the thermoplastic fibre is required for blending with cotton and viscose than with wool, since the cellulosic fibres have poor pleat-retention, whereas wool can be induced to hold pleats reasonably well.

Of course, if triacetate, which is thermoplastic, is used in a blend instead of polyester, the other properties of that fibre would to some extent be evident. For example, the fabric would have a softer handle, a lower resistance to abrasion, and would be less expensive.

Wool

Wool becomes plastic and mouldable under moist hot conditions. On drying and cooling, the fabric will retain the shape set so long as it is not put in water at still higher temperature. The plastic properties of wool are used in millinery by shaping a flat piece of felt in the form of a hat, and in tailoring when pressing and shaping garments (page 223). Generally, a steam press is used, but in hand-pressing a wet cloth is an essential part of the process in shaping the fabric and introducing pleats and creases. The steam causes the cross-links (disulphide bonds) in wool to break, thus permitting the long-chain molecules to slide past each other and to rejoin in new positions.

Assessment of easy care and pleat retention properties

An objective test for the measurement of the crease recovery of fabrics is given in BS 3086 which is useful for fabric quality control after the application of finishes. However, this test alone does not assess the degree of unwanted creases arising in use. To judge how well the smooth appearance of a fabric is maintained and how soon it recovers after random creasing in use requires a controlled, subjective approach. The surface characteristics of a fabric, the printed pattern, lustre, and texture, can either highlight or subdue the presence of the creases.

'*The recovery from creasing of textile fabrics by measuring the angle of recovery*' BS 3086, requires the folding and creasing of a rectangular specimen, measuring 15 × 15 mm, under a fixed load for five minutes. The specimen is then carefully transferred and mounted in a crease recovery tester which enables the crease recovery angle to be measured after 5 minutes (Figure 160).

The assessment of the dry fabric must include flat specimens from both cloth directions, tested by folding the fabric face in and face out. The significance of this is that a warp faced fabric, for instance, will have different levels of recovery according to the way it is folded. A value of 180° would indicate complete recovery from creasing, but in practice in this test a recovery greater than 120° for lightweight fabrics would be acceptable. Different results would be obtained on fabric in the wet state.

Normally tests are carried out at 65 ± 2% relative humidity and 20 ± 2°C, but investigations into the behaviour of fabric are sometimes required at 90% relative humidity. Limp, thick fabric, and fabrics with a tendency to curl, may require a different method of assessment to interpret the results.

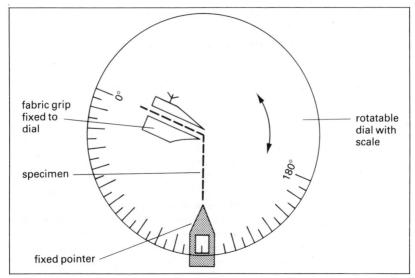

fabric grip
fixed to
dial

specimen

fixed pointer

rotatable
dial with
scale

0°

180°

Fig. 160 Crease recovery tester. The free 'limb' of the specimen is kept vertical, in line with the pointer, by rotating the dial. Crease recovery angle is read off the scale at the pointer.

A *subjective procedure for the assessment of easy care* fabric after repeated home laundering is given in Test Method AATCC* 124, 'The smoothness appearance of textile materials after household wash'. Specimens measuring 38 × 38 cm are washed under defined conditions in a washing machine together with a fixed dummy load of fabric, followed by either line or tumble drying of the specimens. The selected washing and drying cycles are repeated as required, and the specimens, after conditioning, are rated against a set of three-dimensional plastic replicas of graded creased fabric under standard lighting and viewing conditions. Usually more than one observer rates the specimens independently. Grade 1 represents the poorest appearance and successive higher grades denote increasing fabric smoothness.

The *appearance and retention of pressed-in creases* in easy care garments after laundering can be assessed according to Test Method AATCC 88C. The required creases are inserted in the middle of prepared 38 × 38 cm specimens according to the manufacturing procedure in use for the particular fabric and garment. Similar washing and drying methods are followed as outlined above. Finally the appearance of the specimen crease is rated against a graduated set of five standard photographs showing different levels of crease retention. The specimen and standard are mounted vertically and viewed under controlled lighting conditions.

Appearance of seams after repeated home laundering is discussed on page 304.

* *American Association of Textile Chemists & Colorists.*

Handle and drape

The term 'handle' applied to a textile fabric means the sum total of the sensation experienced when it is handled; by touching, flexing in the fingers, smoothing, and so on. The more important of these sensations are those of thickness, softness (or hardness), stiffness (or pliability), and roughness (or smoothness).

Thickness

The thickness of a fabric may be measured easily, but the measurement must be done at known pressures if it is to have any significance, since most textiles are readily compressible.

The thickness of a fabric is dependent on its mass per unit area, the type of yarns used and the weave or knitted structure, and the finish. Hard twisted yarns and plain weave give relatively thin cloths, whereas soft twisted yarns and bulked yarns and looser structures give thicker cloths. For especially thick cloths, constructions such as cellular leno, honeycomb, or velvet may be used. Finishing treatments that apply pressure to the cloth, such as calendering, decrease thickness. Raising and brushing increase thickness.

Apart from its relation to cloth handle, thickness is a factor of prime importance in regard to the protection a fabric will afford against cold conditions; that is, its 'warmth'.

Softness

Softness here is not pliability but ease of compression. 'Hardness' is the opposite to 'softness', and the range from very soft cloths to very hard cloths is considerable. At one extreme are fabrics such as raised blankets, brushed knitted nylon fabrics, and towards the other are filled and calendered materials. Construction features favouring softness are the use of softly twisted yarns, textured yarns, and loose or bulky fabric structures. Certain finishing agents that in effect lubricate, enhance softness. Fabric softness is a property affecting comfort of clothing against the skin.

Stiffness

The stiffness of a fabric is defined as its resistance to bending. Simple methods are available for measuring this quantity in the laboratory.

The constructional features affecting the stiffness of a cloth are mainly its mass, the nature of the fibres, fibre fineness, and the compactness or density of the weave. Weaves such as twills and satins, in which the yarns are only loosely bound, provide limper fabrics than more tightly bound plain weaves. Knitted fabrics are therefore much less stiff than woven fabrics. Fabrics made from fibres that have a high resistance to extension, such as linen, tend to be stiffer than fabrics made from fibres such as wool, which are easily extended.

The stiffness of a fabric is also dependent to a high degree on the finishing treatment it has received. Finishes that tend to compact the cloth or make the fibres adhere promote an increase in stiffness. Among such finishes are calendering, embossing, and schreinering, since they all involve the application of pressure and a reduction of thickness. The addition of finishing agents such as starch, dextrin, or synthetic resins will bind the fibres together and so increase the stiffness of the cloth. These substances are commonly used for this purpose. On the other hand, it is possible to reduce the cohesion of the fibres and the friction between them by the use of suitable softeners which act as lubricants, and also by suitable mechanical treatment of the cloth. The finisher, in fact, has a variety of means at his disposal for changing the stiffness of a fabric and indeed for improving its 'handle' in other respects also. Lamination of, say, two rather thin limp fabrics increases fabric stiffness in excess of the sum of the individual fabric stiffnesses.

Drape

Different fabrics may drape limply like some jersey fabrics, stiffly like taffeta, organza and canvas, in soft graceful folds such as chiffon, or with a richer effect like brocade. All these aspects of drape are appreciated by the eye. A complete description of the diverse draping effects possible in textiles and their causes has not been made, but it may be stated that two factors, stiffness and weight, are of the first importance. While the weight of the fabric provides the force causing it to drape, the stiffness provides the resistance. Thus, a stiff but heavy fabric may drape similarly to a limp but light fabric. It has also been shown that the manner in which a fabric drapes depends not only on the stiffness of the cloth but also on the resistance of the cloth to distortion by change of the angle between the yarns, and the ease with which the cloth may be extended. For these reasons compact fabrics such as taffeta, which has a high resistance to distortion, have a quality of drape that might be described as papery in appearance, compared with the drape of a fabric such as a voile, which has a low resistance to distortion.

Fabrics differ considerably also in their recovery from bending, silk being obviously more elastic than cotton. As a generalisation, it may be said that the more elastic fabrics tend to drape more gracefully than the less elastic fabrics.

Smoothness and roughness

Smoothness and roughness are terms much used in descriptions of fabric handle, but they cover a variety of sensations and are not precisely defined. Cloths may be rough because of an irregular surface arising from the weave employed, such as the crêpe weave; from the irregular nature of the yarns, particularly slub yarns; from the presence of coarse fibres, and so on. Smooth cloths may be obtained by using a regular weave, particularly with long floats such as the satin weaves, and smooth regular yarns such as gassed two-fold cotton yarns, or continuous filament yarns.

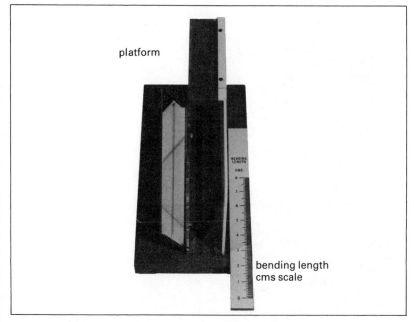

Fig. 161 Cantilever stiffness tester showing scale adjacent to instrument.
(Shirley Developments Ltd.)

Smooth fabrics are produced by using continuous filament yarn in tricot fabrics. Finishing treatments such as calendering and schreinering also confer smoothness.

It should not be assumed that smoothness is always a desirable quality. In fabrics such as hand-woven tweeds, roughness of the right kind may be considered an asset.

Assessment of fabric stiffness, drape and surface friction

Tests for these properties are not routinely included in performance specifications, but serve as useful means of investigation and quality control for certain fabric properties.

BS 3356 describes a method for the determination of stiffness of cloth. A specimen of a given size is placed on the horizontal platform, and a rule marked in 'bending length units' in centimetres is positioned on top. The rule and fabric are together slid forward until the specimen overhanging the platform aligns with two lines engraved at an angle below the horizontal. From the position of the scale projecting from the platform the measurement of the length of fabric (in bending length units) to bend to this fixed angle can be read off. It is one factor contributing to the fabric's draping characteristics. Measurements are made in both directions of the fabric. Flexural rigidity (g/cm^3), that is the stiffness of the fabric or

193

Fig. 162 Fabric drape tester.
(Shirley Developments Ltd.)

resistance to bending in each direction, is calculated from the bending lengths and mass/unit area in g/m^2 of the fabric.

'The assessment of fabric drape', BS 5058 provides a means of quantifying the multi-directional curvature of a circular specimen supported centrally between two discs. The specimen is allowed to drape under its own weight. By means of a light source and a mirror, a shadow of the draped

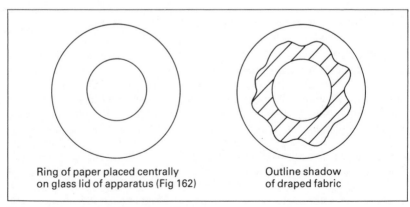

Ring of paper placed centrally on glass lid of apparatus (Fig 162)

Outline shadow of draped fabric

Fig. 163 Assessment of drape coefficient.

specimen is cast on a ring of paper, of the same diameter as the specimen placed centrally on the glass lid above the specimen. The outline of the shadow is traced on the paper, which is of known mass. The paper is cut along the trace, and the inner part representing the shadow is weighed. The 'Drape Coefficient %', is calculated as the ratio of this mass to the mass of the paper, expressed as a percentage.

The concept of such surface properties as fabric smoothness and roughness is very complex and difficult to define. However, specially designed sophisticated Japanese* laboratory apparatus for the measurement of surface roughness and surface friction is available. These are currently used in the study of fabric handle and tailorability.

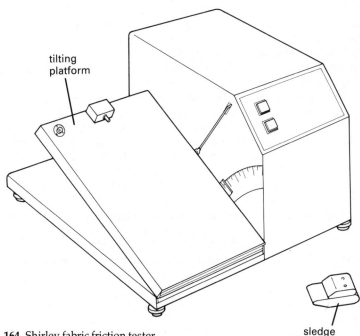

Fig. 164 Shirley fabric friction tester.
(Shirley Developments Ltd.)

sledge

A simple practical approach to the assessment of fabric friction is obtained on the apparatus illustrated in Figure 164 which conforms with BS 3434. The specimen is mounted on a sledge and placed in position on a horizontal platform covered with standard friction fabric. The platform is tilted slowly at a fixed speed and, when the fabric covered sledge begins to slide, the angle is read on a scale.

* *Dr S. Kawabata – KES-F Instruments, Japan.*

Lustre

The influence of fibre and yarn properties and type of weave on lustre has already been mentioned. Cloth finishing also plays an important part in the development or control of fabric lustre in both woven and knitted fabrics. Most of the finishes applied to produce lustre may be described as mechanical, since they usually depend upon the application of heat and pressure to a damp fabric. This is somewhat similar to ironing, where surface irregularities are smoothed out. Under hot, damp conditions the fabric becomes plastic and responds to the mechanical pressure applied. Such processes do not depend on chemical finishing, where an interaction occurs between the chemicals and the fibres in the fabric.

Mechanical finishes are not always durable, but durable effects may be obtained in fabrics made from thermoplastic fibres which are heat-set to achieve the desired effect. Fabrics made from hydrophilic fibres lose their surface appearance or lustre fairly easily in water unless they are assisted by the use of a chemical finish or resin.

Fabrics made from wool are sometimes required to have a sheen, and this can be achieved by having the surface fibres, nap, or pile, laid smoothly in one direction and flattened. Doeskins and superfines are fabrics which exhibit an attractive lustre. 'Blowing', which is essentially the blowing of stream through a firmly wound roll of wool fabric, results in the flattened surface of the fabric developing a lustre. Special machines have, however, been designed for giving an increased lustre to woollen fabric. In order to stabilise the fabric appearance in use and in steam pressing, wool fabrics may be chemically treated to set the fabric and help maintain its appearance.

Calendering of fabrics – the passing of the fabric between a heated metal roller and a less hard non-metal roller surface – has been extensively used. The operation of the heated cylinders at various pressures and relative speeds can produce a wide range of effects. In 'friction calendering', the fabric passes between a pair of rollers rotating at different speeds, and the fabric is not only flattened but also polished. One of the essentials in calendering cloth is to avoid flattening it so much that it feels like paper and loses its characteristic fabric appearance. The flattening and lustre effect is only durable if, in the case of fabric made from hydrophilic fibres, a chemical finish is applied to prevent the fibres from swelling and returning to their natural state when washed. Resin finishes are employed for this purpose. Starch fillings, which are sometimes used to enhance the smoothness and crisp handle of the fabric, can only be regarded as a temporary finish. Calendering fabrics made from thermoplastic fibres produces a durable effect and, in some instances, the process is used to close up the fabric and reduce the fabric porosity, as is required in polyester cloth for sails. At the same time, the fabric looks more opaque. Opacity of very sheer fabrics made from nylon or polyester fibre is sometimes a fabric requirement, and some form of calendering may be used to achieve this.

A different type of lustre is achieved by Schreinering, which consists of impressing parallel lines on the fabric surface by means of a roller engraved with about 150 lines per centimetre. These lines can easily be seen if viewed through a magnifying glass; they increase the lustre of the fabric by controlling the directions in which the light is reflected.

Ciré fabrics come into popularity from time-to-time. These fabrics are often in a satin weave, which is waxed and then calendered, producing a brilliant lustre. Sometimes fabrics with a very high lustre such as vinyl-coated fabrics have been called 'ciré', but this is an inaccurate description.

Beetling is a mechanical finishing process which may be applied to linen fabric. The fabric is wound into a large smooth roll and large heavy wooden 'hammers' are automatically lifted and dropped continuously on the rotating roll of fabric beneath. This flattens the fabric and imparts a lustre.

The use of mercerisation to impart lustre to cotton sewing threads has already been mentioned. The finish is also an important one for certain cotton fabrics, particularly poplins and satins. The cloth is treated with a strong cold solution of caustic soda while under high tension, which is not released until the caustic soda has been washed off. This treatment produces a very high lustre in fabrics of suitable construction, and the effect is quite permanent.

Colour fastness

An aspect of fabrics which is always of interest is how fast the colour is. In use, textiles may be subject to a wide range of agencies such as daylight, washing, drycleaning, perspiration, sea water, rubbing, and hot pressing. These can affect the colour in different ways. Some dyes may be fast to washing and drycleaning but not to daylight. Other dyes may be fast to perspiration and rubbing when wet, but not so fast to hot pressing, and so on.

There is a wide variety of different types or classes of synthetic dyes, each with a range of colours. Information is available on the behaviour, under various conditions of use, of each synthetic dye that is manufactured. This information is provided by dyestuff manufacturers, who carry out exhaustive tests on their products. The dyeing of the fabric must, therefore, be carried out with the probable end use of the fabric in mind, since apart from achieving the desired colour on the fibre, it is necessary to select dyes which have the degree and type of colour fastness required for the intended application, be it evening wear, swimwear, children's wear, curtains or carpets.

Sometimes information is supplied with the fabric, indicating that it is 'colour fast'. This may mean that the colour is particularly fast to one agency, but it does not necessarily mean that it is fast under all conditions of use. It is usually more expensive to obtain fast colours. Home dyeing methods are, of course, quite simple, and it cannot be expected that the dyes used will give an all-round high level of colour fastness.

Tests for the assessment of colour fastness of textiles

The fastness tests which are of particular interest to the textile user are those for fastness to:

burnt gas fumes – exposure to oxides of nitrogen
carpet shampoo
chlorinated water, as in swimming pools
daylight, under dry and humid conditions
drycleaning with a range of organic solvents
perspiration, acid and alkaline, for linings and clothing worn close to the skin
dry heat, as in fusing interlinings or other processes
hot pressing in damp, wet or dry states
rubbing (ie "crocking") in dry and wet state
sea water
washing at various levels of severity
water, as when wet coloured articles are left in a pile.

Whilst there is a long list of agencies to which coloured fabrics and leathers may be exposed, only certain appropriate tests are carried out on a particular fabric intended for a particular end use.

Standard methods of test to evaluate the colour fastness of textiles are published by the Society of Dyers and Colourists,* the International Standards Organisation, and in BS 1006† and these are essential for the professional assessment of colour fastness.

The principles of colour fastness testing will be briefly outlined, and a simple non-standard practical approach to some tests will be given. Where appropriate the test requires that the specimen of a given size be either brought into contact with, or be sandwiched between, standard pieces of white cloth. The test is then carried out by subjecting the specimen to synthetic perspiration, brine, heat, or washing, as the case may be. At the end of the test two observations may be made. One is the change in shade of the specimen, and the other is the degree of staining of the white fabric with which it was in contact. It is difficult to estimate the extent to which the changes have taken place without the aid of the 'grey scales', referred to below, which are obtainable from the BSI and SDC (Figure 165).

Change in colour – use of grey scales

To assess change in colour, specimens of the cloth before and after testing are compared against a 'grey scale' consisting of five pairs of grey colour chips. Each pair represents a different level of contrast, and bears a fastness rating. Fastness rating number 5 is represented on the scale by

* SDC, Perkin House, Grattan Road, Bradford, BD1 1JB.
† British Standards 1006, 'Methods of test for colour fastness of textiles and leather'.

Fig. 165 Grey scales for use in colour fastness testing: assessment of
(A) shade change, (B) degree of staining.
(ICI Colours and Fine Chemicals, Manchester)

two identical neutral grey chips mounted side by side. This, of course, represents no change in colour between the tested specimen and the original material. An identical reference chip is used for each rating Nos. 4 to 1, and these are paired with successively lighter neutral grey chips until the colour difference for rating 1 provides the greatest contrast. It is necessary to make these comparisons under standard lighting conditions. The specimen is rated according to the rating on the grey scale with which it corresponds. If the difference in colour between the specimen before and after testing lies between two contrasts on the scale, the specimen is given the intermediate assessment: 2–3 for example.

Staining

A different 'grey scale' from that described above is required to assess the degree of staining. The scale consists of one pair of white and four pairs of grey and white colour chips. The white pair is rated No. 5 and is equivalent to no staining having occurred. Nos. 4 to 1 have progressively darker neutral grey chips which correspond to increased staining, No. 1 being the most heavily stained. The conditions for comparing the specimen with the scale are similar to that outlined above.

Fastness to light

Colour fastness to light may be tested by prolonged exposure to daylight or, more rapidly, by exposure to a suitable artificial source of light.

Both methods, as standardised by the British Standards Institution, are based on a comparison of the shade change in a specimen of the cloth under test, with the shade changes occurring in a set of eight standard blue-dyed wool fabrics exposed simultaneously to the same source of light. The standards are dyed to provide eight levels of light fastness ranging from fugitive to very fast and are numbered in order 1–8. No. 1 is the most fugitive and each standard is approximately twice as fast as the previous one in the series.

It is obviously more convenient to conduct this test under the reproducible and reliable conditions provided by an artificial source of light. Such a source is provided by the Xenon arc lamp that has been developed for this purpose, and which provides light of sufficient intensity and a spectral distribution that mimics the effect of daylight acceptably.

For a test using the Xenon arc lamp specimens under test and the set of blue-dyed standards, all measuring 5 cm × 1 cm, are mounted on a metal support and covered by an opaque mask as shown in Fig. 166b, the central

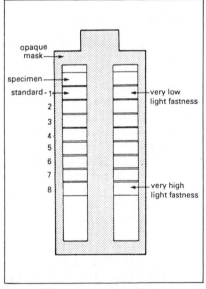

Fig. 166a Light fastness tester, showing test specimens and standard fabrics mounted on inside of cylindrical chamber
(James H. Heal)

Fig. 166b Specimen and eight blue-dyed standards mounted under an opaque' mask, revealing exposed portions (according to BS1006).

200

portions of all being shielded on the inside of a cylindrical chamber at the centre of which is the arc lamp, Fig. 166a. The specimens and the standards are inspected at intervals during the exposure, according to a routine described in BS 1006, in order to observe the development of fading by comparisons made between the exposed and masked parts of the specimens. The development of fading in the standards is used, in effect, to standardise the degree of exposure to which the specimens have been submitted. The result of this assessment of light fastness is expressed by reference to the number of the standard which is the nearest equivalent to the specimen in respect of rate of fading. If the result falls between two standards it may be expressed as 3½, for example, but finer divisions are not permitted. For curtains to be hung at windows a light fastness of 6–7 is desirable, and it should certainly never be less than 5. Some dyed or printed fabrics fade more rapidly in humid rather than dry conditions, and this may be important for curtains where heavy condensation may occur at windows. Provision is made in the apparatus for tests to be made at high or low humidity.

Daylight testing is a rather slow method of determining the level of colour fastness, because of the variability of natural light according to location and climatic conditions. It is necessary for the specimens to be protected by glass covers from the weather, soiling and fumes. Specimens and the standards are mounted on an exposure rack, (in the northern hemisphere, south facing) sloping at an angle to the horizontal equal to the latitude of the site.

Colour fastness to all the elements of weather is of interest for textiles used for awnings, for example, and for this purpose specimens may be exposed to weathering in open-air sites without any protection. The results are obviously influenced by local conditions such as degree and nature of air pollution, and climatic conditions during the test period.

Fastness to hot pressing

Change in colour due to hot pressing of the fabric can be either temporary or permanent, and the degree of colour change depends on the temperature and whether the pressing is carried out in the dry, damp, or wet states.

Many disperse dyes used on synthetic fibres are liable, on exposure to heat, to vaporise directly from a solid state. This is referred to as the 'sublimation' of the dyestuff. The risk is that the released dye may be absorbed by and stain adjacent materials, and this may also be accompanied by a change in shade of the original colour. Apart from heat applied with the hand iron, heat is applied in the processing of coloured textiles and clothing, in fusing embroideries and interlinings, and transfer printing, for example. Special testers are available for sublimation and stability to heat.

For general fastness to hot pressing a simple approach to testing could be as follows:

Procedure. A specimen measuring 10×4 cm and five pieces of suitable undyed bleached fabric, of suitable fibre content, each measuring 14×4 cm are required. The temperature of the hand iron should be at a setting suited to the fabric. The temperature of the iron may be checked by observing the behaviour of crystals such as m-hydrobenzoic acid, which has a melting point of 200°C, citric acid 153°C, or benzoic acid 122°C, on the heated undersurface of the iron. Alternatively, temperature-indicating thermopapers may be used.

Dry pressing. The specimen is positioned on a dry cotton cloth and the iron placed on top for 15 seconds.

Damp pressing. Place the dry specimen on a piece of the dry white cloth. Soak another piece of the white cloth in water and squeeze out the excess water. After positioning the wet cloth on the specimen, place the iron on top and move it to and fro for 15 seconds.

Wet pressing. Place a piece of the dry white cloth on the ironing board and on top of this first put the wet specimen and then a piece of wet cloth, both having been soaked in water and squeezed. Place the iron on top and move it to and fro for 15 seconds.

In each of the three tests the recommended weight for the iron is such as to give a pressure of 30 g/cm^2, and in use no extra pressure should be applied.

The colour change in each specimen is assessed immediately after pressing, and 4 hours later, to allow a dyestuff which has changed colour on heating to revert to its original shade on cooling. When upper and lower white cloths are used, the degree of staining is assessed on the piece that is the most heavily stained.

Fastness to rubbing

This test determines the degree to which colour may be transferred from one coloured fabric surface to another, and this may be aggravated if the fabric is wet. The fabric under consideration may have been dyed in yarn or fabric form, or may have been printed.

For this test the apparatus known as the 'Crockmeter'* is used. The method is to rub one specimen, about 10 cm long, with a dry white cotton cloth, and rub a second specimen with a wet cloth. The white cloth is fixed over a wooden finger on the apparatus and this rubs the specimen underneath it ten times in 10 seconds. Separate tests are made by rubbing the cloth in each direction, i.e. length and widthways. The amount of staining, wet and dry, is rated against the grey scales.

If such apparatus is not available, it is useful to imitate the test by holding a piece of white cloth over the forefinger and, bearing in mind the procedure outlined above, carry out 'the test' in this way. The downward force of the finger in the apparatus is 900 g.

---

* *Obtainable from Shirley Developments Ltd.*

Fig. 167 'Gyrowash' showing stainless steel pots, each containing a test specimen in a wash liquor. The sealed pots are rotated in the temperature controlled vessel. (*James H. Heal*)

Fastness to washing

Some deeply coloured textiles, hand towels, for instance, carry a label advising that the article should be washed separately to begin with. The risk with these and other articles is that some of the dye may be 'loose' and the wash liquor may become coloured and the dye redeposited on other articles or white trims on the garment itself. Printed fabrics can end up with the dark colours being transferred to the lighter areas. The risk of staining is further increased if such coloured textiles are left in a heap whilst wet.

Fastness to washing tests, according to BS 1006, may be carried out in the 'Shirley' Autowash or 'Heal's' Girowash (Figure 167).

Each specimen is sandwiched between pieces of the prescribed undyed fabric, the composite specimen is stitched together, inserted in the wash liquor in the pot, which is automatically rotated to agitate the specimen under controlled temperature throughout the test. Following the test the composite specimen is separated, dried, and assessed against the grey scales for the degree of colour fastness and staining of the undyed fabrics.

Five test procedures of different severities are available, each relating to the laundry conditions required for different groups of fibres. Test No. 1 is the mildest and uses a soap solution as in hand-washing. The methods are progressively more severe. No. 5 is an extremely severe test suitable for cotton only; No. 3 is regarded as a severe test for wool textiles but as an intermediate test for cellulose.

The apparatus illustrated in Figure 167 is also used for the colour fastness testing of textiles in dry-cleaning solvents.

A simple approach to colour fastness in washing, (which does not conform with the standard test methods), is to take a specimen measuring 10 × 4 cm and place it between one piece of undyed cotton and one piece of undyed wool fabric, each measuring 5 × 4 cm. Sew through the three thicknesses, following the edges of the undyed cloth. The undyed fabrics should be wettable. Standard fabrics for this purpose may be obtained from the SDC.

Heat a beaker containing a soap solution of 5 g per litre to 40 ± 2°C. The volume of soap solution in the beaker in ml should be 50 times the weight in grammes of the composite specimen; that is, a specimen weighing 2 g must have 100 ml of solution. Put the specimen in this and maintain the temperature for 30 minutes. Ideally, the specimen should be agitated all the time, but if this is not possible, stir at intervals. Rinse the specimen in running cold tap water for about 10 minutes and then squeeze it. Remove the stitching along one short side and two long sides and open it out. Hang up the specimen to dry with the three parts touching only at the line of stitching. When the specimen is dry, the staining of the undyed cloth is assessed against the appropriate grey scale, and the uncovered portion of the specimen assessed for colour change.

Fastness to water, perspiration, sea water and chlorinated water

It has already been mentioned that if wet coloured textiles are left in a heap, dyed areas can stain other fabric with which they are in contact. A test for showing whether a fabric is likely to 'bleed' is available and is similar to that used for perspiration and sea water and chlorinated water testing, except that water is used instead of artificial perspiration, salt solution, or sodium hypochlorite solution.

A simplified procedure is, as before, to sandwich the specimen between undyed cloth, but here the composite specimen is wetted with the appropriate liquid and kept between two glass plates, under pressure, for 4 hours at body temperature (37°C). The method of drying and assessment is as in fastness to washing.

Generally, a minimum rating of 4 for both shade change and staining is required in performance specifications, where these tests and the wash tests conform with British Standards procedures.

Other aspects of colour

Photochromic effect

Certain dyes may have their colour modified on exposure to light. If the colour reverts to the original when the fabric is stored in darkness, it is said to be 'photochromic'.

Photo-chemical degradation

This describes the chemical damage 'tendering', (page 18) that can occur in fabric as a result of the action of light on some fibres. The presence of certain dyes can aggravate the rate of 'light tendering'. In its most dramatic form parts of a printed curtain fabric associated with a particular colour thus affected will fall into holes. This behaviour is well understood and fabrics intended for curtains are unlikely to show this fault.

Polyester is used for net curtains rather than nylon because of its greater resistance to the action of light behind glass. The difference between the two fabrics is not so marked in direct exposure. The explanation is that polyester is more sensitive than nylon to ultraviolet wavelengths which are filtered out by the glass.

Metameric effect

Certain dyes show the effect known as metamerism, that is the apparent shade of the coloured textile depends very noticeably on the lighting used. It is important, therefore, that dyes are selected which do not exhibit this effect. Metamerism is discussed under 'Colour and Colour Matching'.

Colour and colour matching

Reference has been made earlier to colour fastness and tests for colour fastness with the unwritten assumption that everyone understands what 'colour' is. Colour is a sensation, experienced by an individual and is not communicable in words; that is, it is not possible to know that the sensation of 'green' is the same for all of us, although we can all, with the exception of a few with defective colour vision, agree on what things are 'green'. However, we do now know a great deal about how the sensation of colour arises and it is possible to make measurements on coloured cloths, for example, that will indicate quite sensitively to what extent, if at all, they exhibit perceptible colour differences, and it is possible to standardise colours in numerical terms, so that it is possible to indicate precisely what colour a cloth is to be dyed.

Artists and scientist alike agree that there are three essential aspects of colour, although they are not always referred to in the same terms. They are 'hue', 'saturation' and 'lightness'. The hue of a colour is denoted in common language by the words, red, yellow, green, etc. Saturation refers to the degree to which the hue is diluted (mixed) with white. Thus saturated colours are 'strong' or 'pure'; when white is added they become 'unsaturated' and might be described as 'pastels'. Lightness may be described as the inverse of 'greyness' and shows a range from 'bright' to 'dark'.

Specification of colour

The methods used to specify colour by instrumental means depend on the fact that most colours can be reproduced by a mixture, in the correct proportions, of three primary colours. Such a mixture can reproduce hue, saturation and lightness. There are two types of instrument that may be used for identifying the colour of a dyed fabric, and deriving a specification for it in numerical terms, these are the 'spectrophotometer' and the 'tristimulus colorimeter'. The first measures the reflectance of the fabric for light in each part of the spectrum. The second measures the reflectance of the fabric for each of three or four different colours of light. The results of both systems are expressed in the same way, as three 'chromaticity co-ordinates' (also known as 'trichromatic coefficients'). Two of these numbers taken together specify the hue and saturation of the colour and the third its lightness.

Application of instrumental measurements of colours

By quoting the chromaticity co-ordinates a dyer can be given objective, unambiguous instructions as to the colour to which a fabric is to be dyed, and by putting tolerances on these values the degree of departure from the required colour can be reduced to a level at which it will be of no practical consequence.

It is now possible to feed the specification of a colour to a computer which has in store a large quantity of data on dyestuffs and their behaviour on different fabrics, and which from this information can specify a suitable mixture of dyestuffs to provide the required shade on a given cloth. Even if this does not provide a completely accurate match at the first attempt any necessary adjustment is small, and the saving of time and expense on trial and error methods is considerable.

It should be noted that, in choosing a suitable recipe for dyeing, various factors, besides the required shade, must be taken into account. These include, for example, the required levels of fastness to light, washing, etc. and the fibre composition of the cloth. If the cloth contains more than one type of fibre, it is important that each should dye to the same shade, unless a cross-dyeing effect is required.

The instruments used for colour measurement can now measure differences in colour that are too small to be perceptible. Being so highly sensitive they are very useful for checking deliveries of cloth for conformity with the desired shade, and measuring any differences there may be between pieces in the same delivery, or any variation in a piece along or across its length. If there is any variation between pieces, instrumental measurement enables the pieces to be sorted into lots according to shade, to avoid the possibility of a garment being made up with panels perceptibly different. For this purpose, it is important to know what differences in chromaticity co-ordinates (which as stated above define the colour) correspond to differences perceptible to the eye. This is a topic on which much work has been done and on which there is now some good information.

Another application is in testing for colour fastness, where the instruments may be used in refining on the subjective use of the grey scales, to indicate the nature of any colour change and its magnitude.

A comparison of the two types of instruments that are available for colour measurement shows that while colorimeters are used to the best advantage for shade sorting where the purpose is to match shades of the same colour, spectrophotometers will be used for the identification of dyes and for the formulation of dye recipes, and can also be used for shade sorting.

Subjective colour matching

The use of instrumental means for colour measurement implies a reasonably large establishment with trained personnel. Otherwise subjective means will be employed. This requires experienced observers who have normal colour vision (for which tests* are available) and standardised conditions for viewing and illumination. The conditions of illumination are important because samples that match accurately in daylight, may not be an adequate match in artificial light. This is known as metamerism and is discussed below.

For accurate matching more than one observer should be used; the matching should preferably be done under more than one kind of light (because of the possibility of metamerism) including point-of-sale lighting, tungsten and north daylight, and the surroundings should not be glossy or coloured. Viewing cabinets are available that provide good conditions of viewing and illumination.

Metamerism

The behaviour known as 'metamerism' described above is important because it can lead to such disasters as, for example, choosing an evening dress and accessories in daylight and finding that they do not match in artificial light. It occurs when samples that are required to match have been dyed with different mixtures of dyes. The colour compositions of daylight, tungsten light (the light of ordinary electric lamps) and the light of fluorescent tubes are different, and consequently the colour of a fabric depends on the source of the light in which it is viewed. However, the colour in any particular type of light depends on the reflectivity of the cloth for the different parts of the spectrum; unfortunately, individual dyes do not all change colour in the same way when seen in different lights. Thus, a mixture of dyes may match when seen in daylight but may be quite obviously different when viewed by artificial light. It is for this reason that

---

* *'Ishihara' Test consisting of a series of coloured plates.*

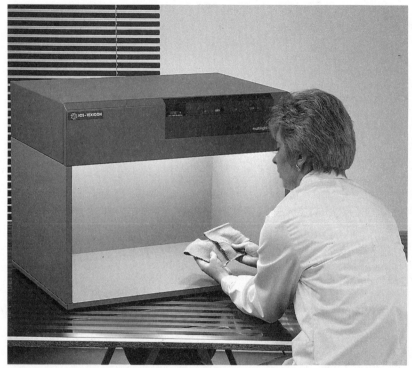

Fig. 168 Colour assessment lighting cabinet with four different light sources (BS950). *(Instrumental Colour Systems – Texicon)*

colour matching should be done by making the comparisons under more than one type of illuminant. Many large retailers standardise the lighting in their stores to approximate daylight more closely.

Colour Atlases

A colour atlas is a collection of coloured patterns arranged systematically. 'Patterns' may be interpreted variously. In the Munsell Atlas painted plastic chips are used, the Methuen Handbook contains printed colour plates. Each pattern is therefore an objective example of a particular colour and is identified by a number. If it is required to identity and specify the colour of a particular sample of, say, cloth, it may be compared with the patterns of the colour atlas. The pattern that matches the sample is then used to identify, by the number of the pattern, the colour of the cloth. This number can then be used to specify and communicate the colour to, say, a dyer if it is required to have a new batch dyed to this shade. Well-known atlases suitable for textile work are the Munsell Colour Atlas, the Methuen Handbook of Colour, and the ICI Colour Atlas, but there are many others.

Soiling

The soiling of fabrics is a universal nuisance which leads to a considerable expenditure on laundering and dry cleaning. Laundering itself is liable to cause some deterioration of the fabric, some shrinkage, and some fading of colours. The amount of dirt in the air greatly affects the rate of soiling, and those who live in industrial regions of the country know how difficult it is to keep a collar clean for a whole day. Fortunately, since the 'Clean Air Act' has been in operation the atmosphere is clearer and brighter.

It has been noticed that some fabrics soil more rapidly than others, and interest has developed in the possibilities of discovering fibres and finishes that will discourage soiling, and make cleaning easier. Research is in progress on the following aspects of the problem:

The nature of the soil

The words 'soil' or 'dirt' cover a range of substances which may contaminate fabrics. Some of the dirt, particularly the dirt found on garments, contains greasy substances; air-borne contamination contains black particles of carbon and tarry substances put into the air when coal is burnt; tobacco smoke contains yellow tarry substances, and so on. When it is known what are the important substances in dirt, it will be possible to understand how they become attached to the different types of fibre and fabric. Figure 169 is a photograph showing greasy dirt on the surface and in the crevices between the fibres.

The mechanism of soiling

Fabrics of open structure will allow the air to pass through, and the dirt may be filtered out. A good illustration of this is found in a skirt hem, which is often cleaner than the remainder of the fabric because, being of double thickness, it does not allow the air to pass through so easily. It must be noted, however, that even if they soil more easily, open fabrics are often easier to launder. The pick-up of dirt from dirty surfaces occurs much more readily if the fabric is rough or hairy. Hence, fabrics made smooth by starching and ironing stay clean longer. A fabric with a hairy surface may look heavily soiled when, in fact, only a small amount of dirt has been picked up. But, being concentrated on the surface fibres, it produces a noticeably dirty appearance.

A static charge on a fabric will attract dirt, and soil acquired in this way becomes very firmly attached. Triacetate, polyester, nylon, and acrylic fibres develop static charges by rubbing in use and retain them for a long time. Therefore, they are particularly liable to become soiled in this way. Giving these fabrics a final rinse in a suitable wetting agent such as 'Stergene' helps to increase the rate of loss of static charges and hence decrease the rate of soiling. (Such a treatment would, of course, seriously impair a water-repellent finish.) Dirt may even be picked up during laundering or dry cleaning. In an unsuitable or heavily soiled solution dirt

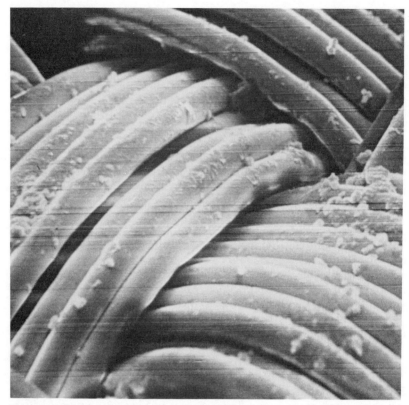

Fig. 169 Soiled nylon fabric as seen by the scanning electron-microscope.
(Dr J. Sikorski.)

may be redeposited after having been initially removed, or it may be transferred from a very dirty fabric to a cleaner one.

The resin finishing of textiles – e.g. for crease-resistance – usually includes other substances, referred to as additives, for purposes such as softening the fabric or improving various properties. Some of these additives are softened by high temperatures and become tacky, picking up soil from the dirty washing liquid. It has been found that the soiling is influenced not only by the additive used but also according to the pH of the soiled washing solution.

General comments on soiling

Until such time as the soil repellency of textiles is improved it is important to remember to clean fabrics frequently and not to allow them to become heavily soiled! Apart from considerations of hygiene, heavily soiled fabrics are more difficult to clean, and if particles of dirt remain in the fabric they act as nuclei to which additional dirt is attached in use.

It is often stressed that fabrics made from thermoplastic fibres should be washed at not too high a temperature; consequently, lukewarm water is frequently used. This is most ineffective; what is generally required is a temperature of about 60°C.

Garment cleansing is required not only to remove soil but also to remove perspiration absorbed by the fabric. If the absorbed perspiration were to remain on the fabric it would decompose and produce an unpleasant odour. Some fabric finishes inhibit the growth of bacteria which decompose the perspiration. One trade-name of such a finish is 'Actifresh'.

Stain repellency

Soiling of textiles specifically refers to the acquisition of dirt and grease. Staining, however, refers to the contamination of textiles by, for example, food, beer, coffee, lipstick, or perspiration, which may be only partially soluble in water and may require special treatment for removal. Most stains remain on textiles not simply because they are mechanically trapped between the fibres and yarns, but because they are firmly held by strong chemical forces. Consequently, special chemical agents are required for the localised treatment of some stains to break down the forces of adhesion before the stain can be removed. Solvents used in dry-cleaning will not remove the water-soluble stains, and this is why garments have to be 'spotted' with a steam-gun to remove such stains.

Here we are not concerned with stain-removal methods but rather with the stain-repellency of textiles and the realisation that some stains are water-borne and others oil-borne. If a fabric is to be 'stain-repellent' it must absorb neither water nor oily liquids. It is much commoner for fabrics to be water-repellent than oil-repellent. For the former purpose it is quite usual to apply a 'silicone'finish, the effect of which is to cause stains such as ink, coffee, and fruit juice to 'pearl off' the fabric surface without wetting it. The fabric to be proofed is passed through the finish in a liquid bath, dried, and then baked at about 150°C for a few minutes. The finish is found to be durable to washing and dry-cleaning, although cotton and acetate show less durability than can be obtained on some fabrics made from other fibres. Silicones, therefore, show a high degree of water-repellency and are extensively used for this purpose in rainwear and suede leather for shoes and garments.

The term 'silicones' was coined by Dr. Frederick S. Kipping of University College, Nottingham, to describe a wide range of substances which he developed and discovered. All are based on the element silicon. Nowadays silicone fluids, resins, and rubbers are used for a wide variety of purposes.

Oil-repellency can be achieved by the use of fluorochemicals such as 'Zepel' and 'Scotchgard', which give both water- and oil-repellency. These finishes are expensive but resistant to laundering and dry-cleaning.

PHYSICAL REQUIREMENTS

Physiological and tactile comfort of fabrics and clothing

Discussion under the heading 'Properties of fabrics' has centred on important fabric mechanical properties and aspects of aesthetic acceptability, both topics being of concern to those involved and interested in the spheres of fashion and functional clothing.

Garment styles presented by the fashion houses emphasise our interest in clothing from a psychological point of view. The designers focus attention first on one and then another feature of the human figure, presumably to excite interest. After a while the eye adjusts itself to the common-place, and the special design feature soon loses its appeal and significance.

The garment style and the fabric are also chosen for decorative effect and, subconsciously, this may be influenced by the desire to please one's associates or to satisfy one's own self-esteem and impress society. One may conform to trends in style according to one's age group, environment, or wealth, and this results in group distinction in dress. On the other hand, if one wishes to reflect a mood, the softness or severity of the fabric and style can easily do this.

We are often judged by the clothes we wear, as in Shakespeare's Hamlet:

> 'Costly thy habit as thy purse can buy,
> But not express'd in fancy; rich, not gaudy:
> For the apparel oft proclaims the man.'
>> *Act 1 – Scene 3*

Apparel and other textile items also have unique functions in providing physiological comfort continuously throughout the full range of human activities. Specially designed fabrics and garments are available for active sportswear, passive spectator sport, everyday wear, and sleep-wear. Such a range of textile coverings for the human form is expected to provide appropriate comfort to the wearer within a wide span of climatic extremes, and must contribute to the regulation of body temperature to avoid the risk of either hyper- or hypothermia.

The 'physiology of clothing' depends on the fact that body comfort can only be achieved if the skin is kept in a dry condition and the body temperature is constant. In order to have some understanding of the possible choice of fabrics and clothing for various activities and climatic conditions, it will be useful to appreciate some of the requirements of the body.

The internal body temperature of 37°C is attained by the chemical processes in the body and by muscular effort. This process is known as metabolism. If the internal temperature varies by more than 5°C either way, death from heat-stroke or exposure will occur. (The temperature of the skin is usually less than the internal body temperature.) It is therefore essential, if the equilibrium of body temperature is to be maintained, for the rate of heat loss from the body to equal the rate of production of heat within the body while the internal temperature is kept at 37°C.

The body, of course, has natural responses to overcoming excessive heat or cold. We have all experienced shivering, the closing up of the pores of the skin (goose pimples) and a 'blue look', which is a sign that the blood circulation is reduced near the skin's surface to conserve heat. To increase the rate of heat loss the blood circulates briskly beneath the surface of the skin and we become flushed, the dilated pores passing sweat to the surface of the skin where it cools the body by evaporating.

The temperature of the body is largely governed by:

- The intake of food.
- Physical activity.
- Clothing which acts as a barrier to prevailing climatic conditions.

Body metabolism will not be discussed here, since it is a topic of human physiology.

Physical activity

Muscular action produces heat and the amount generated will vary considerably according to the degree of activity. The output of heat by the body has been measured under the following conditions, but this will vary somewhat according to the individual's age, height and mass (Table 15). These data are of interest when considering the maintenance of body temperature within the limits of 32° to 42°C. Thus, your output of heat, as you sit reading this page, may be equivalent to that of a 100 watt electric light bulb.

To remain in thermal balance the metabolic heat generated must be offset by an equivalent loss of heat by means of cooling through the loss of sensible and insensible perspiration, radiation and convection of heat from

Table 15   OUTPUT OF HEAT ACCORDING TO PHYSICAL ACTIVITY

	*Kilo-calories/hour**
Sleeping	65
Sitting	100
Rapid typing	140
Walking at 2·6 mph	200
Walking at 3·75 mph	300
Cycling at 10 mph	390
Swimming	500
Ski-ing downhill	540
Level running at 10 mph	900
Sprinting	1250

* 50 Kilo-calories (50,000 calories) per hour is equivalent to 58 watts.

the surface of the skin. About a quarter of the body heat is lost by way of insensible perspiration. Body heat storage of about 80 kcal gives a rise of 1·4°C in body temperature, which would cause an individual to want to stop or reduce the activity causing such a rise.

At times of great physical activity there is a need to remove clothing in order to cool off. This usually means that the body temperature has risen and we are sweating. To accelerate the rate of cooling, top garments are removed to permit evaporation directly from the surface of the skin, giving a maximum cooling effect.

Inactivity may result in insufficient heat production to balance the heat loss to the atmosphere. When one is asleep the generation of heat is at its lowest, and for this reason it is necessary to provide warm bed clothing or sleeping bags to conserve heat. Passive outdoor sport in cold weather requires the use of an anorak and headwear to conserve heat.

Clothing as a barrier to climatic conditions

At different times we may be subjected to air temperatures from below freezing to 40°C. The air may be still or one may be exposed to a gale. It may be dry or humid. In addition one may be surrounded by snow or may be receiving heat from the sun. The function of clothing is to enable us to be comfortable under a range of climatic conditions; that is, it acts as a barrier between our bodies and the climate. Let us consider the properties of fabrics that make them useful for this purpose.

Heat insulation

A most important function of clothing is to reduce the rate of heat loss from the body, and therefore it must be a poor conductor of heat. Now every fabric contains still air entrapped between the fibres, and this air is a very poor conductor of heat. Thus the greater the volume of air space in a fabric, the better it is as an insulator of heat. Fabrics that are thick and soft, such as blankets, contain a large proportion of air, and fabrics may be designed with a cellular structure (e.g. leno) for the same purpose. A raised flannelette sheeting contains more air than ordinary sheeting, as does a brushed knitted nylon fabric used for nightwear, and they are both therefore warmer. It is of course necessary that the fabric should be able to maintain its thickness in use, and therefore, fabrics which spring out after being compressed are the most desirable. This is a property of fabrics made from resilient fibres such as wool, which explains why this fibre and certain textured synthetic fibres are valuable for articles of warm clothing. Polyester fibre filling or wadding is used for anoraks and duvets, and of course down and feathers have been used traditionally for bed covers. To ensure some uniformity of insulation across the cover the uniform layer of filling must be stabilised in position.

Textile fibres are good conductors of heat compared with the still air trapped within fabric structures. This is not of great importance in thermal insulation since the fibre is only a small proportion of the volume of a fabric. The thermal conductivity of fibres is of the order of 200 milliwatt/ metre, at 20°C. Whereas that of a carpet is about 50 and air, at rest, 25.

Polyurethane foam contains a large proportion of air and warm fabrics may be made by laminating this material to a thin fabric chosen for some other property entirely such as wind resistance, shower-proofness, or aesthetic appeal.

It is interesting to note here that the rate at which a person loses heat to his surroundings depends on his size. A thin man has a large surface area relative to the mass of his body, so his temperature drops more rapidly than that of a fat man. In cold weather about 10% of the total heat loss may occur from an uncovered head.

Babies and children need to be carefully protected from the cold by adequate and well-designed clothing because they too have a very large surface area relative to body mass.

Windproof fabrics

The cooling power of the atmosphere on the surface of the body is more than twice as great in a wind of one mile an hour as it is in calm air. Cycling at 10 miles per hour or sailing at 20 miles per hour increases the cooling power, just as do winds of these speeds. A little breeze on a hot day is certainly welcome, since it will cool us by accelerating the evaporation of moisture from the surface of the skin. However, under cold conditions a wind aggravates our discomfort, and a windproof outergarment is valuable, and even essential under really severe conditions as encountered in mountaineering, in the arctic and free-fall parachuting, and for air crew immersion suits. For these purposes fabrics having a high resistance to air penetration have been developed. These are very closely woven, so that the pores through which the air can pass are very small. A fabric which lets no air pass through at all is unsuitable for clothing, since it is essential that perspiration be able to evaporate, for both comfort and health. Vapour permeable coated fabrics, p. 152, now provide wind resistance and vapour permeability for use in ski wear for example.

The importance of maintaining fabric loft was indicated under heat insulation. It has been found that the force of wind on an outer garment can cause compression of the underlying fibre wadding or fabrics, forcing out the air trapped within the clothing assembly. Insulation loss can be as high as 60% according to the wind speed and the permeability of the fabric.

A further example of fabric compression, but unrelated to fabric wind resistance, is the pressure exerted on the underside of an insulated sleeping bag by the user, with the result that the compressed material affords little insulation from the ground.

Radiant heat

The body can receive heat by direct radiation of the sun. If one stands outside on a bright sunny day the sun's heat can be felt directly on the skin, just as one feels the warmth of a fire. This sense of warmth is conveyed by 'radiation', of the same nature as light, but invisible. Fabrics of very open texture will allow some radiation to pass through, but some is absorbed by the fabric and warms it, and some is reflected and has no effect on the temperature of the fabric. Apart from fabric structure, the colour used is important. The heat of the sun's rays is reflected better by white than by black. Consequently, a black fabric will heat up quicker in the sun. Apart from the visible colour, the chemical composition of the dye can influence the amount of heat absorbed or reflected by the surface of the fabric.

In some situations the amount of heat received by radiation may be excessive, as in fire-fighting, and protection can be given by a suit of which the outside is made from a fabric coated with thin aluminium foil. This reflects the radiant heat very effectively indeed, and if the suit is made of a thick fabric, which will limit the conduction of the heat inwards, the wearer can approach the fire closely.

Humidity

Mention has been made above of the role of perspiration in helping to reduce body temperature. It must be emphasised that this role is vital and has an important bearing on the choice of fabrics and the design of clothing.

The ease and speed with which the body temperature is regulated by evaporation under hot conditions or during strenuous exercise depends on the dampness of the skin and the amount of moisture contained in the air; i.e. the relative humidity of the air.

In cool conditions, either in the open-air or in a well-ventilated room, the surface of the skin is kept fairly dry and cool, mainly by convection and radiation. As soon as the heat loss by convection and radiation drops below the heat production level of the body, the other method of heat loss comes into effect – sweating.

The air in contact with a sweating body is warmed and saturated, and, if the clothing allows free movement, convection currents develop. In a crowded room on a calm, muggy, warm day the air is almost saturated with water vapour at body temperature. Consequently, evaporation is hampered, and one feels discomfort because of the 'closeness of the atmosphere'. Circulation of air under such conditions is important, since it brings unsaturated air to the evaporating surface. In addition, air blowing over a porous surface has a suction effect which aids evaporation from the surface of clothing.

Under extreme conditions, when the body is perspiring a great deal, or when the air is so humid that the perspiration cannot evaporate, the skin may become quite wet, and it is essential that underclothes should provide some means of rapid sweat removal to avoid discomfort, due to fabric clinging to the skin, and a rise in body temperature. Previously it was thought that for this purpose only absorbent material should be in contact with the skin. It is true that when the textile absorbs moisture it also provides an increase in surface area capable of evaporation, and so increases the rate of cooling compared with the damp skin alone.

Studies carried out recently in connection with the transport of liquid water from the surface of the skin shows that cotton and acrylic fibres are inherently capable of wicking moisture along the fibre surface, whereas other synthetic fibres and wool do not have this property. However, wickability of synthetic fibres, such as polyester, has been developed by modifying the fibre cross-section and applying a hydrophilic surface coating, whilst still retaining the virtual non-absorbency of the fibre.

Investigations have shown that when a non-absorbent layer, capable of wicking, is in contact with the skin, the capillary transfer of liquid outwards to an absorbent outer fabric layer provides considerable comfort to the wearer.

An example of this phenomenon in common use, but unrelated to active sportswear is the construction of babies' disposable nappies in which a layer of polypropylene wicks the liquid to an absorbent outer layer, thus keeping the skin dry.

Tactile comfort

Sensations experienced through the skin in contact with a garment arise from the stimulation of sensory receptors located beneath the skin. The sensations conveyed by the touch, thermal, and pain receptors make the individual aware of the area and location affected, and the duration of the sensation.

A variety of sensations arising from fabric contact may be expressed as tickle, prickle, scratchiness, localised tightness, initital cold feel of fabric, wet and tacky clinging, fibre shedding, and allergic responses. Individuals vary in their sensitivity – soft skins are more sensitive than hardened skins, and both the presence of water (or sweat) which softens the skin and a rise in skin temperature increase sensitivity.

Reference has already been made to discomfort arising from fabric cling due to a sweaty skin, which may be followed if there is a residue of sweat, by a tacky sensation. It has been found that a very smooth fabric surface is liable to cling under these circumstances and that a hairy surface reduces cling since there is a reduction in the area of fabric contact with the skin. Hairs can maintain a distance between the fabric and skin, facilitating drying and so making a positive contribution to comfort.

Substantial programmes of textile research on 'comfort' have been sponsored by the EC and undertaken in several major research centres as follows: 'Thermophysiological comfort' (German Federal Republic), 'The comfort of semi-permeable rainwear' (Holland), and at the Shirley Institute (BTTG) in the UK 'Sensorial (tactile) comfort of next-to-skin apparel'.

Aspects of fabric construction and garment design have been found to determine most of the discomforting sensations sometimes experienced when certain clothing is worn. So far as claimed allergies are concerned it was found that skin reaction to fabric contact was almost invariably due solely to the mechanical action or impact of fibre ends and the fabric surface on the skin. True allergic reaction has been attributed to the presence of certain plasticisers, stabilisers, epoxy resins, dyestuffs, and residual substances from fabric finishing treatments.

Studies at CSIRO* have shown that the pain receptors are primarily reactive to the force applied to the skin by protruding stiff fibres. It is stated that if the buckling load of the fibre ends in contact with the skin is less than 75–100 mg the significant prickle stimuli will not result. Short coarse stiff projecting fibres are liable to be troublesome whilst longer softer fibres would be more comfortable. Brushing and raising fibres from the fabric can improve this type of comfort, but there is a risk of excessively increasing the number of projecting fibres and so increasing the potential 'prickle'. Chemical processing to de-scale the surface of wool fibres, the application of silicones and softeners are possible ways of reducing the fibres' resistance to bending, so creating less prickly sensations. Of course the individual response depends also on the density and depth of pain receptors in the skin. Individuals sensitive to 'prickle' are advised that they should only wear fine wool garments next to the skin and coarser wool fabrics for outerwear.

To overcome discomfort attributed to fabrics made from manufactured fibres, fabrics made from fibres of multiple staple length equivalent to the length range for combed cotton are produced to reduce the number of contact points between fabric and skin.

The design of clothing, often for specific uses and climatic conditions, will be facilitated by an understanding of the physiological responsiveness of the skin to the nature of the fabrics with which it is in contact.

Choice of garment assemblies

Attention so far has been given to the properties of fabrics required for clothing. For cold conditions they must provide good heat insulation, and this can be obtained by choosing materials that entrap a high proportion of air, such as light fleecy fabrics or cellular fabrics. Thick fabrics are, of course, better insulators than thin fabrics, and in order to maintain their thickness in use, resilient fibres should be used. The cooling effect of wind must be reduced by using a windproof material as an outer layer. For comfort, underclothes and sleepwear should be absorbent or capable of wicking to an outer layer. These conditions help to determine what garments should be worn. These principles are applicable not only to everyday wear but to uniforms and protective clothing. It will be appreciated that such specialised clothing not only has to provide normal levels of

* *Commonwealth Scientific and Industrial Research Organisation Division of Textile Industry, Geelong, Australia.*

comfort to sustain activity and life but requires additional protective properties such as flame retardance and barriers to a variety of agencies.

For wear next to the skin, knitted fabric is ideal because it is extensible and unrestricting, soft to the touch and bulky. It should be made from an absorbent fibre or fibres that promote wicking. Warmth can be increased by the texturing of continuous filament yarns. For reasons of hygiene the material must be washable.

The next layers of clothing are, in cold conditions, those on which dependence is placed for warmth, and bulky fabrics may be used. However, with the interiors of homes and public buildings maintained usually at comfortable temperatures for mainly sedentary activities, the use of multilayers of clothing is preferred to a single warm layer. This facilitates the regulation of body temperature by adjustment of the number of fabric or garment layers. Air entrapped between the layers of clothing is an important contribution to thermal insulation. The 'string vest', which is knitted as a very large mesh from very coarse yarn, worn next to the skin, holds air between the skin and the next garment layer. This insulating layer of air provides lightweight warmth. There is generally a preference for lightweight clothing for almost all activities.

For use out of doors, windproof outer garments may be needed. These are often closely woven with a water-repellent finish to give protection from rain. Wool, cotton, and polyester fibre blends of suitable construction may fall into this category, but of course coated fabrics (page 151) are particularly suitable for long exposure to the elements. The combined benefits of high-loft wadding with a windproof outerlayer provide lightweight warmth but the bulkiness of the fabric provides some restriction on garment styling other than the introduction of colour and some surface design features.

Cold weather clothing became necessary when the human race moved away from the warmer to the cooler regions of the world. So-called arctic clothing was then worn consisting of close-fitting garments covering the whole body, such as trousers and tunic as worn by the Eskimo. This outfit reduces the circulation of air over the body surface and consequent heat loss. On the other hand, warm weather clothing should be open and light and of loose construction, so that it does not impede evaporation and dispersal of perspiration.

Clothing is also used to protect the skin from the sun's rays and of course acts as a barrier to the risk of abrasion in everyday activities. The light reflectance capacity of dyed textiles is of value when considering outer garments for heat protection from the sun's rays. White surfaces reflect light of most wavelengths, whereas black objects will absorb these and heat up preferentially.

It is probably appropriate to consider the worldwide implications of the progressive destruction of the ozone layer in terms of the human physiological needs for protection against the highly damaging UV wavelengths.

Assessment of physical properties relating to comfort

'Method for the determination of thermal resistance of textiles' BS 4745 is widely used for the assessment of fabrics less than 3 cm thick, but for thick and large items such as sleeping bags and quilts the test procedure in BS 5335 is adopted.

A conditioned fabric specimen is placed over a standard insulating board of known thermal resistance, this is heated electrically at its lower face, which is maintained at a known surface temperature. The specimen is covered with a lightweight 'cold' plate. The heat travels upwards from the heated source through the standard board and then through the fabric. Thermocouples embedded on both faces of the board and the topside of the fabric enable the temperature drop across the fabric to be compared with the temperature drop across the standard board, and thereby it is possible to calculate the thermal resistance or TOG value of the specimens. (1 TOG = $0 \cdot 1°$ cm^2/watt). (An alternative unit is 'clo' = $0 \cdot 645$ togs).

Typical values for the thermal resistance of fabric have been given as:

	TOG values
Shirting	$0 \cdot 1$
Underwear	$0 \cdot 3$
Suitings	1
Blankets	1–2
Carpets	2
Continental quilts	4–13

The total thermal resistance of a garment assembly or bed covers may be estimated by taking the sum of the component layers, but a more precise measurement is obtained when the whole fabric assembly, including the intervening layers of 'still' air, is tested.

In the dry state the thermal conductivities of natural and synthetic fibres are about the same, but because of the natural fibres' capacity to absorb moisture, an increase in relative humidity will cause their thermal conductivity to increase. However, if the textile material becomes wet the conductivity for all fabrics will be greatly increased.

The '*Water-vapour permeability Test*' (Figure 170) measures the diffusion of water vapour across the fabric. This is of particular interest for clothing materials. The results are expressed as 'water vapour resistance' which is the inverse of permeability.

Each of the eight dishes in the apparatus serves as a water reservoir and the fabric under test is mounted over four, whilst the other four are covered with a standard permeable fabric only. The fabric is separated from the surface of the water by a known air gap. The dishes rotate for a period of 24 hours at the end of which they are weighed to determine the

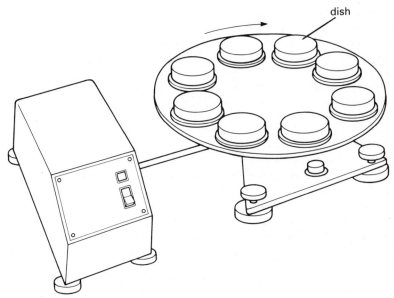

Fig. 170 Shirley water-vapour permeability tester.
(Shirley Developments Ltd.)

residue of water. The rate of weight loss, relating to the water vapour permeability of the specimens, is compared with the rate of weight loss through the standard fabrics. Water vapour resistance is expressed as the thickness in mm of a layer of still air that has the same resistance to diffusion of water vapour. The magnitude of the permeability depends on the size and length of the pores in the fabric structure and the nature of the fibres. As already discussed the resistance of fabric to the passage of water vapour should be as low as possible to permit water vapour to pass through from the skin. Interest in water vapour transmission applies also to 'breathable' coated fabrics as well as clothing fabrics generally.

PROPERTIES FOR GARMENT MANUFACTURE

Following the inception of a new idea of style and intended market, there follows a process of fabric selection and development of a prototype involving a chain of manufacturing processes. There is an interaction between style, manufacturing process and fabric properties that renders the choice of fabric, its specification and finish essential to the success of the operation. The response of the fabric to manufacturing processes, the inevitable adjustment of garment manufacture to the fabric, and the imaginative use of textile properties in the creation of functional and aesthetically satisfying apparel, demonstrate the interdependence of textile and clothing technologies and technologists.

Identifiable requirements of textile materials to satisfy innovative garment manufacturing processes, and design and functional needs can be met by the development of textile specifications for the stated objectives.

Aspects of fabric behaviour in the bulk cutting of garment panels, and seaming and fusing interlinings are referred to under other headings. However it is appropriate to indicate here that difficulties such as lack of dimensional stability, seam slippage and fraying, seam pucker and damage can be avoided by early consideration of requirements in fabric specification and also of the requirements of handling during garment manufacture.

Fabrics required for tailored garments and the production of moulded items need distinctive properties to ensure a satisfactory response to the shaping processes used in garment production. The following indicates some features to be considered.

Tailorability of fabric and garment moulding

Tailorability of fabric relates to its capacity to produce a smooth fit and well-defined silhouette together with freedom and comfort of movement for the wearer.

In dresswear, relatively lighter weight fabric is used with a comparative looseness of garment fit which is generous in accommodating a range of figure types for a given garment size. 'Skin-tight' garments such as swimwear and contour foundation wear have a high level of fabric stretch to permit ease of movement.

A well-tailored garment, such as a jacket, skirt or trousers, requires a 'sculptured' look with unwrinkled contours of fabric and seams. The garment is expected to hang well and smoothly from the shoulders and over the hips with well formed collar and lapels. To achieve this effect, particularly accurate initial planning and pattern drafting of the garment components are needed, together with localised stiffening to form the garment shell. Well controlled methods of fabric and garment pressing, with specially designed pressing equipment, are essential in the garment shaping process.

In order to conform with the human figure the woven fabric itself must be capable of bending smoothly and simultaneously in two directions without buckling – unlike the behaviour of a sheet of paper when handled in this way. To do this effectively the two sets of threads in the fabric must be able to shear or skew (Figure 171).

The stress-strain properties of the fabric and the level of fabric stiffness, resistance to bending, compressive properties in the plane and perpendicular to the plane of the fabric, all determine the response of the fabric to shearing forces in tailoring.

Such physical fabric properties are also particularly important where fabrics are brought together to form a seam, at the sleeve head for instance, where curvature in the direction of the seam itself is required. The fabric in

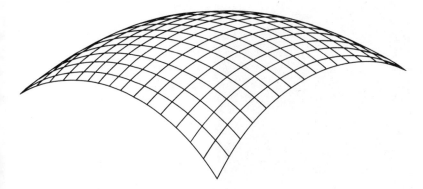

Fig. 171 Simple illustration of double curvature. An initially flat piece of woven fabric skewed or sheared to fit a curved surface. The skewing is greatest at the corners.

the sleeve head will be in excess of the fabric length forming the armhole opening. Such extra fabric needed to achieve fit and ease of movement without apparent excess fullness along the seam line must be capable of being compressed in the direction of the seam without buckling. Alternatively, the shorter layer of fabric could possibly be extended to fit the longer length. Such manipulation of fabric and fabric response is consolidated into the desired shape by steam-pressing and setting the fibres, particularly for worsted or woollen wool fabric or a wool blend.

Whilst woven wool fabric responds well to steam-pressing and the shaping process required for the 'tailored' look, not all such fabrics respond similarly because variables in fabric structure affect such significant properties already mentioned. Investigations based on the study of a wide range of fabric properties have led to theories which assist in the testing and forecasting of the quality of tailorability of a fabric.

Other aspects of importance, apart from the appearance due to shape of a well-tailored garment, are the sharpness of such creases required in the style and the aesthetic quality of fabric handle.

Fabrics destined for mass-production clothing manufactures not only need the fabric to be specified, but also accurate details of garment construction need to be given with precise statements of machines to be used and conditions of processing throughout manufacture.

Garment moulding is a method of inducing shape into a flat piece of material without the introduction of seams. Swimwear, bra cups, leotards, and pantyhose are a few examples of merchandise shaped in this way. Several techniques are available such as compression and vacuum moulding.

Tubular knitted fabric containing thermoplastic fibre may be pulled over a flat metal shape or former, of dimensions related to the garment size. This is then heated in a flat press at a temperature of about 190°C,

Fig. 172 Warp-knitted fabric moulded three-dimensionally into hats. *(Karl Mayer Machinery Ltd.)*

dependent on whether the fibre is nylon, polyester, or elastane, and dependent on the moisture content of the material and other conditions in pressing. Non-thermoplastic materials need the presence of synthetic fibres or the assistance of synthetic resins or special interlinings to retain the shape. The metal former defines the required shape and the thermoplastic material is heat-set in that state.

Three-dimensional shapes such as bra cups and hats (Figure 172) require presses of specially designed shapes. These presses usually have heated positive and negative moulds between which fabric is shaped.

Warp-knitted and weft-knitted, woven and nonwoven fabrics are used in moulding. The loop structure of knitted fabric is easily deformed to conform to a shape, whereas woven fabrics depend for their response primarily on the extensibilities of their yarns and fibres and their ability to skew. Nonwoven structures depend solely on the behaviour of the fibres and resins. An example of the use of nonwoven fabric is for moulded air filters to cover the nose and mouth.

Apart from bodywear, moulding of outerwear has been explored but has not yet become a major aspect of garment production. For instance, trousers with single-seam legs have been shaped over suitably shaped formers. However, care must be taken to avoid developing wide deviations in the spacing of the knitted loops during the shaping of the fabric whilst moulding, as this can detract from the overall surface appearance of the fabric. For the purpose of clothing the elasticity and recovery of the fabric and general performance in its new shape after heat-setting must be functionally and aesthetically satisfactory. Softness of handle must be maintained without any significant change in colour or lustre.

Moulded textile materials are used in car upholstery and for some industrial purposes.

PROPERTIES FOR SPECIAL APPLICATIONS

Water-repellency

Fabrics that are not easily penetrated by water are essential for garments intended to protect the wearer from showers or heavy rain. Such *shower-repellent* fabrics are used for men's and fashion rainwear, and are traditionally woven from cotton, cotton/polyester and wool fibres, and finally finished with a water-repellent treatment which lies on the surface of the individual fibres.

Waterproof fabrics, by contrast, completely prevent the penetration of water and are impermeable to the passage of air and water vapour because of the continuous coating on the fabric. Moisture vapour permeability for comfort, however, can be introduced by modifying the composition of the continuous film. Air vents are usually an essential feature of waterproof garment design. Discussion of 'Coated fabrics and Laminates' (page 151) refers to the impermeability of such materials and the methods for facilitating moisture vapour transmission.

The nature of water-repellency, on which shower-repellency depends, can be illustrated by experimenting with fabric. If drops of water are scattered on, say, a bleached sheeting or handkerchief, they are readily absorbed. On the other hand, small drops of water on a well-'proofed' raincoat remain more or less spherical and will roll about freely without even wetting the surface. This is achieved by applying to the cloth a suitable 'hydrophobic' (i.e. 'water hating') substance. Paraffin wax, if properly applied, gives quite a good effect and has been used for a long time, but modern finishes based on silicone are more efficient and are not easily removed by dry-cleaning and laundering.

To explain how a water-repellent finish produces its effect it must first be understood that molecules attract each other. Each molecule of water in a drop attracts nearby molecules, so that if the drop of water is free it draws itself together and becomes spherical. The water molecules are, however, attracted by the molecules of the fibre where they come together and if this attraction is large enough it separates the water molecules. They will then be drawn between the fibres of the cloth, and the water is thus absorbed. This suction of the water into the space between the fibres and the yarns is known as 'wicking'.

The water-repellent finishes lie on the surface of the fibres, and their attraction for the water molecules is only slight. They are therefore unable to break down the water drop, which is free to assume its natural spherical shape and will roll about in this form on the cloth surface, and can be shaken off easily. (Figure 173). It will now be understood that water repellency is determined by the characteristics of the surface of the fibre. A fibre such as polyester may absorb practically no water, but if the fibre surface is wettable it will make a fabric that 'wicks'. Typical finishes are wax-based 'Mystolene' (Catomance), 'Phobotex' (Ciba-Geigy); Silicone-

Fig. 173 Drops of water standing on a fabric that has been proofed to give three degrees of water repellency. Left, the cloth is least water repellent; right, the most water repellent. *(Catomance Ltd.)*

based 'Phobotone' (Ciba-Geigy); and the fluorochemical finishes 'Zepel' (Du Pont) and 'Sandofluor' (Sandoz). The trade-names here are followed in brackets by the chemical manufacturer's name. The efficiency of the water-repellent finish is liable to decline in use because if the material becomes soiled, the superimposed dirt increases the attraction between the water drop and the fabric, and so permits the easy spread of the water into the fabric. Some garments with a shower-repellent finish are described as washable, but thorough rinsing is essential to remove all traces of detergent which will otherwise reduce the effectiveness of the finish.

In order to make water pass through a water-repellent cloth, it is necessary to apply the water under pressure, equal to a column of water of about 20–100 cm in height. This property is measured according to BS 2823 'Hydrostatic head test'. If the fabric is of open construction, this pressure will be low, but for very closely constructed fabrics it will be at the high end of this range. To obtain good protection against rain, closely woven fabrics must be used. It has been found very advantageous to treat the lining of a shower-proof garment with a water-repellent finish, for if the lining is absorbent the passage of water through the top cloth occurs more readily.

It will be remembered, under the heading 'moisture absorption', that fibres that absorb water swell in diameter. This feature is used to advantage in the production of 'Ventile' cotton fabrics. These fabrics, when subjected to rain, absorb a little water; the fibres then swell and fill the spaces between the threads. For the effective sealing of the fabric in this way it must be woven with a suitable weave and thread spacing. A shower-repellent finish is applied to 'Ventile' fabrics. The special feature of this fabric, arising from its construction, is vapour permeability, which is essential to comfort in wear. 'Ventile' was the name used at The Shirley

Institute, Manchester, when the fabric was developed there, and it was later adopted as a registered trade name.

With the availability now of polyester and nylon microfibres finer than 0·1 dtex, and very fine irregular crimping of filaments, it is possible to construct woven fabric in which the spaces between the fibres are very small and which therefore, together with the appropriate water-repellent finish, provides an effective barrier to the passage of water droplets. It is claimed that this type of light-weight vapour permeable fabric maintains its performance over a long period of time. Fabrics which have a fibrous surface, such as in traditional tweeds, are resistant to immediate wetting by rain. Furs and pile fabrics generally behave similarly.

Assessment of water repellency

Obviously, claims for garment water-repellency might imply merely satisfactory performance in a light shower of short duration or, on the other hand, an effective barrier under more severe conditions. A wide range of laboratory tests is used to assess the effectiveness of fabrics and measure their likely behaviour in use.

The simplest method in use is the '*Spray test*', BS 3702, which in effect determines the resistance of a fabric to surface wetting by water. A given

Fig. 174 Spray test: Resistance of a fabric to surface wetting. *(Shirley Institute)*

227

Fig. 175a Bundesmann water repellency tester: 304 water jets positioned 150 cm above specimens under test. *(James H. Heal)*

Fig. 175b Bundesmann water repellency tester: fabric specimens mounted over four cups showing water droplets having landed from overhead jets. *(James H. Heal)*

Fig. 175c WIRA shower tester in which two specimens are exposed to an artificial shower. *(Shirley Developments Ltd.)*

volume of distilled water is sprayed onto a specimen mounted in a ring and placed centrally at 45° to horizontal beneath a spray nozzle. After the spray has ceased the mounted specimen is tapped to shake off surface water, and the fabric is then visually assessed and categorized into one of five classifications according to the severity with which the test area is wetted. This screening test simply verifies whether or not a fabric has had a finish applied; it does not reflect the likely combined performance of finish and fabric structure. The spray is only 152 mm from the centre of the fabric, and the velocity and volume of drops is far less than in a real shower, or in the prevailing artificial conditions in the following laboratory tests.

In the *Bundesmann test*, for example, fabrics are subject to the equivalent of a rainfall of 45·7 cm/hour, followed by the measurement of fabric water absorption and water penetration. Figure 175a shows the four specimen holders over which the specimen is stretched, while a wiper moves back and forth, on the under side of the specimen, imitating the rubbing that occurs in use.

Other tests for water repellency are the WIRA Shower BS 5066 and the 'Credit' rain simulation tester of Marks and Spencer. Reference has already been made to BS 2823 which measures the pressure required to make water pass through water repellent cloth. Although useful in the development of fabric and finishes it does not often feature in fabric performance specifications.

Whole garment testing

Because the performance of a garment depends not only on the quality of the outer fabric but on a number of features of construction, such as the type of seam, choice of sewing thread, location and style of pockets, position of buttons and zips, and on the effects of interlining and lining, it will be realised that the quality of a garment cannot be assessed by tests on the outer fabric alone. To learn how effective the garment will be it is necessary for it to be subjected for a given period of time to a standard

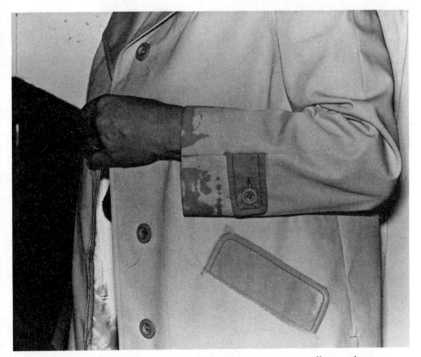

Fig. 176 Garment made from a fabric of satisfactory water repellency after exposure to a simulated rain shower. The wetted areas occur where unsuitable interlinings have been used.

Fig. 177 Waterproof coated fabrics require vigorous laboratory testing and extensive garment wearer trials before ultimate use as competitive sportswear. *(Henri-Lloyd Sportswear)*

shower of controlled, simulated rain under suitably realistic conditions (Figure 176).

This is done by means of a 'wearer trial' in which the wearer walks around in a prescribed manner beneath the artificially produced rain in the 'rain room'. Examination and assessment of the garment after such exposure focuses on identifying: where the water has penetrated in relation to the design and construction of the garment; whether and where penetration is attributable to fabric failure; and to what extent there has been an increase in garment weight due to water absorption. This example of whole garment testing illustrates the importance of considering the totality of the garment: fabric, components, design and garment construction.

Air permeability

The resistance of fabric to air flow is of interest where protective clothing is to act as a barrier to the penetration of wind, and is required to maintain body temperature under cold conditions. Garments used in warm conditions will require high air permeability for ventilation. Air permeability also provides a measure of the openness of a fabric.

Air permeability is determined by measuring the rate of air flow through a specimen when the pressure difference between the two faces of the cloth is equal to 1 cm head of water. The result is quoted as $cc/cm^2/sec$; BS 5636 defines the test procedure.

It should be observed that openness as assessed by an air permeability test will not necessarily correlate closely with other assessments of openness, since the resistance to the passage of air does not depend directly on the percentage of the fabric that is 'open'. For example, 100 small pores of a given total area offer a greater resistance to air flow than fifty larger pores of the same total area.

Flame retardance

The term 'inflammable' meaning 'capable of burning' has been found to be ambiguous, and has given way to 'flammable', carrying the same meaning, in British Standards and in specifications. The term 'inflammable' should no longer be used.

Normally the flammability of textiles is assessed by applying an appropriate British Standard flammability test method to the fabric.

Factors influencing flame retardance

Apart from the severity of the test, the rate and extent of burning will depend on:

1) the choice of fibre and fibre blends used
2) the weight of the fibre
3) whether the fabric is closely or loosely constructed
4) the presence of pile or nap on the surface
5) surface finish applied to the fabric.

The flammability of a garment made from the fabric will be influenced by:

6) garment design
7) laundering of the garment after use
8) the types of materials used in the composite structure

Burning of textile fibres is the result of chemical reactions taking place in the presence of oxygen. First, the heat decomposes the fibres and combustible gases are produced; these gases, whilst burning, generate more heat which further decomposes the fibre. To reduce the flammability of most types of textiles, it is therefore necessary to reduce the flammability or the volume of gases produced. To achieve this, special finishes may be used, which chemically modify the surface or the whole of the fibre, particularly for fabrics made from the natural fibres. Manufactured fibres may have their burning behaviour modified by the introduction of fire retardant (F-r) additives prior to polymerization or extrusion.

Limiting Oxygen Index (LOI)

Information about the potential flammability of a fibre type can be obtained by measuring its Limiting Oxygen Index (LOI) that is the minimum percentage of oxygen needed in the atmosphere to support the combustion of a fibre under the test conditions of BS 2782.

Air contains about 21% oxygen and fibres having an LOI less than 21% are very flammable whilst those with an LOI above this value will burn less readily. The following comparison of some commonly used fibres illustrates the range of burning levels by LOI. However, these do not provide the sole criteria for judging the fire resistance of fabrics in practice.

The high performance fibres tend to be very expensive and often lack the aesthetic properties required for apparel and furnishing. The price of 'Nomex' and 'PBI' being now about £15 and £60/kg respectively. Wool has

Table 16   LIMITING OXYGEN INDICES % OF FIBRES

Fibre type (and trade-name)	Typical LOI%	Possible uses
Polypropylene	18	
Acrylic	19	
Cotton, viscose, acetate	20	
Polyamide, polyester	22	
Wool	26	
F-r viscose	27	Mattress covers
F-r polyester	28	Fire blankets
F-r cotton / ('Proban' finish)	28–30	Clothing, bedding
Modacrylic	29	Clothing and simulated fur
Wool/('Zirpro' finish)	32	Clothing and furnishings
Aramid	28–34	
Chlorofibre (Rhovyl)	35–48	Barriers to heat
Polybenzimidazole (PBI)	>41	and flame:
Polyacrylate/cross-linked	43	Protective
Chlorofibre	35–48	clothing
Semi-carbonised fibre ('Panox', 'Asgard')	>50	Public transport Industry
PTFE	80–90	

a relatively high LOI and its ignition temperature (570°C–600°C), and high moisture content contribute to its low flammability and capacity to withstand simple burning tests.

Asbestos, which poses a health hazard, and glass, because they are inert, are the only textile fibres which can be considered to be completely flameproof. Some finishes applied to glass are flammable. Other fibres in common use can be classified by their persistence and speed of burning when an igniting flame is removed; they broadly fall into the following categories:

Table 17   BROAD CLASSIFICATION OF FIBRE FLAMMABILITY

	Flammability	
High	*Medium*	*Low*
acetate	cotton treated with	aramid
acrylic	flame-retardants	polyvinyl chloride
cotton	modacrylic	'Zirpro' treated
linen	nylon	wool
viscose	polyester	
triacetate	wool and hair	
some blends and		
unions (e.g. polyester/		
cotton, polyester/		
viscose)		

It must be appreciated that the above classification involves a broad generalisation, and the fire hazard presented by any textile is very dependent on its construction and the circumstances at the time. Thus, aramid fibres, although a good choice for a motor racing driver's overalls, cannot be described as non-flammable under all conceivable circumstances. It is also particularly important to discuss the behaviour of fabrics composed of blends of fibres or of yarns of different fibres, since they may be more flammable than fabric made entirely from a single fibre type. Thus the thermoplastic fibres normally extinguish themselves by the falling away of the burning molten material which, of course, may cause secondary ignition. However, if cotton is also present it supports the molten portion and prevents it from dropping and consequently the fabric burns fiercely. It has also been found that if a cotton sewing thread is used in a nylon or polyester fabric, the flame will run up along the length of stitching. That is why the Nightwear (Safety) Regulations 1985 insist that thermoplastic sewing threads must be used below the waist or elbow in nightdresses made from thermoplastic material. Another important point to remember is that combining two dissimilar fabrics in the same garment may result in a fire hazard, even though both are of low flammability. Thus, the under-skirt or lining used in a garment of low flammability fabric preferably should be of the same low flammability fibre as used in the garment.

Fabric weight

For fibres that propagate a flame without melting, the heavier the fabric the better will be its flammability performance. For example, a flame will travel twice as fast in a fabric weighing $100g/m^2$ as in a fabric weighing $200g/m^2$. If the fibre melts as it burns, however, it is found that the molten material drops away less rapidly from the heavier fabrics, and this accelerates the rate at which they burn.

Fabric density

The effect of density of construction on the rate of burning of fabrics made from fibres which do not melt and drop away can be illustrated to some extent by taking a tuft of cotton or wool fibre and observing the speed with which it burns in comparison with a similar but tightly twisted tuft of fibre. Wool, for example, which is usually considered to be a safe fibre, will, in lightweight, open-textured fabrics, be found to have a rather poor flammability performance.

Presence of pile or nap on the surface

Fabrics with projecting surface fibres are liable to be ignited by a sudden flame or flash over the surface of the fabric. The extent or severity of the flash depends primarily on the fibre content, the density and height of the pile, and the composition of the base fabric.

Finish

Some finishes which may be applied to fabrics made from thermoplastic fibres will reduce the shrinkage of the fibre from the flame, and so reduce the flame resistance of the fabric. Some synthetic resins of high melting point applied to fabrics such as nets, and heavy shades of dyes containing chromium have this effect. Finishes containing starch or wax can cause otherwise flame-resistant fabrics to burn.

Much effort has been applied to the development of finishes that will improve the flammability performance of textiles and research continues into the improvement of those that are available. The aim is, of course, to produce a durable finish which will not add greatly to the cost of the fabric, will not spoil the handle of the cloth or reduce its strength or wearing properties, and will not be an irritant or pose health problems. Some years ago, for example, it was discovered that long exposure to 'Tris' an American treatment used extensively in the USA on children's nightwear, could cause skin cancer. There is very extensive information on the two most widely used UK finishes (Proban and Pyrovatex) which indicates that there is no danger from these finishes.

Some finishes work by making the fabric unable to produce fuel vapours that normally feed the flame. Other finishes work by producing vapours that positively suppress the flame. With either type, the flame is transient or absent, and the fabric merely chars.

Two important finishes are available for cellulosic fibres, these being 'Proban' and 'Pyrovatex'. Both are effective in reducing flammability to a low level but they increase the stiffness of the fabric, reduce the tearing strength (page 165), and add appreciably to the cost of production. For wool the Zirpro process has been developed. This finish applies a combination of Titanium and Zirconium which increases the formation of char and reduces the formation of volatile combustible gases. It is claimed to be applicable to garment fabrics, textile furnishings and carpets, and to be fast to washing and dry cleaning. This IWS treatment may be used for protective clothing for industrial workers and firemen, for instance.

The use of a solution of borax and boric acid is to be discouraged, since incorrect application is quite likely to lead to a false sense of security. The finish is not durable and has to be re-applied after each wash. It may be useful, however, for such items as scenery for amateur dramatics. There are now some proprietary home treatments, some based on aerosol application, which are particularly useful for curtains and upholstery. There is little independent information on their efficiency and it is certainly necessary to consider durability (i.e. resistance of the finish to wear and cleansing) as well as their performance. If used, manufacturers will provide detailed instructions which should always be followed closely.

Interest in flammability of textiles extends, of course, beyond clothing to furnishings both in the home and in public buildings, such as theatres, where flammable fabrics may contribute to disastrous fires.

Garment design

Close-fitting garments are less liable to catch fire than loose fitting and flowing garments such as nightdresses, dressing gowns, and full-skirted dresses. Skirts are liable to accidental contact with a flame or an electric fire, and the greater air supply provided by loose clothing can increase the rate of flame spread. The importance of garment design is underlined in the regulations relating to nightwear which allow fabrics of lower flammability performance to be used in pyjamas.

The effects of linings and sewing threads have been discussed above. The regulations already mentioned require that trimmings or any material sewn to a child's nightdress made of thermoplastic fibres below the waist or elbow must also be made of thermoplastic fibres. The reasons for this are the same as that given for the choice of sewing thread.

Cleansing

It is of little use manufacturing a fabric and applying a flame retardant finish if it loses the finish when it is laundered or dry cleaned. Indeed, a fabric that loses its flame retardancy in use is more dangerous than a fabric that has never been treated since the user may be unaware of the change.

Laundering may increase flammability by removing the flame retardant. Some commercial treatments are very resistant to laundering; however, effectiveness may sometimes be impaired by bleaching and boiling.

Certain conditions of laundering may lead to a gradual accumulation of lime soaps, and since these are flammable they can increase the flammability of fabrics in time. The use of synthetic detergents instead of soap avoids this danger.

Types of material used in composite structures

It has already been mentioned that blends of fibres, and yarns of different fibres, may be more flammable than fabric made from a single fibre type. It will be realised that upholstered seating may be composed of foam or other filling, and layers of different fabrics together with an outer covering. Some fabrics and fillings are highly flammable and their combination highly dangerous. Similar concern exists for the combined behaviour of mattress and bed covers, duvets and pillows.

Flammability performance – testing, performance standards, legislation

Exposure of textile materials to the risks of fire occurs in the home, in public places and buildings such as hotels, leisure complexes, residential homes and public authority establishments, in public and private transport, and in such specialised uses as protective clothing for furnacemen and firefighters.

Of fire deaths in the home involving textiles as the first item ignited, a large majority are associated with upholstered furniture and beds and bedding. A large number of deaths are caused by ignition of clothing on the person and whilst in the early 1950's many of these were associated with nightwear, the proportions have altered and improved, partly because of legislation relating to nightwear and fire guarding; partly because of greater awareness; and partly because of the reduction in the number of open fires in favour of central heating.

Cigarettes and matches are the main causes of the ignition of bedding and upholstered furniture. Typically the lighted cigarette continues to smoulder and penetrates the upholstery cover, reaching the foam or filling, thereby starting the fire. The fire hazard associated with standard foam and high resilience foam often several hours after the cigarette has been discarded has been recognised and they have been effectively banned in favour of combustion modified high resilient (CMHR) foam; research into the development of self-extinguishing cigarettes is also in hand.

Over half of all fire deaths result from the inhalation of smoke and toxic fumes (mainly carbon monoxide) emitted by burning materials, hence the value of smoke detectors.

Ceiling temperature can reach 800°C in 3–5 minutes and the heat radiated to the surroundings causes 'flash over' when the whole contents of the room are set alight instantaneously.

Testing and performance standards

Fire and flammability aspects of textiles are treated in a number of British Standards and legislative instruments, in some cases dealing with textiles as garment materials and in some cases as part of a composite structure such as upholstered furniture, or toys. When trying to assess a textile product for a particular end use, it is important to take account of the hazards it will be exposed to and especially its interaction with other materials it will be associated with. For example, a thermoplastic fibre fabric might be very adequate for use in nightwear where it would protect by shrinking away from the flame, but might not be suitable for use stretched over upholstery material when an ignition source might cause it to shrink and expose the underlying material.

For these reasons, there are many British Standard test methods to meet the various end use situations. It should be noted, however, that the development of British Standards is a continuing process and details of any quoted example should be checked at source. Many public university and college libraries maintain complete sets of standards.

The public needs the protection from the risk of fire provided by the implementation of existing and future legislation. The BSI, in parallel with the International Standards Organisation (ISO) publishes agreed 'Methods of Test' and 'Performance Standards' and each carries a BS identification number. This means that the selections of apparatus and test procedures specified are appropriate to the use to which textile materials, or composites, are to be put. 'Performance Standards' prescribe the level of performance. Examples of observations to be made during the tests are:

- how easily the material ignites
- duration of flaming
- duration of afterglow
- whether debris falls and whether it is flaming
- the extent of burning and length of char
- the duration of flaming and smouldering
- assessment of detectable amounts of smoke

Clothing, curtains, drapes and tentage end-uses:

BS 5438: 1976 Methods of test for flammability of vertically oriented textile fabrics and fabric assemblies subjected to a small igniting flame.

This standard test method was published following extensive Home Office sponsored research at the Shirley Institute (now BTTG). It is made up of three separate tests each of which employ a vertically held specimen, pinned around its edges, to the surface or edge of which a small, specified butane flame is applied. (Figure 178 overleaf).

Test 1 (specimen size 220 mm × 170 mm) is used to establish the minimum flame application time to cause ignition.

Properties of Fabrics

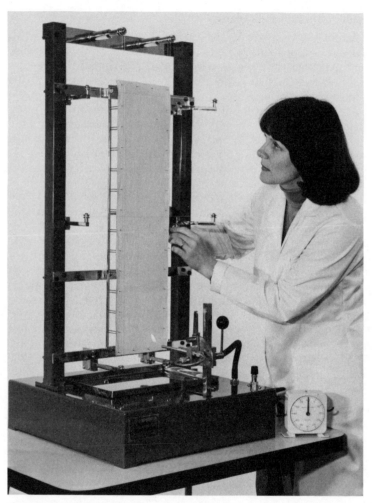

Fig. 178 Flammability testing of vertically positioned fabrics and fabric assemblies. *(Shirley Institute)*

Test 2 (specimen size 220 mm × 170 mm) is used to assess fabrics which, when ignited by the flame after a specified flame application time, do not exhibit flame spread beyond the upper or either vertical edge.

Test 3 (specimen size 670 mm × 170 mm) is used to assess fabrics which, because of their flame spread behaviour, cannot be tested by test 2. It is made more informative by the introduction of cotton trip threads, positioned horizontally at prescribed intervals, which actuate timing mechanisms so that the rate of flame spread can be established.

238

Performance standards

The above test is currently employed in the following British Standard specifications for flammability performance:

Sleepwear – (*BS 5722: 1984* Specification for flammability performance of fabrics and fabric assemblies used in sleepwear and dressing gowns, which is, itself, involved in legislation (see below).

Curtains and drapes – BS 5867 Specification for fabrics for curtains and drapes: Part 2: 1980 Flammability requirements.

Tent fabrics – BS 6341: 1983 Specification for fabrics for camping tents.

Protective clothing – BS 6249 Materials and material assemblies used in clothing for protection against heat and flame. Part 1: 1982 Specification for flammability testing and performance.

Synthetic fibre cellular blankets – BS 5866 Part 3: 1983

Blankets for use in the public sector. Part 3, specification fibre cellular blankets.

Pile fabrics and assemblies having pile on the surface:

BS 4569: 1983 Method of test for ignitability (surface flash)
Pile fabrics and assemblies having pile on the surface.

A specimen 200 mm × 130 mm is mounted vertically with the longer edge horizontal and a specified butane flame is passed across the pile surface at a speed of 150 mm per second. The test is a simple pass/fail test and observation is made during the test as to whether ignition of the surface of the pile occurs substantially over the whole area of the specimen during the traverse of the flame. This test is cited in the regulations governing the safety of toys.

The extent and severity of the flash, and subsequent burning, depends primarily on the fibre content and the density and height of the pile, and, to some extent, on the composition of the base fabric.

Performance standard

Toys (Safety) Regulations BS 5665 (1974) – to be revised.

Textile floor coverings:

BS 4790: Method for determination of the effects of a small source of ignition on textile floor coverings (hot metal nut method)

BS 6307: 1982 Method for determination of the effects of a small source of ignition on textile floor coverings (methenamine tablet test)

These two methods are similar, the latter being a direct copy of the international standard, ISO 6925.

BS 4790 requires that a metal nut, heated to 900°C, be placed in the centre of a specimen 300 mm × 300 mm. The time to extinction of any flaming or

Fig. 179 Hot metal nut used as source of ignition on textile floor coverings – BS4790. *(British Carpet Technical Centre)*

glowing is measured together with the radius of the area affected by flaming, or glowing.

BS 6307, unlike BS 4790 which uses a glowing ignition source, uses a small, flaming ignition source comprised of a flat, 150 mg, 6 mm diameter hexamethylenetetramine tablet placed in the centre of a 230 mm × 230 mm specimen.

The 'hot metal nut' has sufficient mass to penetrate the pile of the carpet, whereas the 'tablet's' flaming source of heat sits on top of the pile. Whilst the 'hot metal nut' method is used extensively in the UK, the tablet test, originating in the USA, has wide international acceptance.

Performance standard

BS 5287: 1976 'Assessment and labelling of textile floor coverings tested to BS 4790 provides a method for imparting information from the test to the consumer and its requirements can often be found on carpet labels.

Furniture, upholstery and bedding

BS 5852 fire tests for furniture

Part 1: 1979 Methods of test for the ignitability by smokers' materials of upholstered composites for seating

Part 2: 1982 Methods of test for the ignitability of upholstered composites for seating by flaming sources

These tests are based on research originally carried out by the Department of the Environment, Property Services Agency, and are based on composite testing of the filling and cover to be used in the final product. The upholstery filling is mounted on an L shaped metal rig to represent a seat/back situation and then covered by the outer fabric under standard tension. Ignition sources are applied at the junction of the seat and back and consist of a series of increasing intensity, namely a smouldering cigarette, three butane flames and four small pine wood cribs. The crib is constructed to include a piece of lint, to which is added a small quantity of alcohol to aid ignition (Figure 180). An assessment is made up of the ability of the whole composite to flame or smoulder progressively over a specified period. Use is made of this standard in legislation affecting the sale of domestic upholstered furniture.

BS 6807: 1986 Methods of test for the ignitability of mattresses with primary and secondary sources of ignition

Like BS 5852, this is a composite test standard consisting of a representative mock-up of a mattress section. However, unlike upholstered furniture, the fire performance of mattresses in use is complicated by the

Fig. 180 Four pine wood cribs used as sources of ignition on upholstery and bedding – BS5852. *(British Standards Institution)*

addition of sheets, blankets, duvets, etc. and so a slightly more complex series of tests is provided.

Test 1. The mattress alone tested with primary ignition sources.

Test 2. Mattress tested with bed covers which act as secondary ignition sources. This is particularly applicable to those end uses where the covers can be specifically identified, as in hotels and hospitals.

The ignition sources for tests 1 and 2 are cigarette, butane flames and pine wood cribs.

Test 3. Mattress tested with secondary ignition sources representing unknown bed-covers and made up of a smoulderable source (cotton wool pad) and a non-smoulderable source (glass fibre pad). For this test, the cigarette and smallest butane flame is used. Unfortunately, at present, there is no control over the choice of bed-covers for tests of ignitability in domestic situations.

Performance standard

The Furniture and Furnishings (Fire) (Safety) Regulations 1988, Statutory Instrument 1988 No. 1324, sets ignition requirements for domestic upholstered furniture.

These regulations, made under the Consumer Protection Act 1987, will apply to new and secondhand domestic upholstered furniture including children's furniture and certain nursery items, as well as re-upholstered furniture. Furniture made before 1950 and furniture re-upholstered before that year will be exempt.

The Regulations will also apply to cushions, pillows and loose covers for furniture. Upholstered garden furniture which may be used indoors, and furniture built into new caravans are also included.

BS 5651: 1978 Cleansing and wetting procedures for use in the assessment of the effect of cleansing and wetting on the flamability of textile fabrics and fabric assemblies

As already mentioned, various finishes are available to improve the flammability performance of textiles. Many are very durable and BS 5651 provides a series of cleansing procedures, (cold water soak, domestic and commercial laundering, dry-cleaning), which can be used to assess the effect of such processes on the flammability performance. Normally, performance specifications require that a fabric is tested after cleansing by one of the specified methods although, to accurately assess the effect, flammability testing should be carried out both before and after cleansing.

Test implementation – 'Health and safety' warning

There is a considerable hazard with these tests and safety precautions must be taken. All the above tests should be carried out professionally and with the provision of a suitable fume cupboard. A fire-proof base, the absence of other flammable materials or vapours, and the presence of fire extinguishers are all essential.

Legislation

The 'Consumer Protection Act 1987' falls in two parts. Part I relates to 'Product Liability' and Part II covers 'Consumer Safety' and includes flammability. Legislation relating to the description of the flammability of textiles has existed since at least 1913 and extant legislation is summarised below. Copies of the legislation are available through HMSO.

Part 1, Product liability

The Act states that, where any damage is caused wholly or partly by a defect in a product, the liable parties are the producer of the product, an 'own-brand supplier' and the importer of the product into the European Community. Liability for a defective product covers death, personal injury and damage to property. In the event of a claim the onus falls on the liable party to prove his proper discharge of responsibility in the manufacture, and marketing of the product.

Clearly the objective assessment of the defectiveness of a product and its potential hazard, when presented in a court of law, can be based reliably only on such established test procedures and specifications as are in operation under British Standards and ISO Standards, and on current technical and scientific data.

The necessity of complying with legislation such as this has led manufacturers to become more conscious of the benefits of managing their enterprise within a framework of 'Quality Assurance' (page 280) based on technical control of production and product, and product performance requirements.

Part II, Consumer safety

Reference is made here to two Statutory Instruments directed at reducing the risk to the public from flammable textiles – Consumer Protection SI 2043: 1985 and The Nightwear (Safety) regulations. These regulations, introduced in 1985, require that children's nightwear other than pyjamas, babies' garments and cotton terry-towelling bath robes, should be made from fabric complying with BS 5722. Trimmings and sewing threads must be made from thermoplastic materials if the main body of the garment is thermoplastic.

Nightwear for adults is required to carry a label indicating whether the cloth used complies with BS 5722. For fabrics complying with BS 5722 the label carries 'Low Flam' in black on a white rectangular background with a green edging, and for fabrics not so complying the words are 'Keep away from fire' in black on a white triangular background with a red edging.

Advertisements that contain direct ordering facilities must include clear information about the flammability performance of each type of nightwear on offer.

Consumer Protection SI 1324: 1988 The furniture and furnishings (Fire) safety regulations

These regulations rely on BS 5852 for test methods but are quite complex in their application, since they apply to various components of the furniture separately, and not to the composite of filling, liner and outer fabric as in earlier regulations.

This extensive legislation provides for the testing of foam fillings, non-foam fillings and composite fillings for mattresses and bed bases, and interliner and outer covers of furniture. It is expected that implementation of the legal requirements will reduce the number of fire related deaths and injuries in domestic environments but, because of the relatively long life of domestic furniture, it is not likely to have a dramatic effect on fire statistics.

Chapter 5

TEXTILE FLOORCOVERINGS

The term carpet is often thought to refer to a woven structure, such as Axminster or Wilton; however, since tufting, needlepunching, bonding, flocking and knitting are other methods of producing floorcoverings, it is now more usual to include all these under the heading of 'textile floorcoverings' or 'soft floorcoverings', as opposed to 'hard' or 'smooth' floorcoverings such as vinyl, linoleum, cork and rubber in the form of tiles or sheets.

Tufting accounts for the greatest market share of carpets because of the advantages of high rate of production and relative low cost. Axminster and Wilton carpets still offer the desirable and aesthetic characteristics of woven structures for which they have been renowned throughout the history of carpeting.

The properties and behaviour in use of soft floorcoverings depends on the fibre and yarn content and construction of the material. Of course the severity of the demands made on carpeting differs according to whether it is for domestic use or for contract applications as in hotels, hospitals, shops and ships, as well as location in use, as on stairs, in bedrooms or reception areas. The automotive industry has special carpet requirements.

Consideration will now be given to the basic aspects of each of these carpet structures and their characteristics, followed by a discussion of related properties and required qualities.

CARPET STRUCTURES AND CHARACTERISTICS

Axminster

Axminster carpets are woven and have a cut-pile, the pile yarn being confined to the upper surface of the carpet. The three main types of Axminster carpet are spool Axminster, gripper Axminster, and spool-gripper Axminster. Each of these terms defines the method of weaving. Gripper Axminster is usually limited to eight colours but may be twelve, whereas spool Axminster weaving permits an unlimited number of colours. With such scope for colouring, carpets in very different styles and patterns may be produced. The dyed yarn is assembled before weaving in the appropriate sequence of colour, related to the required pattern.

Spool Axminster

This is the commonest type and it provides scope for an almost unlimited range of colours and hence a subtle range of shades. The process is more expensive than gripper Axminster because the dyed pile yarns are first wound onto spools in a pre-arranged colour order to create pattern. Each spool corresponds to one row of tufts that extends across the width of the carpet (Figure 181). This means, for instance, that 252 spools are required to form a 252 row pattern repeat.

The process of manufacture involves the presentation of the pile yarn by each spool in turn at the point of weaving where the weft is inserted to form the carpet. A comb pushes the tip of the pile yarn to form a U-shaped tuft round the weft, and scissor-like blades cut the tuft to the required length from the supply of yarn on the spool. As soon as the tuft of yarn has been woven in, the spool is advanced one place and the next spool, carrying the supply of yarn with the correct colour sequence for the next pick, presents the yarn for weaving, and so on.

The backing of the carpet coming off the loom tends to be flexible due to the weave structure, and consequently it is given a backcoating with a synthetic latex or some other stiffener.

Gripper Axminster

This method of manufacture is distinctly different from spool Axminster and the maximum number of colours possible is usually eight. Otherwise the general appearance of the two types of carpet is indistinguishable,

Fig. 181 Spool Axminster weaving showing rows of spools extending across the carpet width. *(Firth Carpets)*

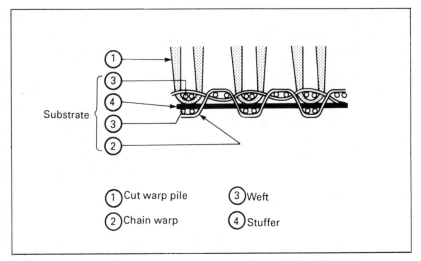

Fig. 182 Gripper Axminster carpet (warpways section – Corinthian gripper weave) showing short ends of yarn trapped by the weft within the structure. Diagram amended from Fig. 9 of BS5557. *(The Textile Institute)*

although the gripper type may have a more ribbed appearance. Its structure tends to be more firm and stable.

Instead of using spools the dyed yarns for the warp pile are withdrawn as required from bobbins arranged in a large stand, known as a creel, at the back of the loom. Jacquard-operated yarn carriers present the appropriate coloured yarns to the grippers which pull off the required length of pile, which is then cut. The grippers, holding the row of tufts, then swing down to insert the tufts at the point of weaving across the carpet width. The Jacquard mechanism now selects the next row of colours to form the pattern, and so on.

There are four main types of ground weave used in the manufacture of Axminster carpets and in each the principle of construction is the same. The chain warp, whilst under suitable tension, binds the cut warp pile tufts firmly into the weave in conjunction with the interlacing of say two or three double shots of weft for each insertion of cut pile. The stuffer warp is held under high tension during weaving and runs more or less straight within the substrate. It provides the body or firmness to the ground weave and forms the bed on which the cut pile rests. The stuffer warp alternates with the pairs of chain warps across the width of the carpet.

Spool-gripper Axminster

This differs from the spool Axminster in that grippers are used to grip the yarn, protruding from each spool in turn, which is then cut and inserted by the movement of the gripper at the point of weaving. This method in effect combines the gripper and spool aspects of manufacture.

Wilton

The distinctive feature of Wilton carpet is that the warp pile yarns are woven into the ground weave or substrate of the carpet and are brought up to the surface when required to form the pile. Cut pile or loop pile, or a combination of two types of pile, are used to create a patterned effect. These carpets can be produced with very heavy weights of pile and high pile density. The method of manufacture allows for special designs and colours to be woven for short production runs to meet customer requirements. The number of colours that can be easily employed for the pile warp is limited to five, in contrast to the high colour range possible in Axminster.

Wilton carpet may be either plain Wilton, sometimes known as 'Velvet', or figured Wilton.

Plain Wilton

Plain Wilton has a cut uniform pile of one colour. This may be produced by 'double plush' carpet weaving, similar in principle to the manufacture of velvet (page 89), in which two carpets are produced face-to-face in the weaving process and then separated by a reciprocating cutter in the loom. The distance between the ground weaves of the two carpets controls the pile height of each carpet after separation. By this method of manufacture a more uniform pile can be produced. Other advantages relate to reduction in manufacturing costs.

Wilton, however, is commonly woven singly, in which case the pile height is created by the introduction of a thin metal strip or wire in the weft direction over which the pile yarns pass during the course of weaving. The metal strip extends across the full width of the carpet and carries a sharp blade at one end which cuts the loops of pile yarn when the wire is withdrawn. The height and thickness of the wire governs the pile height.

A loop pile carpet known as 'Brussels', 'Bouclé' or 'cord' Wilton is produced when the cutting blade of the metal strip is absent.

Figured Wilton

The pattern in the carpet is created by the use of up to five colours (occasionally more) and, as for plain Wilton, the pile is formed over a metal strip.

Figure 183 illustrates how different colours are used to create pattern, and how the pile yarns are integrated into the substantial and consequently firm carpet substrate. Coloured yarns not in use at any one time for the pile can be detected on the back of the carpet, but some such yarns are contained within the ground structure itself until required to appear on the surface to form the appropriate part of the coloured pile.

Figured Wilton is a comparatively expensive carpet. It is woven on a Jacquard loom (Figure 184) in which the two to five frames of pile yarn,

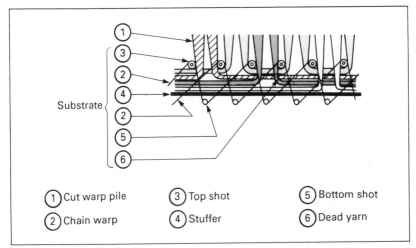

Fig. 183 Figured Wilton carpet, two-shot (warpways section). Diagram derived from Fig. 3 of BS5557. *(The Textile Institute)*

Fig. 184 Wilton carpet Jacquard weaving. *(Wilton Royal)*

each of different colour, are fed into the loom. This type of carpet is more likely to be used for contract installations than in the domestic market.

Textural design effects

To create sculptured single colour designs and 'embossed' effects a choice of methods is available. A combination of normal soft-twist yarns and of high-twist pile yarns which snarl and contract on cutting, produce a pile of different heights. Consequently certain areas of the design differ in appearance and light reflectance.

Earlier it was stated that in singly woven Wilton the pile height is controlled by the height and thickness of the wire (page 248). Special surface effects and patterns can be created by introducing wires with or without the sharp blade, and also possibly differing in size, in a predetermined manner during the course of weaving thereby producing a carpet having various pile heights and/or combinations of cut and uncut pile.

Tufted carpets

Tufting is a very simple, rapid and inexpensive process. Figure 185 shows the creel supplying the pile yarn to the Tufting Machine. Substrate cloth is transported over a supporting perforated plate. Needles, carrying the pile yarns, mounted in line in a reciprocating bar the width of the carpet, plunge down through the substrate and the perforated plate beneath, and then retract. The loop formed under the substrate is held by loopers while the needles are extracted and, if required, the loops are cut by a knife to form a cut pile (Figure 186). The woven, or nonwoven, substrate may be made of polypropylene, polyester or jute. In order to secure the pile, the back of the carpet is coated with a natural or synthetic rubber latex. A secondary backing of a jute or synthetic fibre fabric may be bonded to the back of the carpet to improve stability and stiffness; a latex foam may be

Fig. 185 Tufted carpet: showing creel, tufting machine and carpet emerging on the right. *(Firth carpets)*

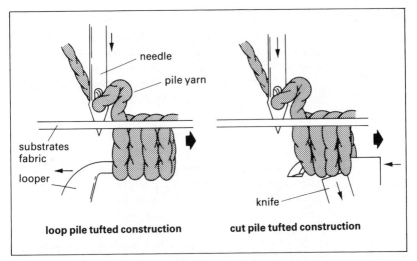

Fig. 186 Tufted carpet (loop and cut pile). *(The Textile Institute)*

used to increase the carpet's resilience. Consideration must be given to the quality of the foam from the point of view of flame retardance and durability in use. The polymer content, density and ageing characteristics determine the extent to which the desirable performance properties are maintained in use.

The quality of a tufted carpet is determined not only by the fibre content of the pile and substrate, but also by the closeness of the loops and the linear density of the yarn.

Colour and range of patterns are of interest when selecting a carpet. Tufted carpets originally offered little variety other than simple designs and self-coloured types. In order to increase the market share of carpets, developments in the control of needle movement during tufting have been introduced in an attempt to create the designs typical of Wilton and Axminster carpets. However, the problem is that such innovations reduce the speed of tufting, thereby increasing costs for long production runs. One method of producing coloured patterning is by the so called 'buried pile design'. This may be formed by high-low pile tufting with alternate needles threaded with different colours so that the high pile forms areas of colour overlying the low, buried, pile of a different colour.

Printing of undyed plain tufted carpets provides a versatility in creating more elaborate, instant designs, to meet customer requirements. Screen printing is only justified for long production runs of a particular design, because of the cost of preparing screens. Jet-'printing' (page 335) is capable of switching designs instantaneously without stopping the process because the dye liquor is fed through individual jets as required. A large store of design data is held on magnetic tape or disc and the machine is programmed to produce instantly a particular design.

Needle-punched floor covering

Fibre bonding is created by the needling method used in the manufacture of nonwovens (page 148), followed by resin impregnation or heat treatment depending on the fibre content. The material of suitable thickness and quality may be used in roll form as carpeting or underlay, or cut into carpet tiles which are given a heavy backing to ensure dimensional stability.

Bonded-pile carpet

Apart from weaving, tufting and needling, textile floor coverings can be made rapidly and inexpensively by bonding pile yarn or sheets of fibre directly on to a backing fabric. The pile can be either cut, loop pile or a multi-level loop pile.

One method is to pleat a sheet of fibres or yarns, and simultaneously cause the base of the loop to be implanted and anchored in the adhesive which has been applied to a textile substrate.

Another method is to fold sheets of fibres or yarn, by means of reciprocating blades, between two parallel downward travelling backing cloths, each of which has been pre-treated on the inside face with an adhesive, usually of the hot melt type (Figure 187). The 'corrugated' fibre web or yarns are bonded to the adhesive surface of the backing cloths. The face-to-face carpet is cut up the middle to form two separate rolls of carpet, as in face-to-face weaving of velvet.

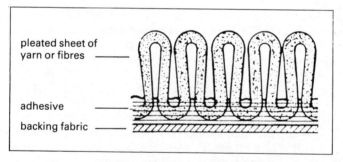

pleated sheet of yarn or fibres

adhesive

backing fabric

Fig. 187 Bonded loop pile carpet.

This type of carpet has the advantage that cut edges do not fray and the security of the tufts can be greater than in woven carpets. Bonded-pile carpets have a particular use as carpet tiles, rolls of carpeting which can be cut easily, and automotive carpeting where pieces of carpet can be pre-formed into the contoured shape of the vehicle interior and stuck in position. In fact, such carpets can be stuck to sub-floors, and the seams bonded to ensure flatness of joins and avoidance of preferential wear.

Flocked carpet

Electrically charged nylon fibres, only 2 to 4 mm long, are projected into an electrostatic field where they align themselves parallel to the direction of the lines of electrical force. Consequently the fibres shoot vertically into a prepared binder film which coats a thin nonwoven fibre-glass base passing beneath the charge.

To increase the thickness and resilience of the carpet the back is coated with an appropriate foam layer which is normally nonporous. Such carpets are often suitable for floor areas subject to wet spillage and heavy traffic.

Raschel knitted carpet

This method of warp knitting (page 103) has not reached a level of commercial significance for floor coverings and carpeting, but it is necessary to be aware of its potential.

The character of the material depends on the details of the lapping movement (page 126) in the knitting pattern, and the choice of fibres for the pile and the ground structure. For instance, in artificial turf the pile consists of dope-dyed nylon ribbon knitted in a nylon and polyester base.

UK sales of carpet types

The sale of machine-made pile carpets and rugs in the UK in 1988 amounted to a total of 132 million m^2 and a value of £819 million (source: Business Monitor – carpets PQ 4384/5, through The British Carpet Manu-facturers' Association Ltd. Report 1988/89). The share of the market by each carpet type being:

Table 18   UK SALES OF PILE CARPETS 1988

	% m^2	% value
Tufted*	85·6	65·7
Axminster	10·4	24·1
Wilton	2·0	6·1
Sundries	2·0	4·1
(Including knitted pile, deep pile, nonwoven).		
* Of which printed Tufted	36·0	23·0

CARPET QUALITY AND PROPERTIES

Rating of fibres

Fibre manufacturers are anxious at all times to promote the use and increase the sale of their particular fibre types. Carpets, with their vast consumption of fibre in the pile in combination with other fibres in the ground structure, provide clear incentives for producers to compete in the production of fibres specially suited to particular carpet requirements in use at competitive prices. Fibre variants and textile finishes offer a range of characteristics that are important for carpeting such as subdued lustre, differential dyeing and flame retardance. Soil-hiding, soil and stain release, and anti-static behaviour can also be controlled.

Apart from the functional features of carpets, their aesthetic qualities in terms of scope for colouration, development of surface texture and carpet styling are important in the stimulation and maintenance of user interest.

The main outlet for wool has been traditionally in woven carpets although now an increased proportion of woollen yarn is being used in tufteds. Nylon, both as staple and BCF yarn (page 68), is extensively used in tufting, but now woven Wilton has been made from nylon 6.6 'Timbrelle' for contract carpeting. BCF nylon and polypropylene yarns provide bulk and pile resilience compared with unbulked filaments.

'Timbrelle', an ICI nylon fibre, is an example of a fibre variant to meet the specific needs of the carpet industry. It is the brand name of a family of nylon fibres including staple and BCF yarn in various dtex filament values, and of various levels of lustre and dyeing effects. 'Tactesse' belongs to this group of fibres, and is a specialised 6 dtex staple fibre for carpets in which variants are introduced by way of modifications to the internal fibre structure, the presence of delustrant, and the development of a 'grainy' fibre surface. These contribute to physical properties and aesthetic characterisation close to that of wool. The presence of anti-static additive reduces its soiling tendency.

Acrylic fibres have been the most wool-like of all synthetic fibres, their principal attraction for domestic use being the soft pile they provide.

Flame retardance may be conferred on fibres by suitable modifications, and this will be indicated by the suffix FR to the brand name of a fibre. Finishes may also be applied to the same end, sometimes even more effectively, as in the case of the Zirpro finish on wool. Resistance to soiling and improved soil release behaviour are conferred by fluorocarbon finishes such as Scotchgard and Baygard. The accumulation of static electricity can be controlled by Permalose and Disperstat finishes, and by the introduction of metal particles or fibres in the pile yarn which provide conducting paths by which any charge may leak away.

The cost of fibres fluctuates in response to commercial factors and generally ranges from viscose and polypropylene, as the cheapest, through acrylic to wool and nylon, the more expensive. To judge value for money, consideration must be given to fibre properties in conjunction with the carpet construction, in relation to the expectations of the customer and the use to which the floorcovering is to be put.

It is now appropriate to summarise in broad terms some of the properties relating to the fibres referred to.

Table 19   RATING OF FIBRE PERFORMANCE IN CARPET PILE
(excluding the influence of carpet structure and finish)

| | Performance | | | |
	Highest ←		→	*Lowest*
Resistance to abrasion	nylon	Pp	wool acrylic	viscose
Resilience and appearance retention	wool	acrylic	nylon	Pp viscose
Resistance to soiling	wool Pp	viscose	acrylic	nylon
Ease of cleaning	acrylic Pp	nylon	wool viscose	
Absence of static		wool viscose	acrylic Pp	nylon
Flame retardance	wool		nylon	acrylic Pp
Ease of dyeing (therefore choice of colours)	wool nylon	acrylic viscose		Pp

Note: Pp – polypropylene

Tufted carpets are available in different qualities, the variables being the nature and quantity of pile fibre, the quality of the base fabric and the backcoating and secondary backing. The production run for any given quality must be long to provide the volume of sales needed for profitability.

Nylon, acrylic and polypropylene are the fibres mostly used, and also wool/nylon or wool/acrylic blends. Wool has been associated with the 'berber' and wool tweed styles.

Carpet widths are up to 3·66 m and 4·57 m and these are described as 'broadloom' carpets. Jet-printing (page 335) and screen printing widen the scope of elaborate surface design and colouration for this type of floor covering. The computer controlled injection-dyeing machine has the facility to change the design frequently without stopping the printing process as in screen printing.

255

Woven carpets range in width from 0·69 m and 0·91 m, (known as 'body' carpets) to widths of 2·74 m and 3·66 m. Wool/nylon 80/20 or 50/50 blends are frequently used and sometimes acrylic fibre combinations with wool or nylon.

Carpet tiles 33½ cm or 50 cm square are usually cut from needle punched carpeting, which is the least expensive, or tufted material. Blends of two or three fibres such as nylon, animal hair, polypropylene and viscose are used for the surface according to the required visual effect, location in use and target cost. The presence of viscose reduces material cost but it is used only in small amounts in view of its low resistance to abrasion. The inclusion of nylon in the blend ensures adequate durability.

To contribute to the stability of needle punched tiles, a woven cotton scrim or fabric is used as a base on which the surface fibres are laid prior to needle-punching and subsequent back-coating. Dimensional stability is most important and this relies on the nature and quality of the backing. Tiles are normally loose laid but some tiles are given a peelable adhesive to locate them in use.

Carpet printing provides great design potential and for contract flooring logos, for instance, can be featured.

Rugs. Apart from the use of quality woven carpet structures and choice of fibres already discussed, inexpensive rugs intended for decorative use are made with such blends as 75% viscose/18% cotton/7% other fibre. Shag-pile rugs with very long pile have an aesthetic role primarily.

In traditional oriental rugs the pile tufts are knotted by hand and these rugs are the most exclusive and aesthetically prized of the range of floorcoverings.

Now polypropylene BCF yarn is made into rugs carrying oriental designs which demonstrates the constant technical inventiveness needed to create style and meet functional demands at a price.

PERFORMANCE RATING OF TEXTILE FLOORCOVERINGS MADE WITH YARN PILE

The properties and performance of a carpet in use are largely dependent on its constructional features. These include the mass of pile yarn lying above the substrate, the thickness (that is length) of the pile, pile density, tuft density and type of fibre in the pile yarn. The nature of the substrate and any underlay also have their effects on carpet performance.

BS 4223 provides test procedures for the determination of constructional details of carpets, and simple definitions of some of the terms used are worth noting, since it is on these that the BS 7131:1989 for 'carpet performance rating' is based. The British Carpet Technical Centre specialises in the evaluation of carpets and uses this British Standard and other test procedures.

Surface pile mass – g/m^2

This is the mass of the pile above the backing and is determined by the shearing away of the pile from a known area of carpet and the determination of its mass. Pile mass is an important factor in the durability of a carpet, but a short dense pile is better than a longer more open pile, and of course there are important differences between fibres. A large part of the weight of a carpet is accounted for by the weight of the pile.

Surface pile density – g/cm^3

This is the ratio of the pile mass in g/m^2 to the pile thickness in mm, under a given load. The surface density of the pile influences the recovery of the pile from flattening. Good recovery is associated with high pile density, and promotes the maintenance of carpet appearance.

Tuft or loop density – number of tufts, or loops per 100 cm^2

The number of tufts per unit area of carpet is of considerable importance in comparing carpets of the same type. As tuft density is decreased surface pile mass needs to be increased to maintain the same level of performance. At 150 tufts per 100 cm^2 surface pile mass needs to be about 50% greater than at 2,000 tufts per 100 cm^2. Cut pile carpets need to have a surface pile mass about 25% greater than loop pile carpets.

The British Standard Performance Rating for a carpet is calculated from the above data together with its appearance retention rating as obtained by testing on the WIRA Hexapod Tumbler Tester.

Fig. 188 WIRA Hexapod tumbler tester. *(British Carpet Technical Centre)*

Appearance retention

The action of walking, together with the striking of the heel on the carpet, flattens the pile and is liable to change the reflectance of light from the disturbed surface. The Hexapod is a laboratory test instrument used in the assessment of appearance retention.

The carpet is fitted to the inside of the Hexapod drum (BS 6659) with the pile facing inwards. An underlay may be fitted beneath the carpet if required. A heavy tumbler with six PU studded feet is then enclosed within the drum which rotates alternately in each direction for a total of 12,000 revs or six hours. After vacuuming the surface to remove loose fibre the appearance of the tested (so called 'fatigued') carpet is compared with a corresponding piece of new carpet. From the point of view of structural change this is done at an intermediate stage of 4,000 revs and finally after 12,000 revs. The differences observed are graded against a 1–5 BS/ISO carpet grey scale, similar to that shown on page 199. Since appearance change at an early stage of use is considered to be detrimental any visual change at 4,000 revs is doubly penalised.

The loss in the thickness of the carpet (BS 4051) is also determined after 4,000 revs in the Hexapod.

Overall performance 'Carpet Rating'

BS 7131: 1989 sets desirable targets for the rating of pile carpets for different purposes. The ratings are derived from constructional features and fibre type, and performance in tests, some of which are described above. Carpets are graded out of a maximum of 30 according to construction, out of 30 according to pile density, and out of 40 for performance in the Hexapod test. The ratings are added to give an overall rating, the maximum of which is 100, Table 20. BS 7131 then classifies the carpet for use according to its overall rating, Table 21.

It will be seen that reference is made, under 'Effective pile mass rating' to the 'Fibre Factor' (Table 20). BS 7131 discriminates between the likely contribution made by different types of fibre when used in the pile of

Table 20 OVERALL PERFORMANCE 'CARPET RATING'

	Maximum rating
Effective pile mass rating: (including adjustments according to different pile fibres i.e. 'Fibre Factor', and the minimum pile mass required for carpets with given number of tufts/unit area)	30
Effective pile density rating	30
Appearance retention rating: – loss in surface structure – loss in thickness	30 10

Table 21   CLASSIFICATION OF PILE CARPET ACCORDING TO USE

Carpet Classification	Minimum required rating	Suitability in use Domestic	Non-domestic	Location in domestic use
4	85	–	Heavy	–
3	70	Heavy	General	Living room/hall/landing
2	55	General	Moderate	Dining room/study
1	35	Moderate	–	Bedroom

Additional performance requirements are listed for carpets for special situations such as level of colour fastness and mildew resistance for carpets and foam backing to be used in the kitchen and bathroom, the tuft withdrawal force, discussed below, for stair carpets.

carpets by attributing values which are used to recognise the high levels of durability expected from nylon in BCF and spun forms, through polypropylene, polyester, acrylic and wool, to modified viscose and modacrylic fibres which have lower carpet performance characteristics. From the 'Fibre Factors' attributed to each of these fibres it is possible to derive a factor appropriate to a given fibre blend. For a particular carpet being rated, the BS 7131 calculation for the determination of 'Effective pile mass rating' is adjusted according to the pile fibre(s) used.

Other aspects of carpet performance

Appearance retention has already been included under 'carpet classification' with particular reference to mechanical action when walked on, but an additional cause of appearance loss is often the non-recoverability of the pile from compression under a static load, such as furniture. Test procedures are given under 'Carpet static loading' (BS 4939) and 'Thickness-compression recovery' BS 4098.

Carpet durability. The 'wear' of a carpet in use is caused by a wide range of many factors that cause deterioration of the floorcovering including stiletto and damaged heels and grit. Abrasion in various forms is the main cause of failure. In carpet design and development work carpet trials are valuable and may be conducted either on stairs or on flat laid floor coverings. The number of step-ons is electronically recorded together with constant assessment of wear life and appearance retention.

Changes in *pile thickness* may be monitored in several ways including the use of the thickness gauge in Figure 189. Six locating pins penetrate the pile to rest on the backing and the central flat probe connected to the dial contacts the pile surface. The pile height is read off the gauge.

Fig. 189 Portable carpet thickness gauge. *(Shirley Developments Ltd.)*

Fig. 190 WIRA carpet abrasion machine. *(Shirley Developments Ltd.)*

More rapid assessments of resistance to abrasion, particularly for quality control purposes in carpet manufacture, are made on a carpet abrasion tester. Here specimens of the carpet are rubbed against a standard abrasive material, and at the end of the test, the amount of abrasion of the test specimen is assessed by comparison with a standard photograph. Another method of estimating the extent of abrasion is by determining the loss in weight of the specimen.

The results, however, need expert interpretation and are not intended to provide an estimate of the service life of a carpet. To judge the effect of a furniture castor in use a special castor chair test is used.

It must be appreciated that the measurement of resistance to abrasion of carpets is difficult since there are so many variables in use. For instance, if the carpet runs the length of a straight corridor the treatment it will receive from the 'walker' will be different from that when located near a door where there is much pivoting and turning of the feet. In other locations there may be shuffling of feet resulting in heavy localised wear and possible carpet pilling. The heel area of a particular shoe will also affect the severity of the impact on the carpet when walking.

The retention of tufts or loops in woven and tufted carpets is an

Fig. 191 WIRA tuft withdrawal tensometer.

important aspect of durability, particularly on stair nosings and risers, and the 'Tuft withdrawal' tensometer (Figure 191) provides a means of assessment.

The carpet is held flat by a metal plate and a tuft or loop in the pile is fixed to a clamp which is connected to the tensometer. Tension is increased until the force needed to withdraw the tuft is noted.

Physical properties

Dimensional stability

Resistance to shrinkage or extension of a carpet is essential under a range of humidity and temperature variations. An increase in size will lead to rucking and preferential wear on the folds. Methods of test for dimensional stability are given in BS 4682.

Flame retardance and its significance for carpeting is discussed on page 239.

Electrostatic properties

The phenomenon of static electricity is discussed on page 14 and under 'the mechanism of soiling' page 209. Carpets that have a low conductivity attract dust and fluff from the atmosphere after becoming charged by the continual contact and separation of the sole of the shoe in walking.

The degree to which static electricity is developed on a carpet depends on various circumstances, including the type of fibre, the construction of the carpet and the type of footwear being worn, particularly the electrical conductivity of the sole, and also the humidity of the air. The latter is important because when the air has a low humidity the carpet contains least moisture, and in this state is a good insulator and therefore any static charge developed leaks away only slowly. All common manufactured fibres, except viscose, are good insulators when dry. A fall of 10% in relative humidity can cause an increase of 3–6 fold in electrical resistance. Under-floor heating dries the carpet and therefore promotes the accumulation of static charges.

Apart from measurement of the electrical resistivity of the carpet (BS 6654), body voltage tests are carried out. A rise in body voltage results from the electrical characteristics of the floorcovering in combination with the use of different types of soles e.g. rubber, PVC, Neolite. The body voltage test requires the 'walker' on the carpet to be connected to a static voltmeter on which the maximum voltage arising in the body is noted. Normally, tests are carried out with three kinds of soles and, since different people have individual responses to charges, tests with three 'walkers' are carried out on each carpet.

Special testing machines have been designed to replace the 'walker' and these incorporate a mechanical device covered with the appropriate sole material to represent the action of the shoe. The voltage developed during a period in which the carpet is subject to the action of this machine is observed. Values of 2,000 volts indicate that the carpet is prone to static.

The computer industry requires the working environment to be specially static and dust free within a given range of humidity and temperature conditions, and for these requirements the properties of floor covering are critical. For general use it is important to ensure the carpet be conductive and thereby discount the variable influence of the sole and heel of shoes on static.

Thermal insulation

Loss of heat from a room through the floor is accelerated by draughts between and underneath the floorboards; the presence of a carpet and underlay form an effective and valuable barrier to such loss of heat. It is largely the thickness of the carpet pile and the presence of air contained within the pile that insulates and hence the pile thickness is important. Carpets which are soon flattened in use do not maintain their energy-saving capacity.

Thermal resistance can be measured in 'tog' units on the 'Shirley Togmeter' (BS 4745) page 220; normally the values for carpets lie between 1–3 togs.

Acoustic properties

Insulation against the transmission of disturbing noise is especially important in apartment buildings, and specific areas of public buildings.

Sound which is air-borne passes through small cracks, windows and doors, and the presence of a carpet has a limited effect in minimising this. Sound transmitted by impact however, such as the dropping of objects on a solid floor, the scraping of chairs and the tapping of heels, can be substantially reduced by the use of carpeting. It has been found that thick pile carpet with particular types of underlay can usefully absorb sound over a wide range of frequencies. Thin pile carpets with no underlay are least effective. Tests for air-borne sound absorption are given in BS 3638, and for impact-sound insulation BS 2750.

Colour fastness

Exposure to light, carpet shampooing, water, wet and dry rubbing are the main causes of staining and shade change of dyes used in carpets. Additionally, contamination by seawater may be a problem in some localities. Reference to colour fastness has already been made on page 259 and to BS 1006 test methods applied to carpets.

Sometimes the colour fastness of carpets is in question when in fact the observed change may be due to soiling and the flattening of the pile. When the pile becomes flattened it is the sides of the tufts that are seen instead of the ends of the pile. Also, if in a blend of fibres the different types of fibre are dyed to different shades, or colours, and the types of fibres wear at different rates, as will happen in a wool/nylon blend, a true change in shade unrelated to fading will occur as the fabric wears.

Examples of basic requirements for minimum levels of colour fastness in tests carried out in conformity with BS methods would be:

Colour fastness specification

Wet shampoo (shade change)	3–4 grey scale
Rubbing fastness (wet and dry)	3
Light fastness (Xenon arc)	4–5 minimum

Some performance levels may be adjusted according to whether the carpet is plain or patterned, and whether it is a pale or dark shade.

Chapter 6

LABELLING

The mandatory labelling of textile products with the generic names of the fibre content (page 58) and the regulations governing the fibre content labelling (page 57) have already been considered, together with the optional additional use of trade-names of the fibres to meet the promotional needs of the manufacturer.

Other mandatory labelling relates to the flammability of textiles (page 243), the purpose of which is to protect the user.

Manufacturers' and distributors' logos can also be coupled with a trade-name, to establish or reinforce the image and 'quality' of the merchandise in the mind of the purchaser, but this aspect of labelling will not be discussed.

Country of origin

The implications of rescinding the earlier Trade Descriptions Order for the labelling of textile goods and clothing with the country of origin is worth touching upon. The regulation was cancelled following a directive by the European court based on the premise that such labelling provides a barrier to free trade. Country of origin labelling is therefore now optional.

Textiles and clothing consist of many components and a garment, for instance, may be made from fabric, lining, interlining and sewing thread, each of which can originate in different countries. The 'country of origin' of a made-up article is defined as the country in which the last 'substantial change' in manufacture occurred – that would normally be the assembly of components. Such a label, therefore, may be unrelated to the origins of any of the garment's components. Country-of-origin labels, if used, need not be durable, but must be honest.

Care labelling

Whilst information on fibre content is useful, there is still much ignorance of the cleansing treatments that should be applied to the different fibres and blends, and how the treatments should be modified according to the dyes and finishes used. Garment manufacturers particularly have a responsibility to take account of all the fabric components, interlinings and trimmings included in the garment when providing advice on the cleansing of the garment.

Instructions on the use or care of textile products is legally required in the USA, but is provided voluntarily in some other countries, including the UK, as a means of assisting the user to get the greatest satisfaction from the garment or household textile.

The Home Laundering Consultative Council (HLCC),* is concerned with the care of textiles and clothing during the processes of laundering and dry-cleaning, and their recommendations are based on available professional and technical data. The HLCC is an active member of GINETEX, the international care labelling association, which is intended to ensure approximate uniformity of treatment of textiles in these processes by users. The 'International Textile Care Labelling Code' is concerned with how the textile should be washed, rinsed and dried, bleached, ironed, dry-cleaned and tumble dried. A symbol for each process has been evolved.

Chlorine bleaching symbols

 The triangle symbol containing the letters Cl signifies that chlorine bleach may be applied to the article. The use of such bleach is more common in continental Europe than in this country. The symbol does not refer to the rather safer bleaches based on sodium perborate and hydrogen peroxide.

 Signifies that chlorine bleach must not be used. Optional phrases may accompany the symbol as follows:
'Do not bleach' or 'Do not use chlorine bleach'.
These symbols should be observed when removing stains, and laundering in commercial laundries.

Ironing symbols

The outline of an iron and the number of dots in the symbol indicate the maximum temperature of the soleplate.

The accuracy of the sole temperature in relation to the iron setting is the responsibility of the iron manufacturer. However, it is possible to check the temperature either by means of a thermocouple and digital thermometer or simply by using '3M Thermo-paperstrips' with self-adhesive backing which, on contact with a hot surface, change colour according to the temperature. (Available from SDL).

---

* *HLCC, 7 Swallow Place, Oxford Circus, London, W1R 7AA*

Table 22   IRONING SYMBOLS

Symbol	Optional word to clarify meaning	General guide to fibre suitability
	Hot	At 200°C – Cotton, linen, viscose and modal
	Warm	At 150°C – Polyester mixtures, wool
	Cool	At 100°C – Acrylic, nylon, acetate, triacetate, polyester
	Do not iron	Ironing detrimental to fabrics.

The behaviour of a fabric in ironing depends on the amount of moisture present, since the water may plasticise the fibre or possibly reduce its melting point. These effects are more marked in some fibres than in others, and the presence of moisture may be desirable or not. Thus untreated cotton is ironed damp but acrylic fibres are pressed dry. Consideration should be given to the effect of 'safe' ironing temperatures on possible change in colour and stiffness of the fabric.

BS 2747:1986 'Code of Practice for Textile Care Labelling' standardises care instructions and lays down the system for the labelling scheme and the interpretation of the five symbols used in the code. Symbols are intended to be the sole means of communication internationally, but for the time being in Britain the symbols will be accompanied by a choice of appropriate explanatory 'required phrases', published in BS 2747, selected to avoid the possibility of contravening the Textile Products (Indications of Fibre Content) Regulations. Optional information about the washing process may be included in the label in some form.

Apart from the effectiveness of the cleansing process it is important that the fabrics are not damaged or creased excessively, and that they do not lose colour or have the finish impaired whilst washing. Alternative or additional care recommendations to the above may be given, such as: 'Drip dry' (instead of final spin), 'Dry flat', 'Do not line dry', 'Wash separately', 'Do not soak'. Creasing can be minimised if washing temperatures and times, size of load, duration of spin drying, that are recommended, are not exceeded. A rapid drop in temperature in the washing and rinsing stages can cause creases to become fixed in a fabric such as polyester; leaving wet fabrics in a heap for a long time, especially when hot, can introduce persistent creases, apart from running the risk of some colours staining adjacent fabric. In many machine washing cycles, fabric is finally left suspended in water to minimise creasing, prior to spin drying.

Table 23 SUMMARY OF WASHING SYMBOLS

Washing symbols	
Wash-tub Number indicates safe maximum temperature in °Celsius Process suitable for the following fabrics:	
95 White cotton and linen articles without special finishes	**40** Acrylics, acetate, and triacetate, including mixtures with wool; polyester/ wool blends
60 Cotton, linen or viscose articles without special finishes where colours are fast at 60°C	**40** Wool. Wool mixed with other fibres; silk
50 Nylon; polyester/ cotton mixtures; polyester, cotton and viscose articles with special finishes; cotton/ acrylic mixtures	Handwash. (Do not machine wash)
40 Cotton, linen or viscose articles where colours are fast at 40°C but not at 60°C	Do not wash

Interpretation of washing symbols BS 2747 'Required phrases'		Optional information which may be given on the label. *Washing process*
No bar beneath	'Wash as cotton' *or* 'Wash in cotton cycle' *or* 'Wash in cotton programme'	Normal machine agitation (maximum) Normal rinsing cycle Normal spinning (water extraction)
Single bar beneath	'Wash as synthetics' *or* 'Wash in synthetics cycle' *or* 'Wash in synthetics programme'	Reduced machine agitation (medium i.e. 40–60% of maximum) Rinsing cycle, with gradual cooling before spinning Reduced spinning (short spin)
Broken bar beneath	'Wash as wool' *or* 'Wash in wool cycle' *or* 'Wash in wool programme'	Much reduced machine agitation (minimum i.e. 20–30% of maximum) Normal rinsing cycle Normal spinning

Drycleaning symbols

Drycleaning is symbolised by a circle. The letter in the circle refers to the solvent which may be used in the drycleaning process. Common solvents in use are perchloroethylene (tetrachloroethylene), white spirit (hydrocarbons, Stoddard solvent), solvents R113 (trichlorotrifluoroethane) and R11. An article carrying a drycleaning symbol can be safely classified for the appropriate process by the commercial drycleaner. It is the responsibility of the user of a 'coin-op' drycleaning machine to check the suitability of the process by comparing the garment label with the guide-lines on the machine.

'Guide-lines for the drycleanability testing' of materials issued by the HLCC is in conformity with ISO3175–1975 (BS 4961) 'Textiles – Determination of dimensional change on dry cleaning in perchloroethylene – machine method' with appropriate modifications for the solvent used.

Each of the symbols listed below may be accompanied by the phrase 'Dryclean' except, of course, for the 'Do not dryclean' symbol.

Care should always be exercised when using solvent-based stain removers. A guide to their suitability is: A – can be used without restriction, P – with some restrictions, and F – not suitable.

Table 24   DRYCLEANING SYMBOLS

Symbol	Features of the process
(A)	Goods which may be cleaned in any of the conventional solvents normally used in drycleaning.
(P)	Articles drycleanable in perchloroethylene, Solvent R113, Solvent R11, and white spirit.
(P) underlined	Articles drycleanable as in (P), but only under restrictions affecting the addition of water, mechanical action, and drying temperature during drycleaning.
(F)	Articles drycleanable in Solvent R113 and white spirit.
(F) underlined	Articles drycleanable as in (F), but only under restrictions affecting the addition of water, mechanical action, and drying temperature during drycleaning.
⊗	Articles unsuitable for drycleaning.

Tumble drying symbols

Tumble driers are increasing in household use and most textile articles can be safely tumble dried, but most wool knitwear and articles containing foam or rubber-like materials are likely to be spoilt in this process.

The presence of a 'may be tumble dried' label may be accompanied by instructions to set the machine at a lower temperature, as for acrylics. The symbol does not provide information about possible fabric shrinkage, which is normally reversible; nor does it specify the level of moisture content of the article at the end of the drying cycle, nor the ease of crease removal from certain fabrics.

When tumble drying is not recommended, use is permitted of such phrases as 'dry flat' for heavy-weight knitwear, or 'drip-dry'.

'Guide-lines for tumble drying testing' prepared by the HLCC link with the revised BS 4923: 1989 'Schedule of Domestic Washing and Drying Procedures for Textile Testing'.

Table 25   TUMBLE DRYING SYMBOLS

Symbol	Meaning
⊡	The circle in a square simply indicates 'may be tumble dried'
⊠	Denotes 'Do not tumble dry'

Precautions in labelling

When an article carries a label it becomes a legal requirement that the recommendations given on the label for its care are appropriate.

Special precautions must be taken in the cleaning of certain fabrics in order to maintain, for example, flame retardancy, water repellency and mothproofness. Only soapless detergents must be used on flame-retardant fabrics, otherwise, with hard water, there may be a build-up of lime soap on the fabric which reduces flame retardance. Soaking in water with a detergent, bleaching, boiling and starching all must be avoided to prevent damaging the effectiveness of the finish. To help maintain water repellency and finish the fabric needs very thorough rinsing to remove traces of the detergent.

A care label should be applied in such a way as to ensure its prominence and permanence throughout the life of the article. Light-weight garments such as lingerie, scarves and socks, for which a conventional sewn-in care label would be cumbersome, may have the care guide-lines given on a loose label.

Inspection of care labels on garments will show a variety of layouts and various combinations of recommendations according to the composition and end use of the garment. An example of a label is given here by way of a summary.

Table 26   EXAMPLE OF GARMENT CARE LABEL

	MACHINE	HAND WASH
[50]	Hand hot medium wash	Hand hot
	Cold rinse. Short spin or drip-dry	
	Wash as Synthetics	

⚠	DO NOT USE CHLORINE BLEACH	☐	MAY BE TUMBLE DRIED	🔥	WARM IRON	Ⓟ	DRY CLEAN-ABLE

Chapter 7

TEXTILE SPECIFICATION AND QUALITY ASSURANCE

Continuous large scale manufacture in the clothing industry demands a continuous flow of fabric of known performance in the making-up processes, and of an acceptable quality in use. These requirements cannot be met without a very clear and explicit means of communication between the textile producer and the clothing manufacturer, to enable the latter to express his needs in terms that will have the same meaning for both parties. A description of a cloth in terms such that any cloth complying with them will meet the purchaser's needs constitutes a fabric specification.

A good specification must conform to three requirements:

1 Sufficiency of information
2 Absence of unnecessary requirements
3 Possibility of checking the cloth for conformity.

Requirement 1 is necessary because otherwise material may be manufactured which although complying with the specification is still unsuitable for the intended purpose.

With respect to requirement 2 it may be noted that any unnecessary stipulation is likely to add to the cost and difficulty of making the cloth. An example would be specifying a degree of light fastness in excess of what is required.

Requirement 3 recognises that a specification is of little value if it is not possible to verify that it has been complied with. It is no use specifying some quality of the cloth for which no test exists.

How can a cloth purchaser describe the cloth he needs? One method would be to specify every relevant detail of construction and finish. For a woven cloth these would include the details of the yarns to be used in the warp and weft (fibre, construction, tex, etc.), the number of threads per cm, the weave and type of finish to be applied. Carried out in sufficient detail this might ensure a satisfactory product, although it must be remarked that the tex values of the yarns used cannot always be determined accurately by an examination of the finished cloth.

An alternative method is based on the view that details of construction are not very important compared with the properties of the cloth that determine its performance in making-up and in use. In such a case emphasis would be placed on properties such as strength, sewability, reaction to pressing, shrinkage, drape, crease recovery, pilling, water repellency, colour fastness.

In practice, specifications are neither purely of 'constructional' nor 'performance' type. For fabrics that are to be used in the visible parts of a garment it is necessary to specify constructional details since these influence the appearance of the fabric in respect of texture, lustre, cover, etc. When nominally identical garments made up from batches of cloth received at different times, possibly from different suppliers, are to be displayed on the same counter it is necessary that they should be practically indistinguishable, and this can be achieved only if they are identical in construction. However, certain properties including, for example, crease recovery, drape and colour fastness, are dependent on details of processing after weaving or knitting, and the specification would therefore include requirements for these properties, as defined by performance when tested by stipulated laboratory tests.

The characteristics of a cloth that are of importance to a clothing manufacturer fall into two classes, namely, those that affect the ease and efficiency of making-up, and those that are important to the user of a garment. In each case the list of characteristics that might be important is very long. Among the former are freedom from visible defects, uniformity of appearance, accurate colour rendering, lustre, bowing, skewing, width uniformity, sewability, dimensional stability, performance in pressing and fusing. In use the cloth must have adequate strength (measured by tensile, tear or bursting methods), resistance to abrasion and other effects of wear such as pilling, good seam strength and resistance to seam slippage, fastness of colour to light, washing, dry cleaning and other conditions, crease resistance, pleat retention, flame resistance, shower or rain resistance, vapour permeability.

To draft a specification it is necessary to be able to identify the characteristics that are important in the making up and use of an article, and this is apt to be a continuing process as experience is accumulated, so every specification is liable to be modified from time to time. In addition, it is necessary not only to be able to recognise what characters should be controlled but to know how to achieve this control. Often, of course, the specification will require that the cloth should show a certain level of performance in a suitable test. The choice of this level is important since to make it too difficult to reach adds to the cost of the cloth, but to make it too lenient courts dissatisfaction. It will be appreciated that the development of a specification for a cloth for which a high level of efficiency in manufacture and use is demanded requires the existence of a widely accepted body of test methods of proved value. To draft a specification acceptable to the cloth producer and the clothing manufacturer demands an understanding of the problems and difficulties of each. It is necessary also to have experience of the practicalities of textile testing, the value and reliability of available test methods and the bearing of test results on the performance of fabrics in making up and use.

The form of specifications

A common form of lay-out of specifications is well illustrated by those issued by the Ministry of Defence and the British Standards Institution. Cloth specifications generally contain the following clauses:

1) *Title.* The title should indicate the nature of the cloth being specified and its intended use as, for example, 'Acetate locknit fabrics for ladies' underwear'.
2) *Introduction.* This may indicate why it has been found desirable to introduce the specification and a reference to any earlier specifications which are now superseded.
3) *Scope.* A statement of the type of cloth to which the specification refers, for example, 'printed cotton/viscose shirting, weighing 150 g/m².'
4) *Cloth particulars.* The requirements may be more or less detailed depending on the use to which the cloth is to be put and the requirements to be made for performance testing. A discussion of the specification of constructional particulars begins on page 275.
5) *Finishing requirements.* This clause would indicate whether the cloth is to be bleached, dyed, printed, and whether it is to be given a special finish to provide water repellency, crease recovery, shrinkage resistance, etc.
6) *Test methods.* The laboratory test methods to which the cloth is to be subjected. Most of the tests will be standard methods such as those listed by the British Standards Institution, but if a special test is to be used it may be necessary to describe the routine to be followed.
7) *Test Results.* Requirements that are expressed as the results of laboratory tests are likely to be tabulated. For each such requirement the required mean result for the stipulated number of tests will be given. It will be stated whether this is a minimum acceptable result, as for tensile strength, or a maximum, as for shrinkage. In certain cases the result of the test will be required to lie within a stated range, expressed as tolerances. For example, the requirement for threads per cm might be '30 ± 1', that is, inside the range 29–31.

8) *Sampling*. It is likely that the specification will contain clauses describing how many samples are to be taken from each delivery of cloth for inspection and how they are to be selected.

9) *Delivery*. It is possible that the lengths of individual pieces of cloth will be stipulated, what identification marks they should carry, how they should be packed, etc.
The maximum number of faults that will be accepted in any full piece may be stated.

10) *Reference Sample*. A reference sample may be attached to indicate dyed or printed shade, handle and any special characteristics.

Origin of specifications

Specifications are usually drawn up by either the cloth purchaser, or purchasing authority for its own use, or by a public authority in the public interest. The latter are commonly referred to as 'Standards'. In the UK the British Standards Institution has issued a large number of standards for apparel, household, contract and industrial textiles. There are also standards for textile testing, statistics and quality assurance schemes, and also for sewing threads, furniture, bedding and furnishings. Each Standard carries a title, a BS number and the year of issue.

The International Standards Organisation, ISO, also publishes standards and these are available through the BSI.

The Ministry of Defence in the UK has published the specifications for the vast variety of textiles and garments that it needs and these are available at the Government Book Shops. The specifications issued by organisations such as the Electricity Council and British Gas are available from the same source.

The main purchasing organisations in the public sector, including Government departments, and local authorities, now publish specifications for many products, including textiles, as 'Public Authority Standards' (PAS), an important aim being to secure cost savings by variety reduction. When published, a PAS replaces existing specifications for similar items issued by the individual organisations. PAS are available from the BSI.

The large chain store organisations and the mail order houses draft many of their own specifications. These are not usually available to the public, but since these outlets control such a large proportion of textile and clothing production, their specifications are important to producers. The close contact between retailers and consumer, and the feedback of information, often in the form of complaints, is of great assistance in the formation of specifications, particularly in respect of the selection of tests to be applied and the levels of performance to be required.

Constructional particulars of fabrics

Woven fabrics

The following are the features of importance in the construction of a woven fabric.

Weave. Simple weaves may be referred to by name, as 'plain', '2/1 twill', etc. but in other cases it may be necessary to provide a point paper diagram.

Mass per unit area, which may be expressed in grammes per square metre. A chiffon would weigh about 30 g/m^2, a shirting 100–150 g/m^2, a cotton denim 400 g/m^2 and a heavy overcoating about 800 g/m^2.

Threads per centimetre. The number of 'ends per cm' is the number of warp threads lying side by side in a strip of cloth, 1 cm wide. The number of 'picks per cm' is the number of weft threads in a similar strip. Threads per cm may vary from fewer than 5 per cm in a scrim to as many as 150 per cm in a satin.

Yarn linear density. It is usual now in specifications to express the linear density of yarns in the tex system. In older specifications, cotton count, metric count, woollen, worsted and other count systems will be found, besides denier. Linear densities must be given for both warp and weft yarns, since they are not always, or even commonly, the same.

Yarn construction. It is necessary to state, for each type of yarn used, whether it is single, folded, cabled or a fancy type; the amount and direction of twist in the various components and the folding and cabling twist; the fibre type or blend in each component.

Yarn crimp. If a cross-section of a fabric is examined, as shown for example in Figure 85, it will be seen that the yarns are 'crimped': that is, they are not straight. Crimp is an unavoidable consequence of interweaving. Theoretically, it is possible for the warp yarns, or the weft yarns, but not both, to be straight, and in some cloths this may be almost the case.

A result of the thread crimp is that the length of a thread taken from a strip of cloth will be found to be greater than the length of the strip. The amount of crimp in the thread is defined as this length difference, expressed as a percentage of the length of the cloth strip, and this quantity is known as the 'percentage crimp' of the threads. Warp and weft crimps must be stated separately, and if there is more than one type of warp or weft yarn, the crimp of each must be found, as would be the case for the terry cloth illustrated in Figure 84.

Thread crimps are practically never stated in cloth specifications, but they are important because the excess of yarn must be allowed for in estimating the amount of yarn that will be used in weaving a given amount of cloth, and in calculating the cloth weight from the threads per centimetre and linear densities. The levels of yarn crimp will influence various cloth properties, such as extension under load, liability to thread slippage, surface texture and lustre.

Relation between loomstate and finished particulars

When a cloth specification is drawn up by a cloth user (e.g. a clothing manufacturer), it is most likely that the particulars given will relate to the cloth in the finished state. Although a specification will have to be drawn up for the loomstate cloth, where the responsibility for this lies will depend on the chain of supply. A large organisation may arrange the supply of yarn to the weaver, the manufacture of the cloth to be supplied to the finisher and the finishing of the cloth also. Smaller users may only be able to specify their requirements in terms of the finished cloth and will depend on other links in the chain of supply to find a source of loomstate cloth.

In any event it will be necessary to ensure the loomstate particulars are such that the finished requirements can be met. There is a change of weight in finishing, due not only to the removal of size and foreign matter from the cloth during processing but also to gain or loss in width or length, which are of course accompanied by changes in threads per centimetre. The particulars of the loomstate cloth therefore must be such that the cloth can be finished to have the desired mass per unit area, width and threads per cm. Furthermore, in the finished state it will be necessary for the cloth to have the required level of dimensional stability (usually expressed as shrinkage behaviour). It must be observed here that whereas fabrics made from synthetic fibre may be heat-set within a range of dimensions to give stable cloth, fabrics from natural fibres must be finished, possibly by a compressive shrinkage process, at dimensions that will be stable in washing. These dimensions are determined by the loomstate dimensions and the conditions of weaving. It is important, therefore, to choose the loomstate particulars carefully so that the cloth may be finished according to the desired finished particulars. This is largely a matter of experience and some trial and error.

Cloth geometry of woven fabrics

The cloth particulars enumerated above are not all entirely independent, and the nature of the relationships between them is the subject of the study of 'cloth geometry'. It is easily seen that the yarn crimps are dependent on weave, thread spacings and yarn diameters. The latter are determined largely by the linear densities of the yarns, but are influenced by yarn construction, twist and the compressions of the yarns in the cloth (The yarn cross-section is usually flattened to some extent.) Yarn crimps are high in 'closely-set' cloths, that is cloths in which the threads are packed closely together, and they are low in open constructions such as cheese cloths. Crimps tend to be high in weaves with frequent intersections such as plain, and lower in weaves with infrequent intersections such as satins.

It is possible to influence thread crimps by the conditions of weaving and finishing, but this possible variation is shown mainly as an interchange of crimp between warp and weft yarns. Thus if the warp crimp is reduced the weft is increased and vice versa. To illustrate this point, if a strip of cloth is stretched in the length direction, the crimp of these threads is reduced, but the crimp of the crossing threads is increased and the strip of cloth becomes narrower. The reduction in crimp that can be achieved by pulling the cloth in both directions simultaneously is limited.

Cloth weight

Cloth weight is related to the other particulars by the formula

Cloth mass per unit area (g/m^2)

$$= \text{Ends/cm} \times t_1 \times \frac{100 + C_1}{1,000} + \text{Picks/cm} \times t_2 \times \frac{100 + C_2}{1,000}$$

where C_1 and C_2 are the percentage crimps of the warp and weft yarns and t_1 and t_2 are the tex values of the warp and weft yarns.

Thus if the mass per unit area of the cloth and the threads per cm have been chosen, it is necessary to calculate what linear densities will be needed. Similarly, if it is desired to use certain yarns in a cloth of given weight the threads per cm must be suitably chosen. It will be noted that these calculations cannot be made accurately without a knowledge of the yarn crimps to be expected. This is largely a matter of experience.

Cover factor

This quantity is easily calculated and is useful as an indication of how closely a woven cloth is constructed. The number is calculated for warp and weft directions separately and it indicates the extent to which each set of threads covers the area of cloth.

$$\text{The cover factor for the warp } (K_1) = \frac{(\text{ends/cm}) \sqrt{t_1}}{10}$$

$$\text{and for the weft } (K_2) = \frac{(\text{picks/cm}) \sqrt{t_2}}{10}$$

where t_1 and t_2 are the tex values of warp and weft yarns.

If a set of parallel cotton yarns just touch, that is, giving perfect 'cover', the value for K is about 27. The corresponding value for spun yarns from other fibres would be somewhat different. If the spaces between the yarns are equal to the yarn diameters, giving 50% cover, the cover factor is about 13·5. The practical significance of cover factor is not absolute but depends on the type of yarn, its twist and fibre composition, and the weave of the cloth. Its effective use therefore demands experience, but this quantity has been found very useful in practice.

It should be remembered that there is a distinction between 'cover factor' and 'cover'. The former is a conventional measure of the closeness of setting of the threads running in one direction. The latter signifies the actual efficiency of the yarns in closing up the cloth. The cover of a cloth may be judged by the appearance of the cloth when held up against the light, and it depends not only on the number of threads per cm and their linear density but also on their regularity, hairiness, fibre composition, twist, and the cloth finishing processes. Any irregularity in construction, as for example in the uniformity of the spacing of the threads, tends to reduce the level of cover. 'Cover factor' is calculated from only two of these quantities and, therefore, cannot provide a complete indication of 'cover'.

Cover factor is, however, useful in making comparisons between cloths, particularly those from similar yarns, not necessarily of the same linear density, but in the same weave. With experience it enables a pre-judgement to be made, from a knowledge of cloth particulars, of aspects of cloth quality such as handle and air porosity, and it helps the manufacturer to judge the ease or difficulty of weaving. The common weaves, such as plain, twill, and matt, cannot have a high cover factor in both warp and weft directions simultaneously. This is a fundamental aspect of the geometry of these weaves. It is possible to attain higher cover factors in cloths with few intersections such as satin and twill weaves than in the plain weave.

The study of the geometry of woven cloths is largely mathematical and is built on basic assumptions relating to the shape of the cross-section of the yarn as it lies in the cloth, the profile of the crimp of the yarn, the compressibility of the yarn, and its retention of an imposed 'set'. Various assumptions may be made, and yield somewhat different results. The geometrical relationships of the characteristics of cloths studied in this way are helpful in the understanding of cloth properties and behaviour but have not yet reached a satisfactory degree of precision.

Knitted fabrics

For all knitted fabrics, whether of weft- or warp-knitted types, it is necessary to specify the basic requirements of width, mass per unit length or per unit area, the construction and linear density of the yarns to be used, including fibre composition, and the knitted construction. The knitted construction may be described by name, or if this is not sufficiently specific, by notation, as discussed in the section on knitted fabrics (page 96). Other manufacturing particulars are the number of wales per cm and courses per cm, and these are quite commonly specified. For warp-knitted fabrics the 'run-in' of the yarns, and for weft-knitted fabrics the stitch lengths of the yarns, can be specified but this would be unusual.

In respect of finishing treatments it is necessary to stipulate colour fastness, and possibly the type of dye, and any special finishes the cloth is to be given. It is usually important to stipulate the dimensional stability of the fabric, that is the maximum dimensional changes acceptable in washing, preferably by an accepted standard method.

Many of the performance tests used for woven fabrics are suitable also for knitted fabrics, although the level of results expected may be different. The strip test for the tensile strength of cloth is usually unsuitable for knitted constructions since these distort to an unacceptable degree when stretched. To ensure that a knitted fabric has an acceptable level of strength it is usual to specify a bursting test result.

Geometry of knitted fabrics

The geometry of knitted fabrics has been slower in development than that of woven fabrics, mainly because it is difficult to describe properly the shapes of the yarn loops in the various states such as the greige state, relaxed or heat set.

Stitch length

This is a parameter of great importance in weft-knitted fabric geometry, since it determines the dimensions of the fabric in the relaxed state: that is, the state in which the fabric is dimensionally stable when washed.

The practical significance of this is that it is possible to control the stitch length during knitting, and hence to knit fabric that will have the required dimensions when brought to the dimensionally stable form in finishing. Without this knowledge, satisfactory fabrics can be produced only by trial and error.

The situation is different for warp-knitted fabrics. These are most commonly knitted from thermoplastic yarns, which can be heat-set. Consequently, these fabrics can be brought to the required dimensions during finishing and heat-set to retain these dimensions during washing. These finished dimensions therefore need not be the relaxed dimensions of the fabric 'as knitted'.

Warp-knitted fabrics are usually stretched considerably from the relaxed state, partly to obtain the increase in area, but also to reduce the extensibility of the fabric, and so to improve its suitability for applications for which it competes with woven fabrics. In this respect warp-knitted fabrics may be contrasted with weft-knitted fabrics, which are used more for articles for which easy extension and form fitting are valued. However, for warp-knitted fabrics also, run-in, which is equivalent to stitch length, is still a basic parameter and controls the relations between the dimensions of the fabric on the machine while it is being knitted and the dimensions to which it is practical to extend it for heat setting.

Tightness factor

Corresponding to the cover factor defined previously for woven fabrics, there is a 'Tightness Factor' for knitted fabrics which indicates the relative looseness or compactness of the knitting. The factor is related to the ratio of the surface area occupied by the yarn in a loop to the area of fabric enclosed by the loop. The study of fully relaxed plain weft-knit worsted structures provided the basis for the experimentally derived formula:

$$\text{Tightness factor} = \sqrt{t} \div l$$

where t: yarn tex and l: loop length (mm).

A fabric with a large loop length and coarse yarn could have the same tightness factor as a fabric with a small loop length and fine yarn.

The tightness of the fabric has an important bearing on such fabric properties as dimensional stability and ease of felting, handle and drape, bursting strength and resistance to abrasion.

Account is not taken of the effect of twist, fibre density, and the extent to which loops overlap each other in the structure, all of which would be considerations in the determination of fabric cover.

The mathematical theory of the relationship between the various parameters that describe a knitted fabric has not been developed to the point where it is suitable for routine application.

Quality Assurance

'Quality' may be defined as fitness for purpose at an acceptable price. Fitness for purpose is defined by a range of performance characteristics, some of which are common to most applications, such as durability, appearance retention and ease of cleansing, and some of which are particular to the product, such as water repellency, or flame retardency.

In the past, 'quality control' has been synonymous, more or less, with inspection and testing of the product at the end of the manufacturing process. This aspect of quality control is discussed on p. 163. If 100% of the product is examined, the purpose is to detect substandard articles that will be rejected. Such a scheme would be applied when it is essential that every single item is satisfactory, as for example, in parachute manufacture. It is however, usually felt to be sufficient to examine only a relatively small fraction of the product, in which case the aim is to ensure that the general level of the product is such that very few substandard articles will reach the customer. However, the production of even a few substandard articles raises the cost of production and introduces the possibility of customer dissatisfaction.

The term 'Quality Assurance' has a broader significance than 'Quality Control'. It implies commitment to the concept of quality from the inception of the design through product development, purchasing of raw materials, the control of each manufacturing process to the testing and inspection of the finished product. It becomes a duty of every member of management and staff to think in terms of 'quality'.

Much thought has been given to methods of implementing such an approach, and British Standard 5750 'UK National Standards for Quality Systems' lays out a model scheme for introducing quality assurance throughout the creative and manufacturing processes. The objective is to 'get things right first time', eliminating the costs of producing unacceptable goods and guaranteeing a fully satisfactory output at an appropriate price.

QA systems demand a detailed and comprehensive specification of the product including specifications of the materials used, of the sequence of manufacturing operations and of the manufacturing equipment to be used. The intermediate products, at each stage of manufacture, are subject to specifications and tolerances, and good records of test results and other data must be kept. Only products that are within the tolerances prescribed by the QA scheme may be passed on for further processing. Such constant and routine monitoring at each stage of manufacture enables early corrective action to be taken and eliminates the waste of processing unsatisfactory material.

BS 5750 (CEN 2900), referred to above, provides for registration of any company that operates an efficient 'Quality System'. To qualify for registration the company must have a documented Quality System that meets the requirements of BS 5750. Before registration, BSI assessors visit the factory to ensure that the scheme is in satisfactory operation. If the firm receives registration as a 'BSI' Firm of Assessed Capability' it will be subject to periodical visits from BSI inspectors to ensure that the scheme is being observed. This scheme is recognised by major purchasers such as public authorities. Registration has considerable advantages to the firm and customers alike. A registered firm may make use of the BSI Registered Firm Symbol on letter headings, advertisements and for promotional purposes, but not for product marking. (Figure 192).

Fig. 192 Quality Assurance: registered firm mark.
BS 5750 (CEN 2900: ISO 9000)

Chapter 8

SEWING THREADS AND SEAMS

SEWING THREADS

It is always stressed, with justification, that to ensure a satisfactory appearance and performance in use it is important to choose the most suitable sewing thread for the fabric to be sewn, and for the part of the garment into which it is to be incorporated. Whilst consideration of the behaviour of the sewing thread in the seam is a high priority in selection, the initial demands made on the thread during the stitching operation in the machine have also to be taken into account. The most critical test of a thread is provided by its behaviour in a lockstitch machine.

Examination of the summary of sewing threads in Tables 27 and 28 shows that a greater range of threads is required by the clothing industry than by the domestic retail market. This is understandable when one considers that the sophisticated machines in industry operate at high speeds and are required to produce a great variety of stitch types for different purposes. The demands made on threads whilst machining and in specialised uses are extremely varied, whereas for domestic sewing the threads do not have to meet such stringent tests.

Different stitches and seam types* may be required according to whether highly extensible swimwear or knitwear, less extensible knitted piece goods, or least extensible woven fabrics are being sewn. In addition, several types of stitch may be required within each garment according to the function of the seam. For instance, strong long side seams, extensible and strong seat-of-trouser seams, and unobtrusive hems require particular stitches and threads.

Garments may be constructed to include fusible interlinings in such a way as to reduce the amount of seaming, as in suits, or an unstructured style of unlined casual suit can be designed which requires particular neatening type stitches for the exposed seams. On the other hand, if instead of lockstitching the seam of a shirt tail the fabric is turned over only once, overlocking will be necessary. Colourful overlocking can be used as a decorative feature in place of binding round the edges of collars and

---

* 'Schedule of stitches and seams' and 'Classification and terminology of seam types' BS 3870 1983.

Table 27 SEWING THREADS FOR THE APPAREL INDUSTRY

Fibre and thread type	Brand name		End use	Ticket number
STAPLE FIBRE SEWING THREADS				
Cotton: Soft	Hilbran	(B)* ⎱ ⎰	General Seaming	24–60
	Highland	(B)		
	Atlas, Eagley, Chain	(C) ⎱ ⎰	Overalls, jeans	24, 30, 40
	Swallow	(C)	Dresses, shirts, etc.,	50, 60
	Atlas rainproof finish	(C)	Rainwear	40, 50, 60
	Eagley (S twist)	(C)	For flatlock machines	60
	Chain	(C)	Overalls, protective clothing	24, 30, 40
	Neilston super	(E) ⎱ ⎰	General seaming according to	24–60
	Eagley fast	(C)	thread number	60
	Swan	(E)		50, 60
	Highland	(E)	Basting	36
	Highland	(B)	Buttonhole gimp	25/9
Cotton: Mercerised	Sylko	(E)	General seaming	36–50
	Anchor Pearl cotton	(C) ⎱ ⎰	Decorative stitching	8
	Sylko Perlé	(E)		
Cotton: Polished	Escort	(E)	Leather trades and footwear	70/4
Linen	Best	(B)	Machine buttoning	60, 70
	Best	(B)	Hand buttoning	35
	Best	(B)	Buttonhole gimp	18
Polyester	Respol	(B) ⎱ ⎰	General seaming according to	80, 120
	Drima T	(C)	thread number.	
	Donistex	(D)	Lingerie, shirts,	80, 120
	Finex	(E)	knitwear	120
	Type M	(G)		50, 70, 100, 120
	Drima	(C) ⎱ ⎰	Decorative stitching	15, 30
	Type M	(G)		11, 30

* *Key to manufacturers are on p. 286.*

Table 27 cont.

Fibre and thread type	Brand name		End use	Ticket number
Corespun (polyester/ cotton)	Terko Koban Don Blend Polyfil Type H	(B) (C) (D) (E) (G)	General stitching according to thread number. Lingerie, shirts, knitwear and heavy industrial sewing	8–120 8–180 25–120 20–180 50–120
Corespun (polyester/ polyester)	DuPol Epic Poly Poly Type A	(B) (C) (D) (G)	General Seaming	25–120 80–180 75–180 80–150
Aramid	Type K Kevlar fibre	(G) (B)	Flame retardant applications	40, 70, 50/2, 50/3, 50/4
Silk	Type S	(G)	Light seaming, decorative stitching	10–100

CONTINUOUS FILAMENT SEWING THREADS

Fibre and thread type	Brand name		End use	Ticket number
Silk	Pero	(G)	Buttonholing and decorative stitching	20–40
Polyester	Weaverbird Type T	(B) (G)	Heavy stitching	6–70 10–80
	Gral Dewhursts Type T	(C) (E) (G)	General seaming	70–140 120–180
	200 Weaverbird Gral Zenith Type U Don Maid	(B) (C) (E) (G) (D)	Underthread, padding, serging, blind stitching, quilting, fur industry	200 200 220 200, 240
	Type U	(G)	Draw thread for knitwear	60
Nylon	Ibex	(D)	Knitwear and general sewing	40, 60, 80
	Dewlon	(E)	General sewing of leather goods	11, 13, 20, 40, 60, 80

Fibre and thread type	Brand name		End use	Ticket number
Nylon cont.	Aptan	(C)	General seaming	20–180
	Lynyl	(B)	General seaming and heavier applications	4–80
	Type L	(G)	Seaming heavy leathers	20, 40
Air-jet Textured polyester	Aim	(D)		20, 35, 50, 75, 90, 120
	Jet-Core	(E)	General stitching	36, 50, 75, 120
	Weaverbird	(B)		160
Air-jet Intermingled or (air-intangled) polyester	Ultimax	(C)	Jeans, upholstery, bedding	20, 36, 50, 75, 120
False twist textured nylon 6.6	Ibex	(D)	Seam covering slacks, foundation garments,	40, 80, 160, 40, 80, 120
	Lynyl	(B)		
	Type D	(G)	swimwear, underwear	40–160
False twist textured polyester	Aptan	(C)		
	Delta	(E)	Seam covering outerwear bedding	40–160
	Ibex	(D)		
	Type E	(G)		
	Weaverbird	(B)	Seam covering	80, 160
Monofilament nylon 6.6	Colorific	(D)	According to thread number suitable for blind stitching and overlocking only, or for general seaming.	80–700
	Monovic	(E)		50–180
	Type Q	(G)		171, 201, 471
	Lindux	(B)	General stitching	80–750
EMBROIDERY THREADS				
Cotton (mercerised)	Tanne	(M)		3, 12, 20, 30, 50, 80
Viscose filament	Decor, Sticku, Madeira	(M)		6, 12, 30, 40

Table 27 cont.

Fibre and thread type	Brand name	End use	Ticket number
Polyester filament 70% acrylic/	Neon, Toledo	(M)	40, 60
30% wool	Burmilana	(M)	3, 12

METALLIC EMBROIDERY

50% polyester/ 45% polyamide/ 5% pure silver.	'FS'	(M)	40, 50
65% viscose/ 35% metallised polyester.	'FS'	(M)	20, 30
70% polyamide/ 30% metallised polyester	'Supertwist'	(M)	20, 30

Key to manufacturers
(B)   Barbour Campbell Threads, Ltd.   (E)   English Sewing Ltd.
(C)   J. & P. Coats (UK) Ltd.   (M)   Madeira Threads (UK) Ltd
(D)   Donisthorpe & Co. Ltd.   (G)   Perivale Gütermann Ltd.

Unless otherwise stated the folding direction of twist is Z

Table 28   SEWING AND EMBROIDERY THREADS FOR DOMESTIC USE

Fibre and thread type	Brand name		End use	Ticket number
SPUN SEWING THREADS				
Cotton: Soft	Chain	(C)*	General stitching by machine	40
	Super	(E)		10–60
	Anchor Soft Embroidery	(C)		
	Miladi	(E)		10, 40
Cotton: Mercerised	Super Sheen	(C)	General stitching by machine	50
	Sylko	(E)		
	Chadwick's (S Twist)	(E)	Mending	
Polyester	Drima	(C)	Machine and hand sewing	
	Mölnlycke	(E)		
	Type M	(G)		100
	Type M	(G)	Buttontwist and decorative stitching	30
	Sylko Bold	(E)		
Corespun (polyester-cotton)	Sylko Supreme	(E)	Machine and hand sewing	
	Strong thread	(E)	Button thread	
	Chain Extra Strong	(C)		
silk	Type S	(G)	Machine and hand sewing	100
	Kinkame	(E)		50
	Silk	(M)	Hand sewing	
EMBROIDERY THREADS				
Cotton	Anchor stranded	(C)	Hand sewing	12–30
	Anchor *Coton à Broder* (S twist)	(C)		
	Six Strand Embroidery	(E)		12–30
	Six Strand Cotton	(M)		
	Anchor Pearl Cotton	(C)		5, 8
	Sylko Perlé	(E)		8
	Anchor for machine embroidery	(C)	Machine, hand, and quilting	30, 50
	Tanne	(M)		12, 80

* Key to manufacturers on p. 288.

287

Table 28 cont.

Fibre and thread type	Brand name		End use	Ticket number
Cotton cont.	Mölnlycke			
	Quilting	(E)	Quilting	
	Crochet cotton	(E)	Crochet and tatting	12, 20, 40
	Mercer-Crochet	(C)		60, 80
Wool	Anchor tapisserie (S Twist)	(C)	Tapisserie	
	Anchor tapisserie grounding (S twist)	(C)		
	Chadwick's wool/ nylon (S twist)	(C)	Mending	
Viscose filament	Decor	(M)	Machine and hand	
	'Rayon'	(M)	Machine	
Polyester filament	Neon	(M)	Machine and hand	
Filament blends	(Metallic)			
	polyester/ polyamide/ silver	(M)	Machine and hand	
	polyamide/ metallised polyester	(M)		
	Viscose/ polyester/ silver	(M)	Hand embroidery	

Key to manufacturers
(C) J. & P. Coats (UK) Ltd.   (M) Madeira Threads (UK) Ltd.
(E) English Sewing Ltd.   (G) Perivale Gütermann Ltd.
Unless otherwise stated the direction of twist is Z

pockets; and the lockstitch, using either single or twin needles, can be used for decorative contrast stitching with coarse threads.

According to type, stitches may have one to six threads in their formation and require particular thread characteristics to contribute to the overall performance of the seam. In some instances, two different types of thread may be included in the one seam as the needle thread and as the under bobbin/looper thread.

Basic requirements of sewing threads

For the sewing process to be trouble free, that is with the minimum damage and breakage of the sewing thread, and an absence of faulty stitching, the thread must be of uniform diameter, free from knots, and must have the minimum tendency to snarl. Threads are generally 2- or 3-ply (folded) or a cord (cabled). For the thread to be balanced, that is to have the minimum tendency to untwist or 'snarl', attention is given to the amount of twist and direction of twist inserted in each component of the plied or corded thread.

Twist

The term 'machine twist' is used to describe the final twist direction of sewing threads; this is equivalent to the usage of 'Z-twist' (Figure 52). There are only a few exceptions when a thread with a final 'S-twist' must be used in a particular type of sewing machine in industry.

Combinations of directions of twist are necessary in folded yarns to attain the requisite strength and to reduce the tendency of the thread to untwist. In a 2- or 3-ply thread the single component would be S twisted followed by Z twist folding (SZ) whereas in cabled or cord threads the twist combination ZSZ (cabled Z twist, on S twist folded yarn, on Z twist singles) is commonly used for glacé cotton thread and crochet yarn.

The significance of having a Z twist thread with the correct constructions and amount of twist is that this ensures that an undistorted loop is presented through the needle to the rotary hook during the formation of a satisfactory lockstitch with the thread supplied by the spool. If the thread untwists and splays out during stitching there is a risk that it will be damaged and the stitch malformed.

Abrasion resistance and strength

Speeds of up to 2000 m/sec can be reached in the sophisticated machines used in industry, and high localised loading of the thread takes place as the needle thread forms the lockstitch with the underthread. Such severe operational conditions, together with a rise in needle temperature arising from the reciprocating passage of the thread through the needle, can reduce the initial tensile strength of the needle thread by the time it is finally incorporated in the seam. Hence the need for high performance sewing threads for the clothing industry and for the stringent requirements of functional apparel.

It is estimated that the strength of the needle thread retained after stitching, given as a percentage of its original strength, is normally about 80% when a lockstitch is used and 95% in chain stitching.

Friction

Another important aspect of sewing thread behaviour in the machine is the build up of tensions in the needle thread due to the friction between the surface of the moving thread and the parts of the machine which it contacts. All sewing threads, especially those made from synthetic fibres, require a lubricant finish to reduce this friction to an acceptably low level. The coefficient of friction of running yarn can be measured against stainless steel or other guide surfaces. A typical satisfactory value for a sewing thread would be $<0.2\mu$

If tensions in a thread rise unduly, there is the risk of the thread being extended excessively, and later contracting and causing seam pucker, or actually breaking whilst sewing. The presence of the lubricant often has other important functions, such as protecting the thread against high needle temperatures and reducing the accumulation of static on synthetic fibre threads. Lubricant is applied by the thread manufacturer, and the type, quantity and uniformity of application of the lubricant is subject to quality control. If the frictional properties are not uniform, unequal lengths of thread will be pulled off the package for each stitch. When thread is stored under unsuitable conditions for a prolonged period, the lubricant can age and the coefficient of friction of the thread may rise. Tacking or basting threads are not subject to stringent use and are, therefore, simply unlubricated, single, carded yarns.

The above discussion suggests some of the properties that a good sewing thread should have: adequate strength and resistance to impact loading, suitable extensibility and recovery from extension, abrasion resistance, uniformity, low friction, and freedom from snarling. These properties are achieved by the correct choice of fibre and construction, which it is proposed to discuss under 'Characteristics of sewing thread types'.

Sewing thread 'Ticket numbers'

Sewing threads are available in a wide variety of constructions that differ in fibre content and have distinctly different characteristics. In choosing a thread for a particular application it is important to select one that has the size and strength appropriate to the weight, thickness and closeness of the fabric to be sewn. It is also essential that it should be suitable to the needle to be used. The size of a sewing thread is given by its 'ticket number' which is intended to help in choosing the correct thread for a particular purpose. It is with this in mind that BS 4134: 1990 'Method for designation of ticket number of industrial sewing threads', has been drawn up.

In this standard a given ticket number corresponds to a short range of tex values, and it is not possible therefore to convert a ticket number exactly to linear density or count or vice versa. The conversion is not the same for sewing threads made wholly or partly from manufactured fibres as it is for all-cotton sewing threads. Manufacturers do not yet follow the system very closely, and the UK system is not observed internationally. BS 6157: 1990 'Specification for industrial sewing threads made wholly or partly from synthetic fibres', specifies various requirements for a number of types of sewing threads containing manufactured fibre, including the ticket number for each tex value, in accordance with BS 4134. There is some latitude in the relationship between tex and ticket number within each category of thread and between categories.

In BS 4134 sewing threads made wholly or partly of manufactured fibres have ticket numbers approximately equal to three times the metric count (Nm) of the thread (that is to say, in the three-fold thread the metric count of the singles component). This is given by the relationship, ticket number = 30,000 ÷ R dtex, R dtex being the linear density of the sewing thread in decitex.

Sewing threads made wholly of cotton have ticket numbers approximately equal to three times the cotton count (Ne) of the thread (again, for a three-fold thread, roughly the count of the single component). The relationship of the ticket number to decitex is given by:

$$\text{Ticket number} = 17715 \div R \text{ dtex.}$$

BS 4134 includes tables showing how ticket numbers should be related to ranges of the total nominal decitex, that is, the sum of the nominal values of all the components of the sewing thread. The values given below have been extracted from these tables.

Sewing threads containing manufactured fibre		Wholly cotton sewing threads	
decitex	Ticket number	decitex	Ticket number
158–178	180	274–324	60
178–200	160	324–398	50
354–388	80	398–468	40
575–635	50	540–665	30
710–805	40	665–810	24
1430–1580	20		

Some sewing threads carry a decitex numbering and this conforms with the standardisation of the tex yarn numbering system within the textile industry. The denier system is used for monofilament sewing threads.

The selection of a thread depends on both its technical suitability and its cost. For a comparison to be made on the basis of price it is necessary to know the actual decitex of the thread, not simply the ticket number, and the length on the package. This is an important consideration in clothing manufacture in view of the quantities of thread that may be used in seams. For example, about 40 m are used in a brassiere, 80 m in a skirt, 150 m in a lady's dress, 150 m in a pair of slacks, 270 m in a raincoat and 400 m in a lady's coat. Thread consumption for a given length of seam is dependent on the overall thickness of the seam, the number of stitches per cm, and the type of stitch. Thus, a 3-thread overlock stitch will consume about 70 cm of thread for 5 cm of seam, whereas in the lockstitch it is about 12·5 cm of thread for the same seam length.

Thread packages

Stitches which utilise long thread lengths relative to seam length must have the thread supplied rapidly whilst machining. Sufficient thread must be available throughout the machining operation to reduce machine stoppages for replenishment to a minimum. To increase the length available on the package larger packages have been designed for industry. The designs of the packages take into account the need for easy withdrawal of the thread at high speed, the control of lively threads such as monofilament, and the necessity to reduce the risk of the thread snagging and 'sloughing off' as it is withdrawn. Packages of various shapes can carry from 1,000 m to over 5,000 m lengths of thread and are prepared to give an even unwinding tension. The effective choice of thread package is linked with the thread and machine type, and the productivity in the sewing room. One advantage in the use of a fine thread is the greater length carried by the package.

For domestic use spools carry sufficient thread length for frequent changes of colour in low speed machines and hand sewing.

For high-speed machines pre-wound cardboard bobbins, wound at a uniform tension, are available to the trade for use as the under thread in lockstitch machines in place of the usual metal bobbin. Apart from an expected economy in re-winding time a greater length of thread can be contained in the ready-wound bobbin. However, judgement on the relative merits of threads and thread packages must be based on performance and technical economy.

Colour

Sewing threads are available in a wide range of colours and these must be considered in respect of adequate colour matching and colour fastness.

Colours, like garment styles, are fashionable for a limited time, but the trends in colour are known in advance by those concerned with textiles and fashion. Thus, the manufacturers of threads, zips, buttons, shoes and so on, can produce their goods in colours appropriate to the fashion to be presented to the public. Usually it is easier, therefore, to match the current popular colours, and black, brown and white, rather than some off-season shade.

Success in colour matching is considerably influenced by lighting conditions and must, therefore, be done under standard reproducible illumination. However, failing this, colour matching for most domestic purposes should be done in daylight, unless the garment is specifically to be used under artificial light. It is also worth bearing in mind when assessing a colour that a thread in bulk on a bobbin looks darker than when stitched.

Good quality sewing threads must have high levels of colour fastness suitable for the use to which they are to be put. For instance, in workwear the dye must not change shade or stain other materials in laundering; nor must the dye sublimate if the garment is processed at high temperatures; and in swimwear the thread must be fast to salt and chlorinated waters. A fuller discussion of colour will be found on page 197.

Characteristics of sewing thread types

Staple fibre thread

Cotton

There are three types of cotton threads; soft, mercerised, and 'polished' or 'glacé'. They are all made from good quality long fine cotton fibres. Combing the fibres during the processes before spinning removes the very short fibres that are present and makes the remaining longer fibres lie parallel to each other, thus improving the regularity and strength of the thread. To reduce the hairiness of spun thread and improve its appearance, the thread is singed with gas flames or electric burners which remove projecting fibres. The constructions of the threads and balance of twist are important to satisfactory performance, as are the dyeing and finishing processes.

The tenacity of cotton threads is about 2·7 g/dtex with an extension at break of about 7%, and the threads can be said to have fairly low levels of shrinkage both in laundering and when subject to heat. They do not melt when heated and generally their resistance to abrasion is good.

Soft cotton thread

This thread is used in the clothing industry but rather more so in the domestic field. Its manufacture follows the outline given above and, as with all threads, the final process is lubrication. This thread is capable of being very effectively lubricated by thread manufacturers to reduce the coefficient of friction.

Mercerised cotton thread

This thread is widely used for domestic sewing, and in the clothing industry. Its chief characteristics are good lustre and increased strength. This is achieved by passing the combed and gassed thread under tension through cold 20% solution of caustic soda before dyeing. This causes the cotton fibres to swell and become rounder in section, and this change is responsible for the improved lustre and something like a 12% increase in tensile strength. The change in fibre appearance (page 49) and properties is permanent and cannot be reversed by washing or otherwise.

Glacé or polished thread

The sewing of leather and fur and the overlocking or 'serging' of tailored garments require threads having a very smooth surface with improved strength, and resistance to abrasion. These characteristics are developed by applying, after dyeing, a solution of starch and waxes to the thread, which is then polished by a series of revolving brushes at high speed to lay the surface fibres and bond the plies. The surface finish is not permanent and is removed by wet treatment.

Linen thread

These threads have restricted use in clothing and are best known as button threads. Coarse linen threads and twines are used in stitching shoes, tents and tarpaulins. If such threads are to be exposed to bacterial action in wet conditions they should be rotproofed.

Polyester thread

Spun polyester threads are widely used and have many outstanding properties. The tenacity of such threads lies between 2·8 and 3·3 g/dtex with extensions ranging from 11–23%. The load-extension properties are controlled in thread manufacture by means of appropriate stretching and heat stabilising processes applied to the threads. Fibre manufacturers can supply a choice of polyester fibres of different tenacities, some of which are pre-stabilised to meet required thread characteristics.

Spun polyester threads are softer than the continuous filament form and the fibrous surface provides easier retention of the lubricant in thread manufacture. The surface characteristics of the spun thread ensure a good 'lock' of the thread in the stitch configuration with the minimum movement of individual stitches in the seam.

The fibrous surface of both cotton, corespun polyester/cotton and spun polyester threads helps to reduce the friction and assist in the cooling of the needle during sewing, in contrast with the behaviour of smooth continuous filament threads.

In some types of seams the stitches are predominantly on the surface of the fabric and are exposed to abrasion in use. Polyester has a high resistance to abrasion and is of value in such circumstances.

Manufacturing thread from staple fibre provides greater scope and flexibility in producing ranges of thread sizes than is possible with continuous filament structures.

Some spun threads are referred to as 'schappe-spun' and others 'cotton spun'. This indicates that the former is made from 'long staple' fibre (25–88 mm) and the latter from 'shorter staple'. Schappe-spun thread is produced by first stretch-breaking the polyester tow to produce a variable fibre length, and then spinning it on machinery of the type formerly used for spun silk. Long staple threads are stronger than shorter staple threads of the same size and have few projecting fibres. All threads are wound onto packages under tension and no matter how low a tension has been applied some relaxation shrinkage, maybe 0·5%, will occur. This is of no significance in seam performance; however stability of polyester thread at about 180°C is ensured by the heat-setting treatment. Polyester thread is particularly free from the risk of discolouration on exposure to heat and light.

Corespun thread

Corespun threads consist of a high-tenacity continuous filament polyester core covered by either a sheath of long-staple cotton fibres (Poly/Cotton), or a polyester fibre covering (Poly/Poly). The thread is formed by twisting several of these corespun yarns together to provide cohesion of the fibre covering. Glacé corespun threads can be produced by a polishing process. The continuous filaments provide high strength and resistance to abrasion.

The Poly/Cotton sheath carries the lubricant and provides the sewability. The continuous filament component allows a finer thread to be used than would be necessary for 100% cotton and yet maintains the required strength.

In high speed sewing of closely constructed fabric, possibly bearing a finish unsuitable for sewing, a needle temperature rise of up to 350°C can be reached on account of high friction as the needle penetrates the fabric. This would exceed the melting point of most synthetic fibres and would cause fusion. When fibres melt, the 'melt' tends to accumulate on the needle itself and thereby increases the friction still further.

The heat sensitive filaments are protected by the cotton sheath from this rise in temperature and in fact the surface fibres tend to dissipate the heat.

Apart from the usual aspects of thread manufacture discussed for spun polyester, special attention must be given to the dyeing process to ensure uniformity of colour of the cellulose and polyester components.

The sheath of fibres does not completely cover the core and may migrate to reveal the core unevenly, and this is likely to show any colour difference between the cotton and the polyester. The Poly/Poly corespun simplifies dyeing and produces greater uniformity of colour along the thread length. The cost of Poly/Poly is consequently less than Poly/Cotton but it does not provide the same protection against rise in temperature at high machine speeds.

The tenacity of these threads, according to manufacture, lies about 3·7 g/dtex with extensions at break between 20–35%. This provides a basis for understanding the choice of thread for particular fabrics and seams. Apart from general stitching some of these corespun polyester threads are especially suitable for blind stitching and linking.

Silk thread

This is schappe-spun from long staple fibre. An important characteristic of a silk sewing thread is its good strength and extensibility of about 20%. Very little silk thread is now used in clothing manufacture, but it is suitable for the seaming of lightweight fabrics and for decorative stitching.

Continuous filament thread

Most threads used for seaming are spun. However, special use is made of polyester and nylon continuous filament threads. These are classed as multi-filament polyester or nylon, textured polyester, and bulked nylon or polyester. In addition nylon monofilament threads are available.

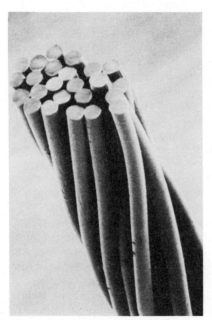

Fig. 193 High tenacity, fully drawn polyester with low twist to avoid liveliness and twist displacement. Adhesives are used to prevent splitting during sewing. *(Tootal Group)*

Fig. 194 3-ply multi-filament, high tenacity type, fully drawn polyester. May be bonded to improve sewing performance. *(Tootal Group)*

Multi-filament polyester or nylon thread

The continuous filaments in this type of thread are neither bulked nor textured. To prevent separation of the filaments and damage whilst machining a number of filaments are twisted together to form a single yarn and these are then folded to form the 2- or 3-ply thread. Another method is to twist the filaments to form a single thread and to bond them together by passing the thread through a liquid polymer to coat them. This is known as a monocord and is suitable for blind stitching in hemming. (Figures 193/194).

The bonded single thread is somewhat translucent and the twisted ply thread is less so. Compared with spun threads they are very compact and fine, and longer lengths of thread can be wound onto the thread packages. Their tenacities are the highest obtainable for sewing threads, with extensions between 20 to 30%. The smooth surface of such threads provides very close contact with the needle which can lead to problems of high friction, temperature rise and hence fusing, and consequently the lubrication of the thread is very important. Plied threads are used to a limited extent as the needle thread in lockstitch and chainstitch machines for seaming light-weight fabrics requiring very fine seams. Single threads are never used for this purpose. Both plied and single threads are used in overlocking and blindstitching.

The single thread is of particular value as an underthread and is used in conjunction with different and more suitable needle threads. One might think that the use of dissimilar threads in a seam would lead to an imbalance, resulting in a reduction of seam strength. In fact, the needle thread suffers greater damage in sewing and the two suitably chosen threads are roughly equal in strength in the finished seam. Occasionally, the single thread can be used in the needle for overlocking where the demands made on it will be less than would be in the main seam of the garment.

Air-jet textured polyester thread

These continuous filament air-jet textured yarns are produced from multi-filament single yarns characterised by loops formed in the filaments which give minute surface irregularities. These irregularities ensure good locking of the stitch and overcome the problem of 'runback' or unravelling. Furthermore they help to give a less intimate contact of the thread with the machine parts compared with that of a smoother 'flat' continuous filament thread. Consequently, they reduce the coefficient of friction between the thread and the surfaces with which it comes in contact. Texturing reduces the high strength which can normally be attained in continuous filament threads, but the thread extensibility is higher. The future prospects for the use of this type of thread are good.

Air-jet Intermingled (or air-entangled) polyester thread

This very recently developed thread is composed of a continuous filament core surrounded by filaments which have been entangled by an air-jet. This intermingling increases the cohesion between the filaments without the development of loops in the filaments as in air-jet texturing above, and reduces the amount of or need to insert twist, thus saving on cost of production. The core contributes to the tensile strength of the thread and the entangled filaments increase the fullness of the thread and contribute to a reduction in yarn friction.

False-twist textured polyester and nylon thread

The very soft and highly elastic properties imparted by the false-twist texturing process are essential for the covering of very extensible seams in knitwear, underwear, swimwear, foundation wear and tights. The comfort of garments which have particularly close contact with the skin is improved by the soft texture.

These highly extensible threads are used in the loopers of overlocking and seam covering machines in which the thread tension is low. The high resistance to abrasion of the fibres is particularly valuable in a stitch in which the thread is so prominently exposed to wear.

Monofilament thread

A monofilament is a thick, coarse, twistless filament which has been extruded and stretched whilst hot to produce the required thread denier. Monofilament threads are made from nylon 6·6 or nylon 6, and because there is only one surface to scatter light they are translucent and the colour of the fabric which is being stitched shows through. It is found sufficient to provide natural, light grey and dark grey threads and this reduces the need to carry the normally large stocks of different shades for the fabrics to be sewn. Whilst the thread has these merits care should be taken in its use.

A monofilament thread is much stiffer than a multi-filament thread of the same size and this difference is even greater in the coarser threads.

Nylon 6 is softer than nylon 6·6 but because it has a lower melting point of 215°C, (as against 250°C for nylon 6·6) it is unsuited to high speed machining. Apart from this risk of fusing, monofilaments tend to shrink and cause seam pucker. The harshness of the thread can be responsible for accelerated wear on machine parts, and the stiffness can create difficulty in securing the ends of the thread in the seam, with the associated risk of unravelling.

Technical considerations must apply to the choice of all threads, and monofilament threads need especially careful selection.

Silk thread

Silk was in use as a thread, in continuous filament form, long before the advent of manufactured fibres, but now very little is used in the clothing industry. There is, however, a retail outlet for such thread in conjunction with the sale of silk fabric, and for embroidery.

Embroidery threads

The large scale production of decorative embroideries on fabrics and garments, and motifs and badges for application by stitching or adhesion, requires the provision of suitable threads for machine embroidery. Threads are also constructed specifically for hand embroidery, which is a recognised form of artistic expression and also now a popular creative leisure pursuit.

Embroidery threads are usually required to be soft and lustrous and for this reason mercerised cotton, silk and viscose filament yarns are used. Polyester and nylon threads are generally too stiff for this purpose. However, the introduction of textured polyester very fine filament yarns, such as 'Tactel', are now successfully in use.

Embroidery threads generally must be lustrous and have the capacity to cover the fabric well. Exceptions are metallic threads for certain types of 'gold work', couching and outlining, and compact threads for special uses. A choice of visual effects, thread sizes and a broad palette of colour contributes to the impact of the embroidery.

Fibres used include cotton, silk, viscose, nylon, polyester, and metallised polyester (page 66). Metallising involves coating a film of polyester with metal and cutting it into narrow strips. The film may be uniformly coloured or be multicoloured. Blends of filaments are also used in order to modify the texture and qualities of the threads.

Cotton embroidery thread is made from a long staple fibre, combed and mercerised; viscose thread is of a higher tenacity than the regular viscose used in fabrics since the thread needs to stand the rigours of machining. Wool, and acrylic/wool blends are used in chenille and loop-pile embroidery, and in the hand embroidery of tapestries.

The tensile strength and elongation of each thread type is controlled, and all are required to have a good lustre, a minimum level of colour fastness to washing, dry cleaning, rubbing and to light. The maximum permitted shrinkage in washing is also defined.

Embroidery thread containing metallised polyester must be washable at 60°C followed by a cool iron. To ensure this, tests on resistance to heat are carried out under ironing, hot water, dry heat and washing with detergent conditions. Similarly, satisfactory drycleaning is ensured by testing the product in perchloroethylene, trichloroethylene, and benzene.

Where pure silver is used its resistance to oxidation is assessed and the care label specifies 'no bleach'.

Influence of fabric characteristics on sewing thread requirements

Fibre content of fabric

It is often suggested that whereas fabrics made from spun natural or viscose fibres may be sewn with threads made from natural and synthetic fibres, fabrics made from synthetic fibres should be sewn only with synthetic fibre thread. The reasons for this are:

- Since fabrics made from most synthetic fibres are not liable to shrink in use, it is very important for the sewing thread to be equally stable in washing. Even though a cotton sewing thread usually has a very low shrinkage, the amount that does occur may cause seam puckering.
- Many fabrics made from synthetic fibres are very lightweight and need unobtrusive seams of adequate strength. Cotton sewing threads are excellent for most purposes but for a given strength they are coarser than the synthetic threads.

A sewing thread must be chosen also with a view to special characteristics of the fabric and the use to be made of the fabric. The following examples illustrate this point.

Extensible fabrics

The extensibility of knitwear garments tends to be greater than garments made up from knitted piece goods, and in addition the style of knitwear often requires the neckband seam, for example, to be extensible enough to withstand repeated passage over the head in use. Other parts of garments, such as shoulder seams and buttonhole stand, may require the seam to be stabilised. This may be done by the insertion of a firm tape or fine nylon ribbon and the use of a less extensible seam structure than at the neckband.

In other garments made from knitted piece goods, seams at armholes and at the seat of stretch trousers would be strained frequently in use and would need the combined contribution of thread and stitch to respond satisfactorily.

Easy care fabrics

Easy care fabrics made from cotton, viscose or synthetic fibres must be sewn with threads of low shrinkage, i.e., less than 1%. Low moisture absorption is also of importance since the seams should dry at the same rate as the garment.

Garments that are subject to high temperatures during garment manufacture must, in addition, include sewing threads which satisfactorily withstand the high temperature. In particular, the dyes used on polyester fibre thread must not sublimate. When resinated fabric is hot pressed, acid may be released and is liable to reduce the strength of cellulose sewing thread. For such fabrics it is advisable to use a slightly coarser, therefore stronger, cotton thread to offset the effect. However, the risk of seam pucker due to the inclusion of a coarser thread must be anticipated.

Shower-resistant garments

Shower-resistant garments can leak at the seams because the holes made by the passage of the needle are not sufficiently well filled by the sewing thread. It is sometimes incorrectly thought that a thread made from a fibre of low moisture absorption, such as polyester, will be water resistant and therefore will contribute substantially to the water resistance of the seam. It is important to remember that such a fibre can pass water along its surface by wicking and so transmit the water to the inside of the garment. Sewing threads are available that have been treated to make the surface of the individual fibres water repellent and so thereby reduce the wicking of water. In waterproof garments, however, clothing manufacturers often seal the underside of seams by taping, using a suitable clear adhesive.

Flame-retardant garments

The effect of sewing threads on the flammability of seams is discussed on page 233. To achieve a flare-free seam it is necessary to use a polyester or nylon thread in a garment made of thermoplastic fibres, or a cotton thread in a cotton fabric of low flame retardance. In the manufacture of flame retardant garments, needle coolants and thread lubricants should not be used, since they increase the flammability of the seam.

SEAMS

Performance of seams in garments

Defective seams may spoil the appearance of a garment and be the cause of its ultimate failure. Good seams are essential factors in garment quality.

A detailed study of seam geometry in knitted fabrics and the effects on seam performance is given in HATRA Research Reports*, and a series of 'Technological Reports' published by the Clothing & Footwear Institute[†] cover a range of studies on seams in knitted and woven fabrics. It is by understanding the relevance of the properties of the fabrics and sewing threads to seam properties that cost-conscious garment technologists can determine the seam specification for a particular garment with a view to meeting performance requirements, and ensuring that a good estimate is made of thread utilisation and sewing time.

The inherent properties of knitted and woven fabrics, the special seam requirements for particular uses such as easy care and swimwear, and the special location or function of seams as in the crotch of trousers and tights, all govern the choice of variables in the seaming operation. For instance,

* Hosiery and Allied Trades Research Association, 7 Gregory Boulevard, Nottingham NG7 6LD.
† CITA, 10 Blackfriars Street, Manchester M35 DR.

the type of seam, the type of stitch and stitch frequency, the selection of the type and 'size' of sewing thread, the choice of needle, and the skill with which the fabric components are handled, assembled and fed through the stitching zone, all contribute to the production of a satisfactory seam.

Some fabrics, however, have properties which make them particularly difficult to sew satisfactorily and it is important to understand these in order to avoid seaming difficulties and defects.

Problems associated with seams are discussed under the following headings:

- Stitching damage and laddering (damage to the fabric along the seam line)
- Seam pucker
- Seam stretch and grinning
- Transverse seam strength
- Seam slippage and fraying

Stitching damage and laddering

When fabrics are being seamed together, it is possible to damage the threads of the cloth. This may have two consequences. First, the cut ends of the damaged threads may show along the line of the seam, making it unsightly. Second, if the damage is severe the seam will be weaker than it need be.

Sewing damage is generally caused by lack of mobility in the fibres of the yarn, due to high twist; by lack of mobility of the yarns themselves due to close construction of the cloth or to the nature of the finish; or to the use of over-large or blunt needles. Even new packets of needles may contain some blunt ones, but generally damage caused by blunt needles can be avoided by changing needles sufficiently often. If a fabric is difficult to sew without damage, it is very necessary to be sure that sharp needles of the smallest practicable size are used.

It will be seen that if a needle passes through the centre of a thread, a diamond-shaped opening is formed and some of the fibres must be stretched to accommodate the thickness of the needle. In a tightly twisted yarn this is more important than in a softly twisted yarn, in which the fibres can move easily. Breakdown of the fibres will occur if they are stretched beyond their breaking extensions. This is more likely in the highly twisted yarns, in which the fibres are more firmly bound, and in yarns made from the less extensible fibres. Wool fabrics rarely show damage because the fibres are so extensible.

When the needle passes between the yarns it may have to push them aside if they are close together. In a densely constructed cloth the yarns can only be moved over a short length close to the needle, and this length of yarn is consequently stretched. If the yarn is inextensible or very difficult to move, stretch applied over a short length may be sufficient to break it. Finishes that have the effect of anchoring the yarns in place or which

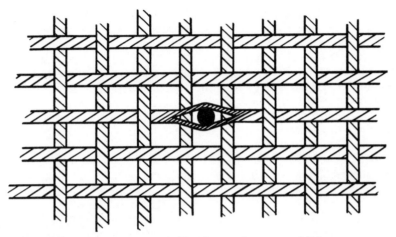

Fig. 195 Effect of yarn twist on stitching damage in a woven fabric.

increase the friction between them making them difficult to move also increase the danger of the yarn being broken. Certain dyes and the resin finishes behave in this way.

In knitted fabrics damage which has essentially the same cause shows as burst loops. If the needle is too large for the size of loop it may be accommodated if the yarn in the loop extends or if extra yarn can be 'robbed' from adjacent loops. If the extra yarn cannot be provided fast enough to meet the speed of machining then the knitted loop will burst. The mobility of the yarns is influenced by their frictional properties and the constraints on fabric extensibility imposed by complicated knitted structures.

It is important to realise that the behaviour of a fabric that is difficult to sew can be improved by controlling the lubrication of the fabric in finishing. Improved lubrication reduces the inter-fibre and inter-yarn friction and consequently increases the mobility of the fibres and yarns in the fabric. Reference has been made in the section on corespun threads to the rise of needle temperature that may be generated in high-speed sewing. The temperature may rise to a level sufficient to damage a fabric containing thermoplastic fibres. It is usually fairly easy to control such damage by the correct choice of needle, and particularly by the application of a suitable lubricant.

Damage is not usually detected by casual inspection of the seam, but shows up when the garment is worn and subject to flexing, and when it is washed. Knitted fabric develops ladders which radiate from the damaged seam and it is the dense, fine-gauge, double jersey structures that are particularly liable to such damage. Garment manufacturers need to test and anticipate the behaviour of fabric in sewing before embarking on bulk production. Testing must be carried out using the number of plies sewn in practice because it is known that the level of damage rises with the number of plies in the seam. This is because the needle drags the top ply of fabric into the second layer and so on, inhibiting the mobility of the yarns, especially in the middle layers.

Weft-knitted fabric needs to be handled in a relaxed state to avoid undue stretching of the loops and laddering. To achieve an adequate quality control the garment design and manufacturing techniques need to be related to fabric behaviour. It is essential that no sewing damage or fabric breakdown should occur along the seam line.

Seam pucker

Puckering or distortion of the fabric along the seam may be apparent immediately after machining or may develop in use, possibly after several launderings. An example of this type of defect is shown in Figure 196.

Lightweight fabrics often have a very uniform surface, especially when made from smooth continuous filament yarns. If the surface of the fabric is disturbed by the penetration of a needle this can affect the uniformity of light reflection from the surface, and this may appear as puckering, even without the sewing threads being present. It is essential, therefore, that the smallest size needle appropriate to the fabric and sewing thread be used to ensure the least possible fabric distortion. Knitted and woven fabrics of close construction, on the other hand, may have insufficient space within the fabric structure to accommodate the sewing threads. This causes the fabric threads to be displaced from the plane of the fabric, with consequent fabric buckling and seam pucker. This difficulty can be minimised by the use of a fine needle and sewing thread, and a reduction in the number of stitches per cm, compatible with the required seam strength. The use of chainstitch instead of lockstitch can also reduce the amount of thread 'bulk' to be contained in the fabric since the interlooping of the sewing thread in a chainstitch occurs on the surface of the fabric instead of in the thickness of the seam. Seams that lie at an angle to the warp enable the inclusion of the extra bulk of the sewing threads to be shared by a series of adjacent ends in the cloth and are, therefore, less liable to show this type of pucker.

Fig. 196 Seam pucker in a twin-needle felled seam after washing.
(*J. & P. Coats Ltd.*)

There is a tendency for seams to pucker when the components of a seam are smooth and slippery. The bottom layer is pushed forward by the feed-dog, but the presser foot tends to retard the passage of the top layer. Since the friction between the layers is low it is possible that the components will move out of phase and pucker. Puckering produced in this way can be overcome by suitable choice of machining conditions.

Puckering due to out-of-phase movement of the fabric layers may arise also by stretching one layer relative to the other when handling the fabric during machining. It is to be noted that deliberate seaming-in of fabric fullness with a view to shrinking to fit during pressing will be effective only when the fabric is made from wool. This technique cannot be used with fabrics made from manufactured fibres, since these fabrics cannot be shrunk in this way which, if it is attempted, leads to persistent puckering. It is, therefore, essential with these fabrics that the garment shape be achieved by accurate pattern cutting.

So far, the behaviour of sewing threads as a cause of seam pucker has not been discussed. Obviously, if the needle and/or under threads have been excessively tensioned during the sewing operation the threads will relax and contract once they are incorporated in the seam. The puckering may show only after several launderings. Polyester is less extensible at low loads than nylon and is, therefore, less liable to cause seam pucker in this way. Various tension measuring devices are available in the clothing industry to control this behaviour.

Clothing made from resinated cotton may be subject to high temperatures in an oven and in 'hot-head' pressing during garment manufacture. This necessitates that the sewing threads used must virtually not shrink when exposed to temperatures in the range of 165°C to 200°C. Spun polyester and corespun yarns are usually heat-set to ensure that they will meet these conditions. This is especially important when a lockstitch seam is used. Compared with other stitch types the lockstitch utilises the shortest length of thread for a given length of seam and for this reason is more sensitive to the reductions in the thread length caused by shrinkage.

Puckering which develops in use is frequently noticeable in those fabrics that are dimensionally stable. It is essential that garments made from fabrics having negligible shrinkage be made up with sewing thread, interlining and lining having similar shrinkage properties. If this is not the case, puckering will develop on washing. Seams may shrink even when made from cloth and sewing thread having 'no shrinkage'. This arises from the increase in thickness of the cloth during washing when the fixed length of the sewing thread can only be accommodated if the seam becomes shorter. Puckering due to this cause is reduced by using the lowest practicable sewing tension.

Assessment of seam appearance in easy care fabric may be carried out according to Test Method AATCC 88B 'The appearance of the seams of garments after household laundering'. Specimens of fabric, seamed in conformity with the seams used for the fabric in the garment, are washed under agreed home laundering or hand-washing conditions and drying procedures. Evaluation of the seam is against five photographic standards of either single or double needle seams, similar in principal to that described on page 190.

Seam stretch and grinning

It is essential for a seam to be able to extend adequately along its length in use without the sewing thread reaching its breaking extension and 'cracking'. Knitted fabrics, as might be expected, are more extensible than most woven structures. Knitwear and specialised clothing, such as sportswear and foundation garments, require the seam to have a very high stretch recovery approaching 100%. Skirts and trousers may require seams to extend up to 30% of their length.

Now the breaking extensions of sewing threads are only about 7% for cotton, 17% for spun polyester, 28% for corespun polyester and about 25% for 'flat' multi-filament thread, and it is because the length of sewing thread is much greater than the length of the seam in which it is contained that the seam does not break at these extensions. An increase in the extensibility of the seam can be achieved by increasing the length of thread in the seam. For example, the zig-zag stitch commonly used in foundation wear and the overlocking stitch which covers the edges of seams in some knitted garments both provide a reserve of thread length which can be drawn upon for extensions of the seam along its length. These stitches are not discreet enough for most outerwear and the choice then often rests between lockstitch and chainstitch structures.

Two-thread chainstitch introduces about twice the length of sewing thread into a seam as does the lockstitch (Figure 197) but this may result in an unwanted gap or 'grin' developing when tensions are applied across the seam. To overcome this 'grinning' and to close the gap the sewing thread tension may be increased, but in so doing the extensibility along the

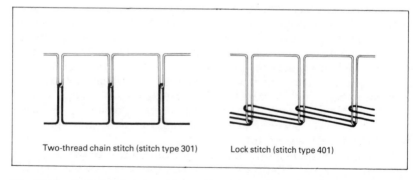

Two-thread chain stitch (stitch type 301)   Lock stitch (stitch type 401)

Fig. 197 Lock stitch (stitch type 301) and Two-thread chain stitch (stitch type 401) – classification according to BS3870: 1982.

seam is reduced. An acceptable compromise must therefore be found between reduced extensibility and tendency to grin.

The extensibility of lockstitch seams can often be increased by suitably increasing the number of stitches per centimetre because of the extra thread length which this introduces into the seam. It is found that there is an optimum stitch frequency and sewing thread tension to give the required seam extension and minimum lateral 'grin' for a given fabric.

Transverse seam strength

As discussed in the previous section, when a load is applied along the length of the seam the important aspect of its behaviour is the degree to which it will stretch without failure of the sewing thread. If this matches the extension of the fabric, or is adequate for the use of the garment, the seam is satisfactory. If, however, a seam is subject to a transverse load it may open ('grin'), it may pull apart by the slippage of the sewing threads over the turnings, or it may break, either because the sewing thread breaks or because the cloth threads break. The load at which a seam breaks for either of the latter two reasons is known as the 'seam strength'. This characteristic of the seam is important, but clearly there is no necessity for the seam to be stronger than the cloth. Most seams in garments are weaker than the cloth and it is important to ensure by proper design, choice of sewing thread and quality of workmanship, adequate performance in use.

Two important characteristics of a sewing thread relevant to the strength of the seam are its 'loop strength' and the variability of the thread. It will be realised that when a load is applied across a seam the top and bottom threads are pulled around each other in tight loops as in Figure 197. The breaking load of a thread where it is looped sharply round another thread is always less than the breaking load of a straight thread, and for this reason alone the strength of the seam is always less than the integral strength of the short lengths of sewing thread connecting the two pieces of cloth. This shortfall of strength is greater for threads made from relatively inextensible fibres such as linen and cotton and least for those made from extensible fibres such as polyester.

The loop strength of a thread may be found by attaching two ends of a length of yarn to the top of a single thread tester, passing a second length through this loop, and attaching its ends to the lower grip. The strength of this specimen is the loop strength of the yarn and will always be found to be somewhat less than twice the strength of a single length of yarn, the theoretical maximum. (See BS 1932 : Part 2 1966). It has been observed that the loops in a stressed seam are usually unsymmetrical, one leg being shorter than the other, and this is a further source of weakness. A test is available for the 'asymmetrical loop strength'.

The variability of the yarn is important because the seam will break first at the weakest loop, so causing failure of the adjacent loops as they become more highly stressed, the rupture of the seam then spreading out rapidly from this point. Thus the strength of the seam is dependent on the strength of the weakest loops, and the less variable the sewing thread the stronger the seam.

For this reason, when tests are made for the 'asymmetrical loop strength' a total of 40 individual tests are made. These are divided into four groups of ten, and the mean value of the lowest loop strengths in the groups is calculated. This result, therefore, is influenced by the variability of the yarn as well as its performance in a loop strength test.

The strength of a seam increases as the number of stitches per centimetre increases and may be calculated from:

Seam strength/cm = stitches/cm × 2 × asymmetrical loop strength.

At a sufficient level of stitches per cm the stitching is so strong that the seam breaks by failure of the yarns in the cloth. Increasing the stitch density beyond this point does not increase the seam strength, which may even be reduced because of increasing sewing damage. In a practical situation other considerations, such as appearance, must be taken into account, besides the strength of the seam, and for this reason the stitch rating used is likely to be less than the optimum for strength.

The strength of a prepared seam in a woven fabric may be measured according to ISO 5082, and may serve as a guide to an aspect of seam quality. In making the test it should be observed whether the seam failure is caused by the fabric or the sewing thread breaking or by seam slippage. Fabric damage along the seam line, although perhaps not visible will reduce seam strength.

Seam strength calculated as a percentage of woven fabric strength is known as seam efficiency percentage and ideally should be at least 85%. A value below this should serve as an alert, and the cause sought. Fabric damage may arise from an unsuitable choice of needle or the use of a damaged needle. An unsuitable finish may be the cause of either sewing damage, as already discussed, or seam slippage.

Seam slippage and fraying

Woven fabrics of open construction, particularly those made from smooth, continuous filament yarns, and weaves with long floats, are liable to develop slippage in those seams of a garment which are stressed during movement. Threads running parallel to the seam are liable to slip (Figure 198) and may even pull out. Such a fabric may be said to have a low seam strength, even though its tensile strength may be good. From the earlier discussion of seam strength it will be seen that in this instance the sewing threads remain intact and simply slide in the fabric at fairly low loads.

Even though a seam appears to have adequate resistance to slippage initially it may slip after a period of use if the fabric is prone to the defect known as 'fraying'. This term describes the loss of threads from a raw edge cut parallel to the threads. If the turnings of a seam lose threads in this way, eventually the resistance of the seam to slippage will be reduced to a dangerous level and the seam may fail. The cloths in which fraying is most

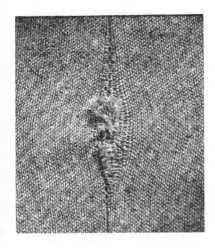

Fig. 198 Seam slippage in a single-lockstitch seam.
(J. & P. Coats Ltd.)

likely to be noticeable are those woven from smooth continuous filament yarns, particularly in weaves having long floats such as satin. If the cross threads have little crimp this increases the danger of fraying. The fault is more likely to be observed in linings.

If seams are liable to slip or fray simple precautions may be helpful, such as providing ample turnings which may be overlocked, or using two lines of stitching about 4 mm apart, or possibly increasing the number of stitches per cm. The textile finisher may reduce the tendency to slip or fray by applying a non-slip finish to the cloth.

The problem may be overcome by choosing a style in which the seams run at an angle to the cloth threads, since they are then unlikely either to slip or to fray. The improvement that this gives is easily demonstrated on a cloth such as a low quality satin lining.

Seam slippage of woven fabrics may be included in performance specifications and determined according to BS 3320 (ISO 5082) which specifies the preparation of the seam and the test procedure. The seamed specimen is mounted in a fabric strength tester so that a load of 12 kg can be applied at right angles to the seam. Upon reduction of the load after a given interval it is expected that for satisfactory performance any seam opening that remains should not be more than 6 mm. Fabrics intended for ski jackets and garment linings must perform adequately at loads of 16 kg and 8 kg respectively.

Welded seams

Discussion so far has been confined to conventional seaming with sewing threads, but reference must be made to the formation of seams without thread, or with thread and the addition of a sealant to produce waterproof seams.

For some time investigations have been made into the possibility of dispensing with the sewing machine and joining fabrics together more economically by welding or the use of an adhesive. However, the basic requirements of quality seams are adequate strength, extensibility, flexibility, and durability under a wide range of conditions in use. Seams welded by using the thermoplastic property of the material alone, or bonded by the use of adhesives have not met all these criteria.

Welding nylon fabric, for instance, depends on the combination of heat and pressure. Whilst the strength across the seam is high the seam is liable to have a low peel strength along the weld line.

The application of adhesives along seam lines in waterproof clothing is a laborious process. The resultant seam is usually stiff and, unless the adhesive is quite continuous and has penetrated the material effectively, water will penetrate with consequent seam failure.

Methods of welding

Welding may be accomplished by ultrasonic vibration which heats and softens the fibres so that, under pressure, they form a bond. Another method is by radio-frequency heating to soften the thermoplastic materials, where the two faces of the fabric meet. The electrodes themselves are cold, but heat is generated within the non-conductive material by the agitation of the molecules when subjected to the high-frequency alternating electro-magnetic field. Where the two layers of fabric are in contact, the molecules flow from one layer to the other and so weld the two surfaces together. PVC is easily welded in this way and has been used successfully in 'plastic' rainwear, provided the seams are designed and located so that

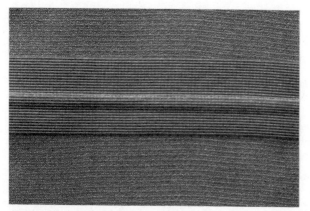

Fig. 199 Triple layer fabric with 'Sympatex' waterproof membrane between outer fabric and lining, seam-sealed with heat-seal tape. The sealing tape consists of adhesive and carrier material covered by a textile layer related to the garment. *(Enka AG West Germany)*

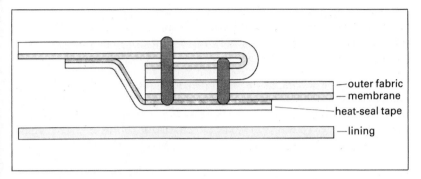

Fig. 200 Diagram of the seam-sealing of a two-layer laminate. The heat-seal tape consists of adhesive supported by a carrier and is applied directly to the membrane. *(Enka AG West Germany)*

they are unstressed in use. Nylon 6 and nylon 6·6 can be bonded under certain conditions of welding, whereas polyethylene and PTFE cannot be so treated.

Hot-air welding is a method of sealing sewn seams from the inside of waterproof high performance garments. A tape composed of a high melting point backing carries the adhesive, which melts at a lower temperature. Hot air is directed at the adhesive side of the tape, immediately before it is brought into contact with the fabric, and pressure is then applied to force the fluid adhesive into the seam and the adjacent fabric. Figures 199 and 200. Silicone spray, sometimes used as a lubricant when machining, must not be used, since it reduces the efficiency of the seal.

When designing waterproof articles, consideration must be given to the types and grades of fabric coatings together with the construction and location of the seams.

Waterproofness of seams

The waterproofness of seams is at greatest risk in locations where seams intersect, and where they join other thicknesses of material, as in pocket flaps and neck seams. Special care and provision for welding is made in these areas. Equally the performance of seams must be maintained during flexing, appropriate washing and dry cleaning, and exposure in use. For this reason the resistance of sealed seams to penetration by water is determined by submitting the seam to a water pressure, for example, of 69 kilopascals (kPa) for at least 5 minutes, after which it is expected that water will not have penetrated the seam.

Seams must perform no less efficiently than the coated fabric itself. The stringency of the test for the fabric and the minimum level of performance expected depends on whether it is polyurethane and silicone elastomer coated fabric, PVC coated, or a fabric coated with natural or synthetic polymer rubber. In BS 3546; 1989, 'Coated fabrics for water resistant clothing' the requirements for each type of coated fabric are specified. Part 3 indicates three grades of rubber-coated fabric and gives minimum levels of fabric resistance to the passage of water ranging from 27–55 kPa with an expected drop after a prescribed exposure to flexing to not less than 14–34 kPa.

Minimum hydrostatic head performance values are also given for less heavy coatings in common use which may be of the order of 100–150 cm head of water for fabrics as received (100 cm head of water equals 9·8 kPa.)

Details of the 'Testing of coated fabrics' are given in BS 3424 which comprises 35 parts covering physical and chemical test procedures.

Chapter 9

GLOSSARY OF FABRICS

(Definitions between quotation marks are taken directly from *Textile Terms and Definitions*, published by The Textile Institute.) All illustrations are shown with the warp or the wale direction running vertically.

Afgalaine 'Plain-weave, all-wool dress cloth, containing (*a*) woollen warp with woollen weft, or (*b*) worsted warp with woollen weft. In both makes, the warp is usually S and Z twist, arranged end-and-end, with S-twist woollen weft.'

Antung A plain-weave, slub-free silk fabric made from wild silk.

Armure A dress fabric having a wavy rib running in the weft direction which is produced by an armure weave.

Astrakhan cloth A curled, lustrous pile is the typical feature of this cloth, which imitates the fleece of the stillborn or very young Astrakhan lamb. The effect may be produced by weaving or knitting.

Baize A light-weight woollen felt used for covering card tables, etc.

Bannockburn tweed *See* Tweed.

Barathea The pebbled appearance is often produced by a twilled hopsack or broken rib weave. Whilst it may be made from a variety of fibres, worsted yarns are often used, or silk warp with a worsted weft. Made in a range of weights.

Batiste A soft, fine, plain-weave cloth of about 80 g/m². Now made from cotton, although originally made from flax.

Beaver cloth A heavy woollen overcoating which is intended to have the appearance of natural beaver skin. The lustrous nap of short fibres is produced by milling the cloth and raising the fibres, which are cut level and laid smoothly in one direction.

Beaverteen A strong, smooth-face, piece-dyed cotton cloth for heavy 'working' trousers. The face of the sateen-type structure consists of up to 150 weft threads per centimetre, and the underside of the cloth is slightly raised. The warp contains about 12 ends per centimetre. It is lighter in weight than a moleskin cloth.

Bedford cord Rounded cords run in the warp direction with fine sunken lines between. The cord may be emphasised by wadding ends. The weave on the face of the cord may be plain or twill. Worsted yarns are generally used for suitings and woollen yarns for heavy trousers such as riding breeches, but there is no restriction on the choice of fibres that may be used in this weave. In the lighter weights the construction may be used for dress fabrics. (*See* Piqué.)

Bengaline A heavy pronounced weft-way rib dress fabric with, for example, a silk or other continuous filament warp and a worsted or cotton weft. The effect may be produced by using a 3/3 warp cord and/or a coarse weft yarn. The rib is rather less heavy than that of an ottoman.

Binding Bindings are classes of narrow fabrics or smallware, and may be woven singly on a narrow loom, or more usually side by side on a broad loom. Each narrow fabric is woven with its own shuttle, thus producing a selvedge on each side. Bias binding is an exception to this method of manufacture.

Bindings are designed to protect, support, and give a finish to garments or other articles.

Bias binding A strip of material cut from a woven fabric at an acute angle to the warp (usually 45°), sometimes folded along one or both edges.

Glacé binding A woven narrow fabric made from polished cotton warp and weft yarns, used principally in tailoring. Usually 3/1 twill weave, ½ in. wide. The stiffness imparted during weaving is sometimes enhanced by subsequent finishing.

Paris binding A binding of warp twill or herringbone double-V twill (usually 3/1). Originally made with silk warp and polished cotton weft but now made with mercerised cotton or viscose warp and weft, and of such a density as to give the article a stiff handle without subsequent finishing.

Simili binding or felling simili A binding made from mercerised cotton yarns throughout, in a 3/1 broken-twill weave in imitation of satin, distinguished by well-pronounced selvedges raised on the face.

Stay binding A woven narrow fabric with cotton warp and weft, 2/2 twill herringbone weave, with one or more Vs. Generally used for the covering of seams and the strengthening of garments. Width 6 mm to 32 mm.

Stay tape A woven narrow fabric, plain weave, usually with linen warp and cotton weft. Generally used in tailoring for stablising garments, particularly at seams. Width 6 mm to 18 mm.

Birdseye *See* Colour and weave effects.

Blanket range In order to offer customers designs with different colour-ways, a pattern is woven in small sections to form a short length of full-width cloth consisting of a variety of designs.

Blazer cloth A heavily milled and raised woollen cloth, which may be printed with bold stripes. Used for sports coats.

Bluette A weft-faced cotton overall fabric made in a 2/2 twill with more than twice as many picks as ends. Typically weighing about 250 g/m^2.

Botany This refers to textiles made from merino wool. The term botany suiting applies to high quality worsted suiting made from this wool.

Bouclé A woven or knitted fabric with an irregular surface created by the use of fancy yarns having a bouclé or 'curled' appearance. It may be produced from a wide range of fibres in dress or coating weights. *See* Figure 201.

Box cloth 'An all-wool, woollen-spun fabric with a fibrous surface and firm handle. The surface should be completely covered with fibres so that no threads show. It is woven in a variety of weaves, depending on the weight of the finished cloth, and, according to weight, used for such purposes as leggings, coachman cloths, and billiard cloth.'

Broadcloth This term may be used in one of three ways. It may simply refer to (*a*) suitings which are at least 135 cm wide in the finished state, (*b*) lightweight poplin type fabric commonly used as shirting in Canada and the USA, or (*c*) a heavily milled woollen cloth made in a twill weave from fine merino yarns. The fabric is given a dress-face finish.

Brocade A fabric ornamented by a pattern produced by Jacquard or dobby weaving, in which warp, weft, or both sets of threads float over the fabric

Fig. 201 Bouclé. *(Hollings Faculty, Manchester Polytechnic)*

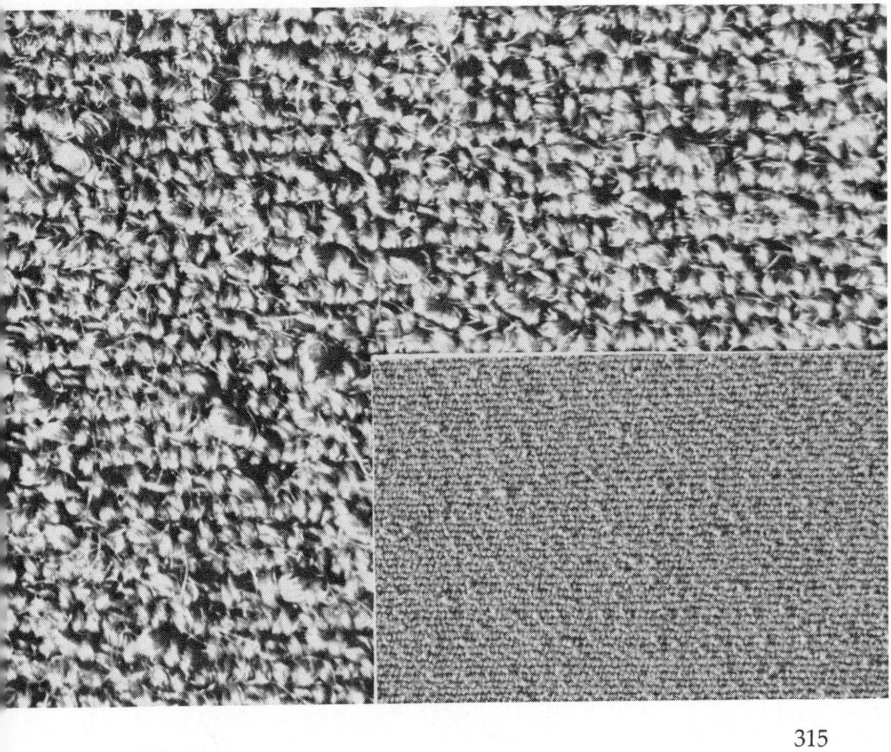

surface to create the required pattern. The basic structure or ground of the cloth is usually a simple weave such as a satin. The woven pattern or figure is often enhanced by the use of continuous filament yarns. *See* Figure 202.

Brocatelle A furnishing fabric carrying a figured pattern in satin weave on a less lustrous ground such as taffeta.

Broderie Anglaise A lightweight woven cloth embroidered by a Schiffli machine. The embroidered pattern includes holes in the design. Often made from cotton.

Buckram A lightweight woven cloth which is stiffened after piece-dyeing. It is usually made from cotton in a coarse plain weave and is used for stiffening.

Calendered cloth This refers to cloth, frequently made from cotton or linen, which has been passed during finishing between pairs of heavy rotating rollers, known as bowls, which may be heated or unheated. Various effects may be produced.

Embossed An embossed pattern is obtained by calendering the cloth between a suitably engraved roller and a soft compressible bowl. The

Fig. 202 Brocade. *(Shirley Institute)*

embossed effect is durable only if the cloth is made from thermoplastic fibres or, in the case of cotton, has been resin-treated.

Flattened To flatten and smooth cloth it may be passed between pairs of bowls which apply sufficient pressure to flatten the threads and close up the interstices of the cloth.

Glazed or lustrous appearance A high lustre may be produced by Schreiner-ing. This is done by impressing very fine lines on to the surface of the cloth from a heated roller engraved with about 150 lines/cm. This finish is not durable unless a thermoplastic material is present. 'Everglaze' was an example of such a finish.

Moiré A water-mark effect produced by calendering. *See* Moiré.

A lustrous appearance is also effected by *friction calendering*. Here the cloth passes between a pair of rollers, the upper one having a highly polished, heated surface which rotates at a greater surface speed than the softer bowl beneath. This difference in surface speed develops friction and consequently lustre on the fabric surface.

Calico 'A generic term for plain cotton cloth heavier than muslins.'

Cambric A fine lightweight, plain-weave cotton or linen cloth which has been fairly closely woven and given a slight stiffening and calendering to produce a smooth surface. Printed, with a crease-resist finish, it is often used for dresses. Very lightweight cambrics (about 65 g/m^2) are used for handkerchiefs.

Candlewick A fabric produced by patterned tufting and used for beds-preads, dressing gowns.

Canvas This firm, rather stiff, strong warp-faced cloth is usually made in a closely woven plain or double-end plain weave from cotton, flax, nylon, or polyester. Its weight can be varied over a very wide range according to its intended use.

Carpet *Velour* or *Velvet* are terms applied to Axminster, Wilton, tufted and bonded carpets which have very smooth, level and velvet-like surfaces. The individual tufts are not visible in the densely packed pile.

Plush or *Saxony* are cut pile carpets with longer and denser pile than velour. Pile height is up to 15 mm. The tufts in the pile appear distinctly separate from each other.

Shag is a tufted or woven long pile carpet with a low tuft density.

Cord has a short loop pile produced by tufting, weaving, or bonding.

Twist pile denotes a high folding twist in the yarn used in tufting and weaving, giving a slightly mottled look to the surface.

Embossed or *sculptured* effects are developed by the combination of cut and loop pile.

Casement cloth A weft-faced, plain-weave curtain fabric weighing about 150 g per sq. metre. It may be woven from cotton or manufactured fibres.

Cavalry twill A firm warp-faced cloth characterised by steep double-twill lines. The cloth is often made of wool and is produced in a variety of weights to meet the requirements of breeches, rainwear, and tailored dresses.

Chambray A plain-weave cotton cloth made with a dyed warp and undyed weft, which gives the cloth a somewhat speckled appearance. Used for dresses.

Cheese cloth A cheap, soft, plain-cloth of open construction and light in weight. Its principal use is as cheese wrapping.

Chenille cloth A cloth woven with chenille yarn in the weft. (Chenille yarn, page 67.)

Cheviot cloth *See* Tweed.

Chiffon A sheer, very lightweight plain-weave cloth of open square construction made from hard twisted continuous filament yarns. Silk or nylon are frequently used. The fabric has a very soft drape. It may be piece-dyed or printed.

Chiné A term applied to woven cloth printed with a design having a soft, blurred outline. This is produced by printing the sheet of parallel warp yarns before weaving, with the result that the printed outline does not

Fig. 203 Woven cloqué. *(Hollings Faculty, Manchester Polytechnic)*

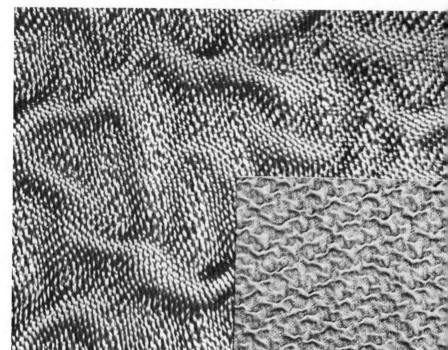

keep exact register during weaving, and the outline appears blurred in the woven cloth.

Chintz A printed plain-weave fabric, usually of cotton and lighter than cretonne. The cloth may be "semi-glazed" by friction calendering, or "fully-glazed" by stiffening with starch or other finish before friction calendering. Use for curtains and chair covers.

Ciré A term used to describe fabrics with a high mirror-like lustre produced by waxing and polishing the cloth by mechanical means. If a cloth with a satin weave is used, it further enhances the lustre by providing a very smooth surface.

Cloqué A fabric with a blistered figure effect. This may be produced by weaving a double or compound fabric, or by knitting a double fabric on a rib Jacquard machine. The choice of fibres is unlimited. *See* Figures 203 and 204.
Weft-knit cloqué Similar blister effects in weft-knit fabrics are produced by increasing the number of loops in the relief areas of the fabric.

Coated fabric A knitted, woven or nonwoven fabric on which single or multilayers of a continuous polymeric adherent coating is applied on

Fig. 204 Knitted cloqué. *(Hollings Faculty, Manchester Polytechnic)*

either one or both faces of the fabric. According to end-use a stiff or flexible coated fabric is produced.

Colour and weave effects Designs in fabric may be produced by the combination of a suitable simple weave and the arrangement of two or more colours in the warp and weft. Fabrics described as birdseye, dog's tooth, hound's tooth, shepherd's check, hairline, step effect, or Glen check pattern (*see* Figure 205) are examples of cloths produced in this way.

Corduroy A cut-weft pile fabric in which the pile forms cords running along the length of the cloth. It is generally made from cotton and the pile may be printed. A velveteen may be cut in such a way as to produce the appearance of corduroy.

Coutil A strong, narrow-striped herringbone cloth of close construction based on the 2/1 twill and used for corsets. It is often made from cotton and may be bleached or piece-dyed.

Covert cloth A warp-faced cloth with a fine, steep twill. Its chief characteristic is the mottled or speckled appearance produced by the use of grandrelle or mock grandrelle yarns in the warp only. Worsted yarns are

Fig. 205 Glen check. *(Hollings Faculty, Manchester Polytechnic)*

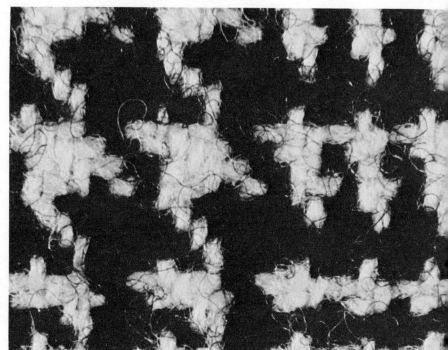

Fig. 206 Crepon.
(Hollings Faculty, Manchester Polytechnic)

often used, although a quality with a worsted warp and a woollen weft is made. Covert cloth is particularly used for light overcoats.

Crêpe Fabrics in this group are characterised by having a surface which is crinkled or puckered to some degree due to the inclusion of crêpe yarn (page 65). Such an effect may be produced either in woven or knitted fabrics.

Crêpe back satin refers to a satin fabric composed of continuous filament warp, which appears primarily on one face of the cloth, and a crêpe weft which is predominantly on the other face.

Crêpe-de-chine This term covers lightweight crêpes in weights and textures suitable for lingerie or dress fabrics. They are made from flat continuous filament warp, and crêpe twist continuous filament weft yarns alternating 2S, 2Z.

Crêpe suzette is equivalent to crepon georgette.

Crepon has the pucker or wrinkles running in the warp direction. This effect may be produced by one of the methods discussed on page 84. See Figure 206.

Crepon georgette is produced by weaving only one direction of twist in the weft of a georgette. The wrinkled effect is, therefore, introduced into fine, lightweight cloth.

Georgette A sheer, lightweight fabric with a crêpe appearance produced in a plain weave from crêpe twisted yarns arranged alternately 2S and 2Z in both warp and weft. Originally made from silk but now made also from wool and other fibres.

Marocain A crêpe fabric with pronounced ribs running in the weft direction. It is similar to but of much coarser texture than dress crêpe-de-chine. Fine, closely woven ends are used with alternating 2S, 2Z crêpe twist yarns in the weft.

Moss crêpe A dress fabric produced from moss crêpe yarn and/or weave. It has a soft, spongy handle, drapes well, and has a characteristic crêpe texture, especially when made from moss crêpe yarn. *See* Figure 207.

Knitted crêpe fabric Crêpe effects may be developed either by the choice of warp- or weft-knit fabric constructions, or by differential shrinkage produced in the fabric by chemical or heat treatment.

Cretonne A printed fabric, heavier than chintz, commonly of cotton. It is usually unglazed and likely to carry a floral design. Used for furnishings.

Fig. 207 Moss crêpe. *(Hollings Faculty, Manchester Polytechnic)*

Damask A reversible figured fabric woven from one type of warp and one type of weft, based usually on a satin weave. Used for furnishings, and in the bleached state for tablecloths, etc.

Delaine A printed lightweight, plain-weave cloth made from wool. It originated from mousseline delaine, which means wool muslin.

Denim A warp-faced twill with dyed yarns, generally blue or brown, in the warp and a white weft. It is often made from cotton in a 3/1 twill weave and pre-shrunk during finishing for use in overalls and 'denims'. Weights range from 200–300 g/m². Brushed denim and stretch denim are also produced.

'Stonewash' finishing, applied to jeans and denims, involves tumbling garments vigorously in a laundry-type washing machine containing pebbles and possibly bleach. The consequent effect is the now well-recognised non-pristine look, which is often graded by manufacturers to ensure uniformity of effect and quality in the garment.

Dimity 'A fabric, usually of cotton, that is checked or striped by corded effects which are made by weaving two or more threads as one.'

Dobby This is a mechanism applied to the loom that enables weaves and patterns to be produced that cannot be woven on a tappet loom, but are much less elaborate than those obtained by Jacquard weaving. Fabrics so woven are referred to as dobby fabrics.

Doeskin cloth A fine woollen, warp-face cloth usually of Merino wool, milled, raised, and dress-face finished. It is similar to beaver cloth but lighter and finer.

Dog's tooth check *See* Colour and weave effects.

Domet An imitation flannel made mostly from cotton. Both sides of the cloth are raised. It is used as an interlining in tailoring.

Donegal tweed *See* Tweed.

Dotted Swiss A fine, fairly stiff cotton muslin-type fabric with a clip-spot effect.

Dress-face finish This term applies to woollen cloth covered with a lustrous nap of short fibres. This is largely the result of milling, raising, cropping, and laying the nap, under suitable conditions, smoothly in one direction. The finish is applied to fabrics such as doeskin, beaver, and pilot cloths.

Drill A warp-faced twill similar to a denim but usually bleached or piece-dyed. It may be mineral khaki dyed for overalls. 'Satin drills' are made in a 5-end satin weave.

Duck A closely woven, strong, plain-weave cloth similar to canvas and used for similar purposes. The term also applies to tropical suitings.

Duffel A heavy, low-quality woollen cloth, napped on both faces. Generally made into short 'duffel' coats.

Dungaree A strong cotton cloth, similar to denim, made for overalls. A 3/1 or 2/1 twill is used. The cloth may be yarn or piece-dyed.

Dupion The cloth was originally made from silk obtained from double cocoons, which gave an irregular yarn. This yarn gives the cloth its characteristic slubby texture. Manufactured fibres are now used to produce fabrics with such effects.

Embossed cloth *See* Calendered cloth.

Epitropic fibre Fibre having particles embedded in its surface to modify one or more of its properties, for example, its tendency to accumulate static electricity.

Faced cloth A general term for cloths, such as box and doeskin, in which the laid pile produces a luxurious effect.

Facing silk A lustrous fabric used for facing lapels in evening suits. Barathea, ottoman, satin, and twill structures are used. Often silk is not used in the cloth, in which case it should not be referred to as a 'silk' facing.

Façonné A term applied to figured fabrics.

Faille 'A fine, soft fabric, woven from filament yarn, made in a plain weave with weft-way ribs formed by the intersection of a fine close-set warp with a coarser weft. Faille belongs to a group of fabrics having ribs in the weft direction. Examples of this group arranged in ascending order of prominence of the rib are taffeta, faille, poult, and grosgrain.'

Felt The cloth is identified by its densely matted appearance. It may have first been woven before the finish was developed, or it may consist of a mass of animal fibres which have been made to felt or mat together to form a continuous sheet of fabric without the aid of yarns.

Figured fabric A fabric having a Jacquard or dobby pattern.

Fishnet An open-work structure, weft-knitted from a combination of floated stitches and plated stitches (p. 108, p. 112). Used for run-resistant stockings.

Flannel A plain or twill weave fabric with a soft handle due to being slightly milled and raised. The cloth was originally made entirely from wool but now commonly contains some other fibre also. Both woollen and worsted flannels are produced weighing about 200 g/m^2.

Flannelette A cotton imitation of the wool flannel. Softly twisted yarns are used in the weft, and these respond to the action of the raising machine. A nap is produced on both faces of the cloth. Flannelette weighs 180–200 g/m^2 and is similar to but heavier than winceyette. It may be piece-dyed, printed, or woven from dyed yarns to produce coloured stripes. Flannelette has been used for children's nightwear, but it is legally required to be made flame-retardant. Heavier qualities are used for sheets.

Flock printed cloth *See* Printed cloth.

Folk weave A loosely woven fabric made from coarse yarn and having a rough surface, often with coloured warp or weft stripes.

Foulard A lightweight 2/2 twill fabric made from continuous filament flat yarns. It is often printed. It is similar to surah, which was originally made from silk.

Frieze A woollen overcoating which has been heavily milled and raised. The nap may be rubbed into small beads or 'pills' to produce a 'nap frieze'.

Fustian A general term used to describe a group of fabrics which have a considerably greater number of picks than ends. Beaverteen, corduroy, moleskin cloth, and velveteen are examples.

Gabardine A warp-faced cloth, firmly woven in 2/1 or 2/2 twill with a greater number of ends than picks. The fairly steep twill lines can be clearly seen, since the yarns used are compact. The fabric is finished to give a clear, clean appearance. Gabardines are commonly made from worsted yarns, all-cotton yarns, unions of wool and cotton, and blends of various fibres. Gabardine to be used for rainwear must be shower-proofed.

Gauze *See Leno.*

Georgette *See* Crêpe.

Gingham A firm, plain-weave, lightweight cloth of nearly square construction woven with dyed yarns to form a check. Commonly made from cotton; used for dresses, tablecloths, etc. *See* Figure 208.

Glen check or Glen Urquhart check *See* Colour and weave effects.

Grey cloth This term is applied to woven and knitted fabrics and is

Fig. 208 Gingham. *(Hollings Faculty, Manchester Polytechnic)*

synonymous with 'loomstate', which refers to the condition in which the woven cloth leaves the loom.

Grosgrain A cloth of about 180 grams/square metre in which the rounded rib runs in the weft direction and is more pronounced than that in a taffeta or poult. The warp consists of closely woven continuous filament yarns. Rather coarse yarn is used in the weft.

Guipure An openwork lace. The method of production is to embroider a ground fabric which is then removed, usually by chemical means.

Habutai A general term applied to silk fabrics that are fine, soft, and have been degummed. Jappe is an example of this group.

Haircord The cloth bears the name of the modified plain weave from which it is made. Fine ribs run in the warp direction of the cloth, which may be printed and is usually made from cotton.

Hairline *See* Colour and weave effects.

Herringbone A cloth made from a herringbone weave. *See* Figure 209.

Hessian A plain fabric of approximately square construction woven from one of the bast fibres, usually jute.

Fig. 209 Herringbone. *(Hollings Faculty, Manchester Polytechnic)*

Holland A thin, glazed, medium-weight plain-weave cloth made from cotton or flax which has been beetled or has received a glazed finish. Used for window blinds, furniture covering.

Homespun Coarse tweeds handwoven from handspun wool yarns in 2/2 twill-weave.

Honeycomb The cloth bears the name of the honeycomb weaves, which are designed to produce a cellular effect. It is made in a range of weights according to its use e.g., dress fabric or counterpane.

Hopsack The cloth of square construction takes its name from the modified plain weave from which it is made. It is synonymous with weaves known as basket or matt.

Hound's tooth check *See* Colour and weave effects.

Italian A lining fabric, usually made from cotton in a 5-shaft sateen weave, with lustrous finish produced mainly by Schreinering. The combination of a cotton warp and worsted weft may also be used.

Jacquard fabric A figured fabric with a large scale repeat e.g. floral brocade which requires a mechanically controlled mechanism, known as a 'jacquard', to select and lift the warp whilst weaving.

Jacquard mechanism A term used in both weaving and knitting. In knitting the mechanism selects the knitting elements in relation to the required pattern.

An electrically controlled jacquard mechanism is now commonly linked directly to a computer which permits increased rates of woven or knitted fabric production and flexibility in design.

Jappe A fine, soft, lightweight (70 g/m^2) plain-woven cloth of approximately square construction. Continuous filament silk yarns are usually used. The fabric is used for lining but is suitable for dresswear if printed.

Jean A warp-faced cotton fabric in 2/1 twill mainly used for overalls.

Jeanette A lighter weight fabric than a Jean and suitable for linings.

Kersey A dense woollen cloth, similar to a melton. Often made from 2/2 twill, milled and finished to give a short lustrous nap.

Lambs' wool Wool from the fleeces of lambs, or young sheep up to the stage of weaning, irrespective of breed or type of sheep. The term lambswool is, however, used commercially to indicate a fabric or garment having a soft handle, made totally of virgin wool, a proportion of which is lambs' wool.

Lamé Applied to fabrics having flat metallic threads which form either the ground or a decorative figure.

Lawn A lightweight, plain-woven cloth of linen or cotton, of a soft, smooth, and sheer character. Spun yarns made from polyester fibres are also used in this type of fabric.

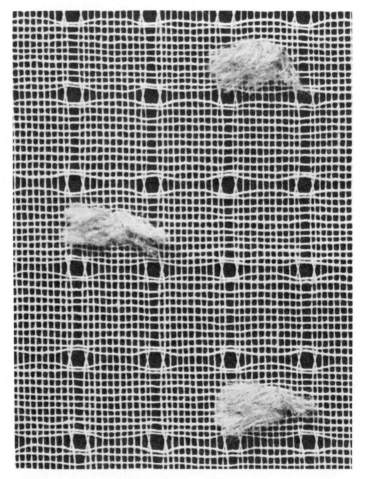

Fig. 210 Voile. Leno used as a decorative effect.
(Hollings Faculty, Manchester Polytechnic)

Leathercloth A coated fabric which is embossed to give a leather-like appearance.

Leno A cellular type of cloth made by crossing warp threads in weaving. Figure 210.

Limbric A closely woven plain-weave cloth. The softly twisted weft is thicker than the warp yarn, and the picks per centimetre exceed the number of ends. The weft is prominent and has a slight lustre because of its low twist. Used as a dress fabric.

Linen This describes cloths woven from linen yarns spun entirely from flax. Many fabrics with the characteristic slubby and thready appearance of linen are made from viscose, polyester, and blends. For this reason it is important to state the fibre content of linen-type cloth.

Linsey-Wolsey A fairly coarse fabric having a linen warp and a worsted weft.

Lisle thread A cotton hosiery yarn, hard twisted, plied (usually 2-ply), gassed and often mercerised. Formerly used for lisle stockings.

Loden A coarse woollen milled fabric of Austrian origin used for outerwear (e.g. coats and capes), and given a water-repellent finish.

Marcella A piqué structure with a fancy or figured woven design. Often made from cotton and used for dress shirt fronts.

Marl *See* Worsted.

Marocain *See* Crêpe.

Marquisette A light-weight leno gauze.

Matelassé A fabric with a quilted appearance produced in weaving. This is achieved by the use of a double or compound structure. It is often used for formal dress wear. Figure 211.

Fig. 211 Matelassé. *(Hollings Faculty, Manchester Polytechnic)*

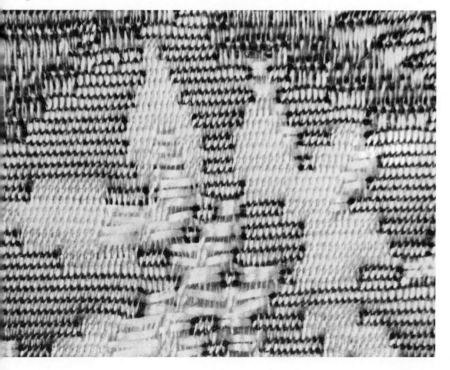

Matt A modified plain weave in which two or more ends and picks weave as one. The fabric may be known as "matt", "hopsack" or "basket weave".

Melange fabric *See* Printed cloth and Worsted.

Melded fabric A fabric made from or containing bi-component fibres. By heating to a suitable temperature one of the component fibres may be softened, producing adhesion.

Melton A heavyweight fabric suitable for overcoats. Lighter weights are used as undercollars in suits. It may be made entirely of wool or with a cotton warp and a woollen weft in a 2/2 twill or other simple weave. It is heavily milled, raised, and cropped.

Mercerised cloth Cotton or linen cloth treated with a cold concentrated solution of caustic soda with or without tension is said to have been mercerised.

Merino wool A fine white wool obtained from the merino breed of sheep, or a fabric made from this wool. The term tends to be used rather loosely (see Botany).

Mock leno A cellular type cloth produced from a mock leno weave in which spaces develop between groups of threads. Figure 212.

Fig. 212 Mock leno. *(Hollings Faculty, Manchester Polytechnic)*

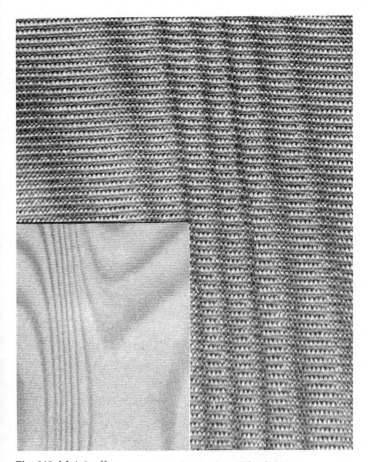

Fig. 213 Moiré taffeta. *(Hollings Faculty, Manchester Polytechnic)*

Moiré A water-mark effect produced on lustrous ribbed or corded cloths by localised flattening of the ribs during finishing. The flattened areas reflect the light differently from the rest of the cloth and consequently produce the distinctive appearance. The finish is generally not resistant to washing. Various styles of moiré can be produced, such as a reversal or mirror-image of the moiré pattern across the cloth and centred on the middle, and a striped moiré produced by suitably engraved rollers. Figure 213.

Moleskin cloth This cloth, used for workmen's trousers, is very much like uncut velveteen. It is heavier than a beaverteen with about 140 picks per centimetre.

Molleton A heavy reversible woollen flannel with a nap on both faces. Now made from other fibres.

Moquette A warp-pile upholstery fabric. The pile may be either cut or uncut, or patterned with cut and uncut pile.

Moss crêpe *See* Crêpe.

Mousseline (de-soie) A French term describing muslin which was originally made of silk. Now mousseline is applied to similar fabrics made from fibres other than silk.

Mull A very fine, soft, lightweight, plain-weave cloth of fairly open texture and almost square construction. Weight about 50 g/m².

Muslin A general term for soft, fine, plain-weave or simple leno weave cloths of very lightweight, open, square construction. Muslins for dress wear may be decorated with embroidery, clip-spot, or lappet designs.

Nap fabric This refers to woollen overcoating of up to 1,000 g/m² which has been rubbed during finishing to produce a beady or pilled surface.

Narrow fabric Sometimes known as smallwares.
'(1) Any textile fabric not exceeding 45 cm in width with two selvedges'
'(2) Any trimming'

Needlecord A fine-ribbed corduroy used for dresses.

Ninon This may be used to describe a voile fabric made from manufactured fibres. Originally it applied to fine, light open silk cloths with highly twisted yarns woven in groups of two or three in both warp and weft, and known as double or triple ninon.

Nun's veiling A very lightweight cloth in plain-weave; usually woven from worsted, silk, or cotton yarns and dyed black.

Ombré A cloth showing graduated colours or shades produced in weaving, dyeing, or printing.

Ondé or Ondulé Descriptive of fabrics having a wavy effect of wavy lines produced by weaving or calendering. In the former, either the weft yarns or the warp follow a waving path.

Organdie A lightweight, plain-weave cotton fabric which has been given a durably stiff transparent finish, preferably by treatment with strong sulphuric acid. Used for dresses and stiffening.

Organza A sheer, stiff, plain-weave cloth originally made from continuous filament silk in the gum, but now also made from continuous filament manufactured fibres. This fabric may be dyed, printed, or machine embroidered.

Ottoman A warp-faced cloth with a fairly flat, bold, smooth, weft-way rib. Originally made from a silk warp and worsted weft. The heavier weight cloths are suitable for tailoring and may have a small fancy design included in the general weft-way rib effect. Figure 214.

Oxford A good quality shirting fabric made in a plain weave with two ends weaving as one. It is generally made from cotton. Stripes of dyed yarn or decorative weaves are sometimes introduced.

Panama A worsted fabric with a clear finish weighing about 200 g/m^2 and used for tropical suiting. The fabric is of a plain weave and square construction. Fibres other than wool may be used. (*N.B.* A Panama embroidery canvas of a hopsack weave which is beetled must not be confused with the worsted Panama.)

Peau de soie 'A French term meaning literally "skin of silk", applied originally to a fine silk fabric in a modified satin weave having a ribbed or grained appearance; sometimes reversible. The term nowadays includes fabrics made from manufactured fibres; it is recommended that in such contexts the name of the fibre should be indicated.'

Percale A plain-weave, good quality, closely woven cotton cloth of approximately square construction. It may be glazed in finishing. Used typically for summer dresses and sheets.

Piece The unit length of fabric removed from the loom. The standard length depends on the type of fabric, but may be such as best suits the purchaser. Piece lengths are generally between 75 and 100 m. According to

Fig. 214 Ottoman. *(Hollings Faculty, Manchester Polytechnic)*

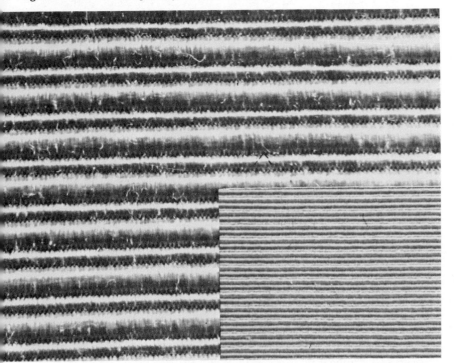

the state of the cloth expressions such as 'loomstate piece', 'dyed piece' may be used.

Pile fabric A fabric with tufts of fibre or loops of yarn projecting from the surface. The most important classes of pile fabric at present are: (*a*) woven, in which case it has cut or uncut warp pile, or cut weft pile, (*b*) knitted, in which case ends of fibres may form the pile or the pile may consist of loops, or (*c*) tufted, which results in brushed, cut, or uncut pile.

Pilot A heavily milled and raised woollen cloth generally used for seamen's jackets and overcoats. It is available in a wide range of fibre qualities. A 2/2 twill is often used.

Piqué Originally a woven cloth with rounded cords running in the weft direction, now often made in a lightweight Bedford cord weave with the cord running in the warp direction. Different widths of cords may be produced in the one cloth to create interest, and the fabric may be printed. A piqué effect may be produced by warp or weft knitting.

Plissé *See* Seersucker.

Plush A cut warp-pile fabric, similar to a velvet but having a longer and less dense pile laid in one direction.

Pongee True pongee is woven from wild silk in a plain weave. It is rather lighter in weight and somewhat less irregular in appearance than shantung. It is now also made from some manufactured fibres and cotton. Cotton pongees are mercerised and Schreinered to develop the lustre. Weight about 75 g/m^2.

Poplin A plain weave cloth with fine weft-way ribs. There are twice as many ends as picks. It is frequently made from cotton or blends, preferably with 2-fold yarns. Poplin is available in various weights, making it suitable for shirts or rainwear, depending on the finish applied. Sometimes it is printed or woven with decorative stripes. An Irish poplin used to be made with a silk warp and a worsted weft.

Poult A plain weave fabric made from continuous filament yarns with a more pronounced, smooth, clear rib than a taffeta and faille because of the inclusion of a coarser weft and about three times as many ends as there are picks. This fabric may be moiré finished. It was originally known as *Poult-de-Soie*. Weight about 140 g/m^2.

Printed cloth A cloth on which a coloured pattern has been printed. Printing may be done in the following ways:
Roller By passing the cloth under an engraved metal roller from which the printing paste is transferred to the cloth to form the pattern. Usually the maximum size of pattern repeat is 46 cm. It should be remembered that some printing techniques, not mentioned here, such as resist and discharge printing, involve dyeing the fabric in the piece.
Screen The colour is passed through a flat or rotary screen on to the cloth, the pattern being produced by masking out parts of the screen. Designs with a large repeat are produced in this way.

Block This method has limited use commercially because it is slow and costly. Engraved blocks of a size that can be lifted by hand are used to apply the colour.

Transfer The dye is applied in a suitable medium to paper and can be transferred under heat to the fabric when required. Since all the colours are transferred from the paper simultaneously, registration is easily achieved on knitted fabric. The method also has the advantage that designs can easily be applied to cloth panels. Also known as sublistatic printing.

Dye-jet patterning Thousands of microjets are positioned over the carpet travelling beneath. Each jet is supplied with a constant stream of a single dye which can be activated by computer to inject dye into the carpet to create the required multicoloured design. Pattern change is instant provided the same colours are used.

Other printing techniques are:

Warp printing Prior to weaving to produce Chiné fabrics.

Vigoureux printing In which bands of colour are printed at intervals across a thick rope of slubbing of fibres prior to spinning. When the slubbing is attenuated during yarn manufacture, a very even blend of dyed and undyed fibre is produced and by this means, if black has been used, a grey yarn results. This is also known as *Melange* printing, and some worsted cloths are known as 'melange fabrics'.

Flock printing Involves printing an adhesive in an appropriate design on to a fabric and then causing finely chopped fibres or flock to fall on the surface. The flock adheres to the printed areas and is removed from the non-printed areas. Metal may also be applied in this way to produce metallic effects.

Burnt out printing *See* Velvet (*Brocaded*). This technique of destroying only one class of fibre in a fabric made from an appropriate mixture of fibres may be used not only on pile fabrics but on any fabric where a design with a shadow-like effect is required.

'Pure New Wool' A description of wool textiles carrying the IWS Woolmark. A maximum tolerance of 5% is allowed for non-wool fibres used for decorative effects and 0.3% for inadvertent impurities.

Ratiné 'Originally a thick woollen cloth with a curled nap. This term *'ratiné'*, the past participle of the French verb *ratiner* (meaning to cover with a curled nap), has also been applied to a cloth, made from a variety of fibres, with a rough surface produced in one of a number of different ways, either by using a fancy yarn in a cloth to which a special finishing technique may or may not be applied or by using ordinary yarns in a cloth to which the special finish is applied.'

Regatta A good quality 2/1 twill fabric of almost square construction and about 180 g/m^2 woven in even width stripes of dyed and white yarns. It is commonly made from cotton or other suitable staple fibre. Often used for nurses' uniforms.

Regina A fine quality 2/1 twill fabric with about twice as many ends as picks, and weighing about 100 g/m^2.

Repp Repp falls into the group of warp-rib cloths. In a true repp the prominent weft-way ribs are produced by having alternately fine and coarse yarns in both warp and weft, with the coarse ends lifted over the coarse picks and the fine ends passing over the fine picks. The fine ends are woven at a high tension in order to accentuate the effect.

Ribbon An attractive woven fabric, characterised in the higher qualities by fine warp yarns and high warp density, and usually of lustrous appearance. Generally for trimming or adornment.
Double satin ribbon A double warp ribbon with a satin or similar weave on each face, the two faces being equally lustrous.
Faille ribbon A ribbon of silk, viscose, or other manufactured filament yarns; usually of plain weave with a definite rib effect to give brightness, and with a selvedge woven in a manner to add a lustrous effect.
Failletine ribbon A ribbon with faille characteristics but of more open construction.
Galloon ribbon A ribbon with transverse ribs, each composed of two or more picks, to give a uniform or pronounced effect. The ribbon has a special selvedge which is normally of tubular weave.
Lingerie ribbon Any type of washable ribbon suitable for use on ladies' and children's underwear. *Note:* It should have a soft, smooth finish and be firmly constructed with strong selvedges.
Petersham ribbon (millinery) A ribbon, usually with a silk or viscose warp, having single picks of relatively coarse weft, usually cotton, to form a rib with the return of the weft making a gimp-like edge. Normally with 10–15 ribs per cm.
Petersham ribbon (skirt waistband) A narrow fabric having a pronounced rib weft-way, composed of one or more picks per rib, and having lateral stiffness produced either by closeness of the weave or by a finishing process. It was woven with or without pockets in which to insert supports. The selvedges are formed by the return of the weft so as to produce gimp-like edges, or they are woven in a contrasting manner.
Sarsnet ribbon A ribbon entirely of plain weave of very fine warp and weft with a high density, the weft density being higher than that of the warp. A true sarsnet is made wholly of silk.
Single satin ribbon A ribbon of silk or viscose warp and silk, viscose, or cotton weft, with a satin weave to give a lustrous effect on one face, and with plain, tubular, or grosgrain selvedges.
Taffeta ribbon A ribbon of silk, viscose, or other manufactured fibre, of plain weave with usually high warp density and very fine, almost imperceptible, rib, generally with a woven tubular selvedge of contrasting weave.

Sailcloth A weft-way ribbed fabric of a character between poplin and repp. It is heavier than a poplin and may be given a crease-resist finish. It feels rather stiff and is used for dress wear.

Sardinian A woollen overcoating weighing 800 g/m^2 based on a twill repeating on 8 threads with 15 ends and 20 picks per cm. The face is raised to a dense nap and rubbed into small beads or 'pills'.

Sateen A weft-faced cloth made in one of the sateen weaves, usually with many more picks than ends. The fabric is often Schreinered to improve the cover and make it lustrous.

Satin A warp-faced cloth made from a satin weave containing many more ends than picks. The fabric is available in various weights and qualities, the heaviest being the Duchesse satin woven on an 8-end repeat. Many satins are made from continuous filament yarns, continuous filament warp and crêpe twist weft, cotton, and many other fibres. The smooth, lustrous surface provides a suitable ground for machine embroidery.

Saxony This refers to a superior quality woollen cloth made from fine merino wool (*cf*. Tweed: Cheviot).

Scrim A loosely constructed, open light-weight cloth, which may be woven, knitted or otherwise. An important application is in the stablization of nonwoven fabrics.

Seerloop A gingham-type cloth in which a few coloured coarse warp yarns are spaced across the cloth. During weaving, these coarse yarns are fed forwards at a slightly faster rate than the ground ends, so that they form loops on the surface of the cloth at regular intervals down the fabric length.

Seersucker This cloth has interspersed puckered and flat areas of fabric forming striped or check effects. Various methods may be used to produce the effect, which is sometimes known as plissé. Figure 215 overleaf.

Serge A piece-dyed 2/2 twill cloth of almost square construction with a clear surface. The twill line runs at a low angle to the weft. It is often made of wool, but other fibres and blends are used.

Shalloon A fabric used for lining uniforms and coats, made from 2/2 twill with crossbred (coarser than merino wool) yarns.

Shantung A plain-weave spun silk fabric made from the rather coarse irregular yarn with slubs produced by the wild silkworm (Tussah). Now made from manufactured fibres which imitate the irregularity of Tussah.

Sharkskin May be woven or warp-knitted and in either case is compact and has a firm handle. The cloth often has a dull appearance, which is achieved in the case of manufactured fibres by delustring. Made in dress and suiting weights.

Shepherd's check See Colour and weave effects.

Shot effect A term applied to such fabrics as 'shot taffeta', 'shot lining' 'shot silk'. The effect is produced in fabrics made from lustrous yarns, when the warp and weft yarns are of contrasting colours. The fabric is usually woven in plain or 2/2 twill weave. The colour of the fabric depends on the angle of viewing, and consequently in use, the two colours will appear simultaneously in different areas of the fabric.

Silesia A smooth lustrous-faced 2/1 or 2/2 cotton twill fabric used for linings in tailored garments. It is usually piece-dyed, but it may be printed or contain colour woven stripes.

Solid worsted *See* Worsted.

Step effect *See* Colour and weave effects.

Suede fabric True suede, made from leather, is produced by abrading the flesh side of the skin to raise a nap and develop a soft, dull effect.

Suede-like fabrics are produced in a number of ways:

Flocking Electrostatically charged, finely chopped fibres are caused to adhere perpendicularly to an adhesive-coated base fabric.

Sueding One or both sides of a plain or twill-weave fabric is mechanically finished by sueding (abrading) to create a fine short nap. The fabric suffers some mechanical damage in this process. Warp-knit fabrics are sueded on one face only.

Fig. 215 Plissé. *(Hollings Faculty, Manchester Polytechnic)*

Coating Base fabrics may be coated by various techniques to produce simulated leather and a sueded appearance.

Surah See Foulard.

Taffeta Taffeta, faille, poult, and grosgrain are all weft-way rib cloths and are listed here in ascending order of prominence of rib. Taffeta is characterised by indistinct weft way ribs, which are the result of using yarns of equal thickness in both warp and weft, and having many more ends than picks. The stiffness of the cloth depends on how closely woven it is, as does the rustling sound it produces when rubbed during wear. Various qualities of taffeta are available, ranging from the lightweight, less stiff fabric used for linings to the closely woven stiff dress taffeta with its tendency to fall into deep folds of a typical character. Wool taffeta is a plain-weave, lightweight fabric produced from worsted yarns.

Tapestry Originally a woollen fabric used in furnishing, particularly wall hangings, having a design in colours produced by inserting relatively short lengths of coloured weft into a uniformly dyed warp, according to the requirements of the design.

The term is now used for upholstery fabrics woven on Jacquard looms from coloured yarns. The construction is close and two or more warps and wefts of different materials may be used.

Tarlatan A stiffened muslin-type fabric.

Tartan 'Originally a woollen cloth of 2/2 twill woven in checks of various colours and worn chiefly by the Scottish Highlanders, each clan having its distinct pattern. Other materials and weaves are now used.'

Terry fabric A looped warp-pile cloth generally made from cotton. It may be colour-woven or printed.

Terry velour After weaving, the tops of the loops are cut off to produce a soft pile.
Warp-knit Terry Cotton loop pile knitted into a continuous filament ground structure.

Tie silk This is a general term applied to silk fabrics used for neckwear. They are produced in a wide range of designs.

Toile An old French word meaning cloth and often applied to plain or twill weave linen fabrics.

Tricotine A fine worsted cloth woven in a weave with characteristics of a whipcord.

Tropical suiting A fabric such as Panama, weighing about 240 g/m^2 used as a lightweight suiting.

Tufted fabric Produced by passing simple woven fabric through a tufting machine, in which a series of coarse needles with eyes punch continuous lengths of yarn through the cloth to form loops on one face of the cloth Used in the manufacture of carpets (page 250) and candlewick (page 317).

Tulle A very fine, lightweight net woven from silk yarns in a plain weave. The term is also applied to net with hexagonal mesh made by twisting the threads on a lace machine.

Tussore A plain-weave dress weight fabric woven from the coarse silk, known as Tussah, obtained from the wild silkworm. The yarns are generally spun and light-brown or écru in colour.

Tweed 'Originally a coarse, heavyweight, rough-surfaced wool fabric, for outerwear, made in southern Scotland. The term is now applied to fabrics made in a wide range of weights and qualities from woollen yarns in a variety of weave effects and colour-and-weave effects.'
Named varieties of tweed are listed below:
Bannockburn A firm cloth woven in 2/2 straight or herringbone twill from Cheviot woollen yarn. Its chief feature is the use of 2-fold yarns alternating with dyed single yarns of equivalent count in both warp and weft; the 2-fold yarns are composed of different coloured singles.
Cheviot A crisp coarse-textured tweed made from woollen yarns of Cheviot or crossbred variety; available in weights suitable for suits and overcoats. Some Cheviot overcoatings are heavily milled.
Donegal A plain-weave fabric characterised by brightly-coloured slubs introduced at intervals into the weft yarn before spinning. The touches of colour are scattered throughout the cloth and show up usually against a light grey or natural coloured ground.
Harris Fabrics known as Harris Tweed carry a certificate stating that the cloth is hand-woven in the Outer Hebrides from yarns spun from pure virgin Scottish wool. The cloth is produced in a wide range of designs, but the blending of dyed fibres to produce the heather mixture is probably the most typical characteristic of Harris tweed. The fabric has a rough fibrous surface and is made from Cheviot wool.
Shetland This tweed is made entirely or partly from Shetland wool, which is fine and lustrous. Raising during cloth finishing adds to the characteristic soft handle.
Thornproof The yarns are more firmly twisted than in most tweeds, and this gives the cloth a firm, hard handle. Two-fold yarns consisting of different coloured singles are commonly used.
West of England This tweed is characterised by its soft, supple handle. It is produced from high quality fine wool of the Merino type.

Twist worsted *See* Worsted.

Velour A term applied to (1) a heavy pile fabric with the thick pile laid in one direction, or (2) a woven or felt fabric with a raised nap laid in one direction to produce a smooth surface. (3) warp-knit velour produced from long underlaps (*cf.* page 134) which are raised and subsequently cropped to produce the cut pile.

Velvet A cut warp-pile fabric in which the cut ends of the fibres form the surface. Originally the pile was of silk but now other fibres are utilised.

Apart from having the pile uniformly distributed over the surface of the cloth, it is possible to produce various styles of velvet such as:

Brocaded velvet (sometimes referred to as Façonné) The pile forms a pattern on a sheer, fairly stiff ground. There are, therefore, areas between each motif or pattern free from pile. The unwanted pile in these areas is removed after weaving by printing a paste containing chemicals which will destroy the pile, but not the ground structure which is made from a fibre resistant to the treatment. These fabrics may be made also, more expensively, on a Jacquard loom.

Chiffon velvet This refers to a very lightweight velvet.

Ciselé velvet In which a pattern is formed by contrasting uncut and cut pile.

Embossed velvet The pile is flattened during finishing by embossing localised areas to produce a pattern.

Genoa velvet This is a figured velvet often in various colours on a smooth satin ground.

Lyons velvet Refers to a heavy, stiff velvet.

Nacré velvet Has the ground structure woven in one colour with the pile in another colour. Consequently, according to the direction of viewing, the ground colour shows through in varying degrees, giving an iridescent effect.

Panne velvet A lightweight velvet in which the pile is laid in one direction. The pile is longer than that in a dress velvet but shorter than in plush.

Pekin velvet A velvet with coloured stripes.

Ring velvet A fine, lightweight velvet.

'Street Velvet' This term has been used in recent times to describe a velvet of suitable weight for use in coats. These fabrics are usually shower-proofed.

Velveteen A cut weft-pile fabric in which the cut fibres form the surface of the cloth. It is usually made from cotton and may be dyed or printed.

Venetian An eight-end cotton satin lining, generally mercerised and Schreinered. The term Venetian is also applied to an overcoating similar to a Covert but made in a modified satin weave.

Vicuna A cloth, usually overcoating, made from the fine downy hair of the Peruvian llama.

Voile This fabric is made from hard-spun yarns in a lightweight, open texture. The weave is plain, approximately square. The yarns are cotton, worsted, silk, or manufactured continuous filament. (*See* Figure 210.)

Whipcord These cloths have prominent steep twill lines formed from the warp threads. There are more ends per centimetre than picks. The cord-like appearance of the twill lines is enhanced by the choice of direction of twist and a clear finish. Whipcord is made in a wide range of qualities, usually from cotton and worsted yarns.

Winceyette A fabric of about 140 g/m^2 in plain or twill weave raised on one or both faces. Usually bleached, piece-dyed, or printed. Often used for women's or children's nightdresses, but for the latter purpose it is now required by law to be flame-proofed.

Woollen 'Descriptive of yarns, fabrics, or garments made from yarns spun on the condenser system and containing wool.'

Worsted 'Descriptive of yarn in which the fibres are reasonably parallel and which is spun from combed wool, or of fabric manufactured from such yarn.'

Additional terms are used to describe worsted yarns with particular reference to the colour. Sometimes the terms are applied to the fabrics in which the yarns are incorporated.

Solid All the fibres are of one colour.

Mixture Different coloured fibres are blended together.

Twist A two-fold yarn consisting either of single yarns of different solid colours or of different mixture shades.

Marl A two-fold yarn consisting of identical singles. The single yarn contains two colours obtained by spinning from two different coloured rovings.

Melange Yarn spun from printed slubbing. (*See* Printed cloth.)

Zephyr Fine, lightweight cotton fabric used for dresses, shirtings, etc., and ornamented with coloured stripes, checks, and cord.

Zibeline A heavily milled and raised woollen coating or costume fabric. The long hairy nap is laid in one direction and pressed flat to give a lustrous satin-like appearance. The inclusion of hairs, such as mohair, enhances the appearance and enables the fabric to retain its appearance rather better in use.

FURTHER READING AND INFORMATION

Textbook availability
Unfortunately some of the books referenced here are out of print. Your library may obtain them through the British Lending Library system.

Fibres

An Introduction to Man-made Fibres, S. R. Cockett (Pitman 1966).
Fibres, C. B. Chapman (Newnes Butterworth 1974).
Handbook of Textile Fibres, 1. Natural Fibres; 2. Man-made Fibres, J. Gordon Cook, 5th Edition (Merrow 1984).
Physical Properties of Textile Fibres, W. E. Morton and J. W. S. Hearle (Heinemann 1975).

Yarn manufacture

An Introduction to the Study of Spinning, W. E. Morton and G. R. Wray (Longmans 1962).
Modern Yarn Production from Man-made Fibres, Edited by G. R. Wray (Columbine Press 1960).
The Woollen Industry, A. Brearley and J. A. Iredale, 2nd Edn (WIRA, Leeds, 1977).
The Worsted Industry, A. Brearley, and J. A. Iredale, 2nd Edn (WIRA, Leeds, 1980).

Fabric construction

An Introduction to Warp Knitting, D. G. B. Thomas (Merrow 1971).
An Introduction to Weft Knitting, J. A. Smirfitt (Merrow 1975).
Bonded Fabrics, J. R. Holker (Merrow 1975).
Carpets: Back to front, (The Textile Institute 1989).
Knitting Technology, D. J. Spencer, 2nd Edn (Pergammon Press 1989).
Manufacture of Wool Carpets, J. G. Crawshaw (Ed.) (The Textile Institute 1987).
Textile Design and Colour, W. Watson (Longmans 1946).
Warp Knitting Technology, D. F. Paling (Columbine Press 1965).
Woven Cloth Construction, A. T. C. Robinson and R. Marks (The Textile Institute 1967).

Dyeing, printing and finishing

An Introduction to Textile Finishing, J. T. Marsh (Chapman and Hall 1947).
Basic Chemistry of Textile Colouring and Finishing, S. R. Cockett and K. A. Hilton (National Trade Press 1955).

Basic Chemistry of Textile Preparation, S. R. Cockett and K. A. Hilton (National Trade Press 1955).

The Chemical and Mechanical Finishing of Textile Materials, P. Carty and M. S. Byrne (Newcastle-upon-Tyne Polytechnic Products, Ltd. 1987).

Dyeing and Chemical Technology of Textile Fibres, E. R. Trotman, 5th Edn (C. Griffin & Co. Ltd 1975).

Dyeing and Printing, S. R. Cockett (Pitman 1964).

Textile Finishing, A. J. Hall (Heywood 1966).

Textile Printing, L. W. C. Miles (Ed.) (The Textile Institute 1981).

General

A Handbook of Textiles, Ann M. Collier (Pergammon Press 1970).

A Student's Textbook of Textile Science, A. J. Hall (Allman and Son, Ltd. 1963).

Manuals of Textile Technology, (The Textile Institute).

Standard Handbook of Textiles, A. J. Hall, 8th Edn (Newnes Butterworth 1975).

Terms relating to fabrics and associated fibres, yarns and processes. (BS 6189: 1989).

Textile Terms and Definitions, 8th Edn S. R. Beech, C. A. Farnfield, P. Whorton, J. A. Wilkins (Eds) (The Textile Institute 1988).

Textiles (Journal) (BTTG, Shirley Towers, Manchester).

Testing and quality assurance

AATCC Standards (American Association of Textile Chemists and Colorists).

ASTM Standards (American Society for Textile Materials).

BISFA The International Bureau of Standards for the Man-made Fibres (Switzerland).

BSI (British Standards Institution – Standards Catalogue).

CEN (European Committee for Standardisation – France).

DIN Standards (Deutsches Institut für Normung – West Germany).

Fiber Microscopy, A. N. J. Heyn (Interscience Publishers 1954).

Fire Tests: Buildings' Products and Materials (BSI 1989).

Guide to the Identification of Animal Fibres, H. M. Appleyard (WIRA, Leeds 1960).

Identification of Textile Materials, 7th Edn D. R. Perry and C. A. Farnfield (Eds) (The Textile Institute 1985).

ISO Standards (International Standards Organisation, Switzerland).

Microscopy of Animal Textile Fibres, A. B. Wildman (WIRA, Leeds 1954).

NF Standards (Association Française de Normalisation – AFNOR – France).

Practical Statistics for the Textile Industry, G. A. V. Leaf (The Textile Institute 1987).

Principles of Textile Testing, J. E. Booth, 3rd Edn (Newnes Butterworth 1984).

Quality Systems, BS 5750 (British Standards Institution 1979, 1981, 1987).

SDC Methods of Test for Colour Fastness of Textiles and Leather (Society of Dyers and Colourists, Bradford).
Statistical Methods for Textile Technologists, T. Murphy, K. P. Norris and L. H. C. Tippet (The Textile Institute 1979).
The Burning Behaviour of Textiles and its Assessment by Oxgen – Index Methods. A. R. Horrocks, M. Tunc and D. Price. (The Textile Institute 1989).

Computers

Computers in the World of Textiles (The Textile Institute 1984).

Marketing and Design

Quality, Design and the Purchaser (The Textile Institute 1983).
Textile Design issue of Journal of the Textile Institute. Vol 80, No. 3, 1989.
Textiles: Product Design and Marketing (The Textile Institute 1987).

Comfort

Clothing comfort, N. R. S. Hollies and R. F. Goldman (Dekker 1978).
Clothing Comfort and Function, L. Fourt and N. R. S. Hollies (Dekker 1970).
Comfort Properties of Textiles, K. Slater (Textile Progress 1977, 9, (4) 1–70, Textile Institute).
Physiology and Hygiene of Materials and Clothing, E. T. Renbourn (Merrow 1971).

Stitches and Seams

A Survey of Literature on Stitches and Seams for Garments 1950–1974, A. P. Worthington (Shirley Institute Publication S22 1975).
Effects of Sewing Machine Needles in Clothing Manufacture, A. P. Worthington (Shirley Institute Publication S38 1975).
Methods of Joining Fabric – A Technical Literature Survey 1950–1982, R. J. Crum (Shirley Institute Publication S47 1983).

FURTHER INFORMATION

To be informed of current and future developments in textiles and apparel it is necessary to be in touch with current literature and the professional organisations. The following publications will assist:

Journal of The Textile Institute
Textile Horizons   The Textile Institute*
Textile Progress   (Manchester)
T. I. Book List and List of Videos

Apparel International   The Clothing and Footwear
CFI Book List   Institute* (London)

World Textile Abstracts   British Textile Technology
                                 Group (BTTG)
                                 Shirley Towers, Manchester
                                 WIRA House, Leeds.

Slides – textile processing,
   fabric structures,
   colour measurement,   BTTG – Shirley Towers,
   testing, seaming,   Manchester
   history of textiles.

   cotton fibre and   IIC – International Institute
   fabric production.   for Cotton, Manchester.

USEFUL ADDRESSES
professional and technical – information, education

British Clothing Industry Association Ltd., British Apparel Centre, 7 Swallow Place, London W1R 7AA

British Man-made Fibres Association, 24 Buckingham Gate, London SW1E 6LB

British Standards Institution (Standards on textiles, clothing, furnishings and footwear), 3 York Street, Manchester M2 2AT

British Textile Employers Association, Reedham House, 31 King Street West, Manchester M3 2PF

Clothing and Allied Products Industry Training Board, 80 Richardshaw Lane, Pudsey, Leeds, LS28 6BN

The Clothing and Footwear Institute*, 71 Brushfield Street, London E1 6AA

Clothing Technology Centre, SATRA House, Rockingham Road, Kettering, Northants NN16 9JH

Confederation of British Wool Textiles Ltd., 60 Toller Lane, Bradford BD8 9BZ

Fabric Care Research Association Ltd., Forest House Laboratories, Knaresborough Road, Harrogate, North Yorkshire, HG2 7LZ.

International Wool Secretariat, Wool House, Carlton Gardens, London SW1 5AE

The Textile Institute*, International Headquarters, 10 Blackfriars Street, Manchester, M3 5DR

* A merger between The Textile Institute and The Clothing and Footwear Institute is expected. If it occurs, the combined professional institution will be known as 'The Chartered Institute of Textiles and Apparel', with the CITA international headquarters located in Manchester. (1990)

INDEX